*Encounters with
British Composers*

Encounters with British Composers

Andrew Palmer

THE BOYDELL PRESS

© Andrew Palmer 2015

All Rights Reserved. Except as permitted under current legislation
no part of this work may be photocopied, stored in a retrieval system,
published, performed in public, adapted, broadcast,
transmitted, recorded or reproduced in any form or by any means,
without the prior permission of the copyright owner

The right of Andrew Palmer to be identified as
the author of this work has been asserted in accordance with
sections 77 and 78 of the Copyright, Designs and Patents Act 1988

First published 2015

The Boydell Press, Woodbridge

ISBN 978 1 78327 070 5

The Boydell Press is an imprint of Boydell & Brewer Ltd
PO Box 9, Woodbridge, Suffolk IP12 3DF, UK
and of Boydell & Brewer Inc.
668 Mount Hope Ave, Rochester, NY 14620–2731, USA

website: www.boydellandbrewer.com

A catalogue record for this book is available
from the British Library

The publisher has no responsibility for the continued existence or
accuracy of URLs for external or third-party internet websites referred to
in this book, and does not guarantee that any content on such websites
is, or will remain, accurate or appropriate

This publication is printed on acid-free paper
Printed and bound in Great Britain by
TJ International Ltd, Padstow, Cornwall

Contents

List of Illustrations	*page* vii
List of Contributors	ix
Acknowledgments	xxv
Introduction	1
Julian Anderson	5
Simon Bainbridge	17
Sally Beamish	27
George Benjamin	39
Michael Berkeley	53
Judith Bingham	65
Harrison Birtwistle	77
Howard Blake	89
Gavin Bryars	101
Diana Burrell	113
Tom Coult	123
Gordon Crosse	135
Jonathan Dove	147
David Dubery	157
Michael Finnissy	171
Cheryl Frances-Hoad	183
Alexander Goehr	195
Howard Goodall	207
Christopher Gunning	221
Morgan Hayes	233

39 entries

Robin Holloway	245
Oliver Knussen	257
John McCabe	271
James MacMillan	283
Colin Matthews	297
David Matthews	309
Peter Maxwell Davies	321
Thea Musgrave	333
Roxanna Panufnik	345
Anthony Payne	357
Elis Pehkonen	369
Joseph Phibbs	381
Gabriel Prokofiev	393
John Rutter	405
Robert Saxton	417
John Tavener	431
Judith Weir	443
Debbie Wiseman	455
Christopher Wright	465
Appendix Advice for the Young Composer	477
Index	487

Illustrations

All photographs are © Andrew Palmer and may not be reproduced without permission.

Julian Anderson, London, February 2012
Simon Bainbridge, London, February 2014
Sally Beamish, London, July 2012
George Benjamin, London, December 2013
Michael Berkeley, London, September 2013
Judith Bingham, London, July 2011
Sir Harrison Birtwistle, Wiltshire, October 2013
Howard Blake, London, July 2011
Gavin Bryars, Leicestershire, September 2011
Diana Burrell, Harwich, February 2013
Tom Coult, London, February 2014
Gordon Crosse, Suffolk, October 2011
Jonathan Dove, London, August 2011
David Dubery, Suffolk, October 2011
Michael Finnissy, West Sussex, April 2011
Cheryl Frances-Hoad, London, September 2011
Alexander Goehr, Cambridgeshire, February 2013
Howard Goodall, London, September 2014
Christopher Gunning, Hertfordshire, September 2011
Morgan Hayes, London, March 2012
Robin Holloway, London, March 2012
Oliver Knussen, London, May 2000
John McCabe, Kent, August 2012

Sir James MacMillan, London, June 2014
Colin Matthews, London, August 2011
David Matthews, Suffolk, October 2011
Sir Peter Maxwell Davies, London, March 2014
Thea Musgrave, London, February 2014
Roxanna Panufnik, Rye, September 2011
Anthony Payne, West Sussex, July 2012
Elis Pehkonen, Suffolk, September 2011
Joseph Phibbs, London, August 2011
Gabriel Prokofiev, London, January 2015
John Rutter, Cambridgeshire, March 2012
Robert Saxton, London, December 2011
Sir John Tavener, Dorset, October 2013
Judith Weir, London, November 2011
Debbie Wiseman, London, July 2011
Christopher Wright, Suffolk, March 2012

Contributors

Julian Anderson was born in London in 1967. He studied with John Lambert, Alexander Goehr and Tristan Murail and came to prominence when his orchestral *Diptych* (1990) won the Royal Philharmonic Society Composition Prize in 1992. He has held Composer in Residence positions with the City of Birmingham Symphony, Cleveland and London Philharmonic orchestras, and with the Wigmore Hall in London.

He has held senior professorships at the Royal College of Music, London (1996–2004), where he was Head of Department for five years, and at Harvard University (2004–07). He is currently Professor of Composition and Composer in Residence at the Guildhall School of Music and Drama in London. His former students include Edmund Finnis, Helen Grime, Ulrich Kreppein, Mark Simpson, Chris Trapani and Huw Watkins. He was Artistic Director of the Philharmonia Orchestra's Music of Today concert series from 2002 to 2011. In 2012 he was appointed Vice President of the Conseil Musical de la Fondation Prince Pierre de Monaco.

Simon Bainbridge was born in London in 1952. He studied composition with John Lambert at the Royal College of Music and with Gunther Schuller at Tanglewood. The success of his *Spirogyra* at the 1971 Aldeburgh Festival led to a string quartet commission, which in turn brought him to the attention of the violist Walter Trampler, who commissioned the Viola Concerto in 1978. A series of large-scale works followed during the 1980s and 1990s, including *Fantasia for Double Orchestra* (1983), Double Concerto (1990), *Toccata* for Orchestra (1992), the horn concerto *Landscape and Memory* (1995) and *Three Pieces for Orchestra* (1998).

He was Head of Composition at the Royal Academy of Music from 1999 to 2007 and received a professorship from the University of London in 2001. He remains on the faculty of the Composition department at the Academy as Senior Professor in Composition. He has taught and lectured at the Juilliard School, the Boston Conservatory of Music, Yale University and Yonsei University in Seoul, South Korea.

Sally Beamish was born in London in 1956. She studied viola at the Royal Northern College of Music, where she also received composition lessons from Anthony Gilbert and Lennox Berkeley. In 1990 she moved from London to Scotland to develop her career as a composer, and she has since written two symphonies, several concertos, chamber and instrumental music, film scores, theatre music and music for amateurs.

From 1998 to 2002 she was Composer in Residence with the Swedish Chamber Orchestra and the Scottish Chamber Orchestra, for whom she wrote four major works. In 2010 she was selected as one of twenty composers to participate in the 'New Music 20×12' project as part of the London 2012 Cultural Olympiad, for which she wrote *Spinal Chords*. She is a visiting lecturer at Leeds College of Music and, with the composer Alasdair Nicolson, she co-directs the annual St Magnus Composers' Course in Orkney.

George Benjamin, CBE was born in London in 1960. In 1976 he entered the Paris Conservatoire to study with Olivier Messiaen (composition) and Yvonne Loriod (piano), after which he studied with Alexander Goehr at the University of Cambridge. His first orchestral work, *Ringed by the Flat Horizon*, was played at the BBC Proms when he was just twenty. He is a Commandeur dans l'ordre des Arts et des Lettres and a member of the Bavarian Academy of Fine Arts. He was awarded the Deutsche Symphonie Orchester's first ever Schoenberg Prize for composition. Since 2001 he has been the Henry Purcell Professor of Composition at King's College London.

As a conductor his repertoire stretches from Schumann to Knussen and from Wagner to Boulez. He has conducted the first performances of works by Chin, Grisey, Ligeti and Rihm and regularly appears with the London Sinfonietta, the Ensemble Modern, l'Ensemble Intercontemporain, the Mahler Chamber Orchestra and the Berlin Philharmonic, Concertgebouw and Philharmonia orchestras.

Michael Berkeley, Baron Berkeley of Knighton, CBE was born in London in 1948. His father was the composer Sir Lennox Berkeley. He was a chorister at Westminster Cathedral, where he frequently sang in works composed or conducted by his godfather, Benjamin Britten. He studied composition, singing and piano at the Royal Academy of

Music but it was not until he was in his twenties, when he went to study with Richard Rodney Bennett, that he began to concentrate exclusively on composing.

He has been Associate Composer to the Scottish Chamber Orchestra and Composer in Association with the BBC National Orchestra of Wales. For ten years from 1995 he was Artistic Director of the Cheltenham International Festival of Music, where he premiered more than a hundred works and initiated a policy of programming a contemporary work in every concert. In 2002 and 2003 he was guest curator of chamber music programmes at the Sydney Festival. Since April 1995 he has presented Private Passions on BBC Radio 3.

Judith Bingham was born in Nottingham in 1952. She went to the Royal Academy of Music to study composition (with Alan Bush and Eric Fenby) and singing. After graduating she studied composition privately with Hans Keller. She sang as an amateur with the then BBC Choral Society (now the BBC Symphony Chorus) and later became a member of the BBC Singers and several other choirs and vocal ensembles. Her reputation as a composer was established by a performance in 1994 of *Chartres*, a forty-minute work for large symphony orchestra.

She left the BBC Singers in 1995 in order to concentrate on composing but continued to sing professionally for some years. She has lectured at the Royal Academy of Music, Trinity College, the London College of Music, the Royal Northern College and Glasgow Academy, as well as in American universities. From 2004 to 2009 she was the BBC Singers' Composer in Association.

Sir Harrison Birtwistle, CH was born in Accrington in 1934 and studied clarinet and composition at the Royal Manchester College of Music. In 1965 he gave up performing in order to devote himself to composition and travelled to Princeton as a Harkness Fellow, where he completed his opera *Punch and Judy*. This work, together with *Verses for Ensembles* and *The Triumph of Time*, established him as a leading voice in British music. From 1975 to 1983 he was Musical Director of the Royal National Theatre in London, and from 1994 to 2001 he was Henry Purcell Professor of Composition at King's College London.

In 1986 he became a Chévalier des Arts et des Lettres and was awarded the University of Louisville Grawemeyer Award for Music Composition. In 1995 he received the Ernst von Siemens Music Prize. His *Panic* for saxophone and orchestra was premiered in the second half of the 1995 Last Night of the Proms to an estimated worldwide television audience of one hundred million.

Howard Blake, OBE was born in London in 1938. He grew up in Brighton, where he sang lead roles as a boy soprano. After winning the Hastings Musical Festival Scholarship to the Royal Academy of Music, he studied piano with Harold Craxton and composition with Howard Ferguson. He then worked as a film projectionist at the National Film Theatre and played piano in pubs and clubs, eventually becoming a session musician, arranger and composer of music for film and television.

His film scores include *The Duellists*, *A Month in the Country* and the animated *The Snowman*, which also exists as a concert work for narrator and orchestra and as a full-length ballet. His other concert works include a piano concerto commissioned by the Philharmonia Orchestra for the thirtieth birthday of Diana, Princess of Wales, in 1991, a violin concerto to celebrate the centenary of the City of Leeds in 1993, and *Benedictus*, given its London premiere in Westminster Cathedral in 1989 with Cardinal Hume as narrator.

Gavin Bryars was born in Goole, East Yorkshire, in 1943. While studying philosophy at the University of Sheffield he became a jazz bassist and worked with the improvisers Derek Bailey and Tony Oxley. As a composer he studied briefly with John Cage in the USA and collaborated with Cornelius Cardew and John White. From 1969 to 1978 he taught in departments of Fine Art in Portsmouth and Leicester; in 1986 he founded the music department at Leicester Polytechnic (later De Montfort University), where he was Professor of Music until 1994. Since then he has concentrated on composition and performance.

He has collaborated on a number of dance and visual arts projects, including the 2002 Valencia Architecture Biennale. He has lectured widely and was Associate Research Fellow at Dartington College of Arts from 2004 to 2008. He has an honorary doctorate from Plymouth University and was awarded a Fellowship of Bath Spa University. He is a Regent of the Collège de 'Pataphysique.

Diana Burrell was born in 1948 in Norwich, where her father was deputy organist at the Cathedral. She studied music at the University of Cambridge and taught for several years in London before becoming a freelance violist. As a composer her reputation was established by her *Missa Sancte Endeliente*, written for the 1980 St Endellion Festival. Her first major orchestral work, *Landscape*, received the 'Encore' award organised by the Royal Philharmonic Society and BBC Radio 3 and sponsored by the Performing Right Society Foundation.

She has taught at the Guildhall School of Music and Drama, and in 2006 she succeeded Jonathan Dove as Artistic Director of the Spitalfields Festival in London. In the same year she was awarded a fellowship from the Arts and Humanities Research Council at the Royal Academy of Music to compose a series of ensemble organ works over five years. From 2011 to 2014 she was Artistic Director of the Harwich Festival of the Arts.

Tom Coult was born in London in 1988. He studied music at the University of Manchester and is currently working towards a PhD at King's College London with George Benjamin. His *Codex* (Homage to Serafini) was premiered by the BBC Symphony Orchestra as the culmination of a year-long Sound and Music Embedded residency in 2013, the same year that he was awarded the Royal Philharmonic Society Prize. From 2014 to 2015 he was a Sound and Music 'New Voices' composer. His *Four Perpetual Motions* was written for members of the Philharmonia Orchestra and premiered as a Music Today event in London's Royal Festival Hall.

He is an Associate Member of the London Symphony Orchestra Soundhub, a platform for emerging composers. In 2014 he was a featured composer at the 'Soundings' festival at the Austrian Cultural Forum in London and was commissioned to write works for the Britten Sinfonia, the London Sinfonietta, and the soprano Claire Booth and the Mahler Chamber Orchestra.

Gordon Crosse was born in 1937 in Bury, Lancashire. In 1961 he gained a first-class honours degree in Music at the University of Oxford, after which he did two years' postgraduate research on early fifteenth-century music. He came to prominence in 1964 when his *Meet My Folks!* (Theme and Relations, Op. 10), a music theatre work for children and adults based on poems by Ted Hughes, was performed at the Aldeburgh Festival. He later held academic posts at the Universities of Birmingham and Essex and was for two years Composer in Residence at King's College, Cambridge. In 1976 he won the Worshipful Company of Musicians' Cobbett Medal for services to music.

From 1980 to 1982 he taught part-time at the Royal Academy of Music but then retired to Suffolk to devote all of his time to composition. In 1984 he extended Benjamin Britten's *Young Apollo* for use as ballet music; the resulting work was premièred by the Royal Ballet. He stopped composing in 1990 and spent the following seventeen years working in computer programming and music technology.

Jonathan Dove was born in London in 1959 and studied composition with Robin Holloway at the University of Cambridge. He then worked as a freelance accompanist, repetiteur, animateur and arranger and in 1987 joined the staff at Glyndebourne, which later commissioned his breakthrough opera *Flight*. His community cantata *On Spital Fields* won a Royal Philharmonic Society Award in 2005 and a British Composer Award in 2006. His operas *When She Died* (about the death of Diana, Princess of Wales) and *Man on the Moon* (about the first moon landing) were commissioned for broadcast by Channel 4 television; the latter won the Opera Special Prize at the Rose d'Or Festival for Television Programming in 2007 and a Gold Medal at the Park City Film Music Festival, 2008.

He is an Associate of the National Theatre and for many years was Music Advisor to the Almeida Theatre. He has written for the Royal Shakespeare Company and for the New York Shakespeare Festival. He was presented with the Ivor Novello Award for Classical Music in 2008.

David Dubery was born in Durban, South Africa, in 1948, and studied piano from the age of five. In 1961 his family emigrated to his mother's home town of Manchester, where he studied piano and composition at the Northern School of Music. He began his career as a solo pianist and accompanist, and in 1969 was awarded a Hesse Scholarship to Aldeburgh. Since 1972 he has additionally worked as a composer, vocal coach, musical director and teacher of piano and voice.

During the 1970s he wrote musicals, and throughout the 1980s he toured as part of the Verlaine Duo with the oboist Jonathan Tobutt. He has coached actors from musical theatre, TV, stage and film, taught cast members from more than twenty-five West End and national tour productions, and worked in the departments of dance, drama and music in further education colleges, the Manchester School of Music and the Actors Centre. From 1985 to 2003 he was staff pianist, vocal tutor and Musical Director of Showcase Productions at the Northern Ballet School.

Michael Finnissy was born in London in 1946. He was awarded the William Yeats Hurlstone Composition Prize at the Croydon Music Festival and then a Foundation Scholarship to study at the Royal College of Music. His teachers there were Bernard Stevens and Humphrey Searle. He subsequently studied in Italy with Roman Vlad. He worked as a pianist for dance classes, both freelance and at the London School of Contemporary Dance, where he founded a music department. He also performed as a concert pianist across Europe.

He began composing seriously in the early 1970s, while he was

Artistic Director of the ensemble Suoraan. In 1987 he joined Ixion, and in both groups he played the piano and conducted concerts. From 1990 to 1996 he was President of the International Society for Contemporary Music. He has taught at the Royal Academy of Music, Winchester College, the Katholieke Universiteit of Leuven (Belgium) and the Universities of Sussex and Southampton.

Cheryl Frances-Hoad was born in Essex in 1980 and studied at the Yehudi Menuhin School, the University of Cambridge and King's College London. At the age of fifteen she won the BBC Young Composer Competition and her work has since won the Cambridge Composers' Competition (UK, 2001), the Mendelssohn Scholarship (UK, 2002), the Bliss Prize (UK, 2002), the first Robert Helps International Composition Prize (University of Florida, 2005), the International String Orchestra Composition Competition (Malta, 2006), the Royal Philharmonic Society Composition Prize (UK, 2007) and the Sun River Composition Prize (China, 2007).

In 2010 she became the youngest composer to win two awards in the same year at the BASCA British Composer Awards. From 2010 to 2012 she was the first DARE Cultural Fellow in the Opera Related Arts in association with Opera North and the University of Leeds, and from 2012 to 2013 she was Music Fellow at Rambert Dance.

Alexander Goehr was born in Berlin in 1932 and came to England with his family the following year. He studied at the Royal Manchester College of Music, where with Harrison Birtwistle, Peter Maxwell Davies and John Ogdon he formed the New Music Manchester Group. In 1955 he went to Paris to study with Olivier Messiaen and Yvonne Loriod. In the early 1960s he worked for the BBC as a producer of radio programmes, and formed the Music Theatre Ensemble.

From the late 1960s he taught at the New England Conservatory in Boston, at Yale University and at the University of Leeds. In 1975 he was appointed to a chair at the University of Cambridge, where he remains Emeritus Professor. He has also taught in China and has twice been Composer in Residence at Tanglewood. He was the 1997 BBC Reith Lecturer and is an honorary member of the American Academy of Arts and Letters and a former Churchill Fellow.

Howard Goodall, CBE was born in Bromley, Kent, in 1958. He was a chorister at New College, Oxford, and a music scholar at Christ Church, Oxford. He began his career as a session musician and programmer, and has been composing music for television and the theatre since the

1980s. His choral works date from 1994. From 2008 to 2014 he was Classic FM's Composer in Residence.

For his six series of television documentary programmes about the theory and history of music he has received a BAFTA and many international broadcast awards. He is also a recipient of the Sir Charles Grove/Making Music Prize for Outstanding Contribution to British Music, the Naomi Sargant Memorial Award for Outstanding Contribution to Education in Broadcasting, and the MIA/Classic FM Award for Outstanding Contribution to Music Education. From 2007 to 2011 he was England's first ever National Ambassador for Singing and led the Sing Up programme to improve the provision of group singing for all primary-age children.

Christopher Gunning was born in Cheltenham, Gloucestershire, in 1944. He studied composition, piano and percussion at the Guildhall School of Music and Drama, where his tutors included Edmund Rubbra and Richard Rodney Bennett, and he gained a Music degree at the University of Durham. He set out to be a composer of serious concert music but soon became involved in the media, arranging albums for Mel Tormé, Cilla Black, Shirley Bassey and other singers, and writing scores for commercials, television dramas and films. He received BAFTA Awards for *La vie en rose*, *Agatha Christie's Poirot*, *Middlemarch* and *Porterhouse Blue*, and Ivor Novello Awards for *Rebecca*, *Under Suspicion* and *Firelight*.

Since 1998 he has also composed concert works, including concertos for saxophone, piano, oboe, guitar, clarinet and flute, and seven symphonies. In 2011 he was presented with a Gold Badge Award by the British Academy of Songwriters, Composers and Authors.

Morgan Hayes was born in Hastings, East Sussex, in 1973 and began to write music at the age of ten. He studied composition with Michael Finnissy, Simon Bainbridge and Robert Saxton and in 1995 won the Guildhall School of Music and Drama's Lutosławski Prize. As 2001–02 Leverhulme Composer in Residence at the Purcell School he created the 'Tatewalks' project, based on Mussorgsky's *Pictures at an Exhibition* and involving young composers in collaboration with the London Sinfonietta and the photographer Malcolm Crowthers. The Sinfonietta commissioned his transcription of Squarepusher's *Port Rhombus* for the South Bank Centre's 2003 'Ether Festival'.

His first orchestral work, *Strip*, was commissioned by the BBC Symphony Orchestra and premiered during the 2005 Proms season. While Composer in Association with Music Theatre Wales he wrote *Shirley and Jane*, an operatic scena based on the career of Dame Shirley Porter. He currently works as a pianist for English National Ballet.

Robin Holloway was born in Leamington Spa, Warwickshire, in 1943. From 1953 to 1957 he was a chorister at St Paul's Cathedral, London. He studied composition with Alexander Goehr at the University of Cambridge, where he later became a lecturer, a reader in Musical Composition and, for the last ten years of his academic career, Professor of Musical Composition. His former pupils include Judith Weir and Thomas Adés.

His doctoral thesis, *Debussy and Wagner*, later published as a book by Eulenberg, discussed a close relationship between music and language as well as romanticism and beauty. Between 1988 and 2010 he contributed a regular music column to The Spectator magazine. Two volumes of his journalistic and other occasional writings were published in 2003 and 2008.

Oliver Knussen, CBE was born in Glasgow in 1952. He studied composition with John Lambert in London and with Gunther Schuller at Tanglewood and in Boston. He was Artistic Director of the Aldeburgh Festival from 1983 to 1998, and in 1992 he established the Britten–Pears Young Artists Programme's Contemporary Composition and Performance Course with Colin Matthews. He was Head of Contemporary Music at Tanglewood from 1986 to 1993.

Having been Music Director of the London Sinfonietta from 1998 to 2002, he remains its conductor laureate. From 1992 to 1996 he was Principal Guest Conductor of The Hague's Het Residentie Orkest, and in 2009 he received the Royal Philharmonic Society's Conductor Award. He was Artist in Association with the BBC Symphony Orchestra (2009–14) and in 2014 he became the inaugural Richard Rodney Bennett Professor of Music at the Royal Academy of Music.

John McCabe, CBE (1939–2015) was born in Huyton, Liverpool. A childhood accident with fire in the home resulted in much time off school, which allowed his musical gifts to develop quickly. When he was eight he started piano lessons with Gordon Green at the Royal Manchester College of Music. He subsequently studied music at the University of Manchester and took composition lessons from Thomas Pitfield. He then returned to the Royal Manchester College for a four-year postgraduate diploma in piano and composition.

After a year of further study in Munich, he was Pianist in Residence at Cardiff University. From 1968 he worked as a freelance composer and pianist, although he was also Director of the London College of Music from 1983 to 1990 and held short tenures as a visiting professor at the Universities of Melbourne and Cincinnati. He was President of the Incorporated Society of Musicians and the recipient of the 2003 Incorporated Society of Musicians' Distinguished Musician Award.

Sir James MacMillan, CBE was born in Kilwinning, North Ayrshire, in 1959. He read Music at the University of Edinburgh and studied for a doctorate in composition at the University of Durham with John Casken. After working as a Lecturer in Music at the University of Manchester he returned to Scotland and settled in Glasgow. The successful premiere of *Tryst* at the 1990 St Magnus Festival led to his appointment as Affiliate Composer of the Scottish Chamber Orchestra. Between 1992 and 2002 he was Artistic Director of the Philharmonia Orchestra's Music of Today concert series.

He worked as Composer/Conductor with the BBC Philharmonic Orchestra between 2000 and 2009, and was appointed Principal Guest Conductor of the Netherlands Radio Chamber Philharmonic in 2010. In 2008 he became Honorary Patron of the London Chamber Orchestra's 'LCO New: Explore' project, which explores links between the arts and fosters emerging creative talent in composition.

Colin Matthews, OBE was born in London in 1946. He studied music at the Universities of Nottingham and Sussex and subsequently worked as assistant to Imogen Holst and Benjamin Britten at Aldeburgh. He is Special Professor at the University of Nottingham, Prince Consort Professor of Music at the Royal College of Music, and Distinguished Visiting Fellow in Composition at the University of Manchester. He received the RPS/PRS Leslie Boosey Award in 2005.

He has been Associate Composer with the London Symphony and Hallé orchestras, a member of the Council of the Society for the Promotion of New Music and a director of the Performing Right Society. He is administrator of the Holst Foundation, chair of the Britten Estate and a founder trustee and Music Director of the Britten–Pears Foundation. In 1992 he and Oliver Knussen founded the Britten–Pears Young Artists Programme's Contemporary Composition and Performance Course. He is founder and Executive Producer of NMC Recordings.

David Matthews was born in London in 1943. He read Classics at the University of Nottingham – which also later made him an Honorary Doctor of Music – and later studied composition privately with Anthony Milner. He also received guidance from Nicholas Maw and Peter

Sculthorpe as a result of doing editing and copying work for them. Similar work for Faber Music led to him spending three years as a part-time assistant to Benjamin Britten at Aldeburgh in the late 1960s. For more than ten years he orchestrated Carl Davis's scores for silent films.

[Britten d. 1976]

From 1997 to 1999 he was Composer in Residence to the Britten Sinfonia, and for thirteen years he was Artistic Director of the Deal Festival. He is Music Advisor to the English Chamber Orchestra. His *Concerto in Azzurro* for cello and orchestra was nominated for a BBC Radio 3 Listeners' Award in 2003. He has written books on the music of Britten and Tippett, and reviews for journals. His published lecture 'Landscape into Sound' explores the relationship of music to painting.

Sir Peter Maxwell Davies, CH, CBE was born in Salford, Lancashire, in 1934. He studied at the University of Manchester and the Royal Manchester College of Music, and in 1956 undertook postgraduate studies with Goffredo Petrassi in Rome. After three years as Director of Music at Cirencester Grammar School, he travelled to the US to study at Princeton University with Roger Sessions, Milton Babbitt and Earl Kim. He then moved to Australia, where he was Composer in Residence at the University of Adelaide. After returning to the United Kingdom he moved to the Orkney Islands.

[d. 2016]

He has been Artistic Director of the Dartington International Summer School and Music Director of the Ojai Music Festival in California. For ten years he was Associate Conductor/Composer with the Royal Philharmonic Orchestra, and he is Composer Laureate of the Scottish Chamber Orchestra. He has guest-conducted the Boston Symphony, Cleveland, Leipzig Gewandhaus, Philharmonia, Russian National and San Francisco Symphony orchestras. In 2004 he was appointed Master of the Queen's Music for a ten-year period.

Thea Musgrave, CBE was born in Edinburgh in 1928. She studied at the University of Edinburgh with Hans Gál and in Paris as a pupil of Nadia Boulanger. In 1958 she attended the Tanglewood Festival and studied with Aaron Copland. She became Guest Professor at the University of California, Santa Barbara, in 1970 and the following year she married the American violist and opera conductor Peter Mark. From 1987 to 2002 she was Distinguished Professor at Queen's College, City University of New York.

She holds honorary degrees from Old Dominion University (Virginia), the University of Glasgow, Smith College and the New England Conservatory in Boston. She received the Koussevitzky Award in 1974 and Guggenheim Fellowships in 1974/75 and 1982/83. She has conducted performances of her music by orchestras that include the Philadelphia, the Los Angeles Chamber, the San Francisco Symphony, the Jerusalem Symphony and the Hong Kong Philharmonic.

Roxanna Panufnik was born in London in 1968. Her father was the composer Andrej Panufnik. She studied at the Royal Academy of Music and began her career as a producer of BBC television programmes about music. She has since written opera, ballet, music theatre, choral and chamber works, and music for film and television, and she has a particular interest in world music and its links to spirituality.

Among her most widely performed works are *Westminster Mass*, commissioned for Westminster Cathedral Choir on the occasion of Cardinal Hume's seventy-fifth birthday; *The Music Programme*, an opera for Polish National Opera's millennium season; and settings for solo voices and orchestra of Vikram Seth's *Beastly Tales*, the first of which was commissioned by the BBC. She is a Vice President of the Joyful Company of Singers and from 2012 to 2015 was inaugural Associate Composer with the London Mozart Players.

Anthony Payne was born in London in 1936. After studying at St Cuthbert's Society, University of Durham, he spent a period as a freelance musicologist before establishing his reputation as a composer. He is the author of books about Schoenberg and Frank Bridge and has written music criticism for the Daily Telegraph, The Independent and Country Life. He has been a visiting lecturer at a number of universities in Britain, Australia and the United States. In 1988 he co-founded the vocal ensemble Jane's Minstrels with his wife, the soprano Jane Manning.

His works include two major commissions for the BBC Proms: *The Spirit's Harvest* (1985) and *Time's Arrow* (1990). His realisation of the sketches to Elgar's Third Symphony was first performed in 1998 and has since joined the international repertory. In 2007 he and his wife were jointly awarded Honorary Doctorates by Durham University, and his String Quartet No. 2 won the Chamber category of the 2011 British Composer Awards.

Elis Pehkonen was born in Swaffham, Norfolk, in 1942. At the age of eighteen he had his first composition lesson with Benjamin Britten and won a composition scholarship to the Royal College of Music, where he studied with Peter Racine Fricker. He also had consultation lessons with Lennox Berkeley, Alan Ridout, Geoffrey Bush, Richard Rodney Bennett and Anthony Payne. His first commission, at Britten's recommendation, was the Incidental Music for *Everyman*, written for the 1966 King's Lynn Festival. From 1967 to 1979 he taught at Cirencester School, where he continued the tradition begun by Peter Maxwell Davies of involving pupils in performing contemporary music. He moved to Suffolk in 1980.

His *Russian Requiem* was conducted by John Sanders at the Three Choirs Festival in 1986 and by Sir David Willcocks at the Royal Festival Hall (with the Bach Choir) in 1993. He is Artistic Director of the William Alwyn Festival.

Joseph Phibbs was born in London in 1974. He studied at the Purcell School and continued his musical education at King's College London and Cornell University, New York. His composition teachers have included Param Vir, Sir Harrison Birtwistle and Steven Stucky. Since 2003 he has combined his composing career with the editing and promoting of Benjamin Britten's music, and he is a director of the Britten Estate Ltd. He is also a visiting lecturer in composition at both the Purcell School and King's College London.

In 2004 his *Lumina* was shortlisted for a British Composer Award in two categories, Orchestral and the BBC Radio 3 Listeners Award, and his *Rivers to the Sea* won the Orchestral category of the 2013 British Composer Awards. He has been Composer in Residence at the Presteigne Festival and at the Exon Singers Festival in Tavistock.

Gabriel Prokofiev was born in London in 1975. He studied composition at the Universities of Birmingham and York and took a particular interest in electro-acoustic music. After graduating he composed garage music and produced dance, electro and hip-hop music under a variety of guises. He was one of the producers of Lady Sovereign's album *Public Warning*. In 2003 he founded the record label Nonclassical and returned to his classical roots by composing his first string quartet.

His Concerto for Turntables & Orchestra (2006) was premiered at the 2011 BBC Proms by DJ Yoda and the National Youth Orchestra of Great Britain under Vladimir Jurowski. It was subsequently toured by the BBC Concert Orchestra as part of its educational programme. He made his conducting debut in 2008 with his concerto for 'dancing' viola, string orchestra, trombones and percussion in the Paradiso, Amsterdam. In March 2009 his Nonclassical club made its New York debut at the Wordless Music series and at the Rock festival SXSW.

John Rutter, CBE was born in London in 1945. He was educated at Highgate School, where John Tavener was a fellow pupil and choir member. He read music at Clare College, Cambridge, and gained wide recognition in the early 1970s for his editorial work on Oxford University Press's Carols for Choirs 2. He later served as Director of Music at Clare College. In 1981 he founded his own choir, the Cambridge Singers, with which he has made many recordings on his Collegium Records label.

He was made an honorary Fellow of Westminster Choir College, Princeton, in 1980 and a Fellow of the Guild of Church Musicians in 1988. In 1996 the Archbishop of Canterbury conferred a Lambeth Doctorate of Music upon him in recognition of his contribution to church music. He was made an honorary Bencher of the Middle Temple while taking part in the 2008 Temple Festival. He is also a Vice President of the Joyful Company of Singers.

Robert Saxton was born in London in 1953. He studied composition with Elisabeth Lutyens, Robin Holloway, Robert Sherlaw Johnson and Luciano Berio, following guidance from Benjamin Britten. He won the Gaudeamus International Composers prize in 1975 and a Fulbright Arts Fellowship to the USA in 1985–86, and was awarded a Doctorate of Music by the University of Oxford in 1994. He was Head of Composition at the Guildhall School of Music and Drama (1991–98) and the Royal Academy of Music (1998–99), and has been Professor of Composition and Tutorial Fellow in Music at Worcester College, Oxford, since 1999.

He has directed the composers' course at Dartington International Summer School and was Artistic Director of Opera Lab. He was a member of the Southbank Centre board for nine years and is Composer in Association at the Purcell School. He was a Frontline Composer for the Park Lane Group Young Artists New Year Series 2015 and will be Composer in Residence at the Presteigne Festival in 2016.

Sir John Tavener (1944–2013) was born in London and educated at Highgate School. He sang in the school's choir and became a sufficiently proficient pianist to perform concertos by Beethoven and Shostakovich. From 1961 to 1975 he was organist and choirmaster at St John's Presbyterian Church, Kensington (now St Mark's Coptic Orthodox Church). He entered the Royal Academy of Music in 1962, where his tutors included Lennox Berkeley. While studying there he gave up the piano and devoted himself to composition.

He came to prominence in 1968 with *The Whale*, premièred by the London Sinfonietta in the inaugural concert of the Queen Elizabeth Hall. He converted to the Greek Orthodox Church in 1977, and theology and liturgical traditions became a major influence on his work.

The Protecting Veil, as recorded by the cellist Steven Isserlis, became a bestselling album, and *Song for Athene* gained worldwide exposure when performed at the funeral of Diana, Princess of Wales, in 1997.

Judith Weir, CBE was born to Scottish parents in Cambridge in 1954. She studied with Sir John Tavener while at school and subsequently with Robin Holloway at the University of Cambridge, graduating in 1976. She held the post of Composer in Association for the City of Birmingham Symphony Orchestra from 1995 to 1998, and from 1995 to 2000 she was Artistic Director of the Spitalfields Festival.

She received the Lincoln Center's Stoeger Prize in 1997, the South Bank Show Music Award in 2001 and the Incorporated Society of Musicians' Distinguished Musician Award in 2010. In 2007 she was the third recipient of the Queen's Medal for Music. She was Visiting Distinguished Research Professor in Composition at Cardiff University from 2006 to 2009. In July 2014 she succeeded Sir Peter Maxwell Davies as Master of the Queen's Music.

Debbie Wiseman, MBE was born in London in 1963. She studied at Trinity College of Music Junior Department and then at the Guildhall School of Music and Drama, where her composition teacher was Buxton Orr. She was awarded Honorary Fellowships at both colleges. She is a Visiting Professor at the Royal College of Music and regularly lectures to schools and colleges about the art of composing music for the screen. She is also a conductor and a radio and television presenter. In July 2015 she was appointed Classic FM's Composer in Residence, a position previously held by Howard Goodall.

Her film music credits include *Tom & Viv* (nominated for two Academy Awards and the Alexander Korda Award for Outstanding British Film, 1994); *Wilde* (nominated for Best Original Film Score, Ivor Novello Awards, 1997); *Arsène Lupin* (Winner of Best Score for a Foreign-language Film and nominated for Score of the Year, Movie Music UK Awards, 2005); and *Flood* (nominated for Best Score for a Horror/Thriller, IFMCA Awards, 2007). In 2007 she was awarded the Gold Badge of Merit by the British Academy of Composers and Songwriters.

Christopher Wright was born in Ipswich, Suffolk, in 1954. After studying music at the Colchester Institute Music School and composition with Richard Arnell, he went to teacher training college in Norwich and taught in state and independent schools in Suffolk and Gloucestershire. At this time he was also involved in community music-making as a trombonist, accompanist and choir trainer. His earliest works, dating from 1979, include his first string quartet and *Patterns* for Brass Band.

By 1993 he was composing full-time, and he has since written more than fifty works in many genres. His music has been commissioned by the cellist Raphael Wallfisch, the Cheltenham International Violin Course, Elis Pehkonen, the Ipswich Wolsey Orchestra, the English Music Festival and the William Alwyn Festival. He was a finalist in the Oare String Orchestra's International Composers Competition.

Acknowledgements

I wish to thank the composers for their time and patience in answering my interview questions and subsequently checking and approving their contributions to this book.

I should also like to thank the following people for arranging interviews and/or helping to ensure that these went smoothly: David Allenby, Elena Anastopoulos and Eleanor Banks of Boosey & Hawkes; Ralph Blackbourn and Andrew Rosner of Rayfield Allied; Sally Cavender and Stephanie Woodworth of Faber Music; Ken Coney; Sakoto Doi-Luck and Caroline Gibbs of Intermusica; Caroline Evans; Anwen Greenaway of Oxford University Press; Svitlana Gunning; Emma Harrison of Collegium Records; Joanna Holland; Joni Hurst; Monica McCabe; Meg Monteith, Caroline Nelson and Victoria Small of Music Sales; Ian Mylett of Schott Music; Anna Power of Harrison Parrott; and Emily Rees Jones of PBJ Management.

In addition, I am very grateful to the trustees of the Ida Carroll Trust and of the William Alwyn Foundation, whose financial support made the publication of this book possible.

AP

Introduction

Some readers will know that this is not the first book of its kind. The precedent was established by Murray Schafer's *British Composers in Interview*,[1] whose enduring appeal lies partly in the fact that while most of its interviewees can no longer contribute to the musical history of which they have become part, we have a sense of their returning temporarily to life as we read their words. Its continuing popularity may also reflect nostalgia for a period in British cultural life that is imagined as simpler and more secure than our own: as classical music becomes ever more difficult to define, some music lovers may yearn for a time when its boundaries were challenged by the young progressives but held largely in place by the traditional values of the old guard.

To look back half a century at the musical Britain that Schafer explored and to discover how much time he spent discussing the twelve-tone method of composition is to be reminded that most composers of the 1960s were required to react to or against a dominant aesthetic trend. While this may have been a stimulus to their creativity, it also risked categorising them according to their degree of commitment to a particular technique. In fact few of them embraced it fully; most adapted it in order to suit their own musical needs, finding that the apparent restrictions it imposed paradoxically empowered them creatively. In contrast, today's music is not judged on its degree of adherence to formulae and it is free to flourish in a multitude of forms and styles.

So one of the most obvious characteristics of contemporary classical music is its diversity. To some music lovers this reflects a welcome breaking down of barriers; to others it brings confusion and a belief that artistic standards have declined. Depending on their optimism or pessimism, they argue that music has either diversified or fragmented: while some suggest that much has happened, musically, since Schafer's book was published, others argue that not enough has happened and that progressive music

[1] London, Faber & Faber, 1963.

has been sidelined by the more conservative. What might surprise some readers today is the apparently modest scope of that book, which featured contributions from only sixteen composers. But what might appear an inadequate sample provided a reasonably comprehensive overview of the music being composed in Britain in the early 1960s, when there were clearer notions of what classical music should be and of how it was developing.

By the time Paul Griffiths compiled a similar book in 1985,[2] the musical world was more complex: the next generation of composers was larger, more varied and arguably more adventurous. But even his selection of twenty composers seems small today. Indeed, he acknowledged that to provide a fair representation of the state of British music would require perhaps five times as many interviews with composers as Schafer published. In the 2010s the task is made even more difficult by the fact that composers are writing many more types of music that are being listened to in many more ways. The cellist Steven Isserlis once suggested to me that

> There's no language of modern music anymore. There was a language of baroque music, of classical music, even of nineteenth-century romantic music, from which composers deviated in their different ways. But now there's pop-influenced music, classical music, a jazz influence, a folk influence, modernistic music, the influence of ancient religious music ... Music is going in all those different directions.[3]

Contemporary classical music, however we wish to define it (and I do not), takes forms that Schafer and possibly even Griffiths could not have anticipated. One and two generations on respectively from the composers they interviewed, the unprecedented range of music being composed in Britain today is one reason for my following in their literary footsteps.

More important was the intention, indeed the necessity, to interview composers as someone who loves music but is not a trained musician or musicologist. Although as a professional writer I concentrate on classical music and musicians, I am a recipient of the music-making process rather than a participant in it, and my response to music is essentially that of the amateur. From this relatively un-analytical vantage point I sense that some composers are writing music with which the majority of the public do not engage because they feel that it has nothing to offer them. But I suspect that the failing is not necessarily that of the composer, who writes music at a time when attention spans are shortening and when gratification is

---

[2] *New Sounds, New Personalities: British Composers of the 1980s* (London, Faber & Faber, 1985).
[3] Interview for *Strings* magazine, April 2011.

increasingly required to be swift if not instant. Why, when many people are unwilling to invest time in listening thoughtfully and adventurously to contemporary music, should composers feel obligated to make their music 'accessible'? On the other hand, what can they expect if they refuse to make concessions to the public – assuming, of course, that they believe their music should have some relevance to society? Naturally, this is not the whole story, for many British composers write in what is considered a conservative idiom. Their problem is not comprehension but competition: what impact can they have in a marketplace that is saturated with a thousand years of Western music?

The experience of hearing contemporary music is often mediated through some form of critical commentary or analysis, but I wanted to establish a more direct and personal connection between British composers of our time and their audiences. And because my interest is in the social, cultural and psychological processes behind composition rather than in the techniques by which it is created, one of my aims in compiling this book has been to explore why contemporary composers write the kind of music that they do – if, of course, they have any choice in the matter.

Schafer's book featured most of the best-known British composers of the time, ranging in age and musical style from the elderly John Ireland to the young Peter Maxwell Davies. As its title suggests, Griffiths's collection had a more contemporary focus and concentrated on composers who were born in the period from 1932 to 1953. My own list of contributors excludes a few well-known composers who were unable or unwilling to participate in the project, but most omissions are due to restrictions of space and time. I was eager to revisit Schafer's youngest contributors, Peter Maxwell Davies and Alexander Goehr, who fifty years later are regarded as senior statesmen of the British musical establishment, and I wanted to interview more female composers (Elisabeth Lutyens was the only woman to be interviewed by either Schafer or Griffiths). My broad aim was to reflect as wide a range of ages, personalities, styles of music and levels of fame as is possible in a book of this size, but I am aware that my selection of contributors is in part a reflection of my own musical interests and curiosity.

Most of the interviews were based on a list of standard questions because I was interested to explore how composers who write very different kinds of music would respond to common issues such as the function and purpose (if any) of their work, their daily routine, the relationship (if any) between their nationality and their music, the extent to which their desire to communicate to listeners affects the practical expression of their musical ideas, how much of their work goes on in the head before being notated, and so on. But this list of questions was only a starting point for conversations, each of which inevitably went off at a tangent that reflected the individuality of its subject.

In order to minimise repetition, my editing of the conversations avoids the question and answer format in which the interviews were conducted; and in order to minimise my presence on the page, it presents the composers' comments in a way that will, I hope, speak directly to readers. My personal contribution is restricted to a highly subjective account of my meeting with each of the composers, including the circumstances in which we talked and, for what it is worth, my impressions of their personality as expressed in the unnatural atmosphere of an interview with (in most cases) a stranger.

I admit that this venture was in one sense destined to partial failure, for composers – like all creative artists, I imagine – can tell us less about their work than we might expect. If they could explain their music in words they would not need to compose it. Furthermore, it might not have the 'meaning' that we believe it has, and some of it might have no 'meaning' at all. I should also point out that the interviews for this book were conducted over a period of nearly four years and therefore that some of the views expressed by the contributors may no longer be relevant. All but one (and in this case, his widow) had the opportunity to approve their contributions, but their comments as reproduced here should not necessarily be regarded as definitive.

'[Schafer's] *British Composers in Interview* is one of my all-time favourite books on music, and another, similar book would be very valuable', David Matthews wrote to me before I interviewed him. And Joseph Phibbs commented, 'I remember coming across the [Griffiths] book *New Sounds, New Personalities* in my school library when I was fourteen and finding it very inspirational. I've felt for ages that an updated version of this book is long overdue.' Since most of the contributors to the current collection expressed similar feelings when agreeing to be interviewed for it, I can only hope that it will be enjoyed for a fraction of the time that its distinguished predecessors have been, or at least until someone repeats the exercise with another generation of British composers.

Andrew Palmer
Brighton, January 2015

Julian Anderson

Julian Anderson, London, February 2012

> **I'd rather be surprised by what I write than merely fill out music according to a pre-decided aesthetic position.**

I'm sometimes asked after conducting an interview, 'How did it go?' And the answer isn't always straightforward because two elements are involved: the technical and the personal. While the first of these can (and must) be prepared for beforehand, the fact remains that some musicians dislike the interview process and engage with it reluctantly; and so I don't automatically expect them to enjoy what's essentially a professional obligation. And I try to remember, each time I switch on my voice recorder and ask my first question, that my interviewee may be having a difficult day or week or month. I'm therefore aware of being both prepared and unprepared for how 'it' will go.

The majority of my most memorable interviews have been with musicians whose personalities were quite different from what I'd expected, and the surprise has nearly always been pleasant. What interests me about this are the mental processes (largely unconscious, perhaps) by which I form a preconception of the character of interviewees. This might be based on their personality as expressed in previous interviews, perhaps their level of celebrity and therefore their accessibility to me, and possibly even the style of music that they write or perform. And sometimes I get it wrong.

The above is an attempt to describe how I approached the task of interviewing the contributors to this book who were previously unknown to me. They included Julian Anderson, who'd been apologetic that the interview couldn't take place at his home but whom I met in February 2012 at a location that has a musical association: the Heights Restaurant and Bar on the top floor of the Saint George's Hotel in Langham Place, London, built on the site of the famous Queen's Hall.

Like many of the composers, he was familiar with Paul Griffiths's book and pleased to be contributing to its successor. But the interview got off to an uneasy start because of the sudden, blaring intrusion of piped music that seemed totally inappropriate stylistically and, in any case, unendurably loud. While I was wondering what to do about this unwanted accompaniment he got up, confronted the staff and told them very firmly about the importance of our conversation; the volume of the music was reduced, he returned to our table and we both relaxed.

'I'm sorry I talked a lot', he said as we finished. 'But anyway, see what you can do with what I've said.' By then it was dark and there was time only to take an inadequate photograph of him standing against the end wall of the restaurant. We left the building sharing anecdotes, I silently hoping to enjoy his company again and feeling greatly encouraged, at a still early stage in the compilation of this book, by the seriousness with which he took his involvement in it. But I must have caught him at a bad time, because when, much later, he sent me a revised typescript of our encounter, he explained, 'This is the interview I would and should have given but, due to pressure of work at the time, did not have the energy to give out properly.'

I'm reluctant to describe him in terms of his integrity because I don't want to suggest that the other composers I interviewed possess less of it, but it's a quality that I'm sure strikes anyone meeting him for the first time. Nor do I want mention of his intelligence, seriousness and impatience with the second-rate to make him appear cold. So for those who aren't fortunate enough to know him, I emphasise his catholicity of taste, his rejection of the political or partisan in the musical world, and above all his warmth and humour, which I feel privileged to have encountered.

―――

I'm partly the child of an émigré lineage, and I grew up with the music that my parents listened to at home: eighteenth- and nineteenth-century Western classical music, and Russian music from the turn of the twentieth century up to and including *The Rite of Spring* – nothing beyond that except some jazz and some prog rock my brothers played. The only British piece I knew was Britten's *The Young Person's Guide to the Orchestra*. It's marvellous, but it had little direct influence on me except in its brilliantly expert professional technique, from which anyone can learn. But I never felt that I was connected with the British tradition, particularly. So I feel I'm a composer who just happens to be British, rather than a 'British composer' as such.

By the age of about fifteen I'd heard a lot of British music from the previous one-hundred-plus years because it was being broadcast on Radio 3 (this was the 1970s and 1980s). There was, for example, a long radio series called *Fifty Years of British Music* (incidentally, since this was broadcast on weekday afternoons I associate it with illness – I only heard it if I was either on holiday or ill, because otherwise I had to be at school at that time of day). To be frank, I didn't like much of what I heard: endless divertimenti and grey 1950s symphonies with flat orchestration and unimaginative melody and harmony. But I recall being interested in Cyril Scott's strange piano concerto, which I recently heard again and still find a rather original (if overlong) piece; some of it sounds a bit like the Ligeti piano studies. Anyhow, hats off to the BBC for giving listeners the chance to discover this sort of repertoire. The idea that William Glock and Robert Ponsonby only promoted a serialist mafia is absolute nonsense. When I was nine or ten the BBC broadcast all of Havergal Brian's symphonies within a year, and they put on his *Gothic Symphony* at the Albert Hall a few years later. So you could hear all kinds of things. And this took music out of the textbooks and into the ears, which is where it should be. The BBC broadcast an amazingly broad range of music, and I owe them a lot for that.

When I was thirteen I visited the British Music Information Centre in London, which at that time was a real hub of musical excitement. It was run with great flair by Roger Wright, who knew everyone and was brilliant at putting people together. All sorts of people would just pop in, both from the UK and abroad. I met Olly Knussen, Harry Halbreich and Michael Finnissy there, for example. Roger was incredibly kind and helpful, in so many ways, both to me as a naïve youngster and to many composers of all ages. With his help and guidance I began to expand my repertoire knowledge and also began to realise, from various things he said, just how very difficult it could be to compose all your life and do nothing else.

Knussen's Third Symphony had very forcefully impressed me when I heard it on the radio a few months before this, and by chance Olly was in the building, score-reading for the Society for the Promotion of New Music, the first morning I went to the BMIC, and Roger introduced us. Olly (I seem always to have known him as 'Olly') was very kind and encouraging, taking huge amounts of time and trouble to help me in all sorts of ways. He looked at my early efforts at composition; and he suggested scores to look at, pieces to hear, plays to read, paintings and films to see – everything. He was terribly supportive, and from him I got an idea of the life of a professional composer. For example, he told me how commissions are paid (you get 50 per cent at the start and 50 per cent upon completion), what the Performing Right Society is, things like that. I realised that this was going to be very difficult, and that the profession was very dangerous because of its total lack of security. It's even more dangerous now.

I was very lucky, I think, to grow up without a sense of there being an official canon, whether contemporary or old, outside which I must not move. I wasn't aware of any sort of stylistic embargo. But I admired very much what I heard of Boulez's concerts in the early 1980s. The red-letter day in my life was probably 25 November 1981, when I heard his dress rehearsal and performance of *Pli selon pli* in the Festival Hall. I'd done my homework – Olly had played me the piece a few months before and I'd borrowed the scores from my local library – and when I heard that music live for the first time I just thought it was the most imaginative and beautiful experience of my life. The variety of harmony, the ornate vocal writing and the staggering range of orchestral colours were unforgettable. At that moment I decided to devote my life to composing music. *Pli* is a remarkable achievement, and I love it still.

I was also very attracted by the latest British music of the time, including Robin Holloway's Second Concerto for Orchestra, Knussen's Third Symphony (as already mentioned), George Benjamin's *Ringed by the Flat Horizon* and Michael Finnissy's *Sea and Sky*. I swam happily in those pieces, and felt very much at home. It was a totally instinctive and strong attraction, and that was terribly inspiring. So I started studying seriously and eventually – on Olly's recommendation – studied with his teacher, John Lambert, for five years, the last three of them at the Royal College of Music.

John was a great encourager: while teaching you he wanted to learn about *your* interests and enthusiasms. I became very involved in spectral music – Tristan Murail, Gérard Grisey, Horatiu Radulescu *et al.* – and in the music of Lachenmann, both of which I'd discovered through listening to French radio in the early 1980s; so I showed John those things. He even let me go to Murail for three months of private lessons in early 1987. John was wonderfully open-minded about all that, but hard to please – which was all to the good. With any piece you took him, he'd immediately spot where it was dragging its heels or would see how to tighten the shape or make its dramatic impact more precise. He was like an expert film editor, and that taught me a huge amount about how to improve a score and how to assess my own music neutrally from the outside. He'd look at your latest orchestral score and say things like, 'Put the beginning at the end, my dear, now throw the middle into the bin, it's treading water, then write a different opening which isn't so obvious, and by the way, haven't you written enough trills already in your life?' All with an amused casualness which was very engaging – you didn't feel 'taught' at all. A lovely man. He also really drilled me in aural, which stood me in very good stead – composers need good ears.

After that it was time for a change, and I decided to study with Alexander Goehr at Cambridge. He was more intellectually tough than

John, and very widely read. He was quite as likely to bring in art or philosophy as other music to lessons. We didn't just talk about notes, although he could do that as well as anyone else. I found his subtle approach to teaching a composer fascinating, and it was very healthy to have almost every assumption about music and culture seriously challenged. I studied with him for three years or so, and he helped me get a better perspective on everything. I owe him a huge amount.

By discovering more music and therefore more of the world, you also discover more about yourself. In the 1983 Proms I heard gagaku (Japanese court music) for the first time, and it was the most startling revelation. I had to find out as much as possible about that music. And without having heard and loved and studied it, I wouldn't have written most of my output. Of course, I don't write fake Japanese pieces – the process of absorption produces something quite different from the original. But the sound of gagaku, its complex modality, its sense of spacing and timing, its particular textures – having the harmony invariably *above* the melody ... all these factors have influenced my work repeatedly. But it doesn't sound like gagaku – why should it? It goes in at all sorts of other levels. Finally, in the first movement of *The Discovery of Heaven*, I paid more direct tribute to gagaku – you hear something more akin to it in one short passage near the end of that movement. It's a little act of homage to gagaku for all that it has done to help me compose. But otherwise, no.

The crucial fact remains: our knowledge of the world has expanded out of all recognition, and this is bound to affect how we write music. If I'd been born in 1867, not in 1967, it would have been much harder for me to know a lot of medieval music such as Pérotin, whereas as a kid I could hear it on the radio. I could also hear Indian raga and learn quite a lot about it – this was the era of the all-night Proms of Indian classical music in 1981 and 1982. Thai classical music also came to the Proms in 1981, and the previous year Donald Mitchell presented three programmes of it on Radio 3; and that has been another long-lasting enthusiasm of mine. Both Javanese and Balinese gamelan came to the Proms in 1979 and again three years later, which got me strongly interested in *that* music as well.

So the musical world has expanded enormously, and personally I can't just sit down and say, 'Right: Symphony No. 2, sonata form first movement in C major, slow movement in A minor, scherzo with two trios in ...'. I've written a Symphony, or rather a piece with that title. But it questions the genre as much as it enshrines it. I mean, what exactly is symphonic about a work whose first two minutes include almost no pitch at all within a texture in which almost every instrument is being played abnormally? And answering that question became, in one way, the journey of the piece. The integration of noise into a complex journey of transforming sound, timbre, rhythm and harmony is what that Symphony's about. Any thematic aspect is just part of working that out.

I admit very happily into my music all the contradictions of the world I see and experience, which basically means I'm not a fundamentalist. In fact, everything I compose is anti-fundamentalist, and the regrowth of fundamentalism that we've seen in so many areas of life in the past thirty-five years is frankly repugnant to me. There's no doubt that new music, too, has its fundamentalists: people who believe that all problems in composition can be solved by subscribing blindly to a single overriding aesthetic, for life. Such people admit no contradictions and are perhaps the greatest single danger to creativity (some of them teach composition, alas). Clearly, some people are very frightened by danger and ambiguity. I grew up in the 1980s, and the hideous political climate of that time – social and sexual intolerance, dogma against dogma, while society went to the bad – gave me a permanent allergy to all extremism and really left me wondering what to expect from politics.

We're still told in art – generally by failed practitioners, admittedly – that it's great to push things to extremes. But, with very few exceptions (Feldman's *Coptic Light* is one), artistic extremism for its own sake results in art that's hopelessly adolescent. And it's too easy – anyone can think up an extreme artistic product these days. Nothing simpler. However, if the music simply emerges as something pushing at the limits, without conscious posing on the composer's part, that's fine and honest; and it's clearly going to happen when it's intrinsically necessary. I tend to feel that the world is more complex and interesting than fundamentalists will allow, and so are our brains. So when I'm composing I'd rather be surprised by what I write than merely fill out music according to a pre-decided aesthetic position.

The result is that I don't write that quickly. I *can't*, given that I've often no idea what to compose when I start a piece, and little notion as to how to compose it. This makes starting a work very difficult and often very protracted; but once I get going, the journey of discovering what the piece will be is terribly exciting. You never know where you'll end up, and I'm usually very surprised by what the finished work is. In fact, if everything went just as expected from the start, I'd suspect the piece was rubbish. I'm not the slowest of composers but, clearly, working in this very heuristic, un-dogmatic way is risky and time-consuming. But I can't see any alternative for me.

When I started work on the ensemble piece *Khorovod*, many years before I completed it, I gradually moved away from my obsession with timbre for its own sake (so typical of the spectral composers) because I became aware that I needed ... well, if I say 'melody' people think of something soppy, and I don't mean that at all. It's simply the power and interest of an unfolding melodic line that attracts me. Around that time I studied Gregorian chant and various folk traditions that are very melodic – the Gaelic psalm-singing traditions of the Hebridean islands of Lewis and Harris were a big influence. And in the early 1980s I'd come across the music of composers like Claude Vivier and Ştefan Niculescu, who had similar preoccupations. Their music was a great support to me while I looked at these melodic issues.

The first piece in which I worked with long, unfolding melodic lines was *Diptych* for orchestra, which was composed between 1988 and 1990. Around then I began to fear that every time I wrote a chord the music would stop in its tracks, so I experimented with heterophony – many variants of the same melodic line all played at once. It produces textures that are at the same time melodic and harmonic, and it seems to bypass the question of whether one's going to write either harmony or counterpoint. It melds the two together. This explains why I wrote much of the piece straight into full score. There was no way of sketching it, because the only shorthand would have been one melodic line amongst several others. Well, there were loose sketches in which I was trying to get a particular section right, but otherwise nothing before the full score, which I wrote in pencil, erasing as I went. More usually, there's a full score sketch (a terrible mess) for each piece, and sketch pads on which I try out a technique or a device.

On the other hand, *Khorovod*, which was composed at the same time as *Diptych*, was sketched quite differently from it, and from any other piece I've written. The first sketch was a single sheet of A2 music paper (forty staves) with one long, changing melodic line going from start to finish. That took me about four hours to compose – which was useful because I could get the timing and musical sequence for the whole piece pretty exact right away. I then spent much of the next five years elaborating and decorating it – devising counterpoints, heterophonies and accompaniments which at times overwhelmed the original melody and erased it – until the full score emerged naturally out of that process.

For me, composing has always been an essentially aural process. But there are levels of imagination and there's aural junk – you have to know the difference between them. I prefer to get rid of the junk by imagining it, then start writing when I've got more of an idea of the piece. Many technical procedures can't be worked out only in your head: you need a piece of paper or a computer to help. A major change occurs when I notice that as soon as I start to notate the music I'm trying to hear in my head, other things become possible. So there's a constant give and take between the paper and the ear.

I explained earlier that I compose without any *a priori* aesthetics, but that doesn't mean there's no technique involved. On the contrary, I've worked very hard at technique. But it doesn't write the music for me. My music is built up from very basic factors: in pitch terms, the degree of consonance or dissonance (in the acoustic sense of roughness or smoothness); in rhythmic terms, the degree of regularity or irregularity and the presence or absence of perceptible meter; and in the field of timbres, the degree of noisiness – again in the acoustic sense of 'white noise'. Clearly, these things don't tell me which note to put down next, nor what chord to write, nor what rhythms to write. They're simple tools with which I can examine what I'm composing and get some kind of perspective on it. As the music is often very polyphonic, there may be more than one change going on in any of these fields simultaneously. When that's the case, I also examine the overall effect of the passage in terms such as: how consonant or dissonant is it acoustically? How predictable or not? And so on.

So the study of the perception of sounds – psychoacoustics – has been very important to me. Also, since about 1986 I've been building up a system of modes which extrapolates the consonance–dissonance factor into different modal areas. Again, this doesn't tell me what notes to write, but it does help me to know where I am in a piece; and, especially, it helps me to modulate between different modes or combine them, which is a great help in building works on a large scale. Since 2001 I've sometimes returned to using pitches outside Western tuning, and I have a modal system for that which is also based on relative consonance or dissonance; so it's all related somehow.

I think the pieces I finished between 1990 and 1998, such as *Diptych*, *The Bearded Lady*, *Khorovod*, *Stations of the Sun* and *Tiramisù*, form a fairly consistent group, because while writing them I was working out these basic concerns very clearly. In other words, those pieces established certain basic things in my music about melody, modes, heterophony, polyphony, polyrhythm, et cetera, and the interaction between them. Then things began to change. *Alhambra Fantasy*, written about a year after *Stations of the Sun*, seemed to me a different kind of piece even though it's clearly by the same composer. It's more abrupt and cut up; the form is more unpredictable and the music goes in many different directions. It's quite unstable.

There was another break around the time of *Fantasias*, a much more recent orchestral work in five movements that took me two and a half years to write – quite a long time for a thirty-minute work. And in that piece I was aware of a complete reassessment of my musical technique. As a result, it has sharper contrasts than previous pieces. When you separate movements out (with pauses between them) you can change your compositional clothes much more, and what excites me now is playing off the very stark against the very rich, the changeable against the static, and so on. Contrasting musical states – and by that I really mean very different ways of building music and listening to it – and then exploring the connections between them is what interests me most. This gives the feeling of an unfolding drama, with different musical characters in opposition to each other; and since I'm writing an opera at the moment, that is a major concern.

Composers need to remember that as soon as the music leaves their desk and goes out into the real world, it has its own existence. We have to let go. I can remember performances of, for instance, *The Stations of the Sun* that went at sharply varying speeds, and I'm fine about that. I try to get my metronome marks correct, but the truth is that they're relative speeds, not absolute ones. I'd never write, as Stockhausen did in *Gruppen*, 'crochet = 53.5'. Tempo is one area where the subjectivity of the performer is even *desirable*. The only thing you don't want is the music to sound careless and arbitrary. But I've generally been very lucky with performers – conductors especially. When you're a kid you think it would be nice to have your music performed under a great conductor, and I still can't quite get over the thrill of it. I just sit there and can't believe it's happening!

I like routine. I have a lot to do, and I like knowing that I'll be doing certain things at different times of the day and week. I teach composition – it's one of the main ways I earn a living – and I enjoy that very much as well. But it all has to be balanced out. For ten years until 2012 I also ran a concert series called 'Music of Today' (from which my own music was pretty much banned) with the Philharmonia Orchestra, presenting almost all of the concerts myself. When it was possible I introduced the composers in person and talked to them about their music, and sometimes we played examples with the ensemble on stage. I enjoyed that, and I'm doing something similar now as part of my duties as Composer in Residence with the London Philharmonic: only one event per year but working with young professional composers towards a concert in which they each get a new piece played. But

I'm truly happy only when I'm at my desk and piano, working at my latest piece. I've got sounds from it whizzing around my head right now. As long as I have that centre to my life, I'm fine.

By nature I'm very shy, but I'm also eager to communicate with people about the music I love. In the UK there's a perception that it's helpful if concert music isn't just flung at the public without some verbal communication that might help them to find a way into it (I'm not convinced this is always true). I enjoy talking to audiences about music, especially if I can introduce them to a wonderful piece – perhaps a contemporary classic they've never heard before. I'm also perfectly happy to talk about my own music. So there's always a battle going on inside me: between the person who'd really like to keep myself to myself and the other person who's very eager to communicate.

Many people like to see a composer talking because they find the notion of writing music very strange – it's not a public activity like conducting or playing an instrument. You can't see it happening. But people shouldn't believe everything composers say about their own music! Ours is only the first (chronologically) point of view. It's not the 'best' or the 'correct' view, if such things exist. My idea of what's going on in my music isn't necessarily what's going on in it; I'm simply the first person to get to know the piece in question. In any case, musical thought is elusive and by nature non-verbal, so naturally many composers find it hard to say much about what they do. But I'm perfectly happy to talk about my music, provided there's an understanding that I can only give a few hints and clues. And that can be useful for an audience who don't know your work.

One of the shocks of my life was taking a two-week summer course with György Ligeti and discovering fairly quickly that, although he was a great composer and I was only twenty-three, his conception of music was clearly not mine. In a sense, his whole output is of very focussed pieces (*études*, really), each of which explores one thing with huge imagination. I realised then that I needed to write music with much more inconsistency on the surface than he would tolerate. I think this remains the case, and that *Fantasias* pushes it even further.

I don't want pick-and-mix eclecticism – a little bit of this and a little bit of that. I'm not a postmodernist (a fashionable label at one time) because I believe in pieces of music being whole. But that whole can and should include sharp contrasts, if they're necessary. As I say, I try to compose without *a priori*. This isn't actually possible – it's an illusion – but I try to keep it in mind!

Simon Bainbridge

Simon Bainbridge, London, February 2014

'It's important to contribute to a culture that survives beyond us.'

There ended up being two interviews with Simon Bainbridge for this book. Both took place at the Royal Academy of Music in London, where he has been a Professor of Composition since 1999, and the venue was appropriate because I wanted to talk to him about how he relates his experience as a composer to that of the students he teaches.

The first interview was arranged for a late afternoon at the end of February 2014, and my arrival at the Academy coincided with the interval of a vocal competition and a flood of audience members surging into the foyer. Bainbridge arrived shortly afterwards, and although I remembered him from a meeting many years earlier as having an authoritative presence – he's very tall and has a deep, sonorous voice – he appeared rather distracted, particularly while attempting to summon the Academy's antiquated and cramped lift. When its doors eventually opened, we manoeuvred around students and their instrument cases and juddered to the top floor, where a composition study had been booked for our meeting. It was virtually filled by an upright piano, a round table across which we talked – to piano accompaniment from a nearby practice room – and shelves full of scores against which he stood to be photographed after the interview.

As I'd hoped, he talked in very practical terms and was concerned to explain his composition processes (which he admitted to sometimes finding frustratingly difficult) as clearly as possible. In short, this was a straightforward, businesslike conversation, whose flow was assisted by his evident sympathy for the thinking behind some of my questions. But I wasn't aware of him relaxing significantly once the interview was underway, perhaps because his mind was on the performance of a horn trio (not his own) by students that he'd agreed at short notice to conduct early that evening.

We met again eight months later because, after reading the edited typescript of the interview, he felt that he hadn't expressed himself as well as he'd wanted to. He suggested starting again from the beginning, and this time he was more relaxed. We talked in a practice room on the first floor of the Academy, a tenor and piano providing distant musical accompaniment, and a few minutes into the interview the horn player Richard Watkins knocked and walked in to return an instrument to a cupboard.

This second conversation was less structured than the first and included a few impromptu questions that (to our mutual frustration, I think) Bainbridge struggled to answer, although this doubtless reflected the fact that a composer's motivations and practices are too intuitive to be expressed easily in words. It felt odd to be asking him the same list of questions when I had the typescript of his earlier responses in front of me, and I wondered how much more satisfied he would be with his new ones when he saw them in print. So we agreed a compromise: the published interview would be based on our second conversation but would include a few comments from the first that I was reluctant to lose.

Although he later made a number of changes to the final edit, clarifying his comments on some of the issues we discussed, the published conversation begins with the very first question I asked him, which was about the moment (if any) in his career at which he was able to identify his compositional 'voice'.

It's interesting that you should ask that, because only recently I gave a talk to students about my Viola Concerto, which I wrote when I was twenty-six and which was my first really big piece. I hadn't listened to it for a long time, as I don't listen to my music very often unless I'm talking about it; but when I played it I realised that, although the way I achieve an end result has changed a lot over the years, there are compositional ideas in that piece which are still very relevant and important to me today.

I came from a visual background – my father was a painter and my brother is a stage designer. And I remember being fascinated by a set of my father's paintings, collectively entitled *Focalform*, that allowed the viewer to home in on one part of the canvas and then to make a journey through it from that point. That idea stuck with me, and it came to musical fruition in the second movement of the Viola Concerto, which I wrote for Walter Trampler. He was a wonderful musician, whom I had the good fortune to know for more than twenty-five years. I remember on one occasion he lent me his beautiful apartment on Riverside Drive in New York City, while he was out of town for a few days, to work on the concerto. I came across a recording he made for RCA with the Polish pianist Mieczysław Horszowski of the two late Brahms Sonatas, and I was knocked sideways by the range of colours he achieved from his magnificent Amati viola. It was both his innate musicianship and his beautiful playing that gave me the initial sound world for the concerto.

While sketching the concerto I became fascinated with exploring musical perspective, and the way one can use distance and the superimposition of background and foreground elements to articulate the musical structure, while defining the ever-changing relationship that exists between the solo instrument and the orchestra. This is a spatial concept, and one that allows the listener to be drawn into a rich and multi-layered musical environment which can be explored in many different ways, magically transporting the listener into the composer's temporal vision.

A composer who did this brilliantly was Luigi Nono. I remember hearing a performance of his *Prometeo* in Germany some years ago and being taken on an extraordinary journey that lasted two and a half hours; the experience was so rich and vibrant that I lost all awareness of time.

In 2007 I wrote a piece that used as its starting point Daniel Libeskind's remarkable architecture. It was called *Music, Space, Reflection*, and it was written for four identical sextets and live electronics. It was designed to be performed in a number of locations, including the Imperial War Museum North in Salford Quays and the Royal Ontario Museum in Toronto. Although the musical continuity remains the same from building to building, the way that listeners hear the work varies depending on the specific building they're within. So the compositional process involved a lot of walking around buildings!

Musical space can also be internalised. I remember years ago having problems finding a way into my first BBC Symphony Orchestra commission: for a few days I stopped writing notes and instead I looked at different ways in which an orchestral layout could be redefined. I came up with the idea of two orchestras of identical instrumentation, positioned opposite each other as a mirror image. The music begins with bass pedal notes from the left and the right of the performing area, and these gradually fan out through the orchestras to meet in the middle before dissolving and re-forming. That initial sound idea – the physical gesture of two orchestras working simultaneously but in mirror image – generated the whole composition, which came to life as *Fantasia for Double Orchestra*, premiered in 1984 at the Royal Festival Hall.

I can't start a new piece until I have a clear and coherent sense of its sound world. I've just finished a string quartet, a most difficult medium to work with, and it took me ages to discover my own way of using the four instruments. I sketched about a hundred pages of score and threw them all away before I began to be aware of a really strong characterisation to the music. But once I could physically hear its sound world I had my starting point, and the time element of the music began to unfold for me.

Identifying or describing that sound world has something to do with the interaction of the four instrumental voices. This involves duets in opposition to each other, fusing contrapuntally to create a four-part texture and then re-forming into duets. Now, this isn't a new idea (Elliott Carter's Third Quartet is made up entirely of two duet groups), but it generated the harmonic and expressive ideas that I needed. It also articulated a very strong visual element in the piece, which was my reaction to the extraordinary paintings of the Ethiopian/American artist Julie Mehretu. They were a kind of trigger that kept the music alive.

I've just started a new piece for the American jazz bassist Eddie Gomez (he played with Bill Evans) and the Britten Sinfonia, and the challenge in writing it is to find a way in which our different musical worlds (there's no hint of a sax or a drum kit, but there are Eddie's extraordinary improvisatory skills) can meet. The piece starts with a two-part invention in which the double bass forms duos with other solo instruments – a marimba, a trumpet, a bass flute, a violin and so on. These duos gradually become trios, quartets, sextets and octets, and eventually the whole piece opens up to the point where the double bass is playing against the *tutti* band. And I knew very early on that in order to control this musical process I needed to create a very rigorous superstructure for the piece.

The first thing I thought about was the *tempi* relationships between the different sections – the duo period, the trio period, the quartet period, et cetera – and then, related to them, the different timbres of the instruments I'm writing for. I've planned the piece very accurately on the page so that I'll know at, say, two minutes fifteen seconds into the trio section that I'm working with a particular trio of instruments. The combination of instrumental colour and the pulse of the music are staging posts; they don't get in the way of the musical development of the piece but they help me to carve and chisel away at the details in the knowledge that I've got the next element there, waiting to be connected.

This is fundamentally a linear process, which is the way I was trained to compose. My teacher, John Lambert, talked a lot about 'La Grande Ligne' and got me to do strict sixteenth-century counterpoint every week. His teacher was Nadia Boulanger, who also insisted on polyphonic studies; and *her* teacher was Gabriel Fauré. Listen to the late Fauré works – particularly the Piano Trio, with its wonderful webs of musical lines!

I start each piece by listening with my inner ear to a gradually evolving sound world. I think, at this stage in the process, the most important information I need is a knowledge of how long the piece is going to be. That provides a thread on which to place and pace the various musical components within a given time frame. You're right to suggest that the process involves a lot of rejecting what I've written. As I said earlier, I threw away a lot of music while writing my new String Quartet. But this is a useful process because it makes me aware of how to draft something differently. And I'm aware that every piece presents a new set of rules that I have to discover. Eventually the music *does* come, which is why you should always avoid getting into a rut and writing the same thing over and over again just because you know it'll work. That's so boring.

I often think about how my music is going to come across to the performers and the audience. It's a composer's duty to develop a technique that will allow his or her ideas and means of expression to be articulate and coherent, and above all to communicate to listeners, allowing them to inhabit the composer's temporal vision. You don't want them looking at their watches every few moments, waiting for the wretched piece to finish!

But the last thing you should ever do is to write down to audiences. They need to be stimulated, and we're living at a time in which they aren't being made to think very much about what they hear. As a result, I find a lot of contemporary music one-dimensional and rather tedious. Writing *for* audiences, but not down to them, means articulating ideas that are explored and developed through coherent musical grammar. This is what informs and communicates to listeners.

For seven years I was Head of the Composition Department here at the Royal Academy of Music. It was an immensely rewarding and stimulating period in my career, although it did take up a lot of my time and energy. These days I have the great pleasure just to be able to teach and lead composition seminars.

Much of my time is spent getting inside a student's creative imagination in order to try to fathom out exactly what he or she wants to do musically. This can lead to discussions about aesthetic or musical ideas, stimulating the students' knowledge and the invention process. In fact, most of the lessons with my most successful students have been long chats about composition, and for me one of the most interesting aspects of teaching is exchanging ideas with them and on occasions learning from *them*.

On a somewhat negative note, however, some of the young composers who are applying to study at universities or music conservatoires actually have very little knowledge of the music of even the great composers, and little knowledge about techniques of composition. This is a problem that seems to have gradually got worse over the years and one that hasn't been helped by the emergence of the amazing Sibelius software, which is often misused and has simply become a means of being able to play back scores. The result of this is that the Academy receives a lot of applications from young students who have no aural perception because they no longer have to use their ears when writing a piece of music or even to understand the grammar of committing it to paper.

I went to study at the Royal College of Music in 1969, which was musically an incredibly exciting time. The giants of the post-Second World War period – Berio, Stockhausen, Ligeti, Pousseur, Kagel and Boulez, to name but a few – dominated the way we thought about music, but it wasn't only the European avant-garde. Peter Maxwell Davies, Harry Birtwistle and Sandy Goehr were equally important to me. I remember hearing the Pierrot Players, before they became the Fires of London, playing many of Max's and Harry's early pieces. A lot of us became involved in what was going on musically at that time and undoubtedly even copied their styles and ideas. And, you know, in some ways it's important for young composers to do that, because finding out how other people's music is made is all part of forming your own musical language.

Forty-odd years later, there seems to be a lack of connection with contemporary composition. When I was a young composer I went to everything, and the Queen Elizabeth Hall was sold out whenever Berio was in town. In other words, there was a sense of real discovery. That's all gone, and I can't explain why that's happened. But I don't want to paint too bleak a picture, because there are some wonderful young composers emerging in this country. And although the ways in which new music is promoted have changed, there are still lots of opportunities for young composers to get their pieces performed by big orchestras such as the LSO, the LPO or the RPO – which is marvellous.

And at the Academy, too. Last year, for example, Richard Watkins devised a project based around the Ligeti Horn Trio, and all the student composers got to work with Richard.

When *I* was a student I never had a piece of mine performed at the Royal College (Benjamin Britten had the same problem!). It was the Society for the Promotion of New Music that gave me my first big performance, in Aldeburgh, when the English Chamber Orchestra performed a short piece of mine called *Spirogyra*, which helped my career quite a bit. Until that point I'd never been in a position to hear any of my music.

I've never quite come to terms with the feeling I get when all the things I've been agonising over are finally fixed on the page and the piece is being taken over by somebody else. I'm transmitting my thoughts to a performer who has to interpret them, and while this doesn't feel threatening there's often a worry about how the piece is going to work when the conductor and musicians take charge. At the same time, there's also the possibility that they'll take my musical ideas even further than I'd imagined. So the beginning of the process of collaborating with performers can be very exciting. But it's still the most terrifying moment when you hear your piece for the first time – when it becomes public domain. That's the point at which you think 'Oh, my God, I got *that* wrong!' or 'Wow, that *works*!' I don't know how much I have to *like* a piece in order to be satisfied with it, but there has to be a feeling of connection and warmth between it and me. And in order to be able to write the double bar at the end I need some sense that the piece has worked.

It's funny: I recently gave a talk on my work and played my *Ad Ora Incerta*[1] from beginning to end, and I had a very strange experience. I was blown away by the harmony in the last movement, 'Buna', which has a very devastating text, and I thought 'How the hell did I *do* that?' I had no comprehension of where the music had come from and how it had occurred in my head. It was almost as though someone else had written it. And it hit me like a ton of bricks, because in the six or seven years since I'd last heard the piece I'd acquired a distance from it. I felt terribly upset by it, actually, as I had been when I was writing it – the subject matter is totally harrowing. Listening to it again I was more objective ... at least, my *emotions* were. But that's a rare occurrence, partly because *Ad Ora Incerta* is less abstract a piece than I would

---

[1] Four Orchestral Songs from Primo Levi (1994).

normally write, and so while I was writing it I was thinking about time and structure (guided by the text, of course) very differently.

I don't feel that being British has a huge effect on my music. In that sense, I don't feel a British composer. Britain is simply where I live and work. But I'd say that each of my pieces has the same function: to act as my interpretation of the world around me and as a statement of my place in it. We're on this planet for a certain number of years, and it's important for composers, like all creative artists, to leave a legacy of commentaries on the world that we're working with, and to contribute to a culture that survives beyond us. Sometimes the results of our work are good, sometimes we make mistakes and the pieces aren't so good. But it's important to write what's inside us.

I think my commentary on the world is an optimistic one, ultimately. But the work itself doesn't get any easier. Every new piece creates its own set of problems, partly because of an increasing expectation of oneself. And I agree with you that most creative people experience periods of great insecurity. I've had moments of darkness when I thought that everything I was writing was rubbish, or when I couldn't write anything at all for a long time, and when I felt pretty damned wretched. This is something that happens to a lot of us. But I've always come through those times, and I'm still writing. I wouldn't carry on if I weren't passionate about it. And writing music is about the only thing I do, really.

Sally Beamish

Sally Beamish, London, July 2012

> **❛ Composers are probably being laughed at today for music that will be iconic in fifty years' time.❜**

When I was asked recently about the possible differences between the music of male composers and that of their female counterparts, I had to reply that I can't identify the sex of a composer from the sound of his or her music. Furthermore, I doubt that anyone who's surprised to discover that a forceful, uncompromising piece was written by a woman would question a male composer's ability to write music characterised by what might be considered typically 'feminine' qualities such as gentleness and warmth. So I hope that the interviews with female composers for this book will challenge preconceptions about the gender of music.

But as I write these well-meaning words I have to admit that the minority status of the female contributors tempted me to look for similarities between them that I didn't look for between male composers. My own perception, although no doubt some of the women would disagree with me, was that there might be something different about the way in which they articulate the mysteries of the creative process, even though the music that results from it cannot be gendered. Is it true that they have a more 'holistic' attitude to this process, one that admits a wider range of influences and more readily finds similarities with the working practices of other disciplines? I'm still not sure. But I was struck by the female composers' emphasis on clarity of expression in both music and words. This is probably something about which male composers are equally concerned, but it seemed to me that they talked less about it. It was certainly a recurring topic of my conversation with Sally Beamish.

On a practical level, however, the clarity of this encounter was often compromised, and although the interview itself was straightforward and enjoyable it was one of the most difficult to transcribe and edit for this book. None of this was her fault. An opportunity to talk to her arose at short notice in July 2012 while she was on a business trip to London; on her last morning there she had a meeting at the Performing Right Society and suggested that we meet afterwards near her hotel in central London, before she and her partner drove back to Scotland, where she has lived since 1990. I discovered just around the corner a sandwich bar with a tiny basement dining area that I thought we would probably have to ourselves, but I was wrong, and by the time she'd arrived and negotiated the narrow spiral staircase it was too late to find anywhere quieter.

The recording of this interview features her talking between mouthfuls of tea and a sandwich, accompanied by animated conversation from the next table and from upstairs the proprietor shouting, a coffee machine gurgling and cutlery rattling. Voice recorders tend to pick up all such sounds with equal clarity (that word again), hence my subsequent difficulty in making out some of what Beamish had said to me. As with all the other interviews for this book, hesitations and self-corrections have been removed as part of my editing of the conversation for publication, but in her case they were noticeably few and far between. I was struck by the extent to which she talked in complete, rounded sentences – doubtless the result of her interest in the written word (she belongs to a creative writing group).

The interview began with my asking about the extent to which she feels that her nationality influences her music. And I wasn't surprised that she responded by returning to her musical roots, for her background is unusual: she began her career as a viola player, was largely self-taught as a composer and managed to establish a composing career without the usual level of support from a manager, agent or publisher.

I started writing music at the age of four, and the composers I was drawn to as a child were British: Malcolm Arnold, Walton and Britten. My father worked for Philips and used to check records for technical faults, and he'd often bring them home in brown paper wrappers. One of them was Arnold's *Tam O'Shanter*, another was the Walton Viola Concerto, played by William Primrose. And repeated listening made me very conscious of my British musical heritage. In fact I can still hear both of those works in my music from time to time. Later, as a viola player, I was involved in *performing* contemporary British music. I went to Dartington, where Peter Maxwell Davies was, and met composers like Olly Knussen and John Woolrich. Martin Dalby was another early encourager and supporter of my music. These days I'm referred to as a Scottish composer, which seems bizarre as I'm from London, but I quite like that.

What most obviously makes me a British composer is, I suppose, the descriptive nature of my music. But there are other influences. My music contains references to traditional folk culture, and since

I've lived in Scotland these have been Scottish rather than English. In addition, I think I've been strongly influenced by Messiaen, Debussy and Ravel. I love the harmonies of French music, and as a teenager I had lessons – they were more like chats, really – with Lennox Berkeley, who was himself almost French.

I began my career as a viola player because it simply didn't occur to me that I could earn a living as a composer from concert commissions. I remember thinking I might make some money out of writing hymn tunes, at one point, but composing was just something that I'd dreamed of doing, not really something that I did. And I was turned down several times when I applied to study composition. Olly Knussen helped me by looking at some of my scores during a London Sinfonietta tour, when he was conducting and I was playing, and Luciano Berio also looked at a couple of my pieces. Later, Harrison Birtwistle gave me a fantastic lesson on my Violin Concerto. But I never paid for a composition lesson. I was really lucky.

However, I didn't come up through the course of study that I imagined all other composers had, and I felt that I didn't hear music as well as some other composers did. I learned to read music at the age of four, before I started to play the piano, so I never played by ear. My mother was very classically trained and regarded perfect pitch almost as a form of cheating – you know, 'We musicians have to *work* at things.' We had to stick to what was on the page, so maybe my ear didn't develop in the way it might have done. Anyway, I found aural training at college very difficult and really struggled with it, and I just thought this meant that I wasn't the genuine article. But I've never been short of commissions and they've nearly all come through playing with colleagues.

I think there's a very strong need in me to communicate, and I've always wanted people to respond to what I do. I composed one vast political piece,[1] which was very much to do with what was going on in my life at the time and my need to get rid of a lot of pain and anger, and I wrote a solo cello piece after I had a miscarriage, in order to help me get through the experience. But I don't set out to transmit messages through my music. After all, the nature of music is that it can't be put into words. So it's always lovely when people respond to something I've written in an instinctive way, without being told what they're meant to feel.

[1] *Knotgrass Elegy* (2001).

I do quite a lot of creative writing, and the thought of writing a poem and putting it away in a drawer is complete anathema to me. Even when I know something's not quite right, I still want someone to read it and comment on it. And I'm very good at taking criticism. I love the dialogue that goes on when you discuss your work with someone else. Joining a creative writers' group has given me insights into making my working processes more conscious, and that can be very helpful in finding ways out when you're 'blocked'. But while writers can ask people to read their work and can get responses like 'I don't understand; who *was* the lady in the red hat?' it's more difficult for composers because we don't get that sort of feedback before our work is published.

It's always easier for someone other than the composer to describe his or her music, isn't it? But I write tonally – I'm very aware of where my tonal centre is at any given moment, and I work with or against that, depending on what effect I want to get. I think there's a collective understanding of tonality – it's just there in the psyche, and you can't pretend it isn't. Just as there are certain words that mean certain things to people, and you can't use them without conjuring up specific images, there are aural expectations attached to certain chords, and so the composer must decide whether or not to break those expectations.

Clarity is important to me, perhaps because I find it hard to assimilate a new work by ear and because I want an audience to be able to do that as much as possible with *my* music. So I have a real need to make things clear, and I don't want to cloud up the sound by adding more and more layers. I once took a very good music theatre course at Dartington, run by Michael Finnissy, in which we experimented with words: when three people each said something different at the same time, you could actually listen to only two of them. You might be aware of the odd word from the third person, but certainly when there were more than three speakers you couldn't take in *anything* – it all got lost. I applied this to my music, and while making my very first attempts at orchestration (my First Symphony) I studied classical scores and discovered that there were never more than two main things and one subsidiary thing going on in the music at the same time.

More recently I took part in a weekend workshop for music theatre writing and loved it. Music theatre has to be absolutely direct – it's no good if someone has to go away and think about it – so you just have to make everything clear the first time. And this isn't only about the words. It's also about the path that each character takes through the piece. I've applied *this* to my music, too. For example, what is the role of this instrument? What's its journey, and where is it ending up? Where's the climax? As the composer you may be clear in your mind about these things, but you need to work out whether you're making them clear to the listener.

In general, the young composers I've taught have felt a need to follow a particular system or ethos, and some of them have become quite dogmatic about this. But then I think *I* was at that age. I suppose I found my voice, as a serious composer, when I was about twenty-nine. Before that, every piece had been a struggle and I hadn't really known what I was doing or whether the result was okay. And there was always an internal voice saying 'This is rubbish.' Then Olly Knussen helped me by giving me some systems to work with that justified where I was getting my material from. Being able to justify every note in pieces like *Commedia* and *No I'm Not Afraid* gave me the confidence to relax a bit and become less rigid about my use of systems. In this way I was able to forge a real language of my own, which included the use of pentatonic themes from Scottish traditional music and themes with ornamentation using the bagpipe scale, and birdsong, too.

The most recent development has been my interest in jazz. I did a two-year jazz course for piano and learned about improvising, which was something that had always terrified me. Having realised that improvising (playing solo in jazz) is in fact composing in real time, and having the confidence to do this when I'm writing music, I'm now freer than I've ever been. I'm just taking the initial idea and running with it, not fussing over it. However, I think I've ended up with a 'voice' that's recognisable in relation to my earlier pieces. It's simply that I write more quickly now, and with less angst (mostly).

When I was applying to study composition I was told that the courses in question couldn't accommodate a composer who tried to write in a tonal way, as I did, but today I'm close to where I was at eighteen: in a very tonal world, constantly stripping the music back and taking out all the clever stuff – again, going for clarity. My recent piece *Spinal Chords*, for strings and narrator, is inspired by Brian Eno and is almost static – it uses the same chords over and over again. I don't think I would have dared to do that twenty years ago.

I started composing full-time when I had my first child, and my work was organised around his childcare. It was a great discipline: four hours a day, and no more. Later, when the children were at school all day, I thought, 'I've got *six* hours now, so I don't need to start just yet.' And now that I don't have *any* boundaries on my time, it sort of drifts on. Sometimes I get to five o'clock in the afternoon and still haven't started my four hours' work. It's shocking. So I'm trying to get a handle on that at the moment and to keep regular working hours. In theory, I now start at nine o'clock in the morning and work until one o'clock.

I discovered recently how much of my work goes on in my head while I'm out walking. I still need the period of silent waiting that I have when I'm walking alone. I'm a Quaker, and just opening yourself and letting the ideas come is very much a Quaker philosophy. Very often it feels as if the ideas *aren't* coming, and then the temptation is to think, 'Oh well, nothing's happening, I'll just go and check my e-mails and do other things instead.' But it's better to sit down and tell yourself, 'No, I'm working. If nothing happens, nothing happens, but I'm still going to sit here and wait.'

I was sent the text for *Spinal Chords* five months before the deadline, but I had no idea how to tackle it and I sat on it until about two weeks before it was due. Then I just wrote it. The piece had been there all the time – that's how it felt, anyway – but I was in total panic. I think you sometimes need that bit of adrenaline. You tell yourself, 'Right, I've just got to start doing *something*', and then you find, as you start to write, that the piece simply needs to be unlocked. It's almost a mystical thing. Sometimes it feels that it's not me doing it at all, that the piece is coming *through* me rather than *from* me. And when that happens, I work really intensely.

It's hard to get a good balance between admin work and actual composition. For example, if you have a new commission coming up in two years' time the commissioners will want to discuss it with you *now*. It might be the only piece they're commissioning in the next few years, and for them it's a really big thing, so they want to make sure that you know what's in their mind. This is the hardest thing for me, because I really don't want to go there while I'm in the middle of the previous piece or maybe three or four pieces back! I don't want to talk about something I'm not yet writing.

Of course, your work doesn't end when you finish writing the music. You have to get the correct acknowledgments into the score, you have to write the programme note, and maybe there'll be some interviews or a pre-concert talk to prepare. By this time you might be composing something else, because there's always a gap between the deadline for submitting a work and when you actually hear it. It could be months. And I've never gone back and studied the score in the way that I always think I will, so I often turn up at the first rehearsal, open the score and think, 'I can't remember anything about this!' I'd like to write one piece and do everything associated with it, and then move on. But you can't. It all overlaps.

First rehearsals are usually terrifying. Sometimes I discover that I've made mistakes, most likely in balance, and that's really annoying. But if the piece makes sense to me, if I can still follow the musical argument through it, I'm more confident. And afterwards I really do let go of the piece.

Although I don't get nervous about performances of my music, I do get nervous about going up to take a bow afterwards. I spend the whole of the performance worrying whether I'll be able to get through the violins and whether I'll forget to shake hands with someone. That kind of thing obsesses me, and so in that respect I find the public aspect of being a composer difficult. When I teach students in Orkney each year and we plan a concert of their music, I say to them, 'Right, you know you're going to go up and bow?' They're absolutely horrified, and reply, 'Well no, I don't want to.' I tell them, 'You have to. It's part of being a composer.' And I have to talk them through it. I say, 'You'll need to shake hands with the conductor. You need to turn and maybe clap to the players, and only *then* do you turn to the audience. And you bow *properly*. You don't fiddle with your jacket, or whatever.' Being comfortable in your own body on stage is an art, and it can be really difficult. I don't think I was a very natural performer, and I didn't *look* good when I was playing. I was always slightly shut off, and I didn't really communicate.

As a talker, though, I could go on forever! I think it's partly because I come from a family of singers and actors – extroverts, very witty people who would compete to see who could be the quickest to make a pun. I think it's also because, having been a performer, I'm garrulous and used to working as part of a large team. This is probably why I love music theatre, because it involves collaborating with so many people. I also like the fact that I was once a performer and so I know all the lingo and what annoys musicians! If, as a composer, you're asked a question by a player, you're expected to know the answer straight away because it's your piece; so even if it would really take you a minute to work it out, you have to give an immediate answer, otherwise they'll lose patience.

There are lots of composers who aren't comfortable presenting or promoting their music, and I'm sure that some have got lost along the way because they just don't find it easy to talk to people, to get to know them and to raise awareness of what they're doing. They need advocates! Having conversations often leads to pieces. I find that nearly every conversation I have gives me an idea for something.

I like frameworks or boundaries when beginning a work because then there are certain givens. For example, when I ask a commissioner something like, 'Is the scoring for two oboes or two clarinets?' and I'm told, 'Oh well, you could have both, or we could change it', I get very frustrated and want to say, 'Just tell me which!' I need to know, because it's my starting point. It puts the colour of the piece in my head. I sometimes give my students an exercise: I put three hats in front of them, one containing different details of instrumentation, one containing different *tempi* and one containing titles or markings, such as *Andante*. They have to pick one parameter out of each hat and then go away and write a short piece from them. And they do this incredibly quickly because I've taken away a lot of the things that they would otherwise have to spend time deciding on.

I also tell them, 'If you get stuck while writing a piece, write the programme note. And if you're *really* stuck, write the review. Then you can describe the piece, and how you want it to sound.' For example, they can write about the delicacy of the string writing, or something like that. I don't think this is a bad way to start a piece, and I often do it because I'm always so late with everything. I get asked for the programme note and I haven't written the piece! Anything that makes the sheet of paper less blank is a good thing.

Since I stopped playing the viola I've found listening to some repertory music quite hard because for me it's tinged with a kind of sadness and regret. I'm much more likely to go and hear contemporary music, because I always come away with something from it. I'm like a magpie: I hear a sound and think, 'Gosh! How did he/she do *that*?' My ear is not that great that I can remember everything, but I get an impression of something, perhaps a colour, and this gives me the idea for something of my own that's related in some way to it.

I don't revise my music but very often I incorporate elements of a smaller piece in a larger piece. It's a great way to work, and a good way of learning about your own material, I think. I certainly learned a huge amount by being asked to orchestrate some Debussy piano pieces for cello and orchestra[2] for Steven Isserlis, because I had to study so many scores in order to get the language right. It was terrifying, and it took

---

[2] The *Suite pour violoncelle et orchestre* (arranged 2006).

me three times as long as writing either of my Cello Concertos, but I loved doing it!

A lot of people respond to new music by saying 'I don't understand that piece', but I sometimes think that it wouldn't have bothered them so much if it had been played as part of a film score because the music would then have been one element among others. Combining music with visual art, or with words, interests me very much. My first major commission was for a score based on six poems by Irina Ratushinskaya, and using words to create music enabled me to expand outside the very small structures that I'd been able to create up to that time. Shortly after that, I did something similar when I took Sylvia Plath's poem 'Winter Trees' and made three instrumental movements (my First Violin Sonata) out of it.

My first experience of really getting to know orchestral music was playing in youth orchestras, sometimes over a whole week of learning, and I remember that when I was thirteen we did the Dvořák New World Symphony. At first I didn't really get it, but then there was that process of absolutely falling in love with it. And when I hear that piece today I get an actual, physical response to it because it's linked to a time in my life when I was *made* to spend time getting inside it. How often does that happen to a piece of contemporary music? You don't usually get the chance to hear it more than once. And even if it's recorded, do we really sit down and listen to it repeatedly? You've got to be *really* dedicated to listen to new music in that way. I find it very difficult because of all the distractions. It's like watching a film that you don't know: you mustn't miss *anything*.

Today we can all listen to Stravinsky without running away, screaming. We couldn't have done that a hundred years ago. Our ears have moved on. But I don't know how far. Composers are probably being laughed at today for music that will be iconic in fifty years' time. If it's good, no one will care that it was written twenty years after someone had done something similar. So it would be very interesting to see which styles of music are still around in a hundred years' time. By then it won't be determined by the charisma of the composer but by whether people actually want to sit and listen to it!

George Benjamin

George Benjamin, London, December 2013

> **'The life of a composer is basically a long journey of discovery, with no destination.'**

My encounter with George Benjamin was postponed twice because of building work in his north-west London house taking longer than anticipated. He offered to be interviewed somewhere nearby, perhaps a café, but I preferred to wait until I could meet him on home territory, partly because I was curious to see where he lives and works and partly because I suspected that he would be more relaxed there. When I eventually visited him in December 2013 the work was virtually complete, and the interview took place in the new ground-floor extension to the back of the house, a living space so substantial as to generate a slight echo as we talked. It was the end of the afternoon, and he looked tired. He was also struggling against a cold. But tea was made, chocolate biscuits were brought out and we chatted across the new kitchen table.

Having never met him before, I had no idea whether his personality still resembles that of the prodigiously talented youngster who at fifteen commuted to Paris to study with Messiaen and Yvonne Loriod and who the following year signed a publishing contract with Faber Music. But what soon became clear is that he's the most articulate of interviewees. The majority of his utterances emerged beautifully phrased and soothingly modulated, as though he was paraphrasing a lecture that he'd given many times rather than spontaneously answering questions with little preparation. And so most of the editing of our conversation for this chapter involved reordering material and deleting what there wasn't room for, not clarifying verbal confusion or hesitancy.

What I hope the editing conveys is that he spoke with both authority and passion – not the infectious, bubbling passion observed by interviewers in the 1980s but a calmer, more reasoned version of it. When he emphasised points that he felt particularly strongly about, the pitch of his voice rose and he raised his eyes to the middle distance like a parson offering a glimpse of the ineffable during a sermon. Yet he was able to use the words 'enchantment' and 'majesty' without appearing remotely old-fashioned or quaint. It seems that my experience of him was typical, because he's invariably described by interviewers as talkative, inquisitive, genial, unassuming, intense, softly spoken and occasionally unable to prevent himself from breaking into laughter.

Sensitive to the purpose of this book, he avoided describing his music in technical detail and spent much of the interview talking about his motivations and working practices. This inevitably led to a number of comparisons with the act of writing words (he's an avid reader) and its reliance on structure, pace, development, narrative and vocabulary. But first we discussed two other, connected issues. One was the pattern and pace of composers' careers, and I suggested that between peaks of public visibility – for example, high-profile performances or the regular release of CDs – they're as busy as ever but working without attracting media attention. This seemed particularly relevant in his case because of the recent success of his first large-scale opera, *Written on Skin*.

The second issue was whether his early successes, which included a Proms performance of *Ringed by the Flat Horizon* when he was twenty, a double first at Cambridge (his teacher, Robin Holloway, is reported to have said, 'In terms of natural endowment he was easily the most outstanding pupil I've had') and further studies in Paris with Pierre Boulez, established unrealistic expectations of what he could subsequently deliver. Was being regarded as a prodigy – a label that I suspect he has always rejected – a help or a hindrance to his career?

I'd been composing seriously since I was seven years old, and because the years seem much larger when you're young, I felt I'd waited a very long time! And although I never felt myself to be a prodigy, I was very hungry to make some sort of mark. So the opportunity to have my pieces published, played by the best musicians and recorded by Nimbus – already from the late 1970s – was simply fantastic. I'd dreamed of such things since being a young child. I must add that I'd had wonderful teachers here in London, then in Paris and finally in Cambridge; and, since my studies, I've been fortunate in that my works have been played widely. But it's also true that the reception for *Written on Skin* has been beyond anything I could ever have imagined.

As for expectations, I set my *own* aims high in terms of craftsmanship from the very beginning. And why not a larger catalogue of published works? Well, inspiration – if that's the word – doesn't always flow reliably for me, particularly as I tend to shed my skin, metaphorically, from piece to piece. Acting as a festival organiser and conducting here and abroad have also taken quite a lot of my time over the last three decades, though I'm now more protective of my diary and – as my productivity seems to be increasing – have cut back on both activities rigorously. In the end I don't see the need for producing dozens of scores, and I've published, on average, a new work every eighteen months; some, of course, achieve their aims more pertinently than others, though I hope each one of them marks out a distinctive terrain.

But I'd also like to add that it isn't easy to write the music I imagine, and so I'm obliged to compose slowly and methodically. More precisely, it takes a large amount of time for me to find the technical, sonorous and expressive world of a piece. But once all that clicks, I actually work very fast. The last third or so of *Written on Skin* was completed in less than four months – that's more than thirty minutes of orchestral music in full score.

When I discovered classical music I fell in love with it very, very violently, and I immediately lost interest in everything else. It took me over and consumed my life – as some things *can* do for a very young person. Even as a child I had an absolute passion for musical scores, and I can still remember which birthday or which Christmas I was given Mahler's Second Symphony and *The Rite of Spring* as presents. So I was utterly convinced, from the age of about eight or nine, that this was the only thing I could possibly do for a living. There was no question within me about that. And yet the whole idea of being a composer was full of terror and the unknown. Would I ever have a piece of my music played? Would I ever hear an orchestra play one? Would I ever see a piece of mine in print?

No one teaches you, when you're young, that although music is the best thing in the world to devote your life to, composing is very hard, very lonely, very solitary and full of moments of blockage and doubt and dead ends. *Every* composer has dark moments – if you were Wagner or Schoenberg, they lasted for half a decade – when they're trying to find something completely new and it doesn't come. Nothing works any more. And those times are very difficult. I remember getting stuck halfway through writing an orchestral piece when I was twelve, and being blocked for the whole of the Christmas holiday. I didn't know what had hit me, or what I was supposed to do about it. And when school started again I hadn't written a single new bar. So, whatever gifts you have, you also need a substantial degree of obstinacy and determination, because it's not an easy path. And you have *no* idea of this when you're a kid.

What else do you need? You need a technique. But technique is nothing unless you also have ideas. And neither ideas nor technique grow on trees. You have to find them and foster them, which means discovering them outside yourself and then nurturing them within yourself. What's more, technique isn't something that you acquire at a conservatoire and then just ride on for the rest of your career. In the end, technique is what enables you to make *new* techniques, to unearth and develop things. And that task is unending. The life of a composer is basically a long journey of discovery, with no destination.

I think teaching has helped me enormously in this journey – I started teaching at the Royal College of Music when I was about twenty-five and I've been teaching at King's College London since 2001. This week I've given two big classes there: one of them was about the history of the staccato dot, and another was about the function and the potential future of parallel harmony. In almost thirty years I've never repeated a single topic, the reason being that I learn so much from teaching. And learning these things fuels me as a composer. Plus, in recent years, the experience of teaching individual student composers, many of them extremely talented, has been hugely rewarding and enjoyable for me.

You also need luck. And you need support: above all, a publisher who believes in you (my long relationship with Faber Music has been extremely happy, and I so value that they print all of my works so beautifully – seeing the first copies of the full score of *Written on Skin* last year was a great thrill for me) and performers who are prepared to play your pieces. I could mention many musicians who have given *wonderful* performances of my works, and to whom I feel unlimited gratitude.

There comes a time when I feel estranged from my pieces – which is a good sign because it makes me hungry to write the next one. And there are ways of helping myself to begin. When I read novels I'm fascinated to see in the first few pages how language is used, what narrative technique is employed, how atmosphere is evoked, how characters (and their names!) are introduced, how the passage of time is handled, and how the tension that will hopefully sustain you throughout the read is instigated and paced. I can see that the first page of a good novel throws up questions that demand answers, at different rates and in different places. Similarly, the composer can plant schisms or breakages, for example in time or in the connection between musical elements, that will demand continuation. I also enjoy exploring the friction between an objective background and foreground liberty. But I've started pieces that went nowhere – pieces which never really became pieces. In my twenties I would sometimes work for *months* on something that seemed highly promising in itself; it wasn't, really, but at the time I believed it was. And now, with the benefit of experience, I understand absolutely why those fragments wouldn't expand into pieces.

It's possible to do a number of things that will block a piece of music from growing. Often I would go down cul-de-sacs and lose the harmonic thread of a piece, perhaps because I don't work in absolutely predetermined forms. And I would have to go backwards to find the specific bar or the specific *beat* where it went wrong. Maybe the logic of the part-writing broke down because I'd made a too-easy decision, or maybe the invention wasn't coherent within the idiom of the whole work. Whatever the reason, only after finding the mistake could I continue to develop the piece. Fortunately that seems to happen less often now.

When a piece is commissioned, you're usually heading for a deadline and a performance, and this pulls you forward through the writing of it. But there comes a point when you have to silence the highly developed critical voice in your mind. So, apart from learning how to write music, being a composer involves finding how to get the best out of yourself. This means discovering what routine fits you best, what type of sketching technique is best suited for which passage, what sort of terrain can be fertile for you, and what not to even *begin* to try because you know it would be a waste of time.

Writing music is such a hermetic experience, and the process from abstract conception, compositional techniques, inner hearing and notation through to score-printing, part-making, rehearsal and eventual performance and audience is a very long one indeed! In the first half of that list everything is connected: if you shift any aspect, however small, the imaginative world of the piece will also shift. And you're in the middle of all that. I suppose one of the reasons why I compose relatively slowly (I often rewrite passages twenty to thirty times in order to get them right) is that I try very hard to step outside the logical and constructional world of the piece and try to imagine, with the most naïve ear, its musical flow.

You're right: the struggle is in maintaining the right kind of distance from your work. And sometimes I get too close to mine. The problem is that the logical connections between the atomic elements of music are so complex; and if you leave the work for a few weeks you'll forget how the piece is written and you may never get back into the required state of mind. So there's something to be said for composing, composing, composing and not stopping, particularly once the piece has acquired momentum. As I said earlier, it's important to know how to manage yourself – when to take breaks and when to trust yourself to come away from your work. But this, too, is difficult to judge, and if you get it wrong the consequences won't be helpful.

Until the age of about forty I would compose – when the work was flowing – until really late at night. I can remember seeing the sun come up in summer while I was still hard at it. And I used to find mornings hopeless for work. I've never had a really stable routine, and I've never been very good at separating myself from my work, as apparently Stravinsky was able to do: he'd have a whisky in the morning and get down to sketching, have lunch and then enjoy other activities for the rest of the day. Nowadays I tend to write when I can, which often means starting work soon after getting up in the morning and just waiting until things become clear in my mind and I'm able to produce something. I tend not to compose late at night now, and from writing bigger pieces I've learned that you have to stop work when your mind loses absolute clarity. If you force yourself to continue when you're tired or confused, you can get yourself into a knot and do great damage to your work. I've learned a little bit how to stop, get some sleep and trust the unconscious to help me the following morning.

I'd like to think that my music has become more subtle in form since I started composing, because my interest in structure has developed way beyond what it was when I was young. I have a more linear, more melodic, more polyphonic approach to composing – a different angle on musical evolution, texture, form. What I've written has become more multi-layered, I think, and I've aimed at greater transparency so that the distinct strata can be clearly audible.

In recent years I've become obsessed with the human voice and have broached a medium I'd always wanted to tackle: writing music for the operatic stage. After a quarter of a century of searching, I finally found an ideal collaborator, Martin Crimp. This has been a definitive change for me and it's made me expand my writing onto a scale that I hadn't achieved before. So: forty minutes for *Into the Little Hill* and an hour and a half for *Written on Skin*. When you're working on such a scale you can say more and risk more, and the greater span of such works means that you can attempt things which are simply inconceivable on a smaller canvas.

One other thing (and we'll get a little technical now) is that my composing technique has changed enormously. When I was eighteen, nineteen, twenty, I believed that instinct alone would lead me through a life of composing, and I was suspicious of logical schemes and objective techniques by which to write music. But then I began to realise that I couldn't write the sort of music I wanted to write using a purely intuitive approach. I eventually found a way to develop the necessary technical armoury to write more multi-layered pieces, and for the last twenty years – since *Upon Silence* and, above all, my *Three Inventions* – abstract and architectural elements have often underpinned the surface of the music. In the end their purpose is not directly to be heard, but I've found them very useful – and indeed liberating. You see, the imagination is strengthened by restriction and by concentration. Besides, to create a complex musical fabric which has multiple points of view and multiple materials co-existing in different timescales – with opposed rhythmical and harmonic strands – is impossible without some form of scaffolding. The number of decisions involved is simply too great.

I still *adore* sound – I find it a tactile phenomenon, and that's what gets me composing. But I'm fascinated with getting the nuts and bolts of music in the right place. I think you'd be quite surprised, perhaps even horrified, as a non-composer, by what goes into producing what can sound a quite simple and direct musical statement. I've learned a huge amount from Webern and Berg, and from Messiaen and Boulez and Ligeti; their sound worlds are wonderful, but the point is that their music isn't just sound. I find the logic of their music – the *science* of it, even – fascinating. And out of that fascination comes inspiration.

People tell me that my music contains my 'fingerprints', but I don't want to identify them. I prefer to concentrate on the material I'm working with. I try to make my pieces sound as different from each other as they can, because I hate the idea of repeating myself and I hate the idea of routine. Routine is the death of anything to do with expression and the arts. So I try to be different from other composers, and up to a point I try to be different from myself, as well!

I remember visiting a museum of modern art in Cuenca in Spain and seeing a room of work by someone who did swirls, a room of work by someone else who did jagged lines and a room of work by another artist who just did spirals. It was quite depressing that these artists seemed to have imprisoned their imagination and done one thing only, perhaps for the whole of their creative life. In contrast, I like to travel – metaphorically – and find new things. But I do have a very, very demanding ear and I can't help the fact that there are some things that I do and other things that I *don't* do, musically. I also, of course, have a personality, and I trust that it will come through loud and clear if I concentrate on the material of music itself – if I distract myself with it, in fact.

I have a very visual imagination and Martin Crimp tells me that images, particularly those involving various forms of light, seem to excite my musical imagination. I love painting, although my attitude to individual artists has changed over the years. For example, Turner was a great favourite of mine when I was young but other painters are now more important to me. I love photography, too, and I used to photograph landscapes when I was young – Messiaen thought this was very important to my composing. But I have many interests inside and outside music. I read a lot – fiction old and new, as well as many books on mathematics, science, history and (of course) music. And I love cinema. There's no dependable source of inspiration for my music; inspiration is capricious and flighty, to a ludicrous degree. I've no idea what might interest me tomorrow and what might spark off a new piece of music.

Nor do I know what any given piece of my music is going to express. This isn't something I'd usually think about, let alone decide in advance. In an age without a functioning vernacular it's very easy to fall into clichés, and in order to stop that happening you have to put obstacles in your path, to create friction between you and the material you're working with. After all, if you're working within a predetermined form whose expressiveness is fixed, how can the imagination take flight? What discoveries, what enchantment can you find along the way? I discover the emotional temperament and trajectory of a piece through its musical material: how the pitches and harmonies relate to each other and to lines and to rhythms and to timbres, across the structure and the evolution of the piece. And on occasion the material itself surprises me, which is the most exciting thing.

I'm not trying to force any form of reaction from the listener, either. Music is such a strange medium – hard to conceive, hard to write and far from easy to fully understand, regardless of the idiom – and that makes it interesting enough in itself. Expression comes from within music itself; it's not forced on it from outside. Of course, writing an opera involves balancing truthful and imaginative responses to the text, but when Martin Crimp and I discuss how we're going to collaborate we don't discuss the message of an opera. We simply devote ourselves to the story in question, and the style and structure used to bring it to life. We're not designing the piece for a specific public or trying to communicate a particular message.

As a kid, you copy the music you get excited by. The music *I* got excited by zipped around: Beethoven followed by Berlioz followed by Mahler, Debussy and Ravel, then back to Schumann and Chopin; then from

Mahler to Berg, and from Berg to Ligeti, and then going backwards to Wagner and Bach. Then, at last, I understood Mozart, and next I discovered Varèse. And the countries where these composers came from were irrelevant to me. But I've been influenced by the French tradition because, beyond my studies there, I've always loved French music and because I've had intense contact with so many wonderful French musicians: Messiaen, Dutilleux and Boulez, as well as other remarkable creative figures nearer my own generation. And my great friendship with the pianist Pierre-Laurent Aimard dates back to my very first days at the Paris Conservatoire in 1976.

However, the idea of following in a particular tradition doesn't preoccupy me. I can understand this issue being important to a nationalistic composer in the first half of the twentieth century, but it hasn't been so during my lifetime. Also, frankly, the British tradition has been ... well, up and down, hasn't it, over the last four or five hundred years. There have been glorious moments and less glorious moments. It's not the same as the German tradition, which seems to have had about three hundred years of unbroken majesty. But I think it's a relief not having that amount of weight on one's shoulders.

I've always written the music I'd like to hear – perhaps walking into a rehearsal, not knowing what it is, and thinking 'I'll stay till the end.' Or switching on the radio and *not* thinking 'I'll turn that off immediately!' In the end the most important thing is that I write what I can, and what I love. And, just like every artist who wants his or her work to be heard or seen, I try to craft what I do as clearly as possible.

I tried to say earlier that the sound of a piece of music – that mysterious attribute – is more than just vibration in the air. And there's no question that the actual *sound* is more of an obsession for me than it might be for some of my British composer colleagues. I'm absolutely aware that music is meant to be listened to, and I very much *want* it to be listened to. So when I'm composing I'm thinking of the performers, even if I don't know who they'll be. I have to imagine the sound, to the greatest degree of precision that I possibly can. I also have to conceive the look of the music on the page so that the conductor can present and direct the music in the best possible way, using my own experience as a conductor as a guide. And if I'm writing a piece for a specific place, its acoustical qualities will in some small way influence what I'm doing. I'm aware of performers' gestures – what they look like when blowing, bowing or striking their instruments – and also try to imagine how the piece will look on stage. For example, if there's a moment when the music's very soft at an important harmonic juncture,

I have to be careful that the fourth percussionist doesn't move from the tam-tam across the back of the platform to the tubular bells with a pair of beaters that he has left on the bass drum, because the platform needs to be very still at that moment.

I think the heart and the mind are inextricably linked. Of course, some music is more cerebral – Webern and some Bach, for example. And there's music, like Scriabin, which is extraordinarily hedonistic and perhaps less inventive in terms of structure – the axis of hearing moves towards the sensual side. But think of the depth of construction, alongside an almost superhuman sensitivity to sound, in Debussy's *La Mer* or *L'Après-midi d'un faune*. And think about Beethoven, who was my greatest musical love when I was a child and whose music I still revere – particularly the Symphonies, which for me are an absolute apex of musical creation. Their architecture required a vast intellect, but the irresistible energy and glowing tone of these works could never remotely be considered cerebral.

All the music of the past that we love tends to have this degree of fusion between architectural and sensual forces. Music that's just pretty sound, with no intellectual engagement or bone structure, is likely to be of little interest. But I have to say that music that's purely cerebral, which doesn't coat you in sound and make your gut buzz in sympathy, is anathema to me. And getting the balance between those two extremes when composing is the big challenge. This will sound a bit weird, even pretentious, but I sometimes think of a piece of music as a sphere filled with sound; and when I'm writing any individual moment, the sound of the *whole* piece is there in my imagination. Every detail of the music connects to that sound, and *makes* that sound.

You can now find, with ease, a thousand years of Western musical history on the Internet, and you can learn a huge amount without moving from your computer screen. But this can also be a major source of inhibition for young composers, because there's so much music to be influenced and excited by, to learn from or to react against. Choice can overwhelm them and make them stubbornly limit the world in which they want to work, almost as a precondition of composing. But this is a false security, akin to the ostrich hiding its head in the sand. And it worries me that many people now only experience music through a pair of miniature headphones, in total isolation, attached to a tiny digital device. A composer must have direct contact with the stuff of music by going to rehearsals and concerts and by meeting performers. Music is written for live performance in the concert hall, which, of course, is a communal experience.

So, in answer to your question, I imagine listeners to my music sitting in silence, watching the platform, seeing the music played and sitting next to other people who are also in silence. As for the *ideal* listener ... well, someone who's really curious and prepared to concentrate (and not to fidget!) while listening. Someone whose imagination – even, I might say, whose heart – is open so that he or she might be willing to follow the journey from the beginning to the end and have some empathy with what's being played. In the end, what can I do but imagine *myself* listening? The best chance I have of writing music that speaks to others is by writing music that would appeal to *me* if I came across it in the way that they do.

I'm very touched if a piece of my music gets through to people, and I'm grateful however they express that. And I can't help being surprised(!), because it's very easy *not* to write pieces and very easy to write them wrongly. Of course, it's also very stimulating to talk to colleagues and composer friends about technical or aesthetic matters, though I tend to shut myself away to a very large degree while writing. I do, however, communicate with my beloved friend Oliver Knussen about the process of composing in a way that I can't with anybody else; and my life would be so impoverished without having at least one person like that in it.

Yes, I'm still thrilled when I hear a piece of my music performed for the first time. Because it's been locked in my mind for a long time, and may have been very hard to write, the distance between the process of writing it and the performance – which one hopes gives the illusion that the music was conceived in a mere second – is enormous. Last summer we rehearsed *Written on Skin* for many weeks with the magnificent singers for whom I'd conceived the score, and then in Aix-en-Provence came the first *tutti* rehearsal with the marvellous, marvellous Mahler Chamber Orchestra: as we ran through the whole opera, three or four years of my life seemed to fly by in a flash. I'd never before written a piece half as big as that, and so that was an afternoon I'll never forget.

Michael Berkeley

Michael Berkeley, London, September 2013

'I quite like the notion that my music provokes and disturbs.'

After twenty years of presenting *Private Passions* on BBC Radio 3, Michael Berkeley knows more than anyone how to lead conversations with people whose response to music is instinctive or intuitive rather than technical or analytical. One of his gifts as an interviewer is his ability to encourage guests to share their enthusiasms without feeling judged or criticised for having tastes that are quite different from his (which, incidentally, are much broader than I'd realised before I met him), and listeners sense his eagerness to establish common ground before contributing insights into the music being discussed. All this is done in a manner that's learned but not over-intellectual, authoritative but not intimidating.

So although it was initially disconcerting to be in the physical presence of such a famous voice, and daunting to be the person asking the questions, my encounter with him in September 2013 was relaxed and informal. It was seven months since I'd first asked if he would be interviewed for this book, and in the intervening period it had been announced that he was to be made a non-political peer in the House of Lords; so it was Baron Berkeley of Knighton who welcomed me into his home – a large, five-storey, bay-fronted Edwardian house in west London. 'Big blue house', he'd described it in his directions, and before I climbed the front steps to ring the doorbell I couldn't help wondering why, on a street of predominantly unpainted brick, the adjoining property is as boldly red as his is blue. But there were more important things to discuss in this interview, which took place in his splendidly spacious and light top-floor studio.

There was the extent to which his decision to become a composer had been encouraged or discouraged by his father, Sir Lennox Berkeley (to whom he refers in interviews as variously 'my father' and 'Lennox'), and the extent to which his dual career as a broadcaster and composer is the result of a conscious choice rather than something that has simply happened. There was his personal and professional relationship with his godfather, Benjamin Britten. And there was his hearing loss, dating from the summer of 2010, and its impact on his music-making. It had little on our conversation, although I tried to remember to speak clearly and to look directly at him in case he was partly reliant on lip-reading. The number of times that he expanded on answers to my questions by going off at a tangent, prefaced by 'I suppose', suggests that he found the interview stimulating and enjoyable; I hope that he did, and that the ease with which conversation flowed didn't lead me to outstay my welcome.

I began the interview by making the perhaps obvious point that some readers of this book will come from families who have little or no connection with the world of the arts and will therefore find it difficult to imagine what it's like to have been the son of a famous composer and the godson of an even more famous one. And I questioned how an aspiring composer could make his own way in such an environment. His creative path would presumably feel less lonely or freakish because his sensibilities would be nurtured – in a sense, he would already be part of the world in which he wanted to make his mark. But what about the pressure to conform or compete, and the need to emerge from shadows that threatened to dominate? Was it an advantage or a disadvantage for this particular interviewee to be the son of Sir Lennox Berkeley?

I think it helped me, for two reasons. First, when I was very young I couldn't help but learn from my contact with Britten, who was an absolutely inspiring figure although socially awkward in many ways. Also, when my father came home from a concert or an opera he would take a score off the shelf and show me how something he loved in the music was achieved. In both cases, this was teaching by sheer enthusiasm. Second, and more important, I always believed that I had something completely different to say. You see, I sometimes felt frustrated by Lennox's music because, although I admired its craft and its elegance, it didn't always seize me by the throat. And, as a young man, I wanted it to do that to me. I'm a much more impulsive creature than my father, in many ways: whereas he eschewed programmatic music, or music in which he wore his heart on his sleeve (it embarrassed him), I was quite the reverse. And I had complete confidence – arrogance, some might say – in my musical sensibility.

I always knew that I wanted to be a composer, and because I played a bit of pop and wrote some film music after I left the Academy, I knew that I could conjure up music that *worked*. The next thing was to write music that was more individually mine, because a lot of personal things were feeding into my character to create a kind of turbulence that I wanted to express. At that time I was very excited by the rhythms and the extraordinary, primitive power of *The Rite of Spring*; I adored Bartók's use of folk music; and I was very moved by Berg and the Second Viennese School. But I needed to acquire a technique in order to write music that was my own.

I wrote a piece for strings called *Meditations*, which won the Guinness Prize, and when I showed it to Raymond Leppard he said to me, 'You've got a lot of ideas, but you need to develop them. And you need the help of somebody who'll be quite tough with you – Lennox is far too nice.' (This echoed exactly what Ravel said to Lennox when Lennox showed him round Oxford in the 1920s: Ravel then took him to Paris to study with Nadia Boulanger.) He said, 'Richard Rodney Bennett would be wonderful for you because he's a consummate technician' (he'd studied with Boulez, of course). And although Richard didn't really teach students, he took me on.

In my first lesson he said, 'The *last* thing I want you to do is to write like me, or indeed in any style that we might explore in order to advance your technique.' Like lots of young composers, I wanted to write something for orchestra, but he said, 'No, I think we'll do something for just two or three instruments, where you can't get away with any gestures. I want you to be able to justify the presence of every note.' I chose to write a string trio (which I'm still quite fond of, actually) and over the next eighteen months I rewrote the whole thing eleven times, until I *could* justify the organic presence of every note. When Richard said, 'I don't think you'll need to do that again', I breathed a sigh of relief! Then he said, 'We're going to use serial techniques to make the most of the notes you assemble, but that doesn't mean you have to be a serial composer.' And we did all kinds of musical exercises, including inversion – turning things upside down and running them backwards. It was exactly what I needed.

Lutosławski also helped me a bit at one time, and I remember asking him how he discovered and developed his use of aleatoric notation (he knew better than anyone how to give players a degree of freedom while controlling the sound of the music). He told me, 'I've never wanted to write like John Cage, but hearing his Piano Concerto opened the door for me to what *I* could do in my own way.' And I think this is what composers do. You see, there's no such thing as total innovation. *Everything* is a synthesis of what we've experienced. I once asked Boulez what he liked about Birtwistle's music and he replied, 'I'll tell you: where does it come from, this music? *That*'s what I like about it.' And yet even in Harry, whose voice is so original, there's early and mediaeval music.

So being surrounded by Britten and my father (and Poulenc) was a great inspiration. Maybe I was crassly immodest, but I can honestly say that I never felt cowed by it. But there was another important influence: as a chorister at Westminster Cathedral I sang a lot of Gregorian plainchant, and its repeated patterns of notes within a melody informed the musical language that I went on to develop.

I'm definitely more articulate – in public – than Lennox was. And I've always had an ability to perform – which I sometimes distrust. For example, I was once at the St Asaph Festival in Wales and decided to attend the eleven o'clock Cathedral service before I spoke to the town's Music Club at lunchtime; and as I walked in, the verger came up to me and said, 'If you'd like to come to the vestry, Mr Berkeley, I'll clip on your microphone.' When I asked why, he told me, 'Well, you're giving the sermon.' And I knew nothing about this! The funny thing is that I spoke for about twelve minutes on the nature of belief, worship, atheism and creativity, whether in architecture or music. (Admittedly, I'd written a newspaper article about this two months earlier.) Afterwards the Archbishop said, 'That was a wonderful sermon. Would you come and shake the hands of the parishioners?' And I felt a bit of a fraud, even though I believed everything I'd said to them.

I have a slightly Geminian character, in that one part of me loves performing while another part is quite reclusive and just wants to compose. In fact, I spend 90 per cent of my time working on my music. It's only the other 10 per cent that I spend broadcasting and talking and at the Lords. But then composing really *is* 90 per cent perspiration and 10 per cent (if that) inspiration. My father taught me that if, in the morning when you go to work, you don't have an idea, you can't say, 'Oh well, tough – I'll go and do something else.' You have to rewrite the opening of something else or re-score it, because that often opens the door back into your piece. And you have to do this every day. It's like being a violinist or an athlete: you have to keep the muscles in constant action, otherwise they atrophy.

Your question about the relationship between a composer's temperament and his music is important, because I believe it's dangerous to concentrate too much on the personal turmoil of the individual concerned. As Tom Adès has written (of Britten), this is an insult to the 'facturing' – as opposed to the manufacturing – of the music. On the other hand, you've only got to look at the texts that Britten chose, you've only got to think about a work such as Janáček's *Intimate Letters*, and you've only got to look at the lives of Tchaikovsky and Rachmaninov to realise that it's *impossible* to dismiss entirely a composer's personal circumstances. Of course, without formidable technique he can't speak about them or transcend them in his music; but I nevertheless think that the music's coloured by them, and that, at a certain level, a composer does plunder them.

It's curious, in an age when people *stream* into Tate Modern to look at all sorts of abstract and expressionist art, that some of them have such difficulty with the language of contemporary music. I think it's because people's aural sense is less developed than their visual sense. Every day we're bombarded with visual images in advertising and on screen that are quite complex, and yet people are still brought up on a diet of tonality. This means that when they're asked to listen to music which doesn't refer to tonality they find themselves in what feels like a completely alien landscape. Yet the more you listen to contemporary music, the more you get from it. And it's interesting that young children are very open to contemporary musical sounds that aren't tonal. This is because they haven't yet had their ears regulated to C major, so they're open to any sound that excites them. I often point out that people listen to music at the cinema – the famous shower scene in *Psycho*, for example – that they would find ugly in a concert hall, because when ugliness is defined by a narrative or visual image, it can become thrilling. So people enjoy *Lulu* or *Wozzeck*, which in places aren't easy, because they understand why Berg wrote what he wrote.

However, it seems to me that the majority of the music being written today is easier to get into than that of twenty or thirty years ago. And while there are still composers like Harry Birtwistle who (admirably) plough their own furrows, many others have slightly moved the ground: adventurous, innovative, avant-garde music has been squeezed out by the popularity of the so-called minimalist school, which the public enjoys and thinks of as 'modern music'. In fact, this is a return to music that's simpler, harmonically, than that of a hundred and fifty years ago, and sometimes close to pop music. That's not a pejorative comment – as I said earlier, I used to play rock music, and I enjoyed it very much. It's just that musical boundaries have become blurred. And maybe that's no bad thing. What's most important is that, as a composer, you're true to yourself. You'll only please an audience if it's convinced that you have your own, individual voice.

You're right: some composers do reach out more than others to their audience. I think of Britten, whose music reached out until he knew he was dying; then there were three pieces – *Death in Venice*, the Third String Quartet and *Phaedra* – that belong more to the world of the interior. But I'm not sure that you can manufacture this 'reaching out'.

There have certainly been times when I've been conscious of writing what I think will be a winning moment, when I've thought 'An audience will enjoy this.' But the guiding motive usually has to be that I can justify my work to *myself*, initially; and then I'm just terribly fortunate if an audience feels the same way about it.

However, I've never forgotten something said to me by Felix Aprahamian, a generous critic who used to write for the *Sunday Times* and who heard and loved my Oboe Concerto. As I began to develop as a composer and to write rather more challenging music he told me, 'Michael, never eschew the lyric gift that you have, because it's quite rare. Yes, you have to push at the boundaries, but don't lose sight of that ability to write a melody that sticks in the mind.' Parts of the Oboe Concerto have an emotional import that I still find moving, even though I'd probably write it in a much better way, technically, today.

I found writing film music very seductive because it's lucrative. You also get to hear your music very quickly. But you have to *write* it very quickly, too – it's usually the last thing that's added to the film, so you may have less than two weeks to write *and* record an entire soundtrack. This means that you've got to trust your first instincts – you simply don't have time to work the material. This can be helpful to composers who've got a bit stuck, but it wouldn't be a good thing to introduce into your concert music all the time because it could make it rather facile. Richard Rodney Bennett was the most brilliant writer of music for films, but he seemed to distrust that side of himself, maybe in the way that I distrust my ability to speak publicly. When I asked him, 'Do you think that some of the music that's closest to the real Richard is in some of those film scores?' he got very angry. And I understand why. But the immediacy of some of that music is wonderful, whereas some of his art music is perhaps less approachable. Richard was a victim of his own staggering facility and technical ability, because when you can write in any language, it's difficult to find the path that you want to hone. Of course, you can't criticise somebody for being so brilliant; but I feel it *is* valid to say that you're a little baffled by which is their real voice.

I'm not conscious of being a 'British composer'. I think you write what you want to write, and if it turns out to *sound* British, fine. It's very refreshing when my music's played abroad, because nobody there knows about the BBC or the House of Lords, and hardly about Lennox or the Britten connection, and so the music's taken at face value. And people tell me that they're struck by its emotional impact, which pleases me.

I enjoy leaving a concert or a theatre or a cinema or an exhibition with the feeling that I've got to think about what I've just experienced because it has said something to me about what it is to be human (and being human isn't entirely comfortable). So I quite like the notion that my music provokes and disturbs. Of course, I've written pieces that were designed to please, but I'm more interested in music that has a kind of rub or edge to it. For example, my Organ Concerto, Clarinet Concerto and Concerto for Orchestra have an emotional import that might make you feel uncomfortable.

I also love setting words, and I feel that writing operas suits my temperament as a composer. Sometimes my operatic or dramatic side feeds into my concert music – for example, the anthem *Listen, Listen, O My Child* that I wrote for the enthronement of the Archbishop of Canterbury, Justin Welby. This is the first choral piece of mine with which people have had a sort of instant connection – it's already sold almost a thousand copies, which is amazing for a piece of contemporary music. Justin Welby asked me to set something from the Rule of Saint Benedict that combined humility and joyous acceptance, and although I wrote an essentially simple, tuneful piece, the music gets quite forceful when the choir sings 'Receive willingly and carry out effectively your loving Father's advice'. And I repeat 'carry out' three times in order to bring an element of drama into the piece – in a way that my father, for example, wouldn't have done.

Repetition can be very important. I remember working on *Love Cries*, which is based on the love music from Birtwistle's opera *The Second Mrs Kong*. It begins with a wonderful flurry of notes – a falling motif – and I suggested to Harry that I repeat this at the end in order to give a sense of returning to the opening. He said, 'Yes, it's a good idea, Michael, but just turn it upside down' – so that at the end the notes form a *rising* motif. It was such a straightforward, simple inversion, yet so effective. And that's why Harry's such a good teacher – after all, you teach children to use building blocks by suggesting that they turn them around or upside down.

I have a strong vertical sense in music, by which I mean that harmony and bass are very important to me. And although I've adopted a slightly more linear approach in some of my recent pieces, melody always *implies* harmony. Because of the way I was taught to compose, I can hear a melody and then visualise it, although I don't think I immediately visualise music as precisely as Britten or Bennett could do. I'm not as technically accomplished as that, by any means.

I start sketching on paper but I very soon put the material onto the computer. I find Sibelius useful for assessing the architecture, not the sound, of the music: I can play a piece and listen to whether the proportions of fast and slow music are correct. Before Sibelius, one could imagine a work's proportions in one's mind's eye, but that could be deceptive; and I'd sometimes get to a performance and feel 'There's not quite enough of it – it has gone by too fast.' What I miss from writing music by hand is the more graphic elements of musical calligraphy, but even with Sibelius I have an almost tactile sense of sculpting the sound as I add or remove texture.

Of course, composers are terribly dependent on their executants for the first performance because the audience doesn't usually know if something's going wrong. Subsequent performances are more relaxing, in a way. I've usually got the confidence to feel that what I'm going to hear is what I wanted to hear and what I thought I'd written; but it's still sometimes the case that a particular harmony sounds much richer than it did in my head.

If you don't believe passionately in a piece, you shouldn't be writing it. In other words, you go through a sort of love affair with it. But when it goes out into the world you have to accept that it must stand on its own feet. And you have to put it to one side slightly in order to create a new sound world for the next piece. I love hearing different performances of my pieces, and even different productions of my operas, and I've always encouraged interpreters of my music to feel quite free with it and to make it their own. There are limits to this, of course, but I'm interested in what people bring to it and I don't want to hear the same thing over and over again.

I like to be able to trace the development of a composer, and I like to think that my progress through music is easy to chart. I'd be very happy if people went on a voyage through my pieces – starting with, say, the Oboe Concerto and gradually working their way through to the Organ Concerto and the Clarinet Concerto, which are much more expressionist – and if they could see a progression and could understand why I've gone where I've gone, musically.

What's particularly interesting is to go back to your work after many years. For example, my early *Meditations* is going to be performed next week, so I've been looking at it again. Although it has imperfections, it also has a kind of youthful honesty, an emotional directness; maybe a naïveté, too, but even *that* is touching, in a way. And for that reason I'm happy for the piece to be played, and I'm not unduly embarrassed by it.

Only a handful of composers in Britain can earn a good living purely from commissions. And it's no longer possible, as it was when I was young, to be all things to all men, musically – to write both concert and film music. People are suspicious of that – which is ridiculous, because most composers in history have had to make money by doing other things. I have a sort of fervent faith that if you believe what you're doing is worth something, and if it's any good, it'll rise to the surface; but it's easy for *me* to say that, because I'm in a quite privileged position – I get performed and commissioned, and I have an income from other activities.

So I worry about (as you were saying earlier) those composers who, perhaps simply for lack of encouragement or opportunity to hear their music, must begin to feel very downtrodden. Because of the current financial situation, I know of a lot of fine composers who simply haven't got any work. In fact all of us, at some time or other, have written music either for no money or for very little money because, ultimately, we're composers. One of the things I'm trying to do as a result of being in the Lords is to find ways of supporting composers who slip between the major commissioning clients in this country. I only accepted the peerage because, having fought so hard for composers in the past, I felt that I couldn't turn down the ultimate 'stage' when I was offered it.

Talking to people for my *Private Passions* programme has taught me that amateurs get more pleasure from music, in some ways, than professionals do. They just like what they like, and it doesn't matter to them about the 'label'. I often find this rather salutary, and it's instructive that somebody who likes the rigour of very highly organised, very tightly conceived music can also completely fall in love with something that's in many ways indulgent and repetitive.

I love most types of music, but I've heard *so* much of it, and I sometimes feel almost as if I've been locked in a cell with it – literally, when I was a continuity announcer on Radio 3, because we did five or six hours at a time and couldn't escape. Now, I have an absolute love of silence, especially of silence *in* music, and I relish those moments where a composer has the confidence to leave a pause or a silent beat. A lot of composers throw notes onto the page, especially when they're young (I did it, too), which means that there's no opacity. But music speaks all the louder for being contrasted against silence.

Losing my hearing was disastrous at first – and still is, to a certain extent, because I can't get the pleasure from a lot of music that I used to get. But we hear with our brain, not with our ears – the ears are merely a conduit. And I've noticed that my brain is adapting to my hearing, and that music is beginning to clarify. It's still not wonderful, but it's less distorted and less painful than it was. And the effect on my composition has been to force me to be much more economical. I now write with more clarity, I think. But then I've *always* believed that less is more, and that limitation is inspiration. People say to me, 'That's a very brave way of looking at it', but it's *not* a brave way. It's the *only* way. And if you've got another hurdle to cross, you're sometimes more creative as a result.

So yes, it's a real bore, and I hate being unable to decipher thick, Straussian harmonies during a concert. But much worse things happen to people, so I'm learning to live with it and to make the best of it.

Judith Bingham

Judith Bingham, London, July 2011

'Writing music is a confused morass of experiences, emotions and note-by-note decisions.'

One of the questions that I asked most of the contributors to this book was, 'Is your memory of your music essentially visual or aural?' Although not the most important topic on my list, I felt it to be valid given that composers make decisions about how to notate their music in order that performers will bring it to life in the way that they intend. Might they not, therefore, both 'see' and 'hear' the music in their imagination?[1] Judith Bingham's immediate response was to laugh and say, 'What a strange question.'

I mention this only because I feel that it illustrates something of her character: alongside the warmth, humour and self-deprecation I sensed a kind of solitary toughness, perhaps defensiveness. She certainly wasn't afraid to challenge the thinking behind some of my questions, and she explained that she has a spider-like knack of drawing people to her before making her point.

We met at her home, a flat that occupies the ground floor of an Edwardian terraced house in East London, in July 2011. We talked and ate chocolate biscuits in the front living room where she works (a shrine-like collection of photos and texts – what she calls a 'visual backdrop' – pinned to a noticeboard next to her electronic keyboard showed that a work was in progress), and afterwards she posed for a photo in the back garden. It was a long interview because she was a very good talker – by which I mean that she spoke imaginatively and eloquently about both the conscious processes of writing music and the unconscious motivation behind them.

She also made some surprising assertions, smiling or laughing as she did so as if to indicate that she knew she was being controversial. One was that composers probably wouldn't describe themselves as music lovers. Another was that the distinction between 'serial' and 'non-serial'

---

[1] Robin Holloway has written about 'eye-music [as opposed to ear-music]' that might be viewed on the page as 'a mass of clearly designated polyphonic parts, or an excitingly black passage of textural complexity' (*On Music: Essays and Diversions 1963–2003* (London, Claridge Press, 2003), p. 381).

composition became redundant as a result of Britain escaping invasion during the Second World War. 'The particular sound of serial music suited the invaded countries better than it did us', she explained. 'It was a very different world here. But then I'm always going on about the War...' Yet another, which I asked her to expand on, was that many composers are unable or unwilling to understand the emotional undercurrents of their own music. This certainly couldn't be said of her, for she appears to know herself very well (and to have a disarming ability to see through others). She was also warm and funny, and I liked her very much.

As she would probably be the first to point out, composers are complex people, and creative because of their complexity. I sensed that in her case self-awareness hasn't been easily won, and that she takes little – including interviewers' questions – at face value. This was clear from her response, at the beginning of our conversation, to my suggestion that all composers, whatever the style of their music, want to entertain or stimulate listeners, and that the majority want to innovate to some degree, if only to avoid repeating what's been done before.

I would challenge what you've just said, actually, because I'm not sure how much I'm thinking *any* of those things when I'm composing. I certainly don't think that I want to innovate, because innovation doesn't happen as a result of making a conscious decision to innovate. Composers who decide to write something really avant-garde tend to sound like all the other composers who have decided to write something avant-garde! And it's the people who stick out and make us feel a bit uncomfortable – the William Blake sort of people – who tend to be the innovators.

It's actually quite hard to do something that no one's done before, and you hear student pieces by young composers that are full of what they think are innovations. But they can be very boring to listen to because what you really want is a memorable *idea*. I mean, some of the great innovators in the past weren't great composers. Locatelli, for example: he had lots of innovatory violin techniques but he was only an okay composer. It was often the next one who came along who took what had been done and then presented serious ideas with it – like Chopin coming after John Field.

Besides, audiences aren't great musicians. They're music lovers. They've come along for a night out. I remember Andrew Parrott telling me that once, as part of a performance, he was required to crawl under the piano and hit it with a hammer; he said, 'I rather felt I lost the audience at that point.' And if you play them something massively complicated they won't be able to digest it and they won't remember it. All the music that has survived has been memorable, even if it's been really difficult, like *The Rite of Spring*. And that memorability is to do with the strength and the truthfulness of the ideas behind it. As a composer you can become distracted by thinking, 'I'd better try to do something a bit different, a bit new, otherwise everybody will think I'm rubbish.' What you *should* be thinking is: 'What have I actually got to say?'

The thing I like to do in my music is to unsettle people with its message. And to that end, I like to entice them in a bit beforehand. I'm like a spider, you know? I kind of draw them in. I want them to think, 'Oh, she seems okay. She's a fat, middle-aged woman and doesn't look too threatening.' So they're in a relaxed state when the piece starts, and then I can give them my unsettling message! Many of the things I write about – the primal nature of things, or the real motivations for war, or what childhood is really like – would make people slightly uncomfortable if you spoke about them directly, and I'm not thinking that I want to entertain them. I'm thinking, 'I've got them sitting there; I want to give them this idea and see how they respond.' So maybe 'stimulate' *is* something that I want to do; but it's more about creating a communal atmosphere in which everybody is quiet and stilled.

This is why I get so fed up with all the interruptions and chatting to audiences before broadcast concerts these days. It's all *rubbish* chat, and it destroys the atmosphere. For example, I had a piece performed at the Proms last week, and apart from the fact that the presenter made three(!) factual errors in her one-minute exposition of it, everything had to be *friendly*. I thought, 'We're not here to be friendly. That's not what it's about! It's supposed to be a very powerful experience.' I mean, if you were walking round an art gallery and somebody kept jumping up and saying cheerily, 'Hey, we're going on to the next picture', you'd say 'Just go away!' It's as if everything's being made ... *trashier*, and that's not what people want. It isn't. They're not stupid. Oh, it makes me so mad.

I don't know when the whole pre-concert talk thing started – when I was growing up I never saw composers at concerts. But it seems that during the 1980s more and more organisers were saying, 'We really like the composer to come along because it makes people feel more comfortable with hearing the piece' and so on. I went down that road myself, and felt that it was a good idea, but now I'm not so sure. I wonder whether composers have given away a bit of their mystique, and whether it actually *does* help people much to be given something to listen out for. The subtext is that the composer's going to be friendly and make them feel 'It's all going to be okay!' It's a bit like religion, in a way. You can give away too much in church, and you can take away an illusory quality that anything artistic should have. There should be a veil there, I think.

How helpful to my career as a composer was my formal music tuition? Absolutely not helpful in any way at all. Well, music O level and A level were what they were, but the Royal Academy of Music was absolutely not one smidgeon of use. In fact, I'd say it was obstructive. Before then I'd had no encouragement at all, not from family or teachers or anybody. The opposite, actually. My music teacher at school told me that if I worked really hard I might end up as second oboe in the Hallé – which, given that I was a terrible oboist and really quite a good singer, just showed the level of advice on offer … In a school in Sheffield at that time a woman composer was thought of as a freaky thing, and everyone just assumed that I would come back home, have babies and settle down.

Yet at the Academy I found that in some ways I was far ahead of anything that was going on there. I'd had a very highly developed listening experience before then, and none of the other students knew any music apart from what they'd studied for their grade exams. When I asked what they thought of Mahler, the response was 'Who's he?' But I was living in cloud cuckoo land about what it was to be a composer. When I was a teenager my role model was Berlioz, so I had a totally romantic notion of what my life was going to be like: it would be a mad and terrific struggle, I'd write huge works and everybody would recognise my genius straight away!

Nobody at the Academy gave me any kind of pragmatic advice. John Carewe had a certain group of composers around him and Paul Patterson was running the electro-acoustical department, but I just wasn't accepted. I was just a freaky girl who was writing bonkers music. I mean, we were supposed to be listening to Stockhausen but I was mad about French baroque music – how weird was *that* in 1970? Mind you, Rameau and Charpentier are, to my mind, far more strange and modern than Stockhausen. Hans Keller was my first real teacher and the first person in my life to take me seriously as a composer. I was about twenty-three when I went to him. It was quite frightening because he expected me to take everything as seriously as he was taking it, and suddenly I felt that I'd dipped my toe into the real world, where people were committed and serious about art. He expected those very high standards from me, and he radically affected the way I thought about everything.

As a composer you've got to be truthful. You've got to try to live by who you are and what you want to say. But this is difficult, because you don't have a massive amount of control over that. You can't change into somebody else. For a lot of composers, this may mean that they attract little attention. They may be wildly misunderstood or they may get only small audiences. If they end up saying 'I don't really care whether people like my music, or whether I'm communicating through it', it may only be experience that's led them to that place. I've heard young composers say 'I don't care whether or not anybody plays my music', but to me that's ridiculous because music is there to be heard.

It seems to me that the high intellectualism of the 1960s and 1970s shrank into a university-based sect of people who today would look with contempt on me writing a piece of music about a crown made up of famous gemstones[2] – something so unintellectual in its basic appeal. But we're all writing about the same deep emotions. That's what I think. We're just finding different surface hooks to hang our work on. So our main focus has to be pursuing our ideas and refining our art, not worrying about how much audiences will love it. I want to embrace audiences with my music, but if they're not interested I'm still going to go on to the next piece. It's like a chimera: you're following an idea the whole time, one that's never within your grasp. Sometimes the musical world can seem to respond to it, but then they suddenly pull the rug out from under your feet and it feels like nobody's interested at all. Most composers have a lot of disappointment, you know, even the well-known ones.

To me, the programme of a piece is just the entry into it. It's opening the door and saying, 'Right, you can come in.' In other words, I distract myself with the programme but I'm *actually* writing about multi-layered feelings that can be hung onto it. I like to think that my music contains a lot of ambiguity and *sub*-subtext, a sort of Jungian basement that you can get into if you really want to. But I think a lot of composers are duplicitous when they talk about their music, and they don't trouble to think too hard about what they're really expressing. They can concentrate on form, and can talk about mathematical

---

[2] *The Everlasting Crown* (2011) for organ.

constructs, golden sections and the whole caboodle, as a way of not acknowledging that they're writing about their massive anguish over their dysfunctional childhood, or whatever. I hear pre-concert talks in which composers speak in the most abstract, intellectual way about what we're going to hear, and then the piece sounds like somebody screaming their head off. And I think, 'Well, this is clearly a very emotional work.' But then it's easy to be out of touch with what you're writing about. And even if you do make clear that you want to write a piece about your dysfunctional childhood, nobody will be interested in listening to it.

I find that I have to do an enormous amount of pre-composition before writing a piece; otherwise it will judder along and keep sticking. But it's not writing music; it's thinking about my ideas. I create a visual backdrop for the piece and spend an enormous amount of time thinking about that. What happens, I think, during this pre-composition period is that I'm almost being told to go off and play while my subconscious works out what's going to happen in the piece. I'm having lots of different thoughts and I'm putting all the data – such as the brief for the piece that I've been given – into my mind, and my subconscious is somehow brewing all this in a cauldron, or fermenting it. Somebody once said it's like waiting for the bubble to come up on a hot mud pool! I may think I know how I'm going to start the piece, but when the day arrives to start it I can sit down and find that I have a totally different idea about it, and this makes me think that I've been put on hold while my subconscious has worked it all out.

For me, a piece of music inhabits its own self-contained world. Composing is like entering that realm, and by the time I'm ten or fifteen minutes into a piece it's acquired its own kind of momentum. I'm not really thinking about expressing myself; I'm on a juggernaut that's rolling along. So writing music is a confused morass of experiences, emotions and note-by-note decisions. It's a decision-making process within a very emotional sphere, you could say. And it's probably the slowest way of creating art, because you might sit for days picking over tiny decisions ('Should I have this semiquaver dotted?') about something that will go past in two seconds in a performance. But those decisions are crucially important because everything should be exactly right. I work by continually going back and playing the piece through, even if it's a big one: playing/listening, edging forward two or three bars, playing/listening again. Which means that by the time I've finished it I know it very, very well.

In order to make a living from commissions I have to write between eight and ten pieces a year, so in general I don't have time to do anything except move on to the next one. I always try to get them right when I'm writing them, and if I go back after a performance it's only to titivate them by making slight changes. I find that I can't easily get back into pieces anyway, because I'm generally into another one or maybe even two or three further on. But occasionally I do what I call 'Then and Now'. I take a piece from way back that I think has got good qualities as well as bits I don't like, and I write new things around it or in the middle of it. It's not really a revision; it sort of presents aspects of a piece with new things added.

The experience of hearing a new piece of mine rehearsed or performed is always shockingly different from sitting in this room and listening to it privately. Suddenly it's 'out there' and has taken on all sorts of other qualities. It's not that it doesn't sound like you thought it was going to sound, but that it's somehow out of your hands. It's moved off down the road and has to be voiced through someone else, and it will never get the perfect performance that you heard in your head. This can be quite disturbing, and it causes some young composers to go to pieces because they feel utterly helpless. I've had to scoop them off the floor. Painters or writers don't have to go through this, because what other people can do to their work is much more limited. The extraordinary thing about music is that it's relived all the time, and so much depends on the circumstances of the performance, not least the personality of the performer.

What I call the mystery of notation is that I feel I've been very specific about certain things in the score and have marked them clearly, and yet performers don't seem to get them. Sometimes I just want to say, 'Can you really not tell how it goes?' – particularly when they ignore tempo markings, which I'm always very specific about. I can say, 'Maybe you'd like to do *this*' or 'Could you play that *staccato*?', and they'll say 'Fine'; but then in the performance they may go back and do what they originally did. They're not being unmusical – I'm not talking about bad performances. And they're not being perversely unpleasant towards me. They're simply having their own response to what I've written, and I have to accept this and let go of the piece. I can't force people to feel something exactly the way I felt it when it was in my head.

I find it rather annoying when people say, 'Oh, it must be wonderful to be a composer. It must be so satisfying, so thrilling to write a piece of music.' I think, 'No, you're a music lover. That's what you think when you listen to a piece of music. You come home from work, all stressed out, you put on *The Lark Ascending* and have a glass of wine, and it's brilliant – the piece does its work, and you feel much better.' They assume that's how Vaughan Williams felt when he wrote it. And they don't think about the personal stuff that a composer feels – 'I can't do this, it's so difficult, I can't make it work and it's just crap ...' All that beating-yourself-up stuff.

I wouldn't call myself a music lover because I think that's a bit like a French person saying that they love the French language. I mean, music is my first language. I think I'm at my most articulate in music. Music is 100 per cent of who I am, really. And so I find that when I'm listening to music of the past I hear first and foremost the composer's voice. I feel that I'm listening as one composer to another. I hear emotional progressions, psychological progressions. I think I also hear where things went wrong or got a bit stuck (I remember Benjamin Britten saying that critics never hear the thing that's actually wrong with a piece). In that sense, I feel very close to other composers.

But the term 'British composer' has never really meant anything to me, and I don't think there's such a thing as 'British music' because the different countries within Britain have such strong characteristics. I guess that in America they're more likely to call you a British composer than an English composer, but in this country I don't think the term has much validity, really. I'm very aware that the Bingham side of the family goes as far back as the thirteenth century (in Nottinghamshire) and I feel English in a very profound way. But I've also got some Irish blood from my mother's side, which I like because I think it's rather magical. Somebody once said that my music is English with a French accent, and I think that's very true.

There's more historical precedent for female painters or sculptors or novelists than for female composers, perhaps because a writer or a painter doesn't have to be a very public person, whereas a lot of composers begin their careers as performers. Another problem, I think, is that women don't form themselves into groups to support highly individual, perhaps maverick female artists, whereas men form groups to talk in reverent, quasi-religious tones about composers like Wagner or Stravinsky. I'm generalising, of course, but a lot of women seem to feel very threatened by a woman who isn't taking a traditional path.

Many of the female composers I talk to have extremely difficult relationships with their mothers. My mother wasn't just uncomfortable with the idea of me being a composer; she was really hostile. She thought it was weird, and she couldn't talk about me as a normal woman. She couldn't say, 'Look: she's married, she's got children, and I'm a grandmother' – that whole stupid tradition of what a woman was supposed to be (what my mother was, in fact). She didn't understand it, she didn't *want* to understand it, and so she couldn't find a way of talking about it. If she'd said to her friends, 'Oh, my daughter's a composer', they'd have replied, 'How amazing, how wonderful!' But she didn't think that. Even on her deathbed she said to me, 'You never did what I wanted you to do …'

To be treated as someone highly unusual meant that I saw myself as an isolated figure, and so I didn't take part in group activities with young composers. Today it's very different because young women composers have grown up with equality, and their male peers see them as equal, by and large. And so there are lots of women composers.

I love starting a new piece because I find the whole lead-up to starting very frustrating. Once I start, I think, 'Well, I'm off – I'm off!' It's like a spring that's been released. And I'm relieved, because between every piece I think, 'Maybe I've dried up. I'm never going to write another piece again. I'll never think of anything.' This happens every time, even though I've written three hundred pieces. And I don't feel I'm anything when I'm not writing music. I feel like a useless piece of flotsam, that I have no other function. That's why I'm always pleased when I get going. I've got a use in the world again.

Harrison Birtwistle

Sir Harrison Birtwistle, Wiltshire, October 2013

> ‘I compose all the time. I'm doing
> it right now. Yes, consciously.’

I had more reasons for wanting to interview Sir Harrison Birtwistle than any other contributor to this book, the most obvious being that his music still divides opinion so strongly. To some people it's the supposedly self-evident reason why they turn their backs on contemporary music, and yet the number of performances it receives suggests that mainstream audiences have begun to catch up with it. Since it doesn't seem to me unduly 'difficult', I suspect that the back-turners' problem is not with his music in particular but with contemporary music in general. So I was pleased that, in spite of his apparent disregard for what people think of his work, he agreed to be interviewed by me.

I was aware beforehand that he's one of the most significant figures in British musical life and that it's important not to waste his time; he rightly expects interviewers to know their stuff and to ask him intelligent questions. But when we met at his home in Wiltshire in October 2013 and started to chat across his kitchen table, I was reassured: he explained that what he was going to say might not make a lot of sense, in which case together we would have to *make* it make sense.

Perhaps my first question – whether he *really* doesn't care about the public's response to his music – couldn't be classed as 'intelligent', but he seemed dismissive about my reasons for wanting to include him in this book. When I explained my hope that a record of personal encounters with composers talking about their music would encourage the reader to investigate their work, adding that this hope sprang from my desire to share the excitement of musical discovery, he replied that he couldn't say anything that would persuade people to listen to his music – and, furthermore, that there was no reason why he should. His logic is indisputable, of course, but the fact remains that most of the other contributors to this book make greater efforts to meet their listeners along the way.

As the interview progressed, his mood alternated between combative and genial, bored and enthusiastic. From time to time each of us felt obliged to justify our point of view – I for asking what I believed were legitimate questions, he for insisting that some of them were unanswerable. At one point he got up, rummaged through a pile of post on the table and retrieved his latest royalty statement that listed performances around the world. 'Somebody's playing them because they *want* to play them', he shrugged. I pointed out that I'd earlier suggested precisely that. Things went no worse when I stood my ground, but this was an interview that sometimes felt difficult to keep on track.

Rightly or wrongly, I came away with the impression that what he enjoys about the interview process is not discussing himself or his music but engaging in a good-natured tussle with his interrogator. So when transcribing our conversation I was surprised to discover that the memorably awkward moments of my encounter with him were far outnumbered by those in which he showed great patience in answering my questions and articulating his thoughts clearly. I found it impossible not to like him, and we parted cordially. When I thanked him for his time, he replied, 'It's a pleasure. I've enjoyed talking to you.' Perhaps he had.

The following morning I re-read Paul Griffiths's description of him in *New Sounds, New Personalities*: 'The creature is friendly but on the surface ponderous, though capable of sudden grace, exactness and surprise. To encourage such moments one has to get the conditions right: the appropriate question at the appropriate time in the appropriate terms.'[1] Like Griffiths, I feel I scored poorly.

People have always had a problem with contemporary music, and they always will. So I've never understood the question about whether I care if people like what I write. I seem to have had the emblem of a sort of rebel, and a reputation for being aggressive, but I've never consciously written aggressive music. It's simply that I've never written music in order to be appreciated, and I've never thought about the audience. What I do as a composer is all I have. And it's brought to life by certain ideas about intuition and continuity that I want to explore in music.

Generally speaking, the history of creativity is about people who've had ideas that, very often, were acknowledged only in retrospect. And if there's any artistic truth anywhere, it's associated with historical context. Consequently, there are moments in the historical journey of art where the truth is sacred. For example, we've gone through a period of minimalism in music, but there's also minimalism in *paintings*

---

[1] *Ibid.*, p. 186.

that are completely white. There's one hanging on the wall in the next room that's completely *black*. And they come from a particular time, from a historical context, that's got nothing to do with anybody. It's simply the truth. Would you have told Picasso, 'Don't put that eye there – that's wrong'?

So I just do what I do, and I do it as clearly as possible. What else *can* I do? By suggesting that some people will read my comments about my music and be encouraged to investigate it further, you've already defined a line; and even if there *is* a spectrum of musical understanding – from somebody who's completely stupid to somebody who's very sensitive – I can't, as a composer, pitch what I do to a particular point on that spectrum. I've never been able to do that. It's not as if I send a message in a bottle and say to people 'Listen to this', because by that stage there's nothing I can do about the music. I've finished with it, by that point.

If, as you say, my music's being recognised more than it was, good for it. It's certainly not as extreme as a lot of other contemporary music. But maybe people's ears have changed. You suggest that there can be pleasure even in sad music or brutal music, and some of mine has those qualities; but never self-consciously. I've read books about my music in which I didn't recognise it, because when people have analysed it they've found in it things that I didn't put there. But this doesn't mean that those things aren't relevant.

In the end, I think, it all comes down to the issue of originality. And you can't consciously be original – you either *are* original or you're not. So composing is essentially about ideas, and the struggle to interpret them through musical notation. And it *is* a struggle – there's evidence to show that a lot of composers find the actual writing of music difficult. So you don't need to talk to me about people who refuse to engage with contemporary music. It's not my problem. And there's nothing I can say, sitting here next to you, that's going to make what I do more acceptable. I know *how* to make it acceptable – I know exactly the sort of music that people would like, and what its ingredients are. But I don't write that sort of music, because it's got nothing to do with me. To write it would be a lie.

I discovered music via the BBC's Third Programme when I was about fifteen or sixteen. I heard Hindemith and Schoenberg, and Mahler conducted in Manchester by Barbirolli, and I just thought, 'This is what I want. This is my world.' There was no precedent for it in my family, although they had ambitions for me to be an instrumentalist. That was something that I would have had to be very proficient at in order to make some money, and maybe I wasn't good enough. Besides, being a performer didn't interest me.

I'd written music from the age of eight, as soon as I had the notation to write it with. It never occurred to me *not* to. It seemed to me more interesting than playing. But while I was expecting to write music, being 'a composer' – in the sense of making a living from writing music or being able to develop it in public – was something quite different. I had no role models to follow. I only thought about the pieces I'd written. And at first I didn't know my music would take a direction that a lot of people wouldn't follow. But then I don't know how to compromise. I still don't know what a compromise in my work would be.

I have to come back to the point that whenever I write music I don't have anything better and I don't have anything worse than what I've got at that moment or on that day. In that sense, I could never be 'commercial'. Well, I could, but I wouldn't want to be. Generally speaking, commercialism – in the cinema, at least – is all cliché, and that's all they want from a composer. If you write something that's against the cliché, it doesn't sell, and so you do *more* of the cliché – which makes the cliché more like itself. Waste of time (although I'd make a lot of money). That's why I'm not that sort of composer.

But I accept that these days the role of the composer is partly a public one. At one time I *didn't* accept this, and I think that was because I wasn't sure what I was doing as a composer. And, as a result, my persona suggested a sort of arrogance. I don't feel that way anymore because I can now articulate, more or less, what I'm doing. But I've got to be honest with people, and I want to know that when they get my music they're getting something genuine. However, you don't need to say too much to keep people happy. Earlier this year I wrote a piece for the Proms, called *The Moth Requiem*, and although I didn't feel that I said anything terribly interesting about it, people seemed to like what I said. And when I did a talk on the radio about my Violin Concerto it ended up on *Pick of the Week* because people thought I was opening up and discussing my innermost thoughts. It wasn't that at all. I've just learned not to be too shy about talking in public about my music!

I'd like to have revised more of my music than I have done, because I've never heard anything I've written that couldn't be better in some way. Yet when I come back to a piece later and hear it, it's as if the original problem no longer exists; but there are other problems instead. And this is corrected and solved by the next piece I write – in essence, I could be writing the same piece of music for the rest of my life!

I *know* what I'm going to write next, because my music is very much a continuum. Usually by the time I'm halfway through a piece I realise that I'm on a journey that never reaches the horizon, and so in a way I'm more interested in what I'm going to be doing next than in what I'm doing at present. Although sometimes I suddenly get nearer to my original idea, I never nail it completely, but I always feel that I can get another chance at it. It's like the white painting I was telling you about: the next thing is the sacred thing. You're dead right, though: the context of a piece is usually temporal, like the music itself, because a composer has only a certain amount of time in which to write it.

You're also right that my ideas are generally abstract. I've been influenced by the idea of landscape but in the sense of stratification or what's under the surface. So when I translate an idea like that into music, it's an analogy, not a depiction. Sometimes I write something small and then see ways of making it into something bigger, or perhaps the other way round. I see a way of developing a facet of an idea within a different context. In that sense, one idea generates the next. But the actual work of composing isn't about ideas, really. Ideas are ten a penny. It's about the realisation of ideas through notation. I can encapsulate the whole of a piece in the original idea, but in the process of sitting down and writing it, that idea tends to disappear immediately. And I'm confronted with what Stockhausen described as a 'moment'.[2] However, as soon as there's a context for the piece that points to continuity, I'm flying.

For example, I've recently been talking with the oboist Melinda Maxwell, with whom I've had a musical relationship for many, many years, because I'd like to write another piece for her. Not long ago I was at Dartington and did a public improvisation (for the first and last time in my life) with her; and the relationship between what I was doing and what she was doing, and how it made a whole, was different from anything that I'd ever done before. So now I'm thinking about the relationship between the oboe and the piano, and it's as if the piece is mapped out in my mind. I know how it would begin: the piano wouldn't come in for a long time, you see. I thought that would be interesting. And if I had the time, I could easily sit down tomorrow and write the piece. I'd love to be able to do that, but I can't because I'm busy doing something else. And I guarantee that when I *do* sit down and write the piece it won't be what I'm thinking of now.

---

[2] Any 'formal unit in a particular composition that is recognizable by a personal and unmistakable character' (Karlheinz Stockhausen, 'Momentform: Neue Beziehungen zwischen Aufführungsdauer, Werkdauer und Moment', *Texte zur Musik*, vol. 1 (Cologne, Dumont Schauberg, 1963), p. 200).

It won't exactly be something else, either, because it'll be generated from that initial idea – if you want to call it an idea. I'm never quite sure *what* it is, you see.

At the moment I'm writing a piece for piano and orchestra, and if I hadn't been thinking about the relationship between piano and *tutti*, and piano and various aspects of the orchestra, I might have been thinking slightly differently about the oboe and piano piece. In that way, the two pieces are related. That's how it goes.

I hear quite a lot of contemporary music which simply apes old music in the way that its argument is carried forward – you know, the traditional exposition and development of an idea. I don't think my music works like that. I'm very interested in trying to find ways of expressing time in music, and I've consciously explored the idea of a permanent state of exposition. I've also become increasingly interested in the ideas of linear music and pulse. But those two things are opposites, and the way that I want to exploit them is private, so I'd be hard-pushed to put it into words for you. Describing a piece of music and what I want to do in it is very difficult; and, in any case, I don't find these things very interesting to talk about.

The process of composing can't all be an intuitive, off-the-top-of-your-head thing, because musical notation is very precise. Even if you want to be musically imprecise, you have to write precisely – you have to write a precise imprecision! So what might sound like a musical brushstroke can be a week's work. I'm like a clockmaker, and I'm interested in all sorts of things to do with time and repetition within it – repetition that you don't know you're hearing. Last night in London I was listening to bells ringing the changes, and the process of repetition meant that I tucked into my memory something that had gone before. The result was that although it sounded as though the bells were always playing the same thing, there was actually something slightly different every time the change rang. I'm not saying that I write bell music, but I'm interested in the subliminal details of a piece, because the accumulation of detail equals the whole of *everything* that we do.

For example, I think about the background and the foreground of a piece, and how they relate to each other. My Piano Concerto – it's actually called *Antiphonies* – is about the relationship between the piano and *tutti*. So is my Fiddle Concerto, but it isn't about the orchestra saying something and then the soloist saying something similar; it's more like a protagonist saying things in front of a crowd, and them replying, 'You're wrong. You didn't say that before.' Then the soloist says, 'But wait a minute – I said *this*.' And they reply, 'Oh yes, I agree with you.' In other words, there's a dramatic journey taking place.

The issue of time is often the root of the difficulty that some people have with contemporary music. It's not with the notes, I'm quite sure, because they'll happily listen to horrendous sounds of pop music screaming away on the radio. No, it's about being able to follow the logic of the journey of a piece. But it's not my problem to change the way my music speaks. It's like a narrative that takes me to places I never knew about, or corners that I didn't know were there. Once I have a context for a piece, I see before me hundreds of ways in which I can go as I write it. And the context is the truth that I jump from, whichever way I jump.

So I find my music by writing it – by chipping a bit off here and there and seeing what happens. This isn't the romantic idea of the composer, I realise that. I open the door of the piece: what's in there? Where's that light coming from? Shall I go towards it, or not? One of the characteristics of linear music is that it can only start and stop, but the logic of where it's going can take you in a number of directions. At least, I like to think it can. But, as I said before, these things are difficult for a composer to talk about.

I compose all the time. I'm doing it right now. Yes, consciously. I've no control over unconscious things! For example, in 1995 I won the Ernst von Siemens Prize in Germany and was confronted by a lot of critics and people writing pieces about me, and every one of them asked me if I knew that my music was English. Now, the one thing that I've never consciously done is to write what *I* think is English music. I've not an idea in my head what it is anyway, and I'd be interested to know what *they* think it is. Nor is it something that interests me.

I think we can easily say what French music is, and I think we can say what Russian music is. We can certainly say what German music is. A lot of the flavour of nationalism is found through their folk music – it's easily identifiable. The danger is when you start being self-conscious about it. At the end of the nineteenth century English composers like Vaughan Williams wrote pieces based on folk music in order to cultivate a national identity, and I don't think it always helped them musically. But I don't think Elgar's an English composer; his music's German, no question about that. As for Parry ... in Prince Charles's TV documentary about him there wasn't a note of anything that wasn't Wagner. What's English about that? I have no idea.

Yes, I write music by hand. Why? Because I'm too old to use a computer. There's a generation of composers who wrote by hand and then changed to computers, but they're younger than me. I don't know how it's done, actually, and I don't want to know. And as I can't think in terms of it, I use a pencil and paper. For a lot of kids who write music, using a computer seems absolutely natural; but I noticed during my ten-year professorship at King's College London that when some students' work was printed out it assumed the quality of a perfect object when it was absolute crap. It looked as though it was published by Boosey and Hawkes or whoever, but very often it was nonsense.

I'm often asked how I think about a particular piece of my music, and the answer is that it's rather like the way *you* imagine a piece you know well – Mozart's *Jupiter* Symphony, for example, or even something as simple as the National Anthem. Can you hear it in your mind *now*? What are you hearing? In fact, it's not about how the first tune plays through time. You're hearing the whole piece at the same time, as if all the parameters are concurrent. And in my head I hear *my* music in that compressed form.

As for my experience of first performances, it comes back to something I was talking about earlier. I'm never surprised by what a piece of my music sounds like, but I *am* surprised by how it speaks in time. Although this is an aspect of the piece that I mapped out when I was writing it, it's not something that I can calculate self-consciously. I can only sense it from a feeling about how the piece will speak. And then strange things happen. Surprise in music is the essence of a composer's originality, and it can't be contrived.

Of course, there's a hell of a variation in what different performers bring to your music. At its best, working with musicians that you know, with people who are going to really rehearse (I work a lot with the Arditti Quartet, and it's what I call music-making), is part of the process of what you've done as a composer. With them, you're making the piece live. But although you're still holding the piece, in a sense, there's something about a rehearsal that you're not in control of. And if you have an orchestra, not only is there never enough time to rehearse the piece but you're putting yourself in the hands of a conductor. You just sit at the front of the hall while the orchestra plays your music, and time flies by. You try to say, 'Wait a minute, wait a minute ... Could you just ...' And you have to let go. Then, when it's time for their break, the players get up and walk out past you. They're professionals, of course, doing a job. It's not personal. And the standard of their playing is fantastic.

What I really like doing is working closely with a string quartet or a soloist like Melinda Maxwell or the cellist Adrian Brendel. I wrote a song cycle for Mark Padmore, and working on it with him was like working on a piece of theatre. It was terrific. With a soloist, it *is* personal, and a soloist is on your side. I'm not saying that an orchestra's *not* on your side; it's just that the situation's different.

Do I feel typecast by one piece of music that people know me for? You mentioned *Panic*, and if you want me to talk about it I can, but it won't answer this question. Firstly, that piece has been played everywhere. Secondly, it wasn't written for the Last Night of the Proms; it was programmed by John Drummond. Thirdly, writing a piece for the saxophone soloist, John Harle, made me think about his characteristics as a performer; and since he's a fantastic, full-frontal sort of a player, I had to write something which reflected that. Then I could see that there was a way of writing something Dionysian and ecstatic – it's a dithyramb. Nothing wrong with that, is there? I think it was a good choice for the Proms, because I'd have thought that if you didn't have a problem with contemporary music you'd quite like *Panic*!

Let me answer your question another way: what do I think are my most important works? There are certain pieces that I'd like performed more often, such as *Secret Theatre* and *Carmen Arcadiae [Mechanicae Perpetuum]*, which had a particular focus: it's as if my music developed towards those pieces and then away from them. In other words, those works represent two important moments in my career – although, of course, the periods in between were also very interesting.

I don't know where contemporary music's going. I'm not a weather man. But, in part, it's going where I take it, and where young composers take it. The musical world isn't independent of them – they're *making* that world. And one of the interesting things about creativity is that it never does what you think it's going to do. So music will be exactly what it will be. People will say they have a problem with contemporary music because they'll want it to be something else, but I repeat: that's *their* problem. It's not the problem of the composers. Francis Bacon said that, although very few people understand painting, quite a lot of them have a kind of feeling for it; but the world of contemporary music is different because not many people really understand it. Maybe they don't have to. I don't know. The problem with music is that it's an act – it has to be rehearsed and performed. And in an expanding world, is there room for every composer? I don't know that, either.

I've contributed to the world of music, to a small degree, and I'd like to think that, when you add it all up at the end, what I've written is more important than what some performers have contributed to the world of music. But I don't see what I've done as progress, in the sense of pushing things forward. As I said before, I can't sit down and be intentionally original. And I certainly can't express myself or be self-consciously English.

It would *seem* that my music is appreciated more than it used to be. I've heard it mentioned that it was becoming a bit soft, anyway. And it *has* changed. How? In all sorts of ways, such as the intervals I write. But *I* didn't change it. Music evolves, and you look back and find that you're doing things differently. Music has a life of its own, irrespective of what people think about it. We put it into the world and it flies away.

Howard Blake

Howard Blake, London, July 2011

'I've always thought I've had two lives: one making money, and another writing music.'

Too often, perhaps, we expect an artist's work to resemble his or her character, and so we look for similarities between them that don't exist. But in many ways Howard Blake is just like his music: accessible, unpretentious and communicative, if not without darker moments.

A few days before our meeting in July 2011 he rang to ask if the interview could be brought forward by half an hour because of a subsequent appointment. I agreed, although I felt that there would be plenty of time. In fact there wasn't, partly because on my way there I took a short cut which turned out to not be one and partly because after I arrived he talked a lot. And there was a lot to talk about, because his music has regained much of the popularity that it enjoyed during the 1980s and 1990s. 'What happened to ...?' was in fact one of my reasons for wanting to interview him. Another was his willingness to state that much contemporary music occupies an irrelevant backwater and that the public tends to stay away from the first performances of new commissions because in the past they've felt 'assaulted' and 'depressed and insulted' by the results.

We met at his home in Kensington, London – a top-floor flat, originally two artist studios, which retains a lofty central workspace. The main part of that room, illuminated through glass panels in the roof, contains his piano, work desk, books and scores, and a small sofa; stairs at one end of the room lead up to a small balcony where he keeps his computer and photocopier. On the walls are framed artworks, photos and a platinum disc of his soundtrack CD for the animated film *The Snowman*, the score for which, despite his many achievements in the concert hall, he'll probably always be best known. The extent to which the success of that work has been a hindrance rather than a help to his career was something else that I wanted to ask him about.

In his seventies he retains the demeanour of a much younger man, particularly when talking. He listened carefully to my questions before responding, then illustrated his answers with anecdotes that introduced into the conversation a wealth of characters from the worlds of music, theatre and cinema. His has been a full and varied career, and he recalled people and events with wry humour. For the most part he was, to use an old-fashioned word, jolly. But he also spoke candidly about the trials and tribulations of his career, including the way in which his single-minded approach to work contributed to the breakdown of his marriages. In order to illustrate this he searched through his bookshelves for a book about Ravel and then read me a comment by the French composer which he has underlined in red ink. Later, he talked about the protracted litigation that cost him a great deal of money and severely depleted his creative energy during the 1990s; this answered my question about what had happened to him, and why.

He now publishes and distributes most of his own music, and he mentioned to me that three CDs of his music – his works for string quartet and two albums of incidental music for the 1960s TV programme *The Avengers* – were about to be released, within days of each other. 'That's not bad for one week, is it? I've recovered.' Soon afterwards, our conversation was cut short by the arrival of his next visitor, a theatre director who had come to discuss a new score with him.

Some years ago I wrote, 'I believe with Plato that the composer's function is to try to balance and reconcile the conflicting elements of society within his music, and that by doing so in an accessible and comprehensible language he may then hope to have the vision to uplift and inspire society at large.'[1] Plato said that the melodic line is the intelligence of music, harmony is the emotion of music, and rhythm is the physical energy of music; and that, in order for music to work, those three elements should be balanced in the right proportions. In other words, one of those elements becoming all-consuming is probably going to lead to something rather undesirable. And I think that's very true. For instance, rock music went through a period a few years ago where you had a rhythm endlessly repeated without any variation, seemingly forever, which to me is staggeringly boring. It doesn't engage either the emotions *or* the intelligence.

Similarly, there are composers who write music purely for intellectual reasons. I was listening to a Swedish composer at the Royal College of Music last year who was deliberately setting out to create music that didn't emanate from anything that could remotely be

---

[1] Quoted in *Contemporary Composers*, ed. Brian Morton and Pamela Collins (Chicago and London, St James Press, 1992).

called musical; it was an intellectual experiment, and I've no doubt he had very good reasons for doing it. The intellectual element of music, I would say, is form, which is something I've occupied myself with a great deal. If music is holding the public and being enjoyed, it probably has a very good form – although the public normally is not aware that it *has* a form. Anyway, I've always tried to balance the three elements of the emotional, the intellectual and the physical into my own particular blend.

I believe that music should be in a comprehensible language. If people don't want to listen to it, there doesn't seem very much point in writing it. First of all, I write music that I personally want to hear myself. When people ask me 'Who's your favourite composer?' and I reply '*I* am', they say, 'Isn't that very arrogant?' I tell them, 'Do you really think I spend my whole life writing six hundred and twenty works if I don't want to hear them?' Secondly, I would very much like to share my music with people. I think there *is* a place for what is called ivory-tower composition, where the composer says, 'I'm writing for some mythical audience in a hundred years' time which will understand what I'm saying, but right now nobody wants to listen to it.' And I'm not saying that one shouldn't experiment. I experiment all the time. But personally, I believe that music should communicate to as many people as possible.

I have a gift for writing melody; it's almost embarrassing, because I almost can't write something that *isn't* melodic. I frequently try. I've been thrown off one or two large-scale film commitments and been told, 'Your music is so beguiling and so attractive, and the tunes are so wonderful, that nobody bothers to watch the film, and we can't have that!'

It is possible to be totally unmusical and to write music, because writing music is just a question of putting notes on a stave, or nowadays recording them onto a computer. Anybody can do it. There is much music written in the many different branches of twentieth-century musical styles that don't really come into *my* category of music. I would describe them rather as decorative, in the same way that you might say, 'That's very attractive wallpaper but it's not something I want to look at as a work of art.' There's a place for it, but it's not about my ideal of combining melody and harmony and rhythm in such proportions that they move you.

I write music because I *like* writing music. And I've no idea why I like it, even though I started putting down notes on paper as early as nine years old. I obviously had a gift for music, and found that I enjoyed it after I'd overcome my nervousness about writing it. One day, when I was about ten, I took to my piano lesson a six-page march in D major that I'd written – a terrible piece – and showed it to my teacher. He said, 'Where did you get this?' When I replied that I'd written it, he told me to prove it by playing it to him, which I did. Afterwards he said, 'I've never had a pupil who can do that. I'm going to teach you proper harmony and proper counterpoint.' We sent off for a book called *Percy Buck's Practical Harmony*, and I worked my way through every single exercise, including first species counterpoint, second, third, canon and fugue, by the time I was about fourteen or fifteen.

I won a scholarship to the Royal Academy of Music, but 1958 was about the worst time to want to write melodic music because the powers-that-be had decided that everything should be twelve-tone and that all conventional music was no longer of any value. By the time I went there I'd already had some music published by Chappell's, but the Academy wanted me to start all over again. And I couldn't do that. I did learn a great deal from my composition professor, Howard Ferguson, who was enormously helpful. He taught me to orchestrate and made me go through Gordon Jacob's book of orchestration exercises. It's hard work, that sort of academic training, but it's vital because music has rules, a very considerable number of rules, which have grown up through practice and development over centuries. And you need to know them. You have to learn how notes combine with each other, and you have to learn what is and isn't possible on each instrument, and what's ungrateful to the ear. It's a craft, not something abstract; and to be a composer, which is what I've been all my life, you've got to have the right tools and you've got to work very hard.

In general, though, the Academy was not good for me, and while I was there I stopped composing altogether and turned my attention to film direction, production and writing – anything *except* composing. After a while I got a job at the National Film Theatre as a projectionist, working one day off and one day on, and on my days off I started to write music again. I made a film and wrote the music for it, and after that people started to ask me, 'Would you write for a documentary film? Would you write an arrangement for me? Would you …?' People said that what I was doing was good, and it was wonderful to be asked to write music for a specific purpose.

One of the important things I learned professionally was the art of writing music that fits exactly to film. *The Riddle of the Sands* has one of the really big film scores I wrote for large orchestra – its eight-minute opening section includes a seascape, a German boat coming in, lots of tension and then beauty – and everything had to fit perfectly and sound effortless. And I did this by shifting the metronome mark infinitesimally until all these things happened at exactly the right point of a bar. That was a skill I acquired.

I started to write for a number of feature films, I composed the music for the last series of *The Avengers* and I was Musical Director at Elstree. And I was still only thirty. Having also won the prize for best TV commercial music of the year,[2] I had every job going. But I thought, 'I don't know anything about music. I don't actually know how to compose. I'm going to start all over again.' And I did, despite everyone telling me I was insane. I had a house in Knightsbridge but I gave it up so that I could go and live in the countryside. My wife said, 'I don't want to move. I don't like what's going on at all ...' And when I moved down to Sussex she went off and joined the Royal Shakespeare Company, and that was the end of the marriage.

I visited Brighton University to see if I could study strict composition there, but they told me that I'd have to do 50 per cent sociology – how the musician relates to society. I told them, 'I'm sure I know far more about that than you do, and it's what I wish to get away from!' So I started analysing Stravinsky and Beethoven and Bach and fugue, and began all over again.

You can be taught the technique of composition, but I don't think anybody can teach you how to harness that knowledge to express yourself. And I wanted to express myself. Yes, I was in huge demand, but it wasn't satisfying *me*. I couldn't go on writing only for television series and commercials and films. You may not believe this, but I turned down Stanley Kubrick's film *Barry Lyndon* because I was busy writing a piano quartet. But during that period in Sussex I started to write better music. The first piece I completed in my new guise was *Diversions* for cello, in which I suddenly discovered a way of writing melodic line that was my own, not somebody else's. And that was so exciting!

I'd said I wouldn't do any more films, but I finally crumbled when, in 1977, Ridley Scott rang me up and said, 'I'm working with a bloke called David Puttnam. We want to make a film and we want you to do the music for it.' It was *The Duellists*, and eventually I said yes. So I came back into films in a big way. At the same time I started being

---

[2] 1969 British Television Advertising Awards, Special Award (soundtrack): music for Courage light ale – 'Cannon Shot'.

offered ballets to write for the Royal Ballet, and choral works, including my oratorio *Benedictus*. So after my long time off, a great flood of new compositions suddenly came out. I moved back to London, and the first thing I wrote here was *The Snowman*. I had no idea it would be the hit that it was – although I'd been very successful before, it made me *publicly* successful. But I've been absolutely lumbered with *The Snowman* – it's become an albatross around my neck, because it has made it less easy for me to get my serious music listened to.

When I start to think about a new piece of music it's usually with a feeling – a kind of atmosphere – and a very small idea. For instance, last year I was asked to write a big piano piece, and a feeling for it emerged while I was clearing bushes and weeding the garden of my summer house in Sweden. And I heard two notes – a B flat and a D flat, going to an E flat. That doesn't sound at all interesting, but it was in a certain context, and I gradually realised that I was in E flat minor and that the whole of a big piano piece was developing from those three notes.

Something similar happened with my Piano Concerto, which I was asked to write by the Philharmonia Orchestra for the thirtieth birthday of Princess Diana, who was the orchestra's President at that time. I said I'd love to do it, but I hadn't any idea whatsoever of what to write. I literally had to wait for inspiration. There *is* such a thing. I had some friends to dinner, and they said, 'That's an extraordinary commission; what on earth are you going to write?' I replied, 'Well, Princess Diana has such a *joyful* nature, and she makes people happy. There's also a sort of natural innocence about her, and a playfulness. I just need a tiny motif that I can develop that from.' 'Like what?' they asked. I walked across the room to the piano and said, 'Well, it should be something like: [*plays the first four notes of the Concerto*]. That's it, actually! That is it!' And in fact, the twelve-minute first movement of the Concerto derives entirely from those four notes.

Many of the really great composers begin a piece with a very small seed. The obvious one is 'Da-da-da-daaa'.[3] If you didn't know what happened afterwards, you'd say, 'Well, so what? Three Gs and an E flat – any fool could think of that.' But it's about the ability to take such a small seed and to allow it to grow, to have the ability to invert it, reverse it, put it into counterpoint – all the wonderful boons, as somebody called them, that European classical music spent a thousand

---

[3] The opening of Beethoven's Fifth Symphony.

years inventing – and to develop it into something that has legs and runs away and, hopefully, inspires. That, I think, is a miracle.

I start working and I sort of go on until I finish. I suppose in my life I've spent many, many thousands of hours writing, and it's an intensely solitary business. I've lived pretty much on my own for fifty years. I've been married three times, but none of my wives stayed after realising what it's like to live with a composer. It's extremely boring for other people, because you really haven't got time for anything or anybody else. You're trying to solve a set of very abstract problems, and you just can't leave it alone till you've finished it. Ravel made a wonderful remark about this:

> You see, an artist has to be very careful when he wants to marry someone, because an artist never realises his capacity for making his companion miserable. He's obsessed by his creative work and by the problems it poses. He lives a bit like a daydreamer, and it's no joke for the woman he lives with. One always has to think of that when one wants to get married.[4]

My present partner doesn't live with me but she did for a while, back in the 1990s. She would go out at eight o'clock in the morning and I would be sitting at the piano, writing, and she'd come back at nine in the evening and I would still be sitting at the piano, writing! She'd ask, 'Haven't you been out at all?' I'd say, 'No. I've nearly finished this …' And I would have been sitting there for thirteen hours. Nowadays I usually stop for lunch about half-past three in the afternoon, have a nap and then start again!

When I'm working I sit up there in the gallery and I compose directly onto computer with Sibelius so that I can play the music back. It's wonderful software which saves a vast amount of time. For example, I can write a full orchestral score, just go into 'Flute' and instantly print out the flute part and listen to it back. That saves having teams of copyists working all night in crowded rooms, smoking cigarettes! On the other hand, composing is a more lonely occupation than it used to be. You do it all yourself now. I used to like having teams of copyists, because if I was writing very quickly and made a mistake, they'd notice it and say something like, 'I think you mean A sharp here.' And usually they would be right! A good copyist was actually a sort of instant editor.

---

[4] Quoted in Roger Nichols, *Ravel Remembered* (London, Faber & Faber, 1998), p. 35.

A score has to be written correctly, but it's not possible to write in all of the nuances you hear in your head. Elgar, more than any other composer, tried to write down every single piece of expression, but that didn't really do the trick – mostly because performers tend to say, 'I'm sure he doesn't mean that!' Very often they totally ignore the extra-musical instructions. You might want them to lean on a note, to make it more expressive, and I've tried all sorts of ways of making that happen. You can mark it *tenuto* or *espressivo*, but there's no precise way of writing it.

Then, of course, someone has got to play it correctly. One of the problems of working with musicians at a very high level is that most of them are taught according to a rigid system. I found this, for instance, with Christiane Edinger, the soloist in my Violin Concerto. She's a fabulous performer – she studied with Nathan Milstein – but I had to tell her, 'You're playing my Concerto just like you'd play the Brahms.' She said she thought this was a compliment, but I didn't want her to play it as if it were the Brahms because it would then start to *sound like* the Brahms! Musicians tend to think 'Oh yeah, this is like Tchaikovsky' or 'This is like Bartók', and you have to tell them, 'No, it's not *like* anything. It's Howard Blake, and this is how I want it played.' Fortunately I am a pianist, and I will play it to them.

At this point, a conductor will almost certainly do something different, even if you explain to him what you want, and will put in what is called his own interpretation. That can be extremely good, or not. It just depends. So I'd prefer to conduct a new orchestral work myself, in order to lay it down. Then it will become very clear: orchestral musicians will latch on very fast and say, 'Ah, yes, I see what you're doing.'

I think people in this country find the whole idea of being a composer rather weird. They don't really understand how composers write music – they think there must be some trick to it. In other European countries, particularly Italy and Germany, people are far more at home with composers. When I did a concert in Germany recently, members of the audience came up and talked to me intelligently about the music. I had deliberately written certain things in the music – little humorous touches – and they got them and laughed at them. That doesn't happen to me in England. People think 'That must be a mistake' or 'I wonder what we're supposed to think about *that*?'

In 1998 my music publishers sued me for everything I'd ever written. I understand that they need to make money, and that other composers on their list don't make any for them, but they wanted to take all my children away, all my six hundred works. I had to stop writing for three years and devote myself entirely to defending my compositions and my intellectual property from extinction, and that hurt me more than I can possibly tell anybody. I eventually won the case, but to do so cost me a million pounds, which I didn't have. It nearly killed me. But I've gradually re-established myself. In 2002 I wrote an organ piece for Dame Gillian Weir called *The Rise of the House of Usher*, which was really about me rising back from the bottom of the deepest pit in the world!

I've always thought I've had two lives: one making money and another writing music. I used to have a rule that the recompense for music varies in inverse proportion to its quality! In other words, if you write a half-minute commercial they'll probably pay you a fortune; if you write a twenty-five-hour opera it'll probably *cost* you a fortune! People think you make lots of money from everything, but records don't make much money. They probably *cost* you money. So you have to be very practical, and balance the kind of work you do.

Gavin Bryars

Gavin Bryars, Leicestershire, July 2011

'I write music the way I hear it, which is rather old-fashioned.'

In his introduction to a 2012 radio documentary celebrating the centenary of John Cage, Gavin Bryars commented, 'It's rare for a composer to remain controversial throughout his life', and he might himself be included in that generalisation. During the 1970s he was Britain's best-known composer of experimental and conceptual music, and twenty years later many of his works were recorded during the CD boom that saw the major record labels subsidise specialist projects with profits earned from the core repertory. As a result, many CD collectors knew of Bryars's *The Sinking of the Titanic*, *Jesus's Blood Never Failed Me Yet* and Cello Concerto *Farewell to Philosophy*, even if they didn't buy them. Since then the non-mainstream repertory has increasingly returned to the specialist labels who don't possess the promotional clout of the majors, which may be one reason why Bryars's name seems less prominent than it did. Perhaps, too, some of the composition techniques he experimented with have lost their power to provoke.

There were additional reasons, both musical and personal, why he'd appeared to me a rather remote figure. One is the difficulty in pinning down what kind of composer he is – there's a long tradition of composer-pianists but not one of jazz-based, double-bass-playing composers who explore free improvisation, minimalism, indeterminism and neoclassicism. There's also the contrast between his early, experimental works and his more recent, predominantly slow and often gravely beautiful music, whose shifting harmonies shun sentimentality. The second reason is that he spends the summer on the west coast of Canada and the remainder of the year in a quiet Leicestershire village, so is not part of the regular, London-based concert scene. Third, his e-mail replies to my request for an interview and its subsequent arrangements were brief to the point of bluntness. I wondered how forthcoming he would be when, or if, we met.

Rather to my surprise, the interview took place exactly as arranged, at his Leicestershire home in September 2011. He was straightforward, serious and apparently unemotional; perhaps because of his Yorkshire roots and his performing background in cabaret and working men's clubs he struck me as a grounded, no-nonsense musician. But he was approachable and generous with his time, leading me after the interview to the bottom of a somewhat overgrown cottage garden to show me the secluded studio – formerly a garage – where he works. Inside, two bicycles stood against a wall, every work surface was covered with papers, folders and family possessions, and most of the floor space was taken up by boxes of shrinkwrapped CDs – he now makes his own recordings of his music, many of them featuring him as a performer. There was just enough room for me to sit down next to his work desk while he played me extracts from a recording of his opera G, which was awaiting commercial release.

I can think of no other composer for whom performing as part of a regular ensemble takes up such a large part of his working life, and so it seemed logical to begin our conversation by asking about the extent to which this influences the music he writes.

Being a practical musician is probably more important for me than for any composer I know. I certainly find it difficult when I don't have a strong involvement in the practicalities and performance of my own music. For example, next week I have an orchestral piece being done in Amsterdam, and I'll be at the rehearsals and at the performance; but I can do very little, so I'll be sitting in the audience, just twiddling my thumbs and hoping it goes well. A week after that, I've the UK premiere of a ballet for which I wrote the music, and again, I can do little. But a week later I'm playing in another ballet that I wrote the music for, and I'm much happier about *that*.

In the orchestration of my second opera I deliberately included an improvising jazz bass part because English National Opera didn't at that time have any bass players who were jazz players, and so taking the part would give me something to do during the premiere rather than watching it with everybody else. As luck would have it, the first performance was postponed till the following year, by which time they'd hired a new bass player for the orchestra who was also a very good jazz player. I wasn't going to take away his moment of glory, so unfortunately I did end up having to sit in the audience.

The other, practical consequence is that I think very much about what the performer has to do in a piece of music. And this could be as simple as where page-turns come. For percussionists, I think about their choreography – manoeuvring from one place to another. They may need to play the tubular bells and then immediately move eight feet away to play a marimba chord, and they may have to change mallets; or maybe they'll already have two mallets in one hand but need to use another music desk. So there'll be a switch of attention. And I don't want to have performers rushing around like crazy. I would rather have a second percussionist in order to make the performance more human.

I also think about the hands of the string players – I'm one myself. For example, not having a hand locked in a certain position for a long period, doing lots of cross-string arpeggios. (Well, I did that to Julian Lloyd-Webber in my Cello Concerto, but that was unusual.) I work a lot with guitarists, and that's the instrument I most have to think about in terms of what the player's hands can encompass. It's not like writing for the piano, where you can have two hands and very wide spans. I also think about the difference between a piano and a harp: a tenth on the piano is quite hard to span, while on the harp it's easier than an octave on the piano.

All this comes about because I didn't really become a composer by studying in the conventional sense. Although I did have some lessons, I took a more practical route to composition: from being a jazz and improvising performer. And that's still at the heart of everything I do. I studied mostly with George Linstead in Sheffield, who was rather grumpy and not interested in seeing anything that I wrote. His point was to teach me the *craft* of composition: harmonising a Bach chorale, writing a string trio in the style of Mozart, doing Palestrina counterpoint, those kinds of things. I learnt some of the rudiments of orchestration, but mainly did imitative pastiche writing that taught me how to observe someone's style and get it right, within rules. I've written a lot of pieces based on historical models, and my knowledge of twelfth- or thirteenth-century monody, or the Italian Renaissance madrigal or viol consorts, has been immensely useful. I also learned simple things – like the spelling of notes and which way up the stems go – which many people get wrong, especially if they use computer software. You know, they'll write G flat instead of F sharp because the computer has decided that for them.

You're right that there are extremes of attitudes among composers towards their audience. Many would want to write for fellow professionals, to earn *their* respect and admiration. That's a perfectly laudable thing to do, and I wouldn't be terribly pleased if another composer thought I was incompetent, even if he didn't like my music and found it simplistic. But there was a time when new music festivals tended to be rather like university seminars. I've been told of a composer who had a new piece played and who then put up a chart on the wall to explain how it was written; someone spotted a flaw in the logic (there was actually an error in the calculations) and this completely flummoxed him, and he had to go back and rewrite the piece.

I'm rather un-philosophical about composing. I take the painter Barnett Newman's line that aesthetics for the artist is rather like ornithology for the birds. The moment you start to scrutinise too much, you become incapacitated or you revert to formulae. I've always tried to respond to each musical situation as it comes, and to not do things with a sense of routine. Of course, there are occasions when, because of the pressure of time, you have to pillage your own work. Every composer has done that. But I don't feel any broad stylistic thrust in terms of the nature of the music I write. Some composers write according to certain rules and matrices and systems, or a body of beliefs and structures, which they then use to *form* their music, so sometimes the ear is not the prime determinant of that music. But for me, the way things sound is prime, and I write music the way I hear it, which is rather old-fashioned.

Also, I'm acutely aware that there's an audience. But I don't pander to them – I don't write something because I think it's what they'd like to hear. That would be dangerously close to the ersatz classical music written by someone who's not really a (I hate to use the term) 'proper composer'. For example, I'm sure Paul McCartney's classical music is well meant, but it's just not very good. However, I like to give an audience some help in finding their way into a piece so that it's not completely alienating. One way is to have some association, musical or non-musical, within the piece – rather like being a figurative painter rather than an abstract one. I used to love titles, and I had a book in which I wrote them down long before I thought of pieces to name. People would think, 'Interesting title; what's it got to do with the music?' And the answer was usually 'Nothing'. It was just a game I played. I actually made a rather silly electronic piece out of a line by Samuel Becket: 'To gain the affection of Miss Dwyer, even for one short hour, would benefit me no end.' I thought that was a fantastic line.

Today, I find that titles can be helpful to give some sort of clue to the piece – some way into it – before anyone hears it or reads the programme note. So the subtitles of my Cello Concerto (*Farewell to Philosophy*), Double Bass Concerto (*Farewell to St Petersburg*), Piano Concerto (*The Solway Canal*) and Violin Concerto (*The Bulls of Bashan*) all have, I hope, a certain resonance for the audience.

I'm sometimes called a British composer, and it can be useful, especially when an organisation like the British Council invites me to Japan for a festival of British music. To call yourself an *English* composer sounds as if you're in some kind of pastoral school, but I do think of myself as English even though my heart is much more with Scotland and the Celts. Although I'm not sure about the extent to which 'British composer' identifies any more a *way* of writing music, there is a sort of routine to the way a British composer will manage his life, and that's to do with who performs his music. BBC commissions, the Proms, the London Sinfonietta, all these have a remit for contemporary British music. However, I'd say that I haven't been favoured that heavily by them. I've had a fair number of BBC commissions, but never anything from the Proms – and I don't particularly want it. I'm sure my publisher would be horrified if I refused a Proms commission, but there's something about that representation of Britishness that repels me somewhat.[1] And so I tend to think of myself as a composer who just happens to live in England for most of the time.

When I wrote my very first piece of music I thought I was being adventurous by doing something twelve-tone, but when I played it through I found it of little interest. I always found the twelve-tone system too rigid. People still study it, and of course people play the music of Webern and Schoenberg. But it's of a particular historical moment. Some composers have moved from serial music to what's called the New Complexity, where one's dealing with the same degree of dissonance and different forms of order than purely acoustic ones. But it's not discussed in the same way. I would say that the complexity people are not using *only* serial techniques; they're using many more forms of complexity and mathematical models. And that doesn't interest me massively.

If the chips were down, I would rather touch someone emotionally than intellectually. I would think, ultimately, that has a more profound and satisfying effect on the listener, and I wouldn't want someone simply to think, 'Gosh, what a clever composer in the way he can manipulate notes'. But one doesn't have to move people to tears. There are times when that happens, but the emotion can come from recognising as extremely beautiful something that provides a satisfying sense of absolute rightness. When I wrote my first opera I spent a long time listening to the music of Richard Strauss, Wagner and Busoni; and there are moments in Strauss which make me gasp

---

[1] When approving the editing of this conversation, Bryars added, 'Ironically, I was subsequently given a Proms commission for a medium that I'd never before written for – the brass band – and I wrote the piece.' This was *After the Underworlds* (2012).

at his virtuosity, allied to the extraordinary simplicity of the way the music sounds. I can find that in all sorts of music, actually.

When I hear music that's aesthetically pleasing I have to analyse *why* it pleases me. So I'm always aware of technical detail. When I listen to jazz I always follow the bass line, so I know where a player's hands are at any moment in the piece; and because of the key signature I'll know which are open strings, how certain resonances are produced, and so on. I can't remove myself as a performer from what I'm hearing. As for pleasure in my own music, it goes back to the aesthetics-versus-intellect argument. Getting the structure right, or mastering some technical detail, is what makes a piece sound good to me. A composer will generally find it hard to think 'I wrote a really beautiful piece' because he'll always be aware of the detail within it. It's rather like my wife, who's a filmmaker, always being aware, when watching a film, of the editing, the camera angles and filters and the technical tricks involved.

Besides, a composer will always move on to something else. I would only revise an old work, instead of writing something new, if I wanted to make it more available. For example, my *Cadman Requiem* was written for the Hilliard Ensemble, plus string trio, in memory of my friend Bill Cadman, who was killed in the Lockerbie disaster; and its original, rather special combination of voices and instruments was making the possibility of subsequent live performances more and more remote. So I made a version for choir and organ, which can be performed much more easily. I've also been very careful with orchestral pieces in not insisting on difficult instruments or difficult combinations of instruments, and in not having to bring in extra players just to make sure the piece can have a life. Whether it does or not is another question ...

I always try to pace my music so that an event will stay only as long as its presence is welcome – rather like not having someone at a party who won't leave on time. But I think pacing is something you simply can't be taught as a composer. Maybe it's something one learns from being a performer. Certainly, within jazz and improvised music, things become redundant if they go on too long. When I was a jazz bass player I worked as an accompanying bassist in cabaret and played with all kinds of comedians and performers who worked the hall, as it were; and I recognised the superior skill of certain comedians in the way that they placed their punchlines and sometimes led up to them by differing routes. That sense of balance and rightness is probably what I've worked hardest at because it's intangible and very hard to achieve.

Composers do make errors. Certainly in the earlier days, when I was not as experienced with *all* instruments as I am now, I'd write something and then find that it didn't sound quite how I'd imagined. But sometimes it actually sounded very interesting, so I logged it, and it became a new piece of knowledge. At other times, something happens in performance that brings a new insight to what you've written. When I wrote a ballet based on the music of Gluck and Purcell I specified certain *tempi* but then found that the choreographer wanted some of it to go incredibly quickly – almost twice as fast as what I'd written. So a rather melancholy slow waltz ripped along at a hell of a pace, and I was quite startled. But it worked in terms of the choreography, although if I were to play it in concert I would probably drop the tempo a bit.

Before I was taken up by Schott in 1994 I published all my own work, and I had a habit of saying yes to every project that was offered to me, whether or not I knew anything about it, and then finding a means of actually doing it. The most serious case was probably my first opera, which I said yes to without even considering the facts that: (1) it was in Ancient Greek, a language I neither spoke nor understood; (2) I had only eight months to write it; and (3) I'd only ever seen one opera performed live (Gunther Schuller's *The Visitation*). I'd written nothing for orchestra, nothing for the human voice, nothing for the stage. And the commission was from one of the world's leading opera houses: La Fenice in Venice. *And* I was to handle all my own publishing, supervise the printing, proofread, negotiate the rights with the opera house, deal with part rental, printing, everything. So I learned very fast – including how to write very quickly.

But once I'd gained this facility, the danger was that I'd leave work for as long as possible before starting it. My rule of thumb used to be that I would start composing the morning after I'd woken up in the middle of the night in a cold sweat, thinking, 'It's too late.' Although I have more responsibility towards my editors these days, that tendency has remained with me, to some extent, and lack of time is still usually the thing that forces me to organise myself.

I would say that most of my 'composing' is a mental exercise that precedes writing down the results. There's a sort of mulling-over, thinking laterally and generally having the piece somewhere in the back of your mind. It's not like active research. And then the actual committing to paper is usually the easiest part of the process. I tend to work in the daytime, keeping relatively normal hours. And I don't work in the house: I have a little studio thirty feet away, which is physically separate and gives me a degree of isolation. I write with pencil and paper, photocopy the work and send it to my editor; at the same time I send a copy to Chris Hinkins, who does the computer-setting. My editor looks for any inconsistencies, and queries things such as whether I've missed out a sharp here or a flat there, and whether a particular note is supposed to be on the line or in the space. Chris then sends his version to my editor, who goes through it and comes back to me with any outstanding queries. This means that for my own deadline I have to count back a lot further from the first performance than I would have done in the old days. So I try to work methodically, and I set myself targets of how much music to write each day.

The year before I joined Schott my orchestral piece *The War in Heaven*, for two solo voices, half chorus, full symphony chorus and full symphony orchestra, was scheduled to be broadcast on Radio 3 live from the Royal Festival Hall, and I started writing it far too late – in fact, a month after the deadline for delivery. It was postponed till the end of the BBC season, but I had effectively six weeks to write it, otherwise it wouldn't happen at all. And I was then teaching full-time. So I worked out how much I had to do each day to send off to the team of copyists that the BBC had working on it. That's when I developed huge respect for Malcolm Arnold, who said in an interview that he wrote twenty pages of full score per day. I just found his facility and his optimism incredibly refreshing, and thought, 'Right, that's what I'm going to have to do.' I managed four times to write twenty pages of full score per day, and I did get the piece done in time.

I've been widely recorded, but I found increasingly that decisions about recordings were being taken by company executives, and that what they wanted to record wasn't what I wanted to record, or at least wasn't my priority. So I felt I should really take it over myself. I now have seventeen or eighteen albums on my own record label, and distributors who export them across the world. It's not that difficult, but it takes a lot of my time just to deal with the negotiation of rights and royalty payments and the accounting. Most days, I'm also on the phone to my publishers. Sometimes there are long conversations when we have a catch-up, and we can be on the phone for an hour and a half, which takes quite a lot out of my composing time because it has to be in office hours, you see, and that's when I would normally be writing.

Occasionally, too, I write words. At the moment I'm supposed to be writing an article for a Russian newspaper about my working relationship with the choreographer of a ballet company over there; I'll write the piece and my wife will translate it. I also maintain my website, updating performances and materials and so on. So there are lots of business activities that go on, quite apart from the act of writing music.

A piece of music can enjoy a sort of iconic moment, or become well known as a result of being heard in particular circumstances, after which its composer is always associated with it. People know *The Sinking of the Titanic* and *Jesus' Blood Never Failed Me Yet* better than anything else I've written, but I wrote them more than forty years ago. They're not pieces that I would promote or push for a performance, but they're what people tend to want me to do – rather like the Rolling Stones always having to sing *Satisfaction*, or Percy Grainger always having to play his *Country Gardens* or Satie his *Gymnopédies*. So I do still perform them. And when I do, I still find value in them – even in a piece like *Jesus' Blood Never Failed Me Yet*. It's incredibly simple, yet that old man's voice, which I've heard so many times, still touches me. The other thing one has to acknowledge is that while *I* may have played those pieces endlessly, some people in the audience will be hearing them for the first time. In any case, it's inevitable that some things of more immediate interest to *me* won't interest the public at all, and there will always be people who find works from a composer's distant past more interesting than what he's writing today.

Because composers' activities take place in a public arena, I'm aware that we get into the public's consciousness at some level. But it's not like being so famous that someone stops you in the street. Once in a while that will happen though, and it's really quite startling. I remember being at the checkout at Sainsbury's in the days when one paid for shopping by cheque, and the woman on the till asking, 'Are you Gavin Bryars the composer?' It was the last thing I was expecting, but apparently she'd previously worked at the HMV shop in Leicester. It was pleasantly surprising!

I'm lucky to be one of the very few professional composers in this country who's able to live *only* by writing music. Almost everyone else has some university post or other kind of job. I perform, too, but in a rather *ad hoc* way – not like James MacMillan, for example, who conducts a lot. So this life is terrific, because I'm being paid to do what I really like to do. It's almost like being a professional footballer (if you like playing football, that is!). I'm paid a lot less than a footballer is, but I'm okay.

Diana Burrell

Diana Burrell, Harwich, February 2013

❛I still don't think I've got any kind of reputation.❜

When Diana Burrell and her husband decided to move out of London, they thought they were being over-optimistic in looking for a modern house down a country lane overlooking an estuary (she's a keen birdwatcher), with good local shops and easy access to London, and within walking distance of a railway station. But almost immediately they found all of those things in Harwich, on the Essex coast, and moved earlier than they'd planned to. Although they didn't choose Harwich because of its artistic life, she has since become closely involved in it: 'When you move to a place like this you soon get found out', she told me during my encounter with her, which took place while she was Artistic Director of the Harwich Festival of The Arts.

She offered to meet me in London but I preferred to interview her on home ground because it seemed important that our meeting take place where she lives and works. During the e-mail exchange in which the interview was arranged she described Harwich as 'a wonderful place' and I wanted to know how or if her surroundings influence her working life. When we met there on a murky late morning in February 2013, the view from her first-floor living room across the River Stour was largely obscured by mist, but I could imagine that on a clear day the broad expanse of sea and sky is an inspiration. In fact, she explained, it's just as often a distraction from her work, which people mistakenly think is derived from the sights and sounds of the natural world. Like that of most composers, perhaps, her home is a pleasant backdrop to her work rather than a specific inspiration for it.

When I asked her how much of her work goes on in her head before she writes it down, she started to describe the process by which she begins a new piece of music. After about thirty seconds she stopped, apparently unsure whether what she was saying made sense, and asked, 'Is this going to be useful to you?' I explained that, although the processes by which music is created can seem mysterious, I was interested less in that mysteriousness than in the different ways in which composers attempt to describe it when asked. Like many of the other contributors to this book, she used terms that alternated between the frustratingly vague and the fascinatingly precise; but, although she may not have realised it, she communicated very clearly how and why she works on the early stages of a piece.

For her, there's a strong visual component to composing. She likens the process to fashioning textures, rather like a sculptor discovering her work inside a lump of clay, and she conceives her music in paragraphs even when she isn't setting words. Which is why, surrounded by the abstract contemporary art – strong blocks of colour, pattern and texture – on the neutrally coloured walls of her relaxingly light and airy sitting room, I felt that there was probably a connection between her music and the interior of her home, if not its geographical location.

I think you have to treat composing like a regular job, and so I try to keep office-type hours. This sounds unromantic to some people: they have an idea of me sitting over there, looking across the estuary and thinking, 'Oh, I'm feeling inspired, so I'll write some music.' Quite simply, if that were all that happened I would never get any composition done.

I love contemporary art – abstract art, mostly – and yes, the paintings in this room *are* about shape and pattern and colour. That's very much me. I like a lot of light, too, and that's why this house is so good to live and work in. But I don't think these surroundings influence my work. People try to find them in the music, but they're not really there. Besides, I can work absolutely anywhere. My husband's a singer, so he's often at home practising, which is not at all useful to a composer who needs silence in order to work; but we manage. And in the past I often worked in funny places like friends' basements or someone's garage. I don't need beauty, really!

At the moment I'm busy organising the next Harwich Festival, and this is taking up a lot of time, so normally I'm working on my latest composition (a brass piece for this year's Proms) in the mornings. I don't answer the phone until lunchtime and I don't even turn the computer on until then. This seems to be the best way of working for me. But it's strange: the days when I really don't feel like it are often the days when I do my best work. Some of the work sorts itself out in the subconscious and then it's released while I'm doing something completely different, like digging the garden; but that won't happen unless I've first sat and stared at my blank sheet of paper, trying to get something to write down.

Yes, I think there *is* something I want to express in general terms through my music. But it's not about expressing *myself*. Some people talk of having another book inside them or another piece of music inside them, but that thought would fill me with terror because it can't all come from *me*. In some way my music reflects the outside world and (I know this sounds very grand) natural energies and forces. One of the reasons I enjoy Tippett's music so much is that it's got this sort of life force to it. And I like Nielsen and Martinů because they can express joy and positive energy as well as all the misery that other composers find easier to communicate! I very consciously try to get that into my own music, but the biggest difficulty is in finding the right harmonic language.

I don't necessarily want to write straight tonal harmony any more but I've spent a long time trying to find a series of chords that do what the old major and minor ones used to do – for example, a cadence chord, or one that will drive the music onwards or have some other established function. This occupies me a lot, because, while it *is* easy to write gloomy, slow music and dark, dramatic music, a composer needs to do other things too. I always try to avoid *sentimental* sadness and misery – I never want to have that in my music. If it's there it's probably the performers' fault, because the conductor's taking the piece too slowly!

As I've been doing this work on harmony I've discovered that the chords which I feel are bright and stable, and which can move the music on, often have a minor sixth or a major sixth in the two lowest parts. And it's this very open, stable interval on which the rest of the music's built that produces a sunny effect – for me, anyway. On the same subject, I've often wondered why the one composer I simply can't listen to is Elgar. I admire him, totally, for the structure and direction of his music, but it leaves me feeling terribly depressed, all of it. And I think it's often because his bass lines move downwards, pulling the music with them; whereas a lot of my harmony (sometimes it's over a pedal, and the chords splash outwards from that ground) goes upwards. Complete opposites!

When I was a young composer I thought Xenakis was wonderful because he seemed so unorthodox, and I wanted to be as striking and original as him. My music has never sounded anything like his, of course, and it was his singularity that I wanted to emulate. I still think this is very important, and when I was teaching composition students I worked with them on it as much as on the technical side of things.

My music has often been described as dramatic and colourful, and

I do want people to be a bit startled by it. I also want it to work on several levels so that people don't get everything the first time they hear it. What I really like to do is to take people on a kind of journey so that they emerge slightly different afterwards. In other words, I want them to have an experience that they wouldn't otherwise have. That's certainly what I'm looking for when I listen to other people's music: I want to think, 'I've never heard anything like that before. It's amazing. And as a result of hearing it I think differently about things.'

Musical form is therefore very important to me, even though the forms I use aren't particularly original. I'm old-fashioned enough to want there to be some sort of development through a piece so that listeners have a sense of achievement at the end of it. But you can't predict what sort of music they'll like. You can only write it in your own way, in the hope that what you do is striking enough to communicate immediately and to make people want to hear more. I would never, ever write down to them, and I simply hope that they'll be persuaded by what I'm doing.

I'm not in any musical tradition, I don't think. At least, not intentionally so. Having said that, I think you can always hear where a composer comes from. The music of a Scandinavian composer doesn't sound German or British; it sounds Danish or Swedish or whatever. But, although I've often puzzled over it, I can't identify what *Britishness* in music sounds like. When I say that I sometimes find Elgar (he's the composer who most people say is 'British') rather sentimental, I immediately get set upon, and people say, 'That's just the way it's performed. It's not meant to be like that.' Which I accept.

People tend to think of my music in narrative terms because some of the titles are very colourful. But a title always comes late in the composition process, when I realise that I have to call the piece something. Like *Das Meer, das so groß und weit ist, da wimmelt's ohne Zahl, große und kleine Tiere* [... *great and wide sea, wherein are things creeping innumerable, both great and small beasts*]: people think, 'Ah yes, that one with the long German title'! In fact, the way I write means that a piece is terribly vague in *all* its aspects until quite late. I leave everything fluid, and I don't put in bar lines until the tightening-up process at the end.

To me, the act of composing is almost like translating sculpture into music: I'm thinking about textures and form and shape and density and paleness and movement. It's almost as if I'm delving into bronze or some other material and chipping away in order to bring the piece out. But I am a composer, not a sculptor, so the word 'translating' is probably not quite correct. It's not that I would *rather* be a sculptor.

There *is* a visual element to the process, but it's about shape, pattern and form rather than the depiction of flowers or trees or landscape.

Nor do I think of my music as making a pattern on the page. It's more about touch and density. (Some words work through all the artistic disciplines, don't they? For example, we talk about colours in music, and architects talk about rhythm in buildings.) At the moment, working on this brass piece for the Proms, I'm conscious of a big pot of bright sounds that I'm stirring before the notes come out, and I think, 'Yes, I'll use *that* one!'

I'm not a composer who more or less works a piece out in the head before writing it down. At first I have all sorts of unconnected thoughts about it and a sense of the sound world that it will inhabit, but this often changes. Sometimes there are what I think of as melodies – musical lines, anyway – and if that's what comes to me first I'm likely to shape the rhythm of the piece afterwards. But sometimes it's the intervals that come first. Otherwise, I start off with an incredibly complex, dark bit of music, and I rough out the whole piece in order to establish its shape before filling in the notes. I think of this as quite a messy process, partly because I'm not a terribly good pianist. I can hardly play my own music, anyway, and that's not very useful!

I tend to work in what I call 'paragraph form', where a section of music is based on a particular series of pitches or rhythms and therefore has a certain feel to it. I know that some composers start at the beginning of a piece and fill in the whole of the first page – including dynamics – before they move on to the next, but I'm the complete opposite of them. Sometimes I start in the middle of the piece. And I try to get a lot of horizontal music down in one go. This is a psychological need, I think, because having ten pages that are nearly blank feels better to me than having only half a page that's filled in!

I sometimes write straight into a neat copy rather than a short score that's then orchestrated. But I keep little sketches here and there on old bits of paper, and I rely on being able to rub things out and change them after living with the piece for a while. Yes, I work the old-fashioned way – pencil and paper – because I like to be able to *see* all of the music I'm writing. I can't cope with a computer screen, where you have to keep scrolling backwards and forwards. And if I'm writing a big piece I'll paste it up on the wall so that I can walk from one section to another. It's rather like being a visual artist.

It's always a surprise to me, even after all these years of composing, how much more vivid my music sounds when I first hear it performed. You'd think that by now I'd be able to imagine the sounds – which I can, of course, but they're usually much brighter and more strongly etched than I was expecting. I don't think I've made many major mistakes in my music recently, and that's probably the result of experience; but I love it when performers have their own ideas about how it should go. I don't stand over the conductor's left shoulder, saying 'Can you do this?' and 'Can you do that?' I'm very much a stand-apart composer, who says to the conductor 'Go for it – do it!' I expect my music to have a life of its own, really – I turf the babies out of the nest and make them fly immediately! And I never go back and revise things.

As to how my music has changed or evolved since I began composing, that's difficult to answer. I *hope* it's changed, and that it's sort of grown up with me. I'm sure it has. But I don't know *how* it's altered. I think I would need to ask someone else about that. I also hope that people can still tell that my music is by *me*, and that they still recognise my fingerprints on it. I want it to make an immediate impact of some kind (which will, of course, depend on who's listening to it), while being full of little things to be discovered as its life force and energy pull the listener along with it. Arresting and strong is how I would like it to be thought of. And bright, and life-enhancing.

I never really studied composition at all, and when people ask me about my formal musical tuition the bottom falls out of my world and I think, 'I shouldn't be doing this!' I did an ordinary music degree (which included a little bit of composition), but what was useful about being at Cambridge in the late 1960s was, I have to say, not so much the course itself but the sheer amount of music-making that was going on. Having grown up in Norwich, which had no professional orchestra, and coming from a church music background meant that I didn't know a lot of orchestral pieces. I'd never heard any Mahler, for example. So I played my viola in every concert I possibly could, and I got to know an incredible amount of music. I wrote pieces while I was at Cambridge but my musical education was a bit hit-and-miss, really, and I felt way behind some of the other students who'd already studied at a higher level.

I don't think composers would have been taken seriously in those days if they'd been writing the simpler, tonal, more repetitive music that's being written today. But there was another reason why I wanted to be much more modernist than I actually was, and it was personal: I wanted to write the sort of music I enjoyed listening to. But I hadn't had enough training to do that. After all, you start off with what you *can* do, not what you want to do. I'd hear pieces and think, 'That's wonderful. How on earth does he do that? I want to find out.'

It might have been helpful to be a composition student and to work my way through the various techniques that I learned myself, piecemeal, later on. And I'm still envious of people who studied composition more methodically. On the other hand, I like to think that the way I learned, and the way I did my own thing, means that I'm more individual.

If I'd thought about what the life of a composer was going to be like, I probably would have been quite surprised, because in those days it didn't occur to me that there weren't any women composers. It didn't really occur to me that *I* was one. I just wanted to write music, and I was quite driven. But I had to earn a living, so I began touring as a viola player and I got a teaching job for four or five years. By that time we had two very young children, and we would pay a childminder to have them for one afternoon a week when I wasn't working. And that time was set aside for composition. So I'd have to remember musical ideas from Wednesday afternoon to Wednesday afternoon – and I did, mostly.

While I was away on tour I wrote in funny places, including a caravan in someone's garden in Sheffield one winter, and various awful lodgings. And I used to have to stand up to compose at home some evenings after the kids had gone to bed because I was so tired – had I sat down, I would have fallen asleep! But I remember thinking, 'Ah, good – composition time!' I never thought, 'I can't do this, it's all too difficult.' I wanted to do it *so* much, I think.

It was my good friend Richard Hickox who gave me some chances in the early days by saying, 'Write us something for the Saint Endellion Festival.' I wrote him a huge piece – fifty minutes' music for large orchestra, double choir and five soloists! And when it started I thought, 'I can't sit here for all that time, listening to all this music I've written. This is awful.' But it taught me to manage large-scale form, which I've always been interested in. Someone once said of my *Symphonies of Flocks, Herds and Shoals*, which I wrote for the BBC, 'But it's *huge!*' I suppose women traditionally *have* worked in smaller forms. It didn't occur to me that I was doing something unusual for a woman. But I remember that at the time when I was writing a lot of music and giving a lot of interviews, most male journalists and radio announcers would want me to talk about being a woman composer. To me, this was a form of discrimination, because my male contemporaries were asked to talk about their music.

There was a period in the late 1990s when a lot of projects piled up and I had a lot of big pieces performed: the Clarinet Concerto, the *Symphonies of Flocks, Herds and Shoals* and *Dunkelhvide Månestråler* for mezzo-soprano, cor anglais and orchestra. And then around the year 2000 I started to do slightly different things. *Gold*, a piece for brass and piano commissioned by Huddersfield, was quite a catalyst for moving my style on. You asked earlier about how my music has changed and I couldn't really answer your question, but I think it's busier and more complex than it was.

In 2006 I began a five-year post at the Royal Academy of Music, during which I wrote *The Hours*, a big work for various ensembles featuring organ, accordion and harmonium. It was a research project, really, to present the organ in a different light. However, by the time that post ended I wasn't getting any more commissions, and I assumed that people had forgotten about me because I'd been buried away in the Academy for five years.

During all that time I was still a composer; I was simply out of work. I wasn't afraid to admit that. But I was still writing. And now I've got this Proms commission. I still don't think I've got *any* kind of reputation, though, and I know I'm not a public figure. I do feel more or less forgotten about, and in one way this is quite nice because it means that I can simply get on with the work. I always seem to have something on the go. And I've always felt it important not to get typecast as a composer. For example, there was a time when I got a lot of choral commissions, and eventually I wanted to get out of that area of work. Then I wrote a lot of pieces for young people and didn't want to be typecast as an education composer. Then came all my big orchestral works, and I was very happy to move on to writing more chamber music so that I wasn't typecast as an orchestral composer.

I love the feeling of finishing a piece of music. That's a great moment, although it leaves me very tired for a couple of weeks. But after the first performance is over I never listen to any of my music unless it's to check a recording. It would feel very strange to me to do so. I'm not listening to much of anyone else's music at the moment, either. I love hearing a new piece that I think is very good, but I find it hard to switch off my critical faculties. I tend to think, 'Oh, that's not how *I* would have done it' or 'Gosh, I'm bored with this.' I was really disappointed recently by a particular piece that I'd been looking forward to hearing because it's by a composer I admire. But it was so dull, and I thought, 'Oh no!' Of course, I have my favourites. If I want excitement I'll put on some Nielsen. And if I want great pleasure I know that *anything* by Bach will do!

Tom Coult

Tom Coult, London, February 2014

> **There's much less music in your head than you think there is when you start to write it down.**

It seemed important to include in this book interviews with young, up-and-coming composers who appeared to be going places, who were beginning to establish their careers and who might be at the peak of them when or if a project like this is repeated a few decades in the future. But choosing composers to represent the future of British music – an impossible and unfair burden, in any case – wasn't easy.

One reason was the increasing difficulty in identifying a central musical orthodoxy that young composers are required to react to or against. In the absence of a leading 'disciple' who's helping music to evolve from such a perspective, I assumed that the most I could hope for was a spokesperson for *one* of the directions in which it's evolving. Another reason was the difficulty in predicting who'll be a big name of the future, since so many factors other than musical talent are involved. Not the least of these is a temperament that can survive the demands of an insecure and increasingly competitive profession. There are more composers today than ever before, and the harsh realities of the musical market place mean that even exceptional early promise can't guarantee long-term success. (Re-reading Paul Griffiths's book thirty years after it was published is to be reminded of a number of then prominent composers whose music is rarely heard today.)

For me, there was the additional problem that my chosen representatives of the emerging generation had to be both young *and* sufficiently articulate to discuss their music with a stranger who was unlikely to know any of it. But Tom Coult appeared to tick all the boxes. He'd recently been awarded a composition grant that I was indirectly involved with, and he'd impressed me with his eloquence in a radio interview about his work. I was struck by the range of influences from the wider artistic world that he admitted to and by his confidence in expressing the view that composition, for him, is in part an act of hedonism. And when George Benjamin, with whom he was then studying at King's College London, vouched for his talent and promise, I knew that I'd made a good choice.

I interviewed him at his home, a first-floor flat in south London, in February 2014, and we chatted across his kitchen table while sipping from enormous mugs of coffee. At one point he paused briefly to roll and light a cigarette. Conversation was relaxed, not only because I sensed that there was less at stake for me than when interviewing a senior British composer but also because he answered my questions in a manner that was neither particularly confident nor shy. He was mostly serious and thoughtful, speaking slowly and often hesitating partway through a remark in order to ensure that what he said was exactly what he meant. After the interview I photographed him outdoors on the large roof terrace at the back of the building.

What struck me most strongly about my encounter with him was his vocabulary. This featured a refreshing combination of 'cool', 'whatever' and 'pre-cheese' (referring to early, experimental rather than late, neo-Romantic Penderecki) with terms less expected of the average twenty-four-year-old: 'hubris', 'nexus' and 'grand narratives', which in anyone else might have suggested stuffiness or quaintness but which he delivered unselfconsciously and in contexts that made their use natural, even inevitable.

I'm of a generation of composers for whom classical music isn't the only type of music they grew up with. It wasn't even the *main* type of music that I grew up with: I listened to 1960s rock music and then worked my way backwards and found Delta blues, New Orleans jazz and old country music. Then, when I was in my mid-teens, I discovered Bach, which I sort of juggled with this other, mostly black American, music of the 1920s, 1930s and 1940s.

By the age of eighteen I was listening to a lot of adventurous non-classical music, and then I discovered classical music of the late twentieth century. And it didn't feel like that much of a leap, really, because the best of it made me think, 'This is very similar, in some ways: it's music that's exciting and new and adventurous, written by people who are serious about what they're doing. They don't necessarily make 'serious' music all the time, but they work hard at making their music as good as possible (whatever that means).' Some arts organisations and concert programmers have cottoned on to the fact that if you want to find an audience, especially a young one, for a concert of Xenakis or micro-polyphonic Ligeti you shouldn't necessarily target people who normally listen to Brahms. You should maybe target people who listen to Squarepusher or Aphex Twin or Radiohead. It's easy to hear links between some 1960s electronic or sound-mass classical music and densely textured studio compositions by rock musicians, but of course some classical music has greater appeal to this new, 'alternative' audience. Penderecki fares very well with them, for better or for worse, while Boulez doesn't.

Rock music can be just as disciplined as classical music but its fundamentals are, broadly speaking, simpler. And it doesn't come from the academies, from formalised musical education. But it's difficult to compare the two types of music by mapping one on top of the other, not least because of the performance element. If you're a jazz or pop musician you're a performer, and in the best cases there's a kind of synergy between the song-writing, the sound production, the quality of the voice or the instrumental playing and the persona or charisma of the performer. That's a complex other world that the majority of classical composers aren't involved in. But I certainly credit a lot of non-classical music with the way I've developed as a composer. It was Jimi Hendrix who made me want to be a musician myself, Bob Dylan who made me want to be serious and idealistic about creating music even if I wasn't making music that was 'serious', and The Beatles (and George Martin, their producer) who made me care about attention to detail in terms of notes, chords and instrumentation. These things had a big impact on me even before I knew that I wanted to notate music myself.

How do I feel about composers who want to straddle genres? Well, it's not a doomed project, but ... let's just say that there has been a lot of debris! The problem is usually that you have someone from one musical world trying to work in another musical world without having that great an understanding of it. For instance, Paul McCartney is musically curious so it's obvious that he should want to experiment by writing orchestral music; and I don't begrudge him that. But he's one of the great geniuses of popular music who suddenly became a complete amateur in the classical world. Which is fine, except that it's difficult for anyone in that position to produce really great work in both worlds.

The Internet is my biggest education, musically, and I've always had the experience of being able to hear something immediately. As a result, my listening has been incredibly wide over the last ten or fifteen years, but in some areas not as deep as it might have been had I grown up with a narrower realm of references that I explored in more depth. I've always got a stack of things that I've downloaded but haven't listened to, and because I have an incredibly curious ear I listen to far more music once than I ever do twice. Nowadays I listen to more classical music (in the broadest sense of the term) than non-classical, but even so I'm constantly discovering new composers, new pieces, new recordings of old pieces. I don't keep taking my favourite CDs off the shelf; it's more usual for me to be finding new things and listening to *them*. And I don't know whether this has changed the way I write music myself.

My response to what I hear varies according to what mood I'm in and to what function I want my listening to have at any particular moment. I can't turn analytical functions off completely, and sometimes I listen cynically because I want to solve a particular problem in a piece that I'm writing, or because I want to nick an idea from somewhere. At other times I listen purely for pleasure and enjoyment, although the pieces that I derive the most pleasure and enjoyment from are those that I also have an analytical way in to. For example, listening to Bach brings me both intuitive pleasure and analytical pleasure. It's absolutely breath-taking that music so human – so profound and moving, exciting and thrilling, beautiful and consoling – is built with such finely tuned mechanisms, like a Swiss clock. It's both explainable and unexplainable.

The moment when I knew that I wanted to be a composer was a slightly extended moment, or a very accelerated process. It was in my first year at Manchester University, where I studied with Camden Reeves. He's a fantastic composer, and he oversaw my development from someone who was vaguely interested in composing into someone who really wanted to write music for a living. I hadn't previously been into much twentieth-century music, so when I went to Manchester there was a lot for me to catch up on. But something clicked, and I responded well to studying there. I read voraciously, working my way through the musical history of almost the whole of the twentieth century and re-living the twelve-tone battles, the neo-classicism battles and then the total serialist battles. And you can chart this in my very early pieces – you can see which composer I was reading a book about at that time!

Anyway, I became obsessed with Stravinsky's neo-classical music and his early serial music, and it was probably while listening to his *Cantata* or his *Mass* or his *Symphony of Psalms* that I thought, 'I want to notate music.' But I didn't really know what the life of a composer would be like. Other than the three or four tutors at Manchester I didn't meet any professional composers for a while, and I'm only just starting to do that now. In those days I was basically emulating people who were dead – well, Stravinsky!

Again, the Internet has been a good educator in this respect because it enables you to see what other composers are doing, and also what kinds of opportunities are around. A major part of the business model of an early career composer involves entering competitions, as if you're an Olympic gymnast; it's a strange concept, but unless you're extremely bold and you decide not to participate at all, you've got to play that game. Well, it's not a game, exactly, and many competitions are well intentioned, but entering them still seems to me an odd thing for a composer to do. Most of us need to have an idea of how to get our music out there, but this shouldn't be mistaken for cynicism – writing a certain type of music in order to win prizes or to appeal to certain people. It's certainly not what *I* want to do.

George Benjamin is by far the best musician I've ever come across, and he's also a wonderful teacher. He can teach you so much technically because he's got an amazing ear and an amazing perspective on how music works. He's also good at encouraging you to find out what your character is, both musically and personally, and I've found this exciting and liberating. He can read a draft or sketch of mine and know instantly what the piece is going to be, or what it could be, and he encourages me to be bold about realising my ideas. For example, if the piece needs a twelve-note chord I should absolutely write one. Or if it needs a C major chord I should absolutely write one of those. I've found this very helpful.

When I saw your question about the term 'British composer' on the list that you sent me I thought, 'That's a humdinger', because I don't know to what extent the image of a British composer is that meaningful to me – even though, in a mundane sense, I of course think of myself as being one. People sometimes try to identify the characteristics of contemporary British music by lumping together certain composers, and it's most commonly a kind of Benjamin–Anderson–Adès–Turnage–Knussen axis that gets defined by terms such as 'craft' and 'polish'. And to an extent I can see that musical characteristic. But it obscures the differences between those composers, and in any case it's only a small aspect of British music because there are many other British composers.

The aesthetic that got referred to as 'cowpat music' is difficult for today's composers to identify with, although Jonathan Cross has written very interestingly about how Birtwistle perpetuates some aspects of the pastoral tradition in radically different settings.[1] I think you'd

---

[1] Jonathan Cross, *Harrison Birtwistle: Man, Mind, Music* (London, Faber & Faber, and Ithaca, NY, Cornell University Press, 2000).

be hard-pushed to find a composer, certainly of my generation, to volunteer that they feel part of a quasi-unified British tradition or style. And one reason for this is the British unease at defining yourself too readily or with too much solidarity – which is a paradox, because I've just implied a kind of definition of Britishness. But it's not very British to join a club in order to fight for it wholeheartedly, if you know what I mean. And if I were to nail my colours to any mast, Britishness would be a fair way down the line. I feel that I have more of a French lineage, musically, than a British one.

This is partly because of specific composers who have influenced me: Boulez, Messiaen, Murail and Grisey. It's also because I feel an affinity with musical characteristics that are almost stereotypically French – in particular, a finely tuned sense of harmony. I sometimes have a tendency towards the musically luxurious or decadent that you'd certainly put in the French camp rather than in the German one. And there's a slight distance, a kind of emotional coolness, in some French music that attracts me. It suggests the creation of an object that's perfect but doesn't reach out and grab the audience by the lapels; instead, it sits there and invites them to gaze at it. And I like that.

Something that terrifies me, professionally, is the idea of attempting profundity and failing. I'd find that so tragic. And it's why some of my least favourite music has vaulting ambition but falls short – to my ears, at least. Mahler's Eighth is an obvious example. It might be that I'm setting the bar for my own music a bit low, and that later on in my career I'll attempt something more serious and profound; but for the moment I'm much more attracted to the idea of something with small but beautiful aims, and which fulfils them, than something vast and profound that loses out. Besides, there's something a bit ridiculous about a twenty-five-year-old attempting a world-defining statement in his music! However, I'm aware that many people would think it a crying shame that composers are scared of that kind of thing. And, when composers are determined to make only small objects that don't particularly demand a huge audience, I can see the logic of asking, 'Why are people complaining about classical music not having a big enough role in general consciousness?'

This can be interpreted in two ways: to foes, it's probably a complete lack of faith in your own ability; to friends, it's an avoidance of hubris. But it's also a practical consideration, because who, even out of the established major composers, ever gets a forty-five-minute orchestral piece commissioned? It would be pointless for a young composer to churn out a vast masterpiece that simply isn't going to be heard. I also think there's a wider cultural context that fears idealism, or which associates it with dogma. You no longer get politicians on the left identifying themselves as socialist, and you don't get composers saying that they want to ensure the supremacy of their country's music for a hundred years, like Schoenberg did. There's a postmodern unease with grand narratives and grand statements, which I think is not a wholly good thing. Having said this, I feel that other composers are, in any case, probably better able than I to make them.

Yes, I have non-musical friends, and I also have friends who are making music that isn't classical. The idea of me being a notated composer probably seems a little eccentric to them, but I think I quite like that, really! What seems to be difficult for them to get their head around is the idea of me staying at home during the day and quietly getting on with a piece that has to be completed in six months' time. I recently finished a twelve-minute orchestral piece which I was working on for more than a year, and *that* seems completely bonkers to people. And when they have that reaction I think, 'Yeah, it *is* ridiculous: twelve months of my life for something that's eventually going to take twelve minutes for people to play!' Sometimes I find myself dutifully making an orchestral score by filling an entire A3 page with markings and squiggles that amounts to three seconds of music, and I think, 'What the hell am I doing? This is ludicrous.'

If I didn't want to do that pesky thing of notating music and giving it to people to perform I might be able to write it much more quickly. But I care about it being played by humans, to humans. And although I'm generally not fetishistic about physically creating the sound by hand, I can't orchestrate my music on a computer. I have to do it with a pencil, so I'm forever going back and forth between the computer and the desk. There's something else, too, which *you* as a writer probably experience even more than I do: when you write by hand you have a greater sense of the work's structure and how far through it you are at any point – how many pages are on *this* side and how many on *that* side – than when scrolling through the whole document on a computer screen.

But although you can be lured into making mistakes with computer notation, it's very useful for some things. For example, it's awful at playing melodies but very good at playing rhythms (and I wonder if this has had an impact on the way people write music with it). I use notation software in various ways during the last two-thirds of the composition process, and all my finished scores are computerised.

In my experience, there's much less music in your head than you think there is when you start to write it down. You have a fantastic but fuzzy idea, which you think about and sleep on for a while, and you can fool yourself into believing that the piece is basically written. But then putting it down on the page is a real struggle, and you find that you haven't done almost *any* of the work that you thought you had. This pulling at threads in order to realise your ideas is actually 99 per cent of the business of composing – it's a massive struggle, and you never get exactly what was in your head beforehand. Maybe it's only me, but I don't have enough space in my head to conceive the complete architecture of a piece; it's usually only the opening, or some other short span of music. Then I have to tease out something to give to the real musicians who will play the piece to real people. And this teasing-out process is often what makes the piece morph in interesting ways.

I tend to create paragraphs of music and then organise them by doing a sort of structural feng shui, but the way I work depends on the piece I'm writing. However, I think I've written only one piece for which my initial idea was structural rather than momentary, and that's my Piano Trio, *The Chronophage*. It was inspired by the Corpus Clock[2] at Corpus Christi College, Cambridge, whose time is completely accurate only every five minutes – in between, the 'seconds' are uneven. The mechanism is cranked over a mechanical insect called the Chronophage – the time-eater – and the overall effect is really spooky because it sort of takes the ground out from under you. A clock should be the most reliable thing in the world, so when it starts to change pace it plays with your perception; and my idea for the trio was that the violin begins by playing only every thirty seconds or so and then gradually speeds up until at the end it's flying around like a madman.

There are things that I value in music generally and often want to draw on when composing, and there's a sort of nexus, a little cloud of ideas, that I carry around with me. It includes concepts such as colour, invention, beauty, wit and energy, and I'll probably not be satisfied with any piece that I write unless it contains enough of them. Although the expressive intentions of each piece will vary, I don't think I could write pieces that are so radically different in intention as to require a completely different toolkit.

Finding out about the serial project – after the event, obviously – was very important to me because I have an almost visceral excitement

---

[2] Designed by John C. Taylor.

about the relationships between intervals and the relationships between rhythms, and how these can be manipulated. This is the nuts and bolts of music, really, and it's what I concentrate on when I'm composing, together with the abstract shape and proportions of a piece. What I find more difficult is the pictorial aspect of music. I've never thought, 'I'm going to tell a story through this piece' or 'This piece is going to express *this* kind of feeling or emotion.' So you could say that I'm abstract-minded, if you think of musical relationships as abstract.

I can already identify musical fingerprints or traits in my work – even in the first couple of pieces that I wrote and don't acknowledge any more. But some of them make me think, 'I've done that a bit too much; I'd better not do it in the next piece.' In other words, I feel there's a danger that it'll become a mannerism. For example, I've always been obsessed with *moto perpetuo* – one of the first pieces I ever wrote was called *Moto Perpetuo*, in fact, and one of the most recent is called *Four Perpetual Motions*. I love things chugging along at a constant pace. But, as with *The Chronophage*, I also like the queasy sensation induced by a clock-like ticking slowing down or speeding up. In a number of my pieces I've made sections or movements move in tempo relative to one another, and the feeling that results is rather like when you're sitting on a stationary train while the one next to you starts to move off: it feels as if *your* train is the one that's moving. I don't know why, but these ideas have always attracted me.

When I was a teenager I admired Bob Dylan's attitude to interviews and press conferences, which was nearly always complete contempt. He would taunt interviewers by being fantastically disingenuous and flippant and by making up stories. And I vowed that if I was to ever become a famous musician I would do the same, or be one of those who never give interviews at all. But I don't think I'm hip enough to carry that off. Either that or I feel a basic, British sense of politeness! Besides, I can see the value of a composer being both formidably good at his or her work *and* being able to communicate well verbally.

In many cases, of course, those things don't go together, and I really sympathise. Why *should* people expect a wonderful composer to also be a great spokesperson for his music? But if you *can* be both, it makes a world of difference, especially to people who are coming to your music for the first time. So I'd like to try. And I don't think it's completely at odds with my personality. Although I'm quite a private person I don't hate speaking in public, and I enjoy using language to get across what I mean – and sometimes what I *don't* mean. Just as in my music, I'm not necessarily revealing my innermost emotions, but in whatever I *am* revealing I want to make my communication as elegant as possible. So I don't have a problem with being a semi-public figure. After all, it's not as if composers are ever going to be *that* public!

Last year I had a part-time job at the South Bank Centre, working for 'The Rest Is Noise' festival of twentieth-century music, and I've also done some education work in schools. And the odd bit of copying and orchestration for other composers. At the moment I'm in the luxurious position of having funding to study for my PhD, and so there's a span of time within which I've got very little to do other than composing. And because I know that this will probably never happen again, I'm trying to make the most of it.

As for the future, I don't have specific ambitions other than to be able to write the music I want to write for the rest of my life, to work with great performers and to enjoy what I do. Nor do I have a checklist of career achievements to tick off, or pieces that I want to write. If I can be a composer in twenty years' time, with a list of pieces that I'm cautiously proud of, I'll be happy.

Gordon Crosse

Gordon Crosse, Suffolk, October 2011

> **❛I didn't really know what a composer's life would be like, and everything has come as a horrible surprise!❜**

Some interviews lurch awkwardly from one topic to the next; others go off at irrelevant tangents and have to be steered back on course. The most pleasurable are those that quickly acquire a momentum in which the issues to be discussed arise naturally in conversation. Such was my interview with Gordon Crosse, which flowed so effortlessly that I scarcely needed to refer to my list of questions. But it was lengthy, and editing it for this chapter proved frustrating because I was forced to discard so much of what he said.

For more than forty years he has lived in a cottage in Suffolk that seems remote but in fact is just difficult to find, hidden from the road in gorse-covered heathland. When we met there in September 2011 he was recovering from the death of his wife a few months earlier, and this perhaps contributed to the length at which he spoke, his willingness to make innumerable mugs of tea and his enthusiasm in showing me his office and the computer on which he writes his music. I had no idea of how much time was passing, and hours later was forced to make my excuses and leave as politely as possible for a dinner appointment.

My reasons for wanting to interview him didn't include his temporary abandonment of composition in 1990 but it was inevitable that we would discuss the factors that led to it. He talked about the unsatisfactory first performance of his *Sea Psalms* in Glasgow that year and a crisis of self-confidence compounded by what he believed was a lack of support from his publisher. John Rutter, in his own interview for this book, suggested a possible third factor: the large number of British composers who were born in the 1930s and who came to prominence in the 1960s. Composers don't compete with each other, at least intentionally, but it's easy to imagine how one lacking the confidence and support that he needed might have retreated from a front line that included Richard Rodney Bennett, Harrison Birtwistle, Peter Maxwell Davies, Alexander Goehr, Nicholas Maw, John McCabe and Anthony Payne. 'Perhaps', Rutter suggested, 'there just wasn't enough sunshine to go round.'

Another great name hovered over this interview, partly because of where Crosse lives in Suffolk and partly because of the style of his music, which is often described as 'post-Britten'. And it was I who set that particular ball rolling, at the beginning of our conversation, by asking about the extent to which his move to within fifteen miles of Aldeburgh placed him in the shadow of the best-known Suffolk composer of all. Although most composers admit the influence of others, it's rare, I think, for one to acknowledge such a debt as Crosse does to Britten, whom he recalled in heroic terms not only for the quality of his music but also for his professionalism. In contrast, he was at times outspoken in his criticism of other composers (although never on a personal level), which may reflect the fact that he left the music profession for a period of seventeen years in order to work as a computer programmer.

'Remember Gordon Crosse?' asked the critic Michael White in *The Telegraph* in January 2012. 'I'm never sure if people do, but he always strikes me as one of the worryingly lost figures of British music ...' When compiling this book I discovered that everyone remembered him but that some didn't know that he has returned to composing, largely thanks to encouragement and good-natured badgering from the recorder player John Turner. He hasn't yet regained the prominence that he enjoyed in the 1960s and 1970s, and in this interview the works of his own that he talked most about were *Ariadne* and *Memories of Morning: Night*, both of which he wrote more than forty years ago and neither of which, in his opinion, he has surpassed. But, he agreed, there's still hope.

———

I wouldn't begin to use the word 'shadow'. For me, it was in the *light* of Britten. I found him inspirational as a composer and as a performer. I always felt that when he walked out onto the platform a sort of warmth permeated the building, and I got that from his music, too. Also, he was an object lesson for all the virtues that I expect of a composer. I didn't have very many of them myself, but he was constantly there to inspire me. And one of the great things about the Aldeburgh Festival in those days was that every year a new Britten piece was unveiled. For example, I remember going to a rehearsal in Blythburgh church of the *Cello Symphony* when it was a new piece. It seemed that with each new Britten piece a new musical map was being created, and it was very exciting. I just felt I could learn a lot.

In those days, writing something that sounded even remotely like Britten, or using one of his techniques or one of his forms, was in itself sufficient to damn you as a composer. But with the passing of time we're starting to feel that there's a kind of Britten tradition, and I think it's healthy that less talented composers should be able to stand next to him. Something similar happened with Vaughan Williams. A whole generation was criticised soundly for working under *his* shadow, but the more I hear his music the more I think he was one of the greatest composers of the twentieth century.

The term 'British composer' has meant different things to me at different times. Back in the hell-for-leather 1960s, chattering to people like Max Davies, British meant incompetent and behind the times – which was very silly, because we weren't. Now, I feel it's truer to say that throughout history there's been a sort of natural conservatism in British taste which always tries – hopelessly – to achieve some sort of balance. And I think the musical establishment's xenophobia is not entirely without benefit. The fact that the latest ideas from Germany or Italy or France aren't automatically absorbed here has given us a similar sort of independence to that of, say, American composers who were fighting more positively for an identity of their own. I don't think British music has to do that, but it does benefit from shutting out the other side of the Channel a bit.

I wish I could say I was a composer who just happens to be British. I don't want my music to be played only in Britain. But unfortunately I have no reputation whatsoever in Europe or Scandinavia. It's a gross failing of my publishers, as far as I'm concerned. And I'm deeply envious of people like Max or my friend Sally Beamish, who get performed everywhere!

When I'm asked why I'm a composer I tend to quote Alexander Goehr, who has been a big influence on me intellectually. His response – 'Because there is nothing else that I can think of that I would be happy doing' – seems to me the ultimate answer. Sandy has also said that the alternatives of writing for your audience or writing for yourself are false alternatives, because you can *only* write for yourself. But you must never *forget* your audience. In other words, you must remain aware of an audience being out there but you must never write *for* them. So I don't try to second-guess what my audience will like. I simply want to write something that *I* like. And then I'm very happy if the audience shares that liking. This must affect what I write, I suppose, but not in a very conscious way.

Communication is self-evidently fundamental to music. But it's a complex issue. You mentioned Harry Birtwistle, whose music I admire enormously and whose Violin Concerto I'm looking forward to because I've recently heard its opening and thought it was very exciting! I would say that Harry is a typical Lancastrian: very few words and a rather dry sense of humour. He's very like Walton in that respect. Whereas the other kind of Lancastrian is Max Davies, who's the most communicative of people – his social skills are amazing. It doesn't reflect on the quality or the interest of Harry's music to say that he has a dour personality, or that Max's pixie-like charm and ebullience make *his* music any better. Another example: Richard Rodney Bennett was such a delightful personality that everybody loved him when they met him, but nobody wants to play much of that 1960s serial music he wrote. His great skill was a different kind of communication: a communication of himself. His ability to put across a song, for example, wasn't surprising. He was a wonderful accompanist, too. And I think that's because it was where he felt happiest.

When you ask me whether there's anything in general terms that I've wanted to do in my music, you're looking for the main road that somehow links the earliest pieces to the most recent ones. I think it's a sort of sharpness of focus, a clarity, and it has a lot to do with Britten and my other favourite composers, such as Stravinsky. For me, one of the greatest compliments you can ever pay a composer is to call a piece of his music memorable, and I can't think of anyone other than Britten – except possibly Vaughan Williams – whose music puts its hooks in so deeply the first time you hear it. And that's something that I certainly strive for as a composer. The only technical thing I've noticed that's run from Day One to the present is a curious desire to put very complicated things next to very simple things.

Britten had a sort of Janáček-like ability to capture in music how phrases would be spoken. I think I could probably still sing most of *The Turn of the Screw* through from memory, and what captures me is the fact that the words are totally absorbed in the music. I hope there are good examples of that in a piece I wrote at the beginning of the 1970s, called *Memories of Morning: Night*. At that time, the fashionable exponent of extreme emotion was Max Davies – for example with *Eight Songs for a Mad King*. But I felt that some of those works stepped over the edge. Instead of portraying a scream, they screamed. I was looking for a way of making music extremely dramatic and expressive without losing my cool and while keeping the emotion at the symbolic level or the rational level.

I've always assumed that people have minds and want to use them, but I don't write for people's minds because I don't think I can possibly predict what their level of mental activity is. So my aim is to hit them between the eyes or in the guts with feeling. I want an emotional response. But how that's expressed, and what lies under the surface, I expect to be really intricate. Again, this comes from Britten. Take *Peter Grimes*, for example. At first, what's so exciting is the difference between one musical idea and another. But then, suddenly, at one terrible moment, Grimes sings, 'So be it. And God have mercy upon me.' It freezes on that phrase, which of course is dramatically appropriate, and from then on that phrase is never absent from a single bar of the opera. The way it's constantly revitalised is amazing. Britten hit on a way of working that starts out with the emotional and the dramatic but achieves its effects by careful planning. The same is true of Puccini, who seems to me a total master.

As a composer you have to acknowledge that you can write complete failures, and that you can find yourself going up a blind alley. But I had a very bad, self-critical period during the 1980s in which I tore up pieces, which I never should have done. I was expecting my Oboe Quintet to be well received in 1988, but it seemed to leave everybody cold. It didn't excite *me* very much, even though the performance was wonderful, so I put it in the bottom drawer and forgot about it. Total dissatisfaction with a choral piece in 1990 was the last straw, really. The chorus master was very competent but didn't tell anybody he was going to be away all summer, which was when I'd assumed they'd be rehearsing. So I was suddenly given a demand for scores back in January, when I had nowhere near finished the piece! I had to cobble it together quickly, and it was a total mess. I thought the piece was rubbish, and I hated myself. I thought, 'However prestigious working to commission may be, this is not the way I want to work.' And I stopped composing, because I believe that ultimately you shouldn't just add to the quantity of music. You should add something, however infinitesimal, to its quality and kind.

When I started to compose again I thought I was making a new beginning and that I was going to write very simple music. But then I realised that my music hadn't totally changed because I was still doing the same thing. That is, I'll either start with a tune and think, 'What can I make from this that's interesting, rather than just playing it ten times?' or 'Here's this complicated bit of sound that I've thought up; how can I find the simplicity that's buried somewhere inside it?' I've worked it both ways. But somewhere at the core of every successful piece I've written is something essentially simple that you ought, in theory, to be able to hum. Nice as it is to appeal to people's minds, I suspect that you're looking at later generations to be able to think that way naturally. This doesn't mean that I don't appreciate intellectual music, but it doesn't have the immediate impact that I rather like.

In the last three years only two of my pieces have been commissioned. All the rest I've done because I had a bright idea and wanted to write. As a result, of course, they're unperformed. Anyway, I've been looking at older pieces of mine, including some that I used to think were rubbish, and two years ago I dug out that Oboe Quintet and listened to it. I think it's one of the best things I've ever written! And a lot of what I saw in it was familiar from much older pieces. My friend Alan Garner and I share a joke that we always know we've got a good new piece coming when we think, 'Ah, here we go again!' We *think* we've started going off in a new direction, but we're actually being drawn onto the old path.

Doing is not something that I do well. What I mean by that is: I've never been a performer. My most terrible moment was being asked by Ben [Britten] to go to the Red House and play my new opera to him. Panic! He was most friendly about it, and I got hold of a very experienced repetiteur who came and did 90 per cent of the job, but oh, I never want to feel like that again. I never would have got a place at music college, you see, but Oxford suited me very well because there was no attempt to teach me how to compose. What I *did* get was brilliant traditional harmony and counterpoint (particularly the latter) – a seamless mixture of academic history and how to manipulate notes. I learned most about composition from working in the Playhouse, because every term I'd have one or two plays to write a score for, starting with a very modest little production of *The Alchemist*. Each one was successful, so I got more and more in demand. Fortunately the Oxford system kept out of your way – all you had to do was see your tutor once a week.

I had some idea of what I wanted my life as a composer to be like. I wanted it to be like Ben's: enormously famous, feted everywhere. But then, in order to achieve that, there were certain things that I thought one perhaps had to do which weren't acceptable. So I didn't really know what a composer's life would be like, and everything has come as a horrible surprise!

I've always thought of routine and discipline in my work in terms of deserving: if I didn't put in the hours, I wasn't going to get the payoff. So I would work away on paper, which would all go in the bin at the end of the morning session, in the vain hope that at some point during week three or four a light would come on. And, in fact, while composing pieces like *Ariadne* and *Memories* I'd work away for six weeks and then the crucial passage would be written in five minutes. And those were the most exciting five minutes of my life, because the pencil just took over and everything fell into place. But I always believed this happened only because of all the work I'd done beforehand. You can't determine *when* it's going to happen, that's the trouble!

I get haunted by what Harry Birtwistle once referred to as wounds: pieces that haven't quite worked and which you haven't been able to fix. He said he thought of their continued existence as wounded pieces, and he wanted to heal them. And there aren't many pieces of mine that I *don't* feel that way about. When you believe that a substantial part of a piece is very good but that it's ruined by that page *there*, you want to rip it out and redo just that page. Or perhaps a piece was too ambitious, and underneath it there's a less ambitious but very good piece. I've written quite a few of those. But most of the composers I've talked to seem to distrust revision. Once a piece is done, it's done; and if it's not good, well, go and write something else.

I think I can be moved by my own music, as long as the listening is well removed from the first performance – at which there's so much panicking and nail-biting about whether particular passages are going to work that I'm sort of anaesthetised. I don't hear things going wrong, let alone going right. Total failure to come out correctly has happened from time to time, and sometimes a work has come out unexpectedly but well, and that's a nice surprise. For example, you write a chord for a particular combination of instruments and your imagination tells you how it's going to sound; but when you actually hear it played it sounds beyond what you expected.

This is much less likely to happen today because of hearing the music on my computer while I'm writing it. What I want to know is: does that chord sound right with that kind of colour balance, and does that rhythm work? And, above all, what is the structure of the piece and the duration? One thing I could never master was proportions, so all my ambitious earlier pieces got out of control – too long, too many developments of things. Now I can play a piece through on the computer in real time and get a feel for where the weak points are.

However, Sibelius (the software I use) finds it very difficult to notate some of the things that I used to write very readily by hand. For example, I was fond of things being out of phase but in time, so that elements of randomness started to enter the way they came together. *Ariadne* is full of repeated patterns in the background, textures built up by things not being quite together, and so on. And it's absolute hell trying to persuade Sibelius to notate those things, so you have to resort to all sorts of tricks. And sometimes you have to resort to the piece being unplayable by Sibelius. I think I've been bullied by my copy of the software into writing more straightforwardly – the notation is much more plain-Jane than it used to be. And sometimes, probably two-thirds of the time, that's been a good thing. I've lost a tiny bit of poetry somewhere but I've gained a lot of precision, and that I like!

There's a lovely phrase that Max Davies used in an article he wrote for *The Score* magazine as a really arrogant young man: he said that British musical life was based on 'vested ignorance'. And I think that *was* the trouble. There was a tacit belief that because twelve-tone technique went across a lot of composers it somehow produced the same kind of music from all of them. But there was no such thing as 'serial music'. It was just part of the toolkit, as it were. And there were extreme views of it – notably Elisabeth Lutyens's, which was to get absolutely incensed if you wrote an octave. I reckon that I learned more about twelve-tone and serial ideas from Britten (most of the latter scenes of *Death in Venice* are straightforward twelve-tone writing) than from 'serial composers', even though Egon Wellesz was my teacher at one time. I had the excitement of him showing me Mahler scores with Mahler's own emendations in red ink, and pages of Schoenberg sketches. For a boy from the suburbs of Manchester, that awareness of old Vienna was unbelievable!

My first reaction to Stockhausen was total incomprehension, so I can understand someone finding a particular piece of music difficult today. A lot of people say, 'Modern music's all rubbish', and my response is often, 'You're quite right', because at any one time, 95 per cent of it *is* rubbish. But, to some extent, those of us who grew up in the heady days of the 1960s actually *liked* our music to be hated. It was a weird kind of perversion: to produce a violent audience reaction was highly desirable because we were very jealous of Stravinsky for having caused a scandal with *The Rite of Spring*.

I don't like public interviews. If you'd asked me to talk to you in the Royal College of Music for a Prom interval piece, I'd have said no. I started saying no back in the 1980s, when those kinds of interview were starting to become fashionable, and I got a reputation for being a bit standoffish. But I just don't like doing it. Some composers thrive on it. Max, for example: he loves being asked an awkward question in public and fielding it with a clever answer. But I just get too upset.

It's part of my inability to perform, like trying to play the piano and getting so nervous that one's fingers shake too much to be able to play. It's a particular brand of shyness, not general shyness. It's the 'being judged' part.

I haven't read reviews of my music – good ones or bad ones – since the late 1960s. Very often it was good ones that got me upset, because the critic had got the wrong end of the stick, and that showed me how I'd failed. And sometimes the bad ones were more interesting because in fact they were right. But while a respectable academic notice can be deadening even though it's friendly, I love feedback from an audience. Recently I wrote a string quartet for the anniversary of the building of the Leiston Quaker Meeting House, and I offered to do that because I'd just become a Quaker. Everybody seemed to enjoy the piece, and then I got a professional performance from the Solstice Quartet in Aldeburgh and had some nice responses from people who came up to me afterwards. And a few weeks ago the Solstice played it again at a fairly prestigious chamber music series near here, and played it 300 per cent better than they did in Aldeburgh. I got the warmest reception – people came up and said 'Beautiful piece' and so on – and as a composer, you *believe* that kind of response. And you're reminded why you're in music, which is to communicate to people.

What annoys me is somebody who sort of gushes, because then there's no evidence that they've actually listened to your piece. But if somebody can pinpoint something that they particularly liked – 'that bit about halfway through with the loud trombones', you know – I'm happy. I never used to believe that anyone could love what I've written. I could always believe that they would like it or that they would admire it; but to actually be passionately involved and *love* it was something I didn't entertain for a long time. I've realised that I was wrong and that it *can* happen. And it's unbelievably gratifying if it does happen. There's nothing better.

For a composer today, it's fashionable to be unfashionable – like postmodernism in the visual arts and those pretty, cottagey supermarkets in architecture. Something that's complex for its own sake is not particularly interesting to me any more, and so I rather like the trend towards simplicity that's reflected in the varieties of minimalism that are around. The more I hear of Howard Skempton's music the more impressed I am, and I'd definitely say he was a bit of an influence now. If you can say it with two notes instead of twenty, it's probably a good thing. I fell for Steve Reich's music back in the 1970s – I thought he was one of the few really original voices to emerge in the last thirty years – but Philip Glass, for me, is the utter pits. And yet people lap up his music up, presumably because it makes absolutely no demands. If there's one thing that I think music should never, ever be, it's wallpaper; and it's cynical to assume that the public wants it. End of rant!

On the few occasions that I involve myself as a member of the public and go to a concert I get enormous pleasure from hearing a piece that most of the audience probably knows ten times better than I do. To that extent, I'm an amateur as well as a professional. I have some very good friends who are fanatical about certain obscure areas of classical music – I think of them as nerds, in a way – but that's a mark of amateur enthusiasm. And I've been humbled. I've learned, through amateur friends, to start to question both my professional discounting of certain music and the idea that there's one correct history book, because it hasn't worked out like that. The history of the twentieth century is different from how I thought it was when I was in the middle of it.

Jonathan Dove

Jonathan Dove, London, August 2011

❛We don't have much control over the sounds that we make.❜

A crowded restaurant on a Sunday lunchtime during the limbo between rehearsal and concert is not the best place or time in which to have an in-depth conversation with a composer. So Jonathan Dove, having just attended the final rehearsal of his oratorio *There Was A Child* for the Brighton Festival, sensibly suggested postponing the interview for this book so that he could devote quieter and more considered time to my questions. We talked at length three months later, in August 2011, in the large, airy living room of his east London flat.

He's that rare thing in the contemporary musical world: an opera composer, not a composer who writes the occasional opera. That's not the whole story, of course, because he has also written a large amount of choral music and some concert works – his *Gaia Theory* was given its first performance by the BBC Symphony Orchestra during the 2014 Proms season. But the success of his operas *Flight*, *Tobias and The Angel*, *The Adventures of Pinocchio* and *Mansfield Park* has led him to be regarded first and foremost as a composer for the theatre. He has in fact written more operatic works than Puccini did, and I wanted to know why, at least at the beginning of his career, he established his musical home in the opera house rather than in the concert hall or recital room.

He was relaxed and affable, and on a personal level my encounter with him was easy and enjoyable. On the subsequent editorial level it was more demanding because of the transparency of his thought processes during the interview. At times he remained silent for several seconds while formulating an answer to one of my questions; at others he appeared to be audibly feeling his way through a response, as if testing whether his words were expressing sufficiently accurately what he wanted to say. This verbal hesitancy, which included a tendency to pause halfway through a sentence while working out how best to proceed, was of course a sign of his intellectual integrity, his refusal to express himself approximately or inaccurately, and a reflection of the seriousness with which he approached the interview. But I fear that on some of the occasions when I was unsure whether he'd finished answering one question I didn't resist the temptation to jump in prematurely and ask him the next.

A composer's use of words needn't resemble closely the way in which he expresses himself through musical notation. And although Dove emphasised the importance to his music of pulse – he's perhaps the nearest thing there is to a British minimalist composer – his speech patterns were quite different: *ritartandi* as he sought to express himself more accurately, then *accelerandi* after finding the vocabulary that satisfied him. However, his carefulness with words enabled him to articulate with unusual clarity (and, as anyone who's heard him speak will know, with a sonorous, beautifully modulated voice) the mysterious creative processes by which ideas are fashioned into music or music drama.

As the majority of his work, including non-operatic successes such as *There Was A Child* and the ballet score *Diana & Actaeon*, has a strong narrative element, I asked him to explain where and how the composition process typically starts for him.

I've come to think about my music as a means of telling stories, whether on stage or in song. But, although this may sound perverse or unlikely, I haven't really thought about the people who would then listen to it. The very first aspect of the creative process is a kind of quarrying ideas that please *me*; but this onomatopoeia, if you like – conjuring sounds that suggest something, that convey a specific feeling – is only half of the job. After the impulse of pleasure comes a perhaps slightly more grown-up aspect: organising those ideas into a significant form that satisfies me. It's a sort of balance between sensation and sense. And I think those are right-brain and left-brain activities. Sometimes ideas present themselves in a shaped way, and all you're really doing is transcribing something that's just occurred to you. But at other times there's a bit of exploration, where you feel you're getting warmer or nearer to a particular sensation. Of course, the choice of story to tell is made in relation to the kind of musical sound you want to make; but once you've embarked on that, the story is going to tell you an awful lot about how it wants to be told. And then, part of the challenge is to find a musical shape that corresponds in the right way to the dramatic journey. Ideally, the musical journey *becomes* the dramatic journey.

As a child I used to spend all my time improvising at the piano, but I would often have a story book on the music stand next to me so that I could read while I was playing. So I was able to associate music with action, although when I listened to music I didn't see pictures in the way that some people I knew did. Just the way the sounds unfolded themselves was enough. I experienced even Mahler symphonies as emotional sound. I also grew up playing the organ at the local church, so I was used to choral music. And I played the viola in the London Schools Symphony Orchestra, so as a teenager I was very absorbed with orchestral repertoire.

I can remember seeing *Iolanthe*, *Hansel and Gretel* and *Der Rosenkavalier* as a teenager, but I'm not sure that I'd seen any other operas by the time I went to university. In those days my greatest enthusiasm was for the theatre and for orchestral music. As an undergraduate I went to see a production of *Così fan tutte* that had come up from the Guildhall School of Music and Drama, and similarly a production of *Rigoletto*, plus one or two other operas. But I was not at all steeped in operatic singing. Of course, I studied operas as part of my degree, and discovering Wagner's *Ring* certainly made a big impression on me. But when I started working with opera companies, in my twenties, it was only because I'd run out of money and needed to earn some by accompanying singers. I found the theatre itself very congenial, and while I was working as a repetiteur I was absorbing what the operatic voice can do. So all this was leading me towards writing my own operas.

However, being a full-time composer crept up on me, to some extent. I'd been Assistant Chorus Master at Glyndebourne and was offered the position of Chorus Master, which seemed to me the beginning of a journey that headed towards being a conductor; and I realised then that that wasn't what I wanted to do. At the same time I was being offered more composing work, none of which was at all well paid but which *was* what I wanted to do. That was the point at which I identified myself as a full-time composer.

But I didn't particularly set out to write text-based music. In fact, the first music I wrote that felt really personal was for dance – an unpublished piece based on the four seasons. It didn't seem particularly respectable in terms of its style, and it clearly was never going to be presented by the Society for the Promotion of New Music. It seemed that I was doing something kind of naughty, in a way. But that was fine, because people were coming to watch the dance, not to listen to my music, so I could do more or less what I liked.

American music was very influential in my development. Benjamin Britten was clearly a big influence but so was John Adams. Also, to an extent, Philip Glass and Steve Reich, not necessarily in the sounds they were making but in the permission they gave me, when I was coming of age as a composer, to explore things that were different from what I perceived to be the European mainstream. When I was a student in the late 1970s, writing even an octave, let alone a major triad, was still a questionable activity; and since nearly all my music revolves around major/minor triads, it seemed shocking in relation to my sense of what was happening in Europe. But it's become a British strand now. How you measure Britishness is another matter, but in my own case it's about having some sense of a local tradition and some sense of what's happening in other places. Of course, it's so much easier now to know what's happening on the other side of the world. Next week I'll be sitting with three other judges on a composition panel in Italy, with submissions from all over the world, and I've already been able to listen to all of the music online.

I don't know that a composer has much control over idiom. It's not like going to a supermarket and thinking, 'I'm going to use *this* idiom today.' There might arguably be something different going on when you're writing for a spoken theatre production, but in a situation where you can really do whatever you want you can't help the fact that some harmonies please you and some don't, and that certain combinations of sounds feel right and others don't. I write music that is largely diatonic and certainly modal, usually using only seven notes at any one time rather than all twelve. I didn't find it possible to express myself satisfactorily in a fully chromatic harmonic palette, and it was when I started using fewer notes that I realised that I could write more articulately because I was able to achieve contrast simply by changing mode. And contrast is the essence of drama.

So composing isn't first of all about communicating or about what might give other people pleasure. It's about what seems natural to *me*. But I'm very concerned that an audience understands the piece as a kind of music-dramatic happening. In an opera, for example, I want to make absolutely clear the moment when somebody changes their mind or falls in love (if that's something that *can* happen in a moment) by presenting clearly the twists and turns of the story in music.

I also want people to hear the words, and there are various considerations governing this. If you want to be absolutely certain that every word will be heard, you have to write within quite a narrow compass – I mean, at the lower, speaking end of the voice. But a trained soprano voice is a wonderful instrument and you want to use all of it, so there will be places where you're going to make some sort of compromise. But you must feel that at least a *sense* of the words will be understood.

So I always play a work in progress to certain people to see exactly whether or not it's coming over. Typically, it'll be the opera's director or conductor, or both. When my composer friend Julian Grant lived in England I would often play *him* things because he wasn't completely seduced by my musical material. I think he liked it, but he was detached enough to see whether it was really making sense.

I also want to know if it's boring, because I think that's the cardinal sin of music. The most important composition lesson I had was with Robin Holloway, in my third year at university. I'd written a twenty-page serial organ piece, and on page two he said, 'I'm bored already.' I could feel my lower lip trembling but I realised that he was right, that it *was* boring. And I could imagine more exciting music, so why was I writing this music that *wasn't* exciting?

As students we felt that we *should* be writing serial music, and it certainly seemed to be the answer for some composers. Serialism implies first of all choice about pitch, that you are going to use the chromatic compass and possibly therefore that there will be no fundamental mode; but it also implies certain contrapuntal principles. So it's not just which notes you use, but also that you're only going to use them in a particular sequence. This wasn't helpful to me, and you can certainly choose other constraints on which pitches you use, and indeed the sequence of intervals that you work with.

The minimalist alternative was to create new forms by using a relatively small number of notes – there were a lot of white-note pieces in the minimalist canon. And there was a feeling that rhythm was doing something different and interesting there. I don't feel comfortable, on the whole, listening to music that doesn't have a clear pulse, so music that's rhythmically chaotic or incredibly slow (which is a common trait of new music) doesn't delight me. Of course, there were attempts to relate rhythm to serialism, but they struck me as rather arbitrary. Also, they were connected to an over-controlled or over-determined approach to composition, which I don't think many young composers today are interested in.

Opera involves collaboration with a great many people, but the music takes responsibility for the event and so the composer gets a fantastic amount of air time. And although a big opera with full orchestra can take a long time to write, you're well rewarded because you can see it many times. *Flight* had sixteen performances in its first year and I went to every one of them. As I'd written a piece that I wanted to see, this was extraordinarily rewarding. And *The Enchanted Pig* has had over a hundred and fifty performances. I've written a flute concerto, a trombone concerto and some short concert openers – overtures, effectively, or something between fanfares and overtures – but none of them has had anything like that kind of exposure.

After completing a piece I often realise that its story has some strong autobiographical element of which I'd been completely unaware while I was writing it. Probably any subject that touches me enough to want to turn it into an opera will have some significant personal connection, but I just think about the story, which I suppose places it safely outside myself. I dare say I'm thinking that I'm expressing Pinocchio or the Blue Fairy or Fanny Price, and not really acknowledging that during the period of making the piece I *am* Pinocchio or the Blue Fairy or Fanny Price and that they're a part of me. But thinking about them as outside of myself helps me to develop ideas of what they need musically.

Sometimes I use traditional, formal devices in my music. I'm thinking, for example, of the passacaglia at the end of *Pinocchio*. Actually, there's one in *Mansfield Park* too, and one at the end of my Flute Concerto. That's a musical technique with a very long tradition going back to Purcell, and it's useful in one particular part of *Mansfield Park* which contains a sequence of very short vignettes. I thought there was a danger that this would be too busy and wouldn't hold together. So having an underlying melody that runs through every scene, with different harmonisation and different textures around it, unifies what otherwise would, I think, sound fragmentary. This is really a kind of dramatic necessity combining with a musical necessity. The dramatic necessity is to make each moment vivid; the musical necessity is to make something satisfying out of it that is pleasing in a purely musical way. But to really understand why this is satisfying requires inside knowledge, I think, and audiences don't need to have this. They'll enjoy it because it's working well – a strong structure makes a piece durable. It's not some sort of private game.

I'm glad to say that there were people in tears at the end of the first performance of *Mansfield Park*, and somebody I spoke to afterwards remarked that they didn't know *why* they were in tears. If they'd asked themselves why, it would probably have been because Edmund has finally realised that he loves Fanny and that they're going to be together. And that's enough. My librettist must take some credit for it, the actors must also take some credit and *I'm* going to take some credit. I don't want to do a kind of off-the-cuff analysis of the score, but there's a significant harmonic resolution at the end of the opera which I hope contributes in some way to the feeling that everything's finally come right for the main characters.

I write music that's essentially very simple, which means that I can retain a lot of it in my head during the composition process. So I try and get it right before I commit it to paper. In other words, notation is something I do once I know what it is that I'm trying to notate.

Because I write a lot of operas I'm usually singing at the piano, and my fingers are the orchestra. And by the time I've shaped an idea to my satisfaction I've played it many times, so I'm getting a lot of enjoyment from the physical sensation of this succession of sounds. And among the things I suppose I'm looking for at any moment are ways of making it *more* enjoyable. I don't know if this makes the music 'good', exactly, but I sometimes say, 'Well, there's nothing wrong with that piece.' You know, 'It works.' Maybe that sounds like a rather mechanical approach, as if I've tried to create a machine and am assessing whether it did the things I was hoping it would do.

I don't ever think of my music as good *music*, but I might think that I've written a good piece. In other words, the music is a part of me, so I'm not going to say I'm good; but I might say that I've made something good out of it. I can be satisfied with the *journey* of a piece, and I suppose that's related to a sense of what the possibilities of an idea were, and whether I managed to satisfactorily explore those possibilities and deal with them in a pleasing way. As it happens, there are times when I'm profoundly moved by my own music because it's merely a succession of things that please me.

I usually try to leave the house first thing in the morning and do some exercise before I start writing, and for the last few years I've made a point of not going on after seven o'clock in the evening, because otherwise it becomes impossible to have anything like an ordinary life – to see friends and go to concerts or plays.

When I'm in the middle of writing a big piece I can go for quite long stretches without listening to anyone else's music; but equally, it can be very stimulating to take a break from things that have been going around in my head. For example, I've been to a few Proms this year while I've been writing (I've just been working through the summer on an opera, and I haven't had a holiday). If I'm at a concert and I'm not enjoying the music, I'm quite likely to think about the piece that I'm trying to write; or sometimes it makes me think of the music I would like to be hearing, and so it gives me new ideas.

There's a gregarious impulse and also a quite strong solitary impulse in me. The gregarious impulse sometimes leads me to work in the theatre or to embark on a highly collaborative project such as a community opera. And that inevitably involves spending a lot more time planning with directors, designers and producers, and also meeting participants and devising workshops. I don't conduct my operas any more because I discovered that you need to be able to stand back and see if it's all working. If you're conducting, you're *willing* it to happen, and you can't be absolutely certain that it *did* happen. But I did conduct my second community opera, which had six hundred performers in it – after which I was quite happy to be on my own for a bit. So I get a burst of company, and I enjoy the more social aspect of being a composer; but then comes a point at which I'm longing to be on my own, with just the piano and the sounds, so that I can attend to *them*.

If one identifies very closely with one's own music, it's easier to admit to skill or clarity than to beauty. I mean, nobody refers to himself as beautiful. So maybe it's not that we composers are detached about the music that we write but that through it we're coming up with manifestations of our unconscious.

Singers have some control over the sound they make, of course, but part of it is just what was given to them by nature. They make their own sound, and if it thrills you, that's wonderful, isn't it? And in a way that's also true with a composer. We don't have much control over the sounds that we make, and I don't think we can help what it is that we find pleasing or satisfying (by that, I suppose I mean what appeals to our innate sense of beauty, whatever that is). So it's not surprising that composers are wary about agreeing that their music is beautiful, because that's an invitation for people to throw tomatoes. There will always be somebody who's not having a very good time in one of my pieces – and they're usually writing for the *Daily Telegraph*!

David Dubery

David Dubery, Suffolk, October 2011

> **❛ I don't believe that any composer has the right to be liked, or even performed. ❜**

I first met David Dubery at the opening event of a music festival in October 2011 and was immediately struck by his friendliness, his inquisitiveness about unfamiliar music and his quiet seriousness of mind. I knew none of his own works except for *Mrs Harris in Paris*[1] but over the following few days there were many opportunities to chat, and our conversations convinced me that he had much to contribute to this book.

One reason is that his career as a composer isn't untypical of what might be called a 'lesser-known' of contemporary British music. He has spent much of his working life performing and teaching a wide variety of other people's music and has written his own pieces as time has allowed. And because he wants them to be performed and heard he concentrates on vocal and chamber music – what he knows from the inside, as it were, through his experience as a pianist, accompanist and vocal coach. He might therefore be described as a musical miniaturist, although there's no reason to suppose that he's less ambitious than his composing colleagues.

However, a creative artist's success is dependent on a number of factors that include professional opportunity and position, and financial stability. Also, perhaps, temperament. Most composers are by nature thin-skinned but are required to develop thick skins and to accept that music is to some extent a product that has to be promoted in a crowded marketplace. Some achieve the necessary balance between self-doubt and self-confidence – between introversion and extroversion, perhaps – more successfully than others, and determination doesn't always translate into the single-minded drive necessary for survival at the most conspicuous level of music-making.

Dubery is a softly spoken, self-effacing person who, having worked for many years with singers and instrumentalists, knows all about the egos, insecurities and rivalries within his profession and has sometimes been on the receiving end of them. By way of consolation, he observes that, although the most famous British composers are known *of*, their music

---

[1] For recorder and string orchestra (2003–4).

isn't widely performed or known. In which case, he suggested to me, 'lesser-knowns' like him are probably no worse off for not having obvious success. In any case, two CDs of his songs and chamber music – one released shortly before I met him and the second in 2014 – have brought his music international exposure.

I didn't conduct a face-to-face interview with him, and what follows is compiled from his written responses to a list of e-mailed questions, several long telephone conversations and a number of e-mail exchanges which appeared to be informal chats but which included comments that seemed appropriate for inclusion in this 'encounter'. He set great store by fine-tuning his comments, and even after having approved his contribution to this book he remained concerned that it makes him appear too conservative in his musical tastes and outlook. What's obvious is that he's no less a 'conviction composer' than any of his colleagues for maintaining that important things can still be said in music without breaking new stylistic or structural ground.

―――――――

What's meant by a 'British composer'? One whose music reflects Great Britain in a nationalist sense? One who's British and represents Britain internationally because he's in vogue? Or simply a British composer whose music is categorised as 'classical'? Sorry, I'm answering your question by asking more of my own! But am I a British composer because of my British heritage? I've lived in Manchester since 1961 but I was born in Durban, South Africa. My music can be pictorial or programmatic and it's influenced by nature and dance, but the influences are eclectic: travel, photography, jazz, theatre and film. My music isn't consciously British, though there's likely to be an English quality to it if I'm setting an English poem – just as in my Dante settings *Love Sonnets/Sonetti d'amore*, written for the counter-tenor James Bowman, I tried to capture something of the Italian Renaissance and the city of Florence. That's simply a response to text.

Had I remained in South Africa, I dare say that the landscape of my music would have been different: there might have been an African resonance to it, which suggests that composers refer in some way to the culture that surrounds them. But I don't feel confined by *any* boundaries. Because I enjoyed a performing career as a pianist and accompanist in both traditional classical recital repertoire and in theatre and cabaret, my musical tastes are very varied.

My earliest musical memories are of my parents' LP collection: Schubert, Grieg, opera arias, Mario Lanza, Ivor Novello musicals and light music balladeers such as Nat King Cole. My thirst for music was insatiable, and by the age of fourteen I'd acquired a sizeable knowledge of the classical repertoire from Haydn through the romantics to Britten, Walton and Bartók. In fact it became an obsession, and after arriving in Manchester I spent much of my time sight-reading music from the public library – sometimes several volumes in a week.

When I went to music college my biggest disappointment was that it didn't have a serious faculty of composition, and after four years I left without a practical knowledge of orchestration. I didn't even think about what life as a composer would be like; I just wanted to write a piece of music. While I was training to be a concert pianist I had a notion of what *that* would be like, and as a result I changed my focus towards becoming an accompanist – not because it was an easier option but because it seemed a less isolated career. Since then, composing has been for me a continuing journey of development and discovery.

My very first piece was for piano, a pathetically naïve and poorly written page influenced by Beethoven. Within a few years I worked through the influences of Weber, Schubert, Debussy and (later on) Britten, Shostakovich, Walton, Richard Rodney Bennett and Bernstein. But it took time for my musical preferences to settle and for me to feel fluent as a composer. Music college was rather stuffy and conservative, and although the Sixties was an experimental age most of my colleagues wouldn't have dared to write some of the music I was writing in my late teens and early twenties. I went through an experimental phase and dabbled in electronics, prepared pianos and twelve-tone music, but this didn't last long because it was almost too easy to do things that I thought hadn't been tried before, or which seemed a bit mad. It was easier to create chaos than order, and I craved to create order in my music. I still do. I suppose some people would say, 'Oh, you've just gone soft'; but although I could probably still write something very experimental, it really wouldn't be 'me' any more. The American composer Kenneth Fuchs, whose music I admire, once wrote to me and told me that he's always asking himself the question 'Have I written something beautiful today?' I like that!

You often hear composers bemoaning their lot because they don't get performances or because nobody buys their recordings. But the language of some contemporary music is too extreme for listeners, too far removed from their experience. I feel that 'contemporary music' has become almost a separate genre, in the sense that – like conceptual art – it's not recognisably based on what went before it. It's almost a new breed: it exists in its own space and you can't call it 'modern' in relation to anything from the past. I applaud Britten's comment in his Aspen Award speech: 'It is a composer's duty, as a member of society, to speak to or for his fellow human beings.'

If I began addressing you in a language that was totally foreign to you, you'd probably switch off, or you'd have to go on some kind of crash course to learn it. And I think some composers are asking rather a lot of audiences, particularly at a time when people have *less* time, not *more*, to get to grips with new music. I don't mean to imply that what these composers are writing is worthless. On the contrary, it's through advanced techniques that new ideas enrich musical language. But because those techniques are often very method-orientated, they lose favour with audiences who find the results rather tortured. Yes, a composer has to be true to his nature and idiom, but if this results in him writing music that he knows will be perceived as difficult he has to take whatever comes to him. After all, he can't force people to like what he writes. He might be a pioneer of all manner of brilliant techniques, but the issue is whether his music encourages repeated hearings because of its content. And if it encourages people to leave the auditorium (and turn the lights out), is he really being useful in any way?

It's not mandatory that audiences should have to work hard to get something out of music, and a piece that requires a lot of work is likely to be either an academic exercise for a specialised audience or an over-indulgent ego trip. I want all music, not just my own, to reveal its magic without needing to be dissected. There's a time for dissection and analysis, of course, but that time can be later. Initially, music must be a pleasure. You see, I don't believe that any composer has the right to be liked, or even performed. Writing music is an act of personal expression, sometimes for others and sometimes as an extension of the composer's own musical development. And if he's able to share his creation with others who respond favourably to it, then it has become useful – even if listeners find in it something quite different from what he intended them to find.

The composer David Arditti talks of a new tonal movement: composers who wish to retain the aesthetic principles associated with traditional classical music. But I don't believe it's new. It's easy to forget that the composing of tonal music continued throughout the twentieth century in spite of critics labelling it old-fashioned. Nor do I believe it should be seen as 'retro'. It's still a valid global musical language. Not every composer is an innovator, and only a few in any century are regarded as geniuses. But, as in any other art form, the creator has to have something to say that's rewarding in some way for a public that wants to listen. My music has been described as 'new British lyrical', but I feel that the current obsession with labels and analysis can inhibit the freedom of composers *and* their audiences. Regardless of the musical genre, what's important is whether the music speaks to an audience and whether there's an audience for it. It therefore needs to contain something that will meet the audience at least part of the way, if not necessarily halfway. Music is a three-way process: composer, performer and audience.

As you'll have gathered by now, the issue of communication is very much in my mind when I compose. This is particularly the case when I'm setting texts, because I want the communication of the words to be as natural as possible – by which I mean that they should be easily understood in musical sound. I don't see the point of setting a poem if the words are rendered meaningless. Similarly, I have a low tolerance of singers who can't communicate text by enunciating clearly!

It occurs to me that composers of the past who were also performers built closer links with their audiences: Bach, Mozart, Beethoven, Chopin, Liszt, Mahler, Strauss, Rachmaninov, Prokofiev, Britten and Bernstein, for example. I've certainly found that being a performer has been beneficial to me in providing opportunities to programme (sometimes multiple performances) and record my own music. There are lots of conductor/composers today, but their music appears not to captivate audiences or receive multiple recordings like their predecessors' did. And I think there could be many reasons for this. At the moment I'm reading a biography of Richard Rodney Bennett, who seems to have discovered something special when he started to perform as a singer/pianist: audiences responded to the marriage of intelligent, witty, human lyrics to memorable melody, and I find it interesting that he talked about never wanting to put anyone through the kind of misery he endured when going to performances of contemporary music in the 1950s! I have a lot of sympathy for these thoughts, because I sometimes sit through similar misery today. Many of his later works brought people more pleasure than his pieces from the 1960s did, and is that such a bad thing?

In one of his television programmes Howard Goodall gave the impression that music should represent or reflect the time in which it's written, adding that of course this wasn't what happened with Mozart and Haydn. But *why* does it have to reflect the time in which it's written? It's important that *some* music does that, but not every composer is writing a historical documentary in musical terms. Music is much wider than that. Geographically, historically and socially, it creates many different kinds of experience.

I like to express shapes and contours, emotions, moods, and movement, but a lot of what I write is determined by subject matter. I try to write music that's well constructed and balanced in an architectural sense, and perhaps this makes me rather unadventurous. I certainly don't set out with the deliberate intention of being 'different'. My music has a kind of tonal home, but it's not always the expected one and I get satisfaction from writing something that travels on a journey to *other* homes. As it's not difficult to improvise or to create music that's self-indulgent and rambles along, outstaying its welcome, I also make a conscious effort to aim for concision.

For me, the process of composing is often like creating a piece of artwork (my teenage education was at an art-biased school): I start with a blank canvas and try to map out my design in order to get the broad picture. Gradually I work in the detail, refining and altering as I go. Sometimes I make a start and simply allow the music to lead me – and the results can surprise me. If I'm setting a text, I like to read it in the way that an actor might read a script in order to discover a character, and to try different interpretations until I find something that seems truthful and natural. Then the most important task is to find the right musical colours to express the emotion of the text. Actually, I often find that when I read a poem for the first time I immediately start to hear it in my head as a song, both melodically and rhythmically. What's frustrating is that by the time I've worked my way spontaneously through the poem (and I can do this quite quickly) I can't remember the musical idea that I started with!

Composers develop mannerisms, just as actors and singers do. And I suppose these become recognisable ways in which composers speak. I think I'm only just beginning to be aware of them in my own work. Sometimes I think my pieces sound very different from each other, but then people tell me that no, they can hear something recognisably 'me' in them. Perhaps it's my construction and my harmonic palate – after all, one's ear does favour certain types of sounds, and I'm aware of wanting to use particular colours in a number of my works.

I've been thinking about your question as to whether I like or enjoy my own music. And my answer would have to be: yes, I do, but only when it's performed well. Of course, some pieces work better than others. And I like my music to be 'right', so something that sounds odd or 'out of step' niggles. I worry about whether I could possibly write it with more clarity and economy, while envying composers who have greater experience and better technique. But when a piece is as complete as I can make it at that time (one does go back to it years later and think, 'I could rewrite that bit'), it starts to become detached from me, rather as if an umbilical chord has been cut. And the piece starts to have a life of its own. It's like a potter creating a bowl from clay: when it has left the wheel and been fired, or even better when it has been fired and glazed, he thinks, 'Yes, that looks like a pot. It does what I want it to do.' I'm always learning more about the craft of composition, and when I look back at some of my early works – which I quite liked when I wrote them, because they were probably the best things I'd written at that time – they now seem very naïve. Either the construction's terrible or the lyrics are terrible, or there's too much repetition. Those pieces were sometimes successful from the public point of view, but I'd be very worried if I were still writing in exactly the same way today.

But am I *moved* by my own music? As I said earlier, that could depend on the performers. On a few occasions I've had pieces played so beautifully that I *was* really moved and felt so grateful towards them. On the other hand, a poor or under-rehearsed performance undermines my confidence and makes me doubt my abilities to express the music clearly in the score. I find that performers who are very gifted are not only in command of the technical issues but often have a real empathy with the music. But others tend to be too academic – and, as a result, unimaginative in their playing. Of course, the amount of rehearsal time available and how familiar the performers are with the scores has a big impact on this. Far too often there isn't enough rehearsal, and so first performances sound like read-throughs (and sometimes that's what they are). And since composers don't always get the chance of further performances, this can be very disheartening and discouraging.

The fact that it takes more than one performance before a work starts to fully live is one reason why I prefer to compose music that's small in scale – it stands a better chance of being performed more than once. But I don't, in any case, see myself as a painter of big canvases. I've written vocal and chamber music because that's the area I worked in as a performer. I was accompanying a singer, a violinist, an oboist or a flautist, and working repeatedly with particular musicians encouraged me to write pieces for them. Reviewers and interviewers often ask me if I've written any symphonies or concertos, which feels rather like a test of my ability – as if a composer has only come of age after writing large-scale pieces. It doesn't particularly bother me that I haven't, and I don't think I'm driven to push myself in that direction for its own sake.

Composing is a lonely pursuit unless you're collaborating on a theatre project, and have a lyric writer or librettist, or working collaboratively with a particular performer. It can also be daunting in its demands to produce a piece that's up to the occasion and appropriate to what else is happening in the concert. But it can be exciting, too. You may suddenly find yourself working with brilliant performers, or perhaps your music's being performed in a prestigious venue. Having been a performer since my early teens in recital, theatre, cabaret, opera, radio and television, I'm used to being in front of audiences and giving interviews, so I'm reasonably comfortable with the public aspect of being a composer. But I suspect that most composers who haven't been performers would rather be left alone. A lot of them like to work quietly, out of the limelight. Then there are those who cultivate their personalities in order to make their mark in public, perhaps because there's a great deal of competition in the musical world and so they're constantly looking for that 'something' that will make them more noticeable. Promotion in the media plays an increasingly large part in determining whether a composer acquires – and maintains – a public profile. It's a highly competitive market, which is one reason why computer technology has had an influence on the way that many of us actually write our music.

When I began composing in 1962 I drew my own staves onto blank paper, later progressing to manuscript pads. I used to compose a lot at the piano. Now, Sibelius software enables me to create a score quite quickly, and in quality print. It also enables me to hear instrumental combinations and orchestrations immediately, even though the human element of performance and the true instrumental sound are absent. This has expanded my aural perception and given me a confidence I previously lacked, and I'm no longer [piano] keyboard-bound. But, however good the software is, it remains merely a useful practical tool, not a piece of technology that composes for you. It can lead you astray!

I find that some pieces are committed quickly and seem almost to write themselves, while others can take a long time because the ideas have to settle in my mind during a kind of gestation period. An idea can occur to me in the dead of night, and I've been known to scribble a phrase or two on a scrap of paper immediately afterwards. At other times I might be travelling on a tram, train or plane when something sparks my imagination. More often than not I lose an idea before I'm able to write it down; and while some kernel of the initial thought might remain, the sequence of notes that results will probably change. Maybe it would be a good idea to sing phrases into a voice recorder so that I've captured something to start working with, because the more you work on the music, the more studied and the less natural it feels.

Some pieces of mine have taken me by surprise, and I find them unexplainable, in the sense that they just took wing and kept on flying to their conclusion. Examples are my four movements for string quartet, *Cuertetto Iberico*, which I wrote because I just had to get something Spanish and Latin out of my system. It seemed so natural for me to be writing this music, and it expanded easily into a twenty-two-minute work. And my Cello Sonata changed direction: it started life as a work for double bass and piano.

Alas, I don't have a regular routine for composing. Writing music can be an expensive and time-consuming activity, and so external funding, paid commissions or independent personal wealth can have a huge impact on whether a composer manages to find a space in the car park of musical life. There are many whose music we wouldn't know had it not been for their financial security. Because I had to earn a living from teaching and performing there were many times when I wanted to compose but couldn't, and that was frustrating.

My composing is still done whenever there's time – sometimes just a snatched moment. When I was writing musical theatre in the mid-1970s I composed a large amount of music, but life was all work in those days! These days I try to maintain a personal life as well. Having said that, compromises have had to be made if I've been writing to a commission, although it's often been the case that a commission has helped the flow of musical ideas. When there's been no pressure, writing a piece has sometimes lingered from weeks into months, which has displeased me.

Often it would have been beneficial to have uninterrupted time to compose, because after too long a gap it's difficult to get back into it. But there are times when breaks from the work can actually be helpful. You can be too close to your music while you're writing it, and sometimes you need a bit of distance in order to realise that something doesn't sound or look right, and that alternatives will make things clearer. I suppose this is why I tend to fiddle around with a lot of my pieces. Some people would call this 'revision', but it's often a minimal tweaking of things here and there. I believe that the score should be as helpful as possible, so the process of tweaking involves making sure that I've kept to recognisable rules that performers can instantly recognise and execute.

In addition to this, preparing scores and parts, creating MP3s and PDF files, mailing scores and notes to performers, researching texts and poems, dealing with applications for permissions, writing programme notes, and preparing and proofreading for publication are all part of a composer's work. And they're enormously time-consuming.

It's easy to be overawed by the greatness of the past, but we have to remember that, before the age of Enlightenment, composers were employed by aristocrats to undertake set tasks throughout the year: quartets, symphonies, operas, church cantatas and so on. And having to earn their living by continuous creation – a learning process over many years – must have greatly aided their musical development. There are similar assignments today but they tend to be isolated commissions, composers' residencies or film composers writing to strict deadlines. Other than this, a composer fumbles about as best he can, trying to encourage a performance here and there. And he keeps on writing for himself, in the hope that he's developing his skill and technique.

As a composer, you can always strive to learn more. But you can only express yourself to the limit of your ability at any particular time. There'll always be composers who have a greater facility and who've benefited from more advantageous training or opportunities which inevitably elevate them to the top of the pot, as it were. In the eighteenth century, when music was written to certain formulae, there must have been countless sonatinas by composers whose names are now unfamiliar because the music wasn't distinguished or memorable enough; and something similar is happening today. But then the success of a piece depends upon numerous factors, none of which has anything musical about it: luck, opportunity, funding, promotion and contacts. Without these, music isn't performed, broadcast, published or recorded, and no one has an opportunity to acquaint themselves with it.

Am I driven to compose? I suppose I am. But I don't know what compels me to do it. It's certainly not the money! It could be an urge to engage in an act of creation of some kind. I've lived with music all of my life, but I wouldn't die if I stopped writing it. I suspect that I'd miss doing so, though. So I'm probably writing for now, rather than for posterity. One has to, I think, because nobody knows what posterity will bring. Composers of the future will be writing music in their own time, and they might not be creating anything that would sound familiar to us today – just as today's composers don't write in the way that Monteverdi did. What survives might not be a composer's most important work; but if it finds a place in people's lives, that's all that matters.

Michael Finnissy

Michael Finnissy, West Sussex, April 2011

❝ I'm on the margins of a world dominated by commercial constraints. ❞

Michael Finnissy is the first composer I interviewed for this book, a fact that may have limited the usefulness of my encounter with him. Nervous interviewers, feeling the need to impress or at least to relax their subjects, can be tempted to concentrate on directing a smooth flow of conversation in which one topic segues neatly into the next, at the expense of listening sufficiently carefully to what's being said; and I may have fallen into this trap with Finnissy. I went to him armed with a list of standard questions to which he supplied some decidedly non-standard answers. It was only later, while transcribing our conversation, that I realised how patiently he'd interpreted my questioning to reflect his outlook and experience. Nevertheless, he later asked to make significant changes to his contribution because he felt that he hadn't expressed himself clearly enough.

As with Julian Anderson, I hesitate to say that he has enormous integrity both as a person and as an artist because this would imply that the other contributors don't; but it's one of the qualities that I feel most strongly define him. And it's linked to what I perceive as his sense of being, or at least feeling, an outsider. Although he's firmly grounded in the real world, it contains much that he dislikes and disagrees with, and his musical responses to it can be demanding and provocative. Presumably it's this instinct that prevents him from suffering fools gladly and enables him to state, quite reasonably, that he sees no reason to waste his time on people who don't interest him.

He now lives on the north Norfolk coast, but at the time of this interview his home was on the edge of a small town in West Sussex; and it was there, on an unusually warm and sunny April morning in 2011, that we talked in the shade of his back garden. He spoke earnestly, analytically and sometimes obliquely, only once fazed by the insistent buzz of his next-door-neighbour's strimmer. I wondered whether his own garden – compact, orderly, densely stocked and full of detail – could have been said to resemble his music, but I was probably making connections for their own sake. Perhaps he simply had a small, neat, well-planted garden.

A more useful observation might be that beneath the surface of both his personality and his music there's great generosity of spirit. After the interview was officially over we spent the afternoon chatting about a number of topics, some of them unrelated to music, while he made innumerable mugs of tea, and there was a lot of laughter. But listeners shouldn't be beguiled by the titles of his *Casual Nudity, Necessary and More Detailed Thinking, Not Envious of Rabbits, That Ain't Shit* and *Après-midi Dada* (for two keyboards, ensemble, coffee grinder and (nude) actors), for he knows that the most serious things sometimes have the greatest potential for humour, and that humour isn't the same as silliness.

I began the interview by introducing a topic that I discussed with every contributor to this book: the identifiable function, if any, of his or her music. He subsequently mentioned more than once his annoyance with the way in which composers are 'labelled' so that their music will fit neatly into predetermined categories, and I suggested that many novelists feel the same way about the rigid classification of fiction-writing for marketing purposes. I explained that if a novel is neither pure 'Horror' nor 'Thriller' publishers don't know which sector of the market to promote it in and booksellers don't know which shelf to display it on. He replied, 'I think I'd be quite happy, halfway between Horror and Thriller!'

I was just over four years old when I started composing. It was spontaneous: just as some children gravitate to painting pictures, I made up pieces of music – telling all sorts of stories with sound and, typically, imitating other pieces of music (either accidentally read or heard). I had no professional tuition. I listened to the radio a lot, and gravitated towards 'modern-sounding' works – eventually finding Bartók, Ives, Satie and Varèse when I was eleven or twelve. Part of this was a rebellion against my father's enthusiasm for Bach and Beethoven, and both my parents' love of Mantovani and Victor Sylvester. So the 'function' of my music at this early stage was mainly to create a bubble in which I could become self-sufficient, like Robinson Crusoe, or in which I thought it was safe to hide. I got enthusiastic support from my great-aunt Rose Louise and from my mother's sister, both of whom took me to concerts and ballet, so sometimes the function was to entertain or to provoke a response.

When I was fifteen or sixteen I won a trophy at the Croydon Music Festival, which made a slight dent in the way my parents thought about my composing. And then, during sixth form, I found a role model in my form teacher, Alan Brownjohn (eventually a much respected poet). I started to dream that I could be a *real* composer, my imagination answerable to people other than myself. I enjoyed the cut-and-thrust of the debating society, and the mid-1960s were great times to be in London: Ban the Bomb, Better Books, the Arts Lab and Film-Makers Co-op, Living Theatre at the Round House, Theatre of Cruelty and all the attendant journals and discussion. So I then felt that the 'function' of my music ought to be to provoke fierce controversy and that it ought to embody social and political ideals. That had been pretty much the viewpoint of Brecht and Eisler during the 1930s, and thirty years later it was pretty much the viewpoint of Nono, Cage, Boulez and Stockhausen, whose voices were listened to and respected while I was at college.

I think that an ethical dimension, perhaps also a didactic one, is important to me in what I write; so the 'function' of my music is to try to inform and stimulate, as well as to allow (perhaps to liberate) the sensuality of the sounds themselves. I also continue to try to push the boundaries, and to explore. This involves carrying through a couple of resolutions that I made when I was at the Royal College of Music between 1964 and 1967: to reconcile disparate materials (I don't admire 'exclusivity') and to make a 'cabinet of curiosities' containing specimens of each genre of music that I encountered and liked in some way, but as viewed 'darkly' through my own, personal glass. I see this as an 'exemplary function' of my music, proving that such things are possible – and ideologically desirable.

In the course of my life I've also found that music can be a salve and a tonic. So I now think about its 'healing function', because music makes things whole that would otherwise not be whole for me.

No, when I started to write music I had absolutely *no* idea of what the life of a professional composer would be like. And I *still* don't know, because for many years I was a professional repetiteur and now I'm a professional university academic. I feel I've utterly failed as a professional composer. Composing is, for me, an obsessive hobby, and I'm effectively an amateur. At the start of my first ever composition tutorial at the Royal College of Music, Bernard Stevens asked me if I came from 'family money': did I have inherited wealth? No, I didn't. 'You're going to find life very difficult indeed', he said. And he was right, in no small measure. But what else could I do? Other than music, I have no inherent gift. In fact, I was useless at everything else, and I'd already been turned down by all the teacher-training colleges I'd applied to as a prospective teacher of English.

I was self-taught until I studied with Stevens and Humphrey Searle.

At eighteen I was just a fairly well-read and sophisticated grammar-school oik, and it's a great tribute to Stevens that he thought I was worth teaching at all. I must have been a total trial to him, but he was a thoughtful and subtle teacher, atypically esoteric in his tastes and slightly diffident about his own work. (I continue to think that his music has been treated appallingly by the mainstream music world, for whom it has, so far, never ticked the right boxes.)

Much later on I had a letter from Michael Tippett, telling me that composing in England was like crossing a desert without a map and with no company! And I had not, in my early twenties, yet realised that quite so many people would take such delight in telling me how dreadful, irrelevant, impossible and meaningless they thought my work was. There's a lot of rejection for composers to get used to, because the classical music business doesn't need new ones; they have Vivaldi and Tchaikovsky, whom the public adore and continue to flock to.

I'm on the margins of a world dominated by commercial constraints, and I'm really only interested in 'carrying the torch' and writing at the highest possible level of accomplishment. It would be quite possible, watching television, to think that England, where I continue to live, was entirely sleazy and trivialising, entirely complicit with capitalism and entirely passive about politics or religion. Fortunately, this is no more true than the myth about 'ordinary people' not understanding modern music. However, I can't control who my audience is, and I wouldn't want to. I'd prefer to think that *anybody* who wanted to could find a way to listen to my music. They won't find it on the South Bank in London, but they can (and do) find it on YouTube or on CD recordings. And they'll find it played by amateurs more often than by professionals, because most of the people who trumpet 'accessibility' for a wider public actually operate within a very narrow cultural sphere.

Composing is partly – perhaps *mostly* – to do with the quality of someone's imagination: how their intuition and wisdom interact with pitches, durations, dynamics, timbres and structures. You ask whether technological advances have changed the way in which I notate music, but I think that larger issues are involved. Anyone who hasn't already done so should read Walter Benjamin's essay about works of art in an era of mechanical reproduction. Literary criticism has long considered that the shift towards scepticism about form and language occurred in the mid-nineteenth century and resulted in a kind of guerrilla writing (usually called 'modernism') whose perceived moral duty is to attack the stultification of society and commonplace assumptions about literature, or the arts generally. Writers went on to choose topics that disturb, disrupt and threaten the status quo and everyone's most cherished sentiments. Others see the shift happening rather later, after Symbolism and Aestheticism. It probably doesn't matter all that much, because the main fact is that it *happened*. Is art separate and 'apart' from life? How can it become involved, and *should* it seek to be involved, without towing institutionalised party lines? Such questions seem to me more significant than whether one's using a pencil, a digital stun gun or an Apple Mac.

People need to try to understand the ambition for power that obliterates most things in its path. Concert halls that are desperate to make money and entertain their audiences will obviously try any way they possibly can to render composers complicit; and new technologies could be just another distraction, something else bright and shiny to swagger about in.

You're right: I don't think of myself as a public figure in the sense that I'm recognisable to people in the street. But I'm not uncomfortable with public appearances. I used to 'show off' with my music when I was a child, to get affection or to make an impression; and I teach, so I've learned how to speak effectively and to think on my feet. And I'm quite gregarious. But I prefer being invisible. It's good to be able to observe, to watch rather than be watched.

Do I make a distinction between ideas and their execution? The first thing to say is that music is music, not *ideas about* music. (That being said, it's better if the music's halfway intelligent.) In fact, ideas can be a bit of a nuisance; and since concepts can be so seductive in themselves, why pursue them into the harsh light of pragmatic trial-and-error? As with pre-compositional sketching, one must be careful to reserve one's *real* energy for the act of composing itself, not to waste it on the limbering up! You mentioned David Hockney's distinction between 'poetry' and 'craft', and I'm a massive fan of Hockney and his abundant wisdom about the practice of art. The craft and ethics of composition can be taught in many ways, sometimes quite obliquely. One has to learn as much as possible about as many instruments as possible, about what notation represents to a wide range of performers. So a blend of philosophy, mathematics and cooking would prepare you fairly effectively for studying composition!

I consciously *avoid* thinking about my technique as I'm sure it would inhibit composing – it would make composing like 'scoring points' or acrobatics. Impressive, maybe, but trivial. And in fact I have an uncomfortable relationship with technical accomplishment: in spite of being fairly perceptive about my students' work and, I hope, helpful with advice on how to surmount problems they might be having with it, I never seem to have sufficient technical resources for my own writing, and I'm frequently puzzled and frustrated by things that I initially can't solve. I tell myself that this is because I haven't tried to do the particular thing before, so I should expect it to be difficult to deal with. But it's tempting to simply attribute the failure to incompetence!

Perhaps you know the very well-known anecdote about Picasso visiting a children's school, shortly before his death, and saying that he'd spent his entire life wishing and trying to draw as they did. I'm increasingly conscious of how much 'education and culturisation' I have to erase before my work is as honest and authentic as I'd like. Because my father was a photographer and surveyor, I dare say these were my initial templates for writing music; and whether or not they were suitable models, I had few other choices. I learned about aesthetics from seriously studying film, and I think of my 'processes' as forms of editing, as types of assemblage and montage. In fact, I've learned about composing music from my studies of Hockney and Robert Rauschenberg, and Degas and Stan Brakhage. Yes, from Bach and Beethoven too, and from Berlioz and Schoenberg.

My preoccupations with the energy and diversity of musical line remain pretty constant, and so I'm conscious more of *change* than evolution in my music. And I advise my students to select very carefully the vocabulary that they use when discussing their own work. I don't find words like 'development' (as in standard accounts of sonata principle) very helpful, and I still prefer 'exploring' or 'investigating'.

When you ask me about density or complexity in music, I assume you have in mind the period in the mid-1970s when *Neue Einfachheit* (New Simplicity) was launched by the WDR in Cologne and Walter Zimmermann. It was widely thought to be a European subset of American minimalism, and of course those who were appalled by the proximity of simplicity to vacuity were likely to fight back. Harry Halbreich and Richard Toop were just two of them, and they advocated 'New Complexity'. But what do the words 'density' and 'complexity' *mean*? Probably something different to everyone who reads or utters them. Which is why words can be dangerous.

To its admirers, 'complex music' doubtless seems exciting and challenging; but to its opponents the word 'complex' means 'unnecessarily obtuse' or just plain confusing. Fortunately I'm not, by profession, a 'phrase-maker', but I have to live, as some sort of jobbing musician, through the ill-considered fall-out from these catchpenny terms. It doesn't help that our culture divides people into opposing factions, reducing a wide spectrum of ideas to easily digested stereotypes. I don't suppose 'dense' is any more intelligible than 'complex' when referring to music. Royalty once complained to Mozart that there were too many notes in his work; and, like him, I like to think that I write 'just the right number', and that complexity isn't an issue.

After all, the universe is complex. People are complex, and their reasoning can be complex (or, perhaps, convoluted). Most things in my life have both simple and complex aspects to them; and I don't want to censor my work and exclude things from it because they might be 'difficult', tangled up or muddled. Nor do I want necessarily to 'resolve' problems – I believe that what I do frequently poses questions rather than providing answers. Of course, I also strive for lucidity, economy and clarity. And I'm fully aware of the penalties of hiding behind enormous swathes of notes (hoping that if *one* doesn't work, there's a ten-thousand back-up). But just try to get out of the box the bastards choose to put you in!

Yes, my surroundings *are* important to my music, but it's difficult to say how much they're reflected in it other than simply being conducive to doing the work. It's sometimes tempting to pursue visual analogies: the tangled textures of a hedgerow, the empty plain stretching to the horizon ... Leonardo da Vinci said, 'Let Nature be your master', and it feels wholesome and comforting to unify with the natural world in the way that Thoreau and Whitman did. This is rather different from Arcadian pastoral, which is largely imaginary, idealised and artificial. But of course I also work a lot on trains and at airports, or wherever there's a well-insulated private space to concentrate in. However, I can write effectively only when I really want to. It doesn't exactly switch on at will, like a tap!

I once wrote two or three scores at the request of the London Contemporary Dance Theatre, and in one of them I was asked to mix the essence of Bach's Brandenburg Concertos with the Beach Boys! They were dire and embarrassing pieces, and I hope I succeeded in destroying all trace of them. Everything else in my portfolio, good or bad, is what I wanted to write. So, to answer your question, commissions don't make any difference at all to what I write, though they can be very useful if they limit the options available to me. I'm sometimes put under pressure to complete work too quickly, and sometimes I lack the requisite technique to do the job – vision is often stronger than competence. So I might withdraw a piece (commissioned or not) if it seems unsatisfactory after being left for a while, in order to try to draw out, more successfully, what was implicit in the work but clouded on the first attempt by a lack of expertise. But maintaining any balance between these two aspects of the work is difficult. Also, publishers make it very awkward to revise works and they charge composers for the privilege of doing so; so changing one's mind is sometimes a luxury!

How much of 'composing' takes place in my head? Thought processes, like 'technique', can actually obscure a certain kind of spontaneity, can 'obscure the iconic essence', as Alaric Sumner put it. I've spent a lifetime researching musical notation, so I try to think with the pen in my hand. Anything else becomes a kind of transcription. There's a fine essay by Busoni about transcription of the thought by the pen, of the work by the performer, of the performance by the audience: Chinese whispers. In other words, my music isn't there before it's written down. As John Cage put it, I write music in order to hear it.

As for my routine: well, there's training that keeps the ear, the hand and the eye fit and ready for action. But I like best the early morning for writing, because nothing has yet got in the way. This somewhat contradicts Nadia Boulanger, who told the students on her Easter courses at the Royal College of Music that they should play the *48 Preludes and Fugues* every day before breakfast. That would clutter up my brain, most days, and remind me of my intellectual and technical inadequacies. (Perhaps that was her intention.) I usually manage to stay on schedule but, in truth, I'm a little disorganised; and because of my other responsibilities, to university and students, I can't be 'regular' in my composing.

You're right to suggest that performers memorise music visually, to some extent. But only if they perform from a score. In improvised music, in jazz or in folk music, the performance will probably not, or at least not entirely, originate from notation. And in *all* music the prevalent conventions, whether or not they're historically aware, are also significant: 'authenticity' in performance has encouraged performers to return to the score and look more closely. But a surprising number of others rely on current, and sometimes entrenched, 'performance praxis'. The notation, and how it's contextualised, should make an enormous impact on performance, not least because there's a vast array of possibilities for notating every sound. For example, it makes a difference whether you notate something as a demisemiquaver or a minim, even if – at different *tempi* – the sound will be the same. But of course music is also about something *more than* sound. The first notational symbols in Debussy's *Clair de Lune* are not sounds, and the first 'sound' is actually a rest!

As for my own music, my initial memory is of its sound. But if I think about a piece I also remember the work of making the score – not of visualising sound in the abstract but of choosing appropriate symbols to stimulate the performers so that they can make the sounds that I want. From my contact with a large number of performers I've learned what works, what's variable and might be worth a risk, and what definitely *doesn't* work. And of course there's plenty of experience encapsulated in scores in libraries. Up to a point, the visual and aural aspects of my music are identical for the listener, since the succession of sounds provides a sense of the music's form. But, as with all music, there are also more or less familiar clues to follow, codes to learn, more and more information to filter in order to interpret the sounds. You need to make quite an effort to continue listening 'innocently', or without curiosity; and, at first, you need to make quite an effort to 'follow the plot'. But isn't that true of most worthwhile human activities?

No, I'm not frustrated by the transience of musical performance. Sound dies, and it's important to acknowledge mortality. We should cherish things while they're there, and work at remembering significant things. But we're lazy. And no, there isn't a piece of my music that sums me up as a composer. I'm still trying to write it. I suppose that some have turned out, and *will* turn out, to be better than others. Frank Lloyd Wright was once asked which of his building designs was his favourite, and his answer was 'the next one'. The same applies to me and my music: my favourite of my own pieces is my next one.

Cheryl Frances-Hoad

Cheryl Frances-Hoad, London, September 2011

> **It seems insane, but I don't think I ever really considered the possibility that I wouldn't be a composer.**

Long before Tom Coult came onto my radar I'd wanted to interview for this book one or two young composers who were considered to show particular promise but whose names wouldn't yet be known to most readers. But who? (Are *any* of the contributors household names, in the generally accepted sense of that term? During his conversation with me John Rutter pointed out that it's many years since a composer has been a national figure in the way that Vaughan Williams was – when *he* wrote to a national newspaper his comments would be published as the leading letter of that day.) The problem is that, while many young British composers are beginning to establish a reputation, it's difficult to predict how their careers will develop.

But I kept reading about Cheryl Frances-Hoad – this was in 2011, around the time that the first CD of her music was released – and the consensus of opinion was that she was destined to go places. She was also happy to contribute to this book and suggested that I interview her at her home near Cambridge after sending her a list of questions to mull over. 'I probably will e-mail answers', she replied after reading them, 'as I'm better writing than speaking! But I'm very happy to meet, as answers might throw up additional questions/clarifications etc.' With this meeting in mind I asked her to respond to my questions spontaneously, as if she were talking on paper, rather than formulating written replies that might be too carefully considered.

A few days later I'd arranged to interview Jonathan Dove in London, but because of a vehicle hitting a railway bridge somewhere up the line all trains to London were cancelled or delayed indefinitely, and I returned home very grumpy. Waiting for me was an e-mail from Cheryl containing replies to my questions, and because they were so unpretentious and funny and believable they cheered me up immediately.

Four weeks later, in September 2011, we met at the Heights Restaurant and Bar at the Saint George's Hotel in London so that I could ask her some further questions and seek clarification about some of her earlier, written comments. It was late afternoon, and after the 'interview', which was really more of a chat, she was going to meet friends for a concert on the South Bank. I couldn't help thinking that I'd never interviewed anyone who looked less like a classical composer, even though this begged the question of what such a creature is supposed to look like. And I wondered what non-musical friends make of her career choice.

As the bulk of questioning was already out of the way this encounter was more relaxed than it might otherwise have been – and very memorable because she displayed an endearing mixture of shyness (she made little eye contact while talking to me) and quiet self-assurance. In spite of her slight reticence she was more forthcoming than most of the other contributors to this book about her own personality and the day-to-day realities of making a living from writing music. She was also very funny.

Because I hadn't yet had the opportunity to get to know much of her music we talked more generally about the life of a young composer who's attempting to establish a career, and I began the conversation by asking about her musical education and training.

When I was eight I went to the Menuhin School to study cello and piano, and I had an amazing training in practical musicianship – doing Hindemith rhythmic exercises, dictation, harmony and so on. Learning to play to a high standard also really benefited my composing. I had a mixture of composition teachers, some of whom just let me get on with it (the best thing when you're little, I think – you just have to churn out music in order to learn how to write) and others who did more intellectual/analytical work with me when I was older. By the time I got to university I was quite happy to reject things if I didn't think they worked for me. That's not to say that I didn't value tremendously all the advice I was given; it's just that I didn't end up like a copy of any of my teachers.

Uni really helped me, mostly by making me write, write, write. I didn't think that writing a fugue a week would influence my composition, but the rigour of it really did, as well as things like writing in the style of Palestrina, which really made me think about line. And I remember what my teacher, Silvina Milstein, said about going through a score in her head and being confident that it would work if it 'breathed' correctly. I have a decent enough voice that I use only when I know no-one can hear it, and so I just go through a score over and over again, playing it and singing it, to work out if it flows in the right way. Little tweaks like adding a quaver to a bar length or altering the length of a note at the end of a phrase can make all the difference, I think.

My PhD was also really useful, and one of the biggest benefits to me was time. I started composing to commission quite young – at fifteen – and I had something to write every school or university holiday. But in no way could I have afforded to live off it in those days, and after graduating I would have had to go and teach or do something else to bring in money. Fortunately my Arts & Humanities Research Council grant enabled me to just take time to write. So I suppose I had a notion of what the life of a composer would be like, although I didn't really think about what I was going to do after university. Looking back on it now, it seems insane, but I don't think I ever really considered the possibility that I wouldn't be a composer.

To me, composing is about harnessing and distilling emotions – usually heightened emotions. I feel that over the years I've become more and more specific about the various hues of emotions involved, to the extent that when I write performance instructions in a score I find it very hard to articulate them in words. Sometimes I go mad and write things like 'passionately glorious yet desperate', but you can't put such rambling directions in too much because then there would be more words than notes! To be honest, it doesn't matter to me if the instruction isn't interpreted by listeners (although it's good if they're in the ballpark!), but I do think it's important during the composing process to be incredibly specific about what emotion you're trying to portray. As for the function of my music, primarily I want it to move people. I also find myself thinking more and more about the performers: I want my music to bring out the best in them.

At the moment I feel that my music is refining, more than changing or evolving, and I've given up being paranoid about being original. But I think that the *way* I compose has changed. Whereas before I tended to add more notes if I wanted to achieve greater intensity, nowadays I'm more likely to try to give the performers more space to fully express the music. And I've found that bits of my music that I thought might be a bit boring as a result turned out to be really affecting emotionally because the performers didn't have to worry about complicated technical details like a quintuplet with lots of double stops in. I've realised that if I want to write something really anguished it might be better to write one long note than two dozen really fast ones that involve scrambling around the keyboard or the fingerboard.

I think I'm more concerned with the heart's response to my music than the mind's response. But this doesn't mean that I don't need a great deal of technical expertise. Musical compositions are like some modern architecture: a building that seems to defy gravity has complex science and maths behind it, as well as sturdy foundations. This is what I aim for in my music, anyway. When I write something that to me is quite intellectual I worry that I'm not being spontaneous and emotive enough; and when I write something straight from the heart, as it were, and don't worry so much about form, I feel I'm being stupid. So I find the best thing is just to stop thinking about this and write! Everything I compose is written heart on sleeve, actually, but some pieces are more planned than others.

Yes, I would say that my music brings me pleasure. I mean, when you're writing it you *have* to think it's wonderful, otherwise you'd stop. I do write the kind of music I'd like to hear (isn't it impossible for a composer *not* to do that?), but I wouldn't like to hear *only* my kind of music. There's lots that's much more stereotypically 'modern' than mine that I really like – James Dillon, for example, and Ferneyhough. And because I'm very 'melody and harmony' I take ideas from composers who are more 'timbre'. What I aim to do is make the emotional content of the music come across as clearly as possible, whether that's distressing or sad or happy. There's a lot of pleasure to be derived from writing something that portrays emotion well, which means that you can get pleasure from being upset by writing a really miserable piece!

My hero is Benjamin Britten, so it means something to me to be a British composer. And I think that the British character or sense of humour sometimes comes through in my music. But other than that, I can't say I've ever really thought about any relationship between my music and my Britishness. When I first started composing I don't think the *audience* even occurred to me (I was only eight!), but as time has gone on I've become more conscious of my intention to communicate through my music. I enjoy composing for people who either aren't professionals or aren't used to contemporary music, and I've recently written a piano concerto for professional pianist and amateur orchestra. I saw no point filling it with complex harmonies that everybody would interpret as a load of wrong notes. And I've just finished a piece whose function is to introduce children aged eight to eighteen to contemporary music, so I thought it was better to veer on the safe side, harmonically, than to write a load of notes that they would be less likely to understand and then might hate. Parts of the piece are very tonal and there are lots of major triads, but you can still do quirky things that make the music interesting and modern. And if you craft a phrase or a series of harmonies well enough, they can directly communicate *something* to most people.

I'm quite happy with the label of 'composer' but the reaction it gets is quite amusing. You can dine out a lot on it, and you can appear much more interesting than you actually are a lot of the time. Of course, people think you just look at the sky and write notes down, whereas in reality it's hard, frustrating work. Although I would never do anything else, I find it's a bit sadistic(!) in a way, because a lot of the time I don't really enjoy it. It's crazy: something that I love doing so much but find so difficult. That's not strictly true, because things 'click' after a while and I find myself writing quickly after what seems like an age of procrastination, obsessive e-mail checking and Internet shopping. But for most of the time I find it very hard to concentrate on composing.

When I begin work on a new piece I feel really inspired and I write a lot of word notes. But when I have to start the musical notes I panic, and usually I procrastinate for a week. Once I've got going I'm usually okay, but I need to start well in the morning, otherwise the whole day goes to pot. And I have to have a pretty similar routine, too. This is probably because I've been spoilt – during my PhD I literally had nothing to do except compose and go to the odd lecture, so I didn't have to structure my time. These days I find that if I have a few days off it takes me quite a while to get back into the work. I don't know how people do other things at the same time as composing, or how they can be both composers and performers.

When a piece is underway I'm fairly disciplined: work in the morning, gym or out somewhere around lunchtime, and more work in the afternoon. I try to treat it like a 9–5 job, and unless it's going appallingly I sit at the piano even if I'm not feeling inspired. When I'm just putting notes on Sibelius I can sit there for hours at a time, but when I'm composing it's rare for me to have more than ten minutes of unbroken concentration. So it's ten minutes on and two minutes off, throughout most of the day. Having said that, I sing a lot when I compose, and if I'm writing a particularly passionate song I'll sing my guts out, which I suppose isn't something that one can do for hours without a break.

My music tends to change time signature a lot, and I often improvise rhythms that I don't consciously understand. So I spend a lot of time working out what the bar lengths will be so that I can put down on paper what I've heard in my head. I love the craftsmanship of composing – working out what note goes where, and who will play what. One thing I've learned is to never finish a section of music at the end of the day. If I do that and have to start a new section the following morning I mess around delaying things for much longer because I start to panic. I think I'm secretly petrified that I'll never be able to compose anything ever again. Certainly, when I finish a piece I look at it in disbelief, wondering how the hell I managed to get it all down on paper. It's unfortunate, really: I spend all my time thinking that I'm not being productive enough, and then (as recently), when I'm confronted with the evidence of a one-hundred-page score, I'm slightly incredulous.

Luckily I don't get lonely, because composing is a very solitary activity, and the busier you get the more cut off you can become. I was struck, when doing some proofreading for a week or so, how lonely I got, and then I realised that this never happens when I'm composing, or at least when composing is going well. It's partly because I make noises on the piano and partly because I'm so absorbed in what I'm doing – when I'm not more absorbed in being unable to concentrate on what I'm supposed to be doing, that is! I still don't know what the perfect solution is. I do some teaching, which I mostly enjoy, but I'm not a natural teacher. Again, I can't really win: when I have to teach regularly I moan about it; but in the holidays, I miss it – well, some of the time. Later this year I'm helping to produce a CD of someone else's music, and hopefully there'll be more things like that to break the solitude of composing.

Just after finishing a piece I can usually both hear the music and see the score in my head. But with some pieces, the memory of the structuring and planning is stronger. I'm thinking of a piece from 2004 which I can't sing through in my head any more although I can remember the amount of pre-composition that went into it. With more intuitively written pieces I'd hear the sound of the music in my head. And I remember the emotions of a piece after the visual image of the score and the exact notes have gone from my memory.

One of my friends, who's a performer, says he believes that until the moment when he walks out on stage he can probably still make the piece better; but as a composer you can't do anything about it at the performance because the work's already been done. So I'm worried – to a ridiculous degree – about my song cycle being performed in Leeds shortly. I'm paranoid about what people will think of it, because my music's quite unusual – it's more traditionally modern than what most of my contemporaries are writing. But I never revise anything I write, because I spend such a long time composing (each bar takes ages and ages) that when I've finished a piece I'm usually happy with it. And, to be honest, if I weren't, I'm not sure that I'd be bothered to alter it. It would depend on how recently I'd written it, I think.

When I go to a rehearsal of a piece I've recently finished I have very strict ideas about its intepretation. But after a year or so, when the piece has gone out there and there's more space between it and me, I become much more relaxed about it. People can play things at different tempos (obviously, only to a degree) and I don't mind. Performing my work so much in my composing room, and having been a performer myself, helps to eliminate any massive surprises. But I may think differently when I've written a huge orchestral piece or an opera.

I'm pretty comfortable with the public aspect of being a composer, really. I don't mind being the centre of attention! Premieres get you out of the house, let you meet lots of lovely and interesting people and allow you to buy more dresses and shoes than would otherwise be permissible. And that suits me very well indeed!

It's great if composers can get out there and do workshops and pre-concert talks, and talk to children about what it's like to be a composer. Just the fact that you're not dead is often a shock to people, and I think that if you're approachable this makes your music more approachable. And I've found that nobody expects composers to be particularly outgoing or socially adept, so there's never very much pressure. But I haven't really done much public stuff other than going to premieres, where everybody's nice to me. I was trained as a performer, so I've been doing the big-smile-and-bow thing since I was little. I get incredibly nervous about giving pre-concert talks, because I'm not used to verbalising about my music and I don't know how to even describe it; but when you've spent six months alone in your room with no reassurance whatsoever, it's quite nice just to lap up the attention. After the composer awards I got a fair amount of publicity and was on the cover of BASCA magazine; I feigned embarrassment and modesty but secretly loved it!

Being a composer has also helped me to come out of myself because of things I've had to do. For example, I won a prize in Florida and as a result I had to give an hour-and-a-half lecture. I'd never spoken in front of *anyone* before, but I wasn't going to turn down the prize because of that. So if being a composer involves becoming more confident in order to do certain things, fine! I know that I'm quite young to have this CD of my music out, but it's only because I raised all the money (about £11,000) to fund it. It nearly killed me and it took up a ridiculous amount of time, and I had to be really quite business-minded about something that's completely un-businesslike – and unprofitable! I remember feeling very self-conscious about blowing my own trumpet in that way, but then everybody else is blowing theirs.

I'm very determined not to run out of work, and I'm aware that in order to get jobs and apply for things you have to kind of turn on the charm. I'm very good at completing application forms, and I know several people who probably aren't so successful just because they can't fill in things for a deadline. Professionally, I've always been very pragmatic, and I lived at home while I was doing my PhD and saved up so that I could put down a deposit on a house. But I'm an only child, and my mother has been ridiculously supportive. I feel quite guilty now about her being almost shut in one room of the house a lot of the time while I was writing. We didn't do *anything* in the holidays. And it was probably only about five years ago that I became truly self-sufficient.

I've been so lucky: since I was eighteen I haven't written anything that wasn't commissioned, apart from an orchestral piece that I needed in order to balance my PhD portfolio. People ask me if there's a dream piece I'd write if I could, and of course I'd like to write a big orchestral piece. But that's unlikely to happen at this stage of my career. If I didn't have any commissions I probably wouldn't write *anything* for at least six months, mainly because I've never had a proper break from composition. And then, I'm sure, I'd be desperate to write something and so would write outside of commissions. The truth is that I find a deadline and a brief really inspiring.

I do find myself getting busier and busier. I'm currently in a two-year post as DARE Cultural Fellow with Leeds Uni and Opera North, and as part of this I've taught one day a week and organised a concert, which took up an inordinate amount of time. Nowadays – thrillingly – more people are commissioning me who either have the money already or are willing to apply for it themselves. So recently most of my non-composing time has been spent proofreading scores for publication or teaching. I've yet to find the right balance between composing and non-composing activities, I think. I spend a *lot* of time writing e-mails about projects, but that's quite fun.

There's something in all types of music, I believe, and I almost use it as a drug. It's almost alarming how music can induce more powerful feelings in me than the rest of life does – this is either a big plus or a big minus, depending on how you look at it. Because I went to the Menuhin School so young I was very sheltered, musically, and I didn't hear any pop music till I was about fifteen. Although I like the way that you can evoke any emotion you want in classical music, I also like the energy and the directness of pop music. It's less complex than classical music, a fair amount of the time, but it has a kind of visceral impact, and so I like the idea of taking some of that into contemporary classical music without dumbing it down in any way. I like everything, basically, apart from painfully inane pop music with *truly* diabolical lyrics, or anything that's ridiculously pretentious for no discernible reason. If I hear certain harmonies or certain colours that I like, then I like them wherever they come from.

One of my friends was talking to a very eminent composer at Cambridge and asked him, 'Do you know Cheryl?' He replied, 'Oh yes, she's that girl who never listens to anybody and does what the hell she wants.' And I do have a reputation for not giving a toss what anybody thinks. I've always just got on quietly with things, and I've never written anything that I felt I *ought* to write. I didn't come into composing because I liked contemporary music, and my own music isn't wildly rebellious. But I've been lucky that other people like what I do. A lot of people come up to me and say that although they didn't think they liked modern music they really enjoyed mine. And my CD was classical chamber music choice in *BBC Music Magazine*! I don't know what I would have done if it had been universally panned. Maybe, if I found that listeners suddenly hated my music, I would find myself consciously changing it. I'm not interested in writing pieces that don't get performed. But it's impossible to appeal to everybody, and while I want my music to appeal to as many people as possible, I'm not willing to lose subtlety or necessary complexity.

My music is naturally quite accessible. I don't think it's particularly super-*now* – it's not very fashionable, or of the moment. But I'm under no illusion that it's mass-market stuff. And, to be honest, I try not to think about this too much as I know I just have to write. So I try to put my head in the sand in order to protect my sanity. Composing is so important to me that I don't want to think about things that might make me believe otherwise. I'm aware that this is a bit selfish and a bit ignorant, but there's the whole question of 'Why write music when there's enough already?' Certain aspects of composing *are* very selfish, and I probably *could* do something more helpful to society. But I don't think too much about how useful or useless writing music is, because I don't want anything to undermine my faith in its importance. Otherwise I might stop. And I don't want to stop!

Alexander Goehr

Alexander Goehr, Cambridgeshire, February 2013

❝Listening to music is a leisure activity, so I don't see any moral imperative to it.❞

I wasn't exactly nervous about meeting Alexander Goehr but I was prepared to be intimidated by his reputation. The son of the conductor and Schoenberg pupil Walter Goehr (1903–1960), he became a central figure in New Music Manchester, the group of avant-garde composers and performers who, while studying at the Royal Manchester College of Music (now part of the Royal Northern College of Music) in the 1950s, sought to radicalise the post-war renewal of British music. And from the late 1960s until his retirement thirty years later he taught composition at the universities of Boston, Yale, Southampton, Leeds and Cambridge (his list of students includes Julian Anderson, George Benjamin and Robin Holloway). A senior figure in the musical establishment, then; and, to someone largely outside it, not the most obviously approachable.

On the other hand, his music had suggested to me an element of moderation, as if his desire for progressiveness is tempered by an acknowledgement of the need for intelligibility. I certainly didn't feel that it could be described as 'uncompromising' in the same way that the works of his fellow 'Manchester School' composers Birtwistle and Maxwell Davies could. And this is confirmed by some of his public statements, for example the open letter to Pierre Boulez in which he argued, 'If one wishes, one can just say that music has to be autonomous and self-sufficient; but how to sustain such a view when people who sing for pleasure are deprived of true satisfaction in the performance of new work?'[1] When I discovered that he'd told the journalist and broadcaster Tom Service that his academic reputation was 'all bullshit',[2] I was optimistic about my encounter with him.

Sure enough, when we met at his home – a seventeenth-century cottage

---

[1] Alexander Goehr, 'A Letter to Pierre Boulez', *Finding The Key: Selected Writings of Alexander Goehr*, ed. Derrick Puffett (London, Faber & Faber, 1998), p. 16.
[2] Tom Service, 'Alexander Goehr Takes on *King Lear* for His Swansong', *The Guardian*, 23 September 2010.

in a village near the Cambridgeshire/Suffolk border – in February 2013 he was welcoming, patient, unstuffy and jocular. Over coffee in the living room he asked me to tell him all about myself and then explained that, as with all interviews, he would answer my questions as directly as possible. He added that he is prone to indiscretion (a number of his subsequent comments were indeed prefaced by 'This is not for your book, but ...') and that he would therefore like to approve his edited contribution. I began by asking him whether he has much contact with amateur music lovers – bums on seats or CD buyers; and, expecting him to express intolerance of those who have little time for contemporary music, I was surprised by his response.

After the interview we moved across the entrance hall into his study so that he could pose for a photo. On one wall was a framed, signed musical scribble by Messiaen, but he chose to sit next to a photograph of Schoenberg surrounded by his students, including the young Walter Goehr. 'My wife always complains that I look grumpy in photos,' he remarked, 'so I'd better keep her happy and smile for you.'

Oh yes, many of my friends are bums on seats. But not necessarily on *my* seats. They respectfully acknowledge that I am a composer but they don't necessarily have much time for what I write. Amateurs seem to have a limited range of musical appreciation: it's basically Bach till Britten, and with difficulty and suspicion they listen to other things. I regard them as people who are basically not interested in contemporary music, though I might be wrong. However, I don't entirely argue with the notion that only composers of the past wrote 'proper' music. Perhaps that's true, because the culture of classical music as we know it is based on a musical language which evolved between the seventeenth century and the early twentieth century and then became possibly something else. And listening to music is a leisure activity, so I don't see any moral imperative to it.

There was certainly a time when one wanted to re-educate the audience. In fact, one wanted to re-educate *society*. I wanted to be a revolutionary, I wanted to march with a banner and upset the regime. And I was rather aggressive. But I was young, and I was young at a particular moment in history. I'm still aggressive, actually, but in a slightly different way. Or at least I'm aware of the limitations of my aggression. And these days I'm inclined to look for blame in myself or in what I do rather than in an audience's response to my music. The way that musical culture has developed publicly in terms of live performance is almost entirely bad, and it's clear that modern music isn't doing what it ought to be doing. People can't find in it the signposts which lead them to the perception of the product in such a way that it gives them any aesthetic pleasure. And that's the fault of the music, isn't it? We have to ask ourselves why this is so. What have we done inadequately, that our music doesn't communicate itself?

Incidentally, there's another kind of music lover, whom I must admit to disliking, who exhibits what I call Hot Bath Syndrome: he thinks of music as having one single effect that excites him in a certain way, and he wishes it to have only that effect. I notice this particularly in films, when a director hires a composer because he needs music that's got to last forty-seven seconds, or whatever, and he inevitably has in his mind a piece of music that he has heard recently – it's generally Sibelius, Tchaikovsky or Mahler. And he wants the composer to rewrite *that* piece.

I'm sure it's true that a taste for modern music can be acquired, but it's difficult for me to comment on this because l don't share your musical background. I come from an environment in which modern music – admittedly, modern music of a certain kind – was taken for granted. When I was young, Schoenberg, Stravinsky, Bartók and Webern were familiar names in our house, and Tippett more or less lived with us. My problem was that I didn't know much about the classical repertoire, because my father didn't conduct much of it. Oddly enough, he did mostly modern music and light music, and so that's what the record cupboard at home contained.

However, one has to distinguish between the categories of modern music and contemporary music, because a great deal that's being written now doesn't appear to have any of the premises of modern music at all. Contemporary, as the word indicates, has to do with time, neither more nor less. But modern – in terms of music – belongs to a period which begins about 1910, ends in 1930, more or less, and then revives in the post-war period and lasts until the 1970s. Modern music is a coherent culture which has its own ways of performing and its own repertoire of ideas, and consequently of sound. And it is roughly the culture that I belong to, if I belong to any culture.

There are two types of ideas that made up the repertoire of modernism. The first, which you could say begins with Brahms, is a certain longing for something that appears to have gone: a nostalgia for an uncommercial, pre-industrial life and for a relationship to nature which the ordinary population supposedly had. (Of course, the peasantry lived in nasty homes, ate bad food and *hated* their environment.) In terms of British composers, Elgar – certainly as he is *perceived*, because he's a complicated case, isn't he? – and Britten were largely conditioned by a vision of how music had been and how it should be. Whether it ever *was* like that is another matter. It's not a question of what it was; it's a question of what people *think* it was.

The other, more revolutionary, element was a desire to get away from the heavy rucksack of dead tradition: pastoral posturing, nymphs and shepherds, purple prose and poetry set to music – all the stuff that actually didn't mean anything any more. There was a sense that traditional music was in decay because it was fundamentally false, and we were prepared to say that certain things being taught in the conservatoires at that time were untrue and pointless.

Now, there was a slight difference between early modernism and post-war modernism, if I may just interpose it. The early modernists – up to 1930 – were well educated and superbly trained, technically, but after the War there was a kind of a blank: we had to find out how to do it. Hence the third spirit of modernism, which was a return to fundamentals, cutting off residual received opinions and culture and trying to build it all again. One went back to the year zero, which is what 1945 felt like for most people in Europe, if not in England. Everything had to be re-examined.

I'm now eighty years old, which is a very depressing thing to have to say, and I realise that I know even less than I thought I knew before. What motivates me, I think, is the hope that one of these days I'll find out how to compose. I suppose I'm always trying to do the same thing properly, which may explain why I'm thought of as more traditional than most of my contemporaries. But I know nothing about tradition. I wish I did.

I try to keep myself informed about what's going on musically, but I can't say with much interest. It's more a professional duty. I'm not easily shockable, because the music that I grew up with in the post-war period was, I think, more radical than anything being written now. I'm more easily bored than shocked; and most contemporary music seems rather wishy-washy to me. It's like women's fashions: there used to be long skirts, then there were short skirts and then there were long skirts again. Now, women can wear *any* length of skirt. And anybody who wants to be a composer can be one by saying 'I want to be a composer.'

My main criticism about a great deal of contemporary music is that it's sound-orientated. To me, sound – the external form of a piece – is fool's gold, because in itself it will *never* create great music, or only very occasionally. This is a very traditional thing to say (Stanford could be saying it), but the stuff of music is the thoughts and ideas – proportions, harmony and counterpoint, and so on – *behind* the sound. Great music results from these internal elements working outwards. The other day I was interviewed by a well-known critic who said that he was struck by the imaginative sound world of a particular piece that I'd written, and he was surprised when I told him that I didn't conceive the piece with a sound at all. I conceived it as a piano score in terms of harmony and counterpoint and melody, and it was only later, at the second or third stage of its development, that it got its clothes.

So I don't listen to much music. But I'm very interested in the craft aspect of composition, in how composers of the past did it. So I can be busy listening to one fugue of Bach for a long, long time because I'm trying to find out how it was written. I don't overrate the importance of technique – by which I mean knowing how to write for instruments, how melody's constructed, how to set words and so on. Composers without technique ought to be regarded with deep suspicion, and yet today it's almost a badge of honour. It's the other side of amateurism – which is a negative word only when applied to people who are simply not doing their job properly.

Do I think of myself as a British composer? By background we were half Russian, half German Jewish, and my father had the good fortune to get a job with the Gramophone Company in London in 1932. English was my first language, although I'm quite good at German, too. So the simple answer to your question is: I'm my own biography. You can't become English, but you can get a British passport; and German émigrés used to say that GB stood for *Geworden Britische*! But I don't think of myself in those terms at all.

What was clear, when I was young, was that I wasn't gifted musically in the way that my parents were. And because I was quite good at everything else, my interest in studying composition was regarded by them as a slightly lunatic eccentricity. My father told me, 'You're mad. You can do anything else *except* that.' So I felt that I had to invent it from scratch, because I didn't know anything. And one of the peculiar characteristics of English cultural life is that if you express yourself radically enough you get a job. I became an academic not because I have any degree – I haven't even got a BA. I didn't bother to turn up for my finals at university because my feeling was, 'There's nothing I want that they have to offer!' So I didn't go. You kindly addressed me as 'Doctor', and I've got several honorary doctorates, but I never became a doctor as a result of my own efforts. I got a job as a professor at Cambridge because I mocked the establishment – I said that what they were doing was worthless. And as they had more or less come to agree with that point of view they said, 'You'd better come and see if you can do any better.'

It was a time of great change, and people who previously would have been rejected suddenly found their views being listened to. I hit lucky. My father said, 'You mean to tell me that they give you money to write the sort of music you're writing? Schoenberg never got a penny for it.' But society became generous – music in England was in a very good situation in the 1960s and 1970s. And I happily benefited (the price of that was, of course, a decline in the radicalism). That ended with Mrs Thatcher, not because she was a particular kind of music lover but because her views and policies led to bureaucratisation and sterilisation. Things became less exciting. And at Cambridge deeply reactionary points of view which no-one would previously have dared say at high table were expressed. This was when the scorn against modernism started.

I think there are certain crises in the development of modern classical music, and minimalism seems to me a movement which came into existence as a reaction to the complexity of contemporary music. But its origins go back a lot further. Orff was writing minimalist pieces in the 1930s, and you could say that *The Rite of Spring* has elements of minimalism in its repetitive structures. They represent that aspect of modernism which I describe as nostalgia – a kind of doffing their hat to simpler music of the past.

I'm always reacting against the complexity of modern music. When I'm sitting in the room next door, where I do my composing, I'm perpetually saying, 'Wouldn't it be better to repeat this chord or this rhythm more times, in order that people might grasp it?' After all, I sit there, repeating it over and over again until it's in my ear, but they'll hear it only once. On the other hand, I don't write for audiences. My pieces of paper mean nothing to them. In the first instance I write for the performers who play or sing my music, because it's *they* who communicate with audiences. I'm not conscious of trying to express any particular aspect of my personality, and I'm not trying to change the world through my music. I don't think I would succeed even if I *did* want to change it. But I'm aware that, because of CDs and the Internet, performers now reach many more people than they do in a concert, where people who hear a new piece only once get little from it.

I rarely go to concerts myself because I hate them so much. I wouldn't even go to performances of my own music if this weren't impolite. First of all, I'm nervous. Then my attention is almost always on looking at a pretty girl or being irritated by someone sitting in the row in front of me, nodding their head out of time with the music. And often the audience is full of other composers who want to have *their* pieces played and who don't care what you're doing. Of course, someone occasionally says something genuine which moves me and makes me think, but I don't read the critics and so I have no idea what they say about my work.

My favourite form of music-making is in the recording studio. It's mostly been Olly Knussen who has conducted my pieces recently, and he knows more about them than I do. So he and I never sit down with the scores to discuss my intentions; I go to the rehearsal and it's all fine. When I've got him and the performers he works with regularly we reach a level where my piece becomes more or less the piece that I wrote; whereas when it's performed in a concert hall it's half or possibly slightly more than half of the piece that I wrote. But I don't feel that I know everything about my own music. In fact, I don't know *anything* about it because I don't know it. Once the performance is over, it's over. Pieces either disappear and catch dust or they get performed occasionally; and I don't follow them.

The contemporary musical world is organised in order that there should be perpetual new pieces, but this contradicts everything that the composer is trying to do. I try to write a piece that can be repeated five hundred times, but it's played only once. I had a very wealthy friend who knew a lot about contemporary music and who told me, 'Every so often I go to the CD shop and look to see what's new, and I come back with twenty-five CDs. Over the next few days I play them all – or however much I can stand of them – and when I've done that, I throw them away.' I said, 'That's a fine description of your leisure life, but it makes what I do completely pointless!' And this is why I hide behind the performers. I say that if a piece of mine is well written for them, and if they don't dislike it, it's good enough.

You suggest that my music is known *of* rather than known, and the obvious, cynical explanation is that I'm not good at show business. Maybe I'm prejudiced against the people who run the music profession, but I don't feel that they have any views about the music at all. Meanwhile there's all sorts of ways for composers to get themselves known, and some are particularly bad at it. I know some who are deeply hurt because they want to be popular but aren't; I suppose I deeply *don't* want to be popular! And in this I'm probably helped by the fact that I was at Cambridge for so many years. It's perhaps perceived as a form of elitism which defies popularity.

In fact, I taught people long before I had a job as a teacher. When I returned to England from Paris and joined Morley College I probably inspired Max and Harry – they brought me their pieces to comment on. (I didn't bring them mine. For some reason, that's how it was.) And we were playing a stupid adolescent game of being the Second Viennese School: I was pretending to be Schoenberg and they were pretending to be Berg and Webern. Since then they've been promoted much more than I have, but maybe they're better composers. Who knows?

I admire Ligeti and Kurtág very much but, like all Hungarian composers, they had extremely fixed ideas about how their pieces should be performed (Bartók specified 'Two minutes, nine seconds' at the end of a piece from *Mikrokosmos*). I used to specify too much; then I learned to cut it out because I became more interested in seeing what happens when a piece is performed. Perhaps I'm too un-prescriptive now, but for me the act of composition and then hearing a piece for the first time should always be a discovery. If it's *not* a discovery, it's like filling in your income tax return, isn't it?

A piece of music changes during the period between writing it and hearing it performed. And hearing it colours the intentions you had about it. When I was young I used to remember my pieces only as they sounded in performance, and to me they often sounded quite awful because by then I'd forgotten why I wrote them. So I used to revise a lot, but then found that I was spoiling my pieces. Nowadays I tend to leave them alone once the act of composing (which in itself includes continual revision) is complete, because it's so easy to spoil.

Music must always be new, but whether or not one is *original* is in one's genes. I haven't the least idea whether what I do is original, but it surely should be *inventive* because otherwise it's going to be boring. I'm more interested in your use of the word 'concession', because for the composers of the generation before me – Liz Lutyens, for example – it was very fashionable to talk about *never* making concessions or compromises of any kind. I remember going to visit Schoenberg's widow, long ago, and being presented, after a rather drunken dinner, with a Photostat score of his *Jacob's Ladder*, on which she wrote, 'For Sandy Goehr, *kein Kompromiss!*' I just laughed, because the composer is trying to compromise all the time. *All* art is a concession or a compromise. I always say, rather rudely, that I'm longing to be a prostitute but nobody ever asked me!

Of course, there are certain compromises which are very ugly. When an artist tries to communicate an effect that he has anticipated, that's propaganda, a form of compromise that I despise.

I have to have an idea of the piece I'm going to write, but then I have to get rid of that idea because otherwise I'm in the business of trying to fulfil an intention which is already formed. In other words, I have to destroy something in myself in order to write successfully. I have an idea, the idea dissipates itself and I just write dots on paper. And it's an article of faith that those dots somehow represent the original intention. But I don't know *how* they do that. I'm deeply committed to unintentionality and chance – not chance in the sense of dear Mr Cage, who was too naturalistic about it, but in allowing the mind to operate freely. Francis Bacon said that when something dripped onto his canvas he didn't remove it; he made it part of the picture. Well, I drip onto *my* canvas, and it becomes part of the music.

I sometimes have the feeling that when the act of composition is successful the piece is writing itself. And I just go with it, even though this doesn't necessarily mean that the piece will be successful. Otherwise, there's a procedure to follow and signals to obey, because it's very difficult to get rid of a piece once you've started to write it. I live with it until it either gives me up or I give *it* up. Some pieces refuse to be written – they die on me. Everything suddenly goes wrong and the pencil won't sharpen. Sometimes I know as soon as I begin work in the morning that it's not going to be successful, and then I start writing the same bit over and over again in slightly different forms, only to find that the original form was better.

I hate posturing and I hate trying to cut a figure of a certain kind. When I was teaching at Cambridge and going about my business – attending meetings, seeing various people, teaching here, giving a lecture there – I was unaware of myself; but obviously, if I'd thought about it rationally, I would have realised that people couldn't *not* know who I was. I was Head of the Faculty. But I'm invisible to myself. If I attend a public event, I'm just doing my job. And when I'm interviewed by Mr Service or whoever, I just try to answer questions as I'm trying to answer yours – so as not to be foolish. I'd rather not be a personality.

The only work of mine that my father conducted was *The Deluge*, a cantata with a small instrumental ensemble. It was the first piece of mine that was successful, and I remember going to the BBC studios in Farringdon where it was rehearsed. Standing next to me in the lift was a famous trumpeter called Harold Jackson, who was obviously very embarrassed because he realised that he had to say something to this young composer but didn't know what – he presumably knew nothing about me and had simply been booked for the performance.

Eventually, when we got to the top floor and the doors opened, he turned to me and said, 'Good tune.'

I love that story because that's all I want to be, as a composer: I want Harold Jackson to say to me, 'Good tune.' Pleasure is what music is for – it's one of the many advantages of our culture. And I see no differentiation whatsoever between pleasures of the mind and pleasures of the heart – except that, as I'm just out of hospital with a pacemaker, my irregularity of heartbeat has been removed and from now on I'll write only in 4/4 and 3/4!

Howard Goodall

Howard Goodall, London, September 2014

> **My attitude is that I write things because I'm asked to and that I want to make them better than they're expected to be.**

There's a sense in which Howard Goodall can be thought of as a very modern composer: he has a high media profile and a number of musical constituencies. Most readers will have heard some of his theme music for television programmes, which include *Blackadder*, *Mr Bean*, *Q.I.*, *Red Dwarf* and *The Vicar of Dibley*. Many will have watched some of his television documentaries about musical history and theory, and many are likely to have heard some of his choral music, much of it written after he was appointed Classic FM's Composer in Residence in 2009. Fewer, perhaps, will be familiar with his work for the stage and musical theatre, even though he has been active in that field for more than thirty years.

What became obvious as soon as the following encounter began is his down-to-earth approach to the act of composing: he believes in honing his craftsmanship rather than consciously pursuing art. It's from the former, he suggests, that the latter is most likely to emerge. Before I interviewed him I was unsure whether I should refer to him as a 'commercial composer', but he soon used the term of himself and I imagine that he wouldn't object to the title 'jobbing musician'. To some extent, in fact, he sees this as the historical norm for composers, even the 'greats' of the pre-modern era.

Seeing composition in this historical context allows him to make an unlikely connection between Monteverdi and *Britain's Got Talent*: 'Monteverdi composed his choral masterpiece, the Vespers of 1610, to win a competition to become Director of Music at St Mark's Basilica in Venice, the biggest job in music at the time', he has explained elsewhere, adding that 'all of the famous French composers of the 19th and early 20th centuries … started their careers by entering and hoping to win the Prix de Rome composing competition'.[1]

In keeping with the collaborative and corporate nature of his career, his regular working day is spent not at home but in an anonymous studio/

---

[1] Music for Youth Schools' Prom programme, November 2009.

office in a business centre in south-west London, surrounded by similar units occupied by accountants, architects and property management companies. When I interviewed him there in September 2014 he was relaxed, confident and talkative. 'When I was younger', he told *The Guardian* in February 2009, 'I was impatient, impetuous and arrogant, which affected the way I wrote. I had too much swagger. Some people would say I still do.' This wasn't my experience of him, but he was certainly opinionated and full of energy. Before the interview he half-ran down the stairs to greet me, and after it he half-ran back up them, calling out 'Nice to talk to you, Andrew!' in order to check his e-mails before lunch.

His roles as a writer and television presenter seem to me well defined: they're essentially revelatory, in the sense that he uses his insight and communicative skills to reveal why and how music has some of the effect on us that it does. So I began the interview by asking him whether he's aware of his music, too, having a particular purpose or function.

───

There's an approach to music in which the composer feels such a need to express himself through his chosen medium that he would do it no matter who asked him (or didn't ask him) to. But while I feel I have to express myself through music – that's absolutely true – I don't now write anything that hasn't been commissioned for some function or purpose. And I haven't done for a long time. I realise that to some extent this is a luxury, because I'm sufficiently in demand to be able to make a living from writing music; but I consider myself, as a composer, to be a craftsman, and I don't see the point of writing music that no-one will hear. I think it's also a kind of philosophical conviction, in that I like to convert my need for self-expression into something that will be beneficial to somebody else. But I don't have a world-spinning-around-me view that my music is needed by anybody other than the people who *say* they need it. I don't think it's somehow locked into a treasure trove of posterity that someone will one day discover and find wonderful. I'm more practical than that. And in learning about composers of the past I've found this view widespread.

Handel and Bach, for example, weren't particularly precious about what they did, and they were very pragmatic about *why* they did it. They wrote pieces because they were asked to and because the music had a function to fulfil. And they weren't overly distressed by the idea that a piece would be heard over two weekends and might not then be heard again for a while, if ever. It's shocking to us, in a way, that they might have thought this, because we consider their music to be so wonderful. But I believe that they saw themselves as craftsmen doing a job that was necessary, and which they did as well as they possibly could. That's not to say that they weren't divinely inspired or had tremendous creative freedom. But what they came up with was often so much better than it needed to be!

I remember reading in H. C. Robbins Landon's book about Mozart's last year[2] about the five-hundred-or-so tunes that he composed for the dance mania that had gripped the ballrooms of Vienna, and a comment to the effect that this was a terrible shame – that he shouldn't have wasted his time writing such music. I think that's very much a commentator's perspective. I doubt that Mozart was thinking, 'This is the best music I've ever written', but I don't think *he* would have felt that it was a waste of his time. He did the work properly and seriously because it was something that he could earn money from and something that gave people joy.

As a composer, you can do that type of work well, indifferently or badly – it's up to you. But it's very dissatisfying to just spin it off so that you can go and write what you *really* want to write. You should treat every job as equally important. So my attitude is that I write things because I'm asked to and that I want to make them better than they're expected to be. And this applies almost across the board, including writing the theme tune for a TV programme – I feel that a thirty-second TV theme should be as interesting and as fine, in the form that it's in, as possible. In the last few weeks my big projects have been a choral work in two languages to commemorate the hundredth anniversary of the beginning of the First World War, performed at St Symphorien military cemetery in Belgium by a German choir, an English choir and the band of the Coldstream Guards; music for fifty-two ten-minute animated *Mr Bean* films; and a West End stage musical of *Bend It Like Beckham*. Those three things are about as different from each other as it's possible to be, but I don't see them in a hierarchy of importance. I just do the things that need to be done each day, with as much seriousness and attention to detail as the next.

I'm aware that my Requiem, <u>Eternal Light</u>, has been a great help to some people, and I know this because they've written to me or have told me at performances. But that function of the piece is actually a by-product, because I wrote it as a ballet for the Rambert Dance Company. I didn't sit up one day and think, 'A twenty-first-century requiem needs to exist, and it needs to be written by *me*'; someone

---

[2] *1791: Mozart's Last Year* (London, Schirmer/Macmillan, 1988).

asked me to write a piece and suggested a requiem. I thought a great deal about the point of a requiem today (there are quite a few already in the repertoire, obviously!) as we move into a sort of post-religious age, and I made some decisions about what and who the piece was for. I'm not interested in saving people from Purgatory, because I don't believe that's what happens, but I *am* interested in the living who are dealing with loss and grief and in how they cope with the shocking and appalling reality of interrupted lives.

It's very reassuring that the intention and outcome of that piece have become aligned. But it might have been the case that I wanted it to be comforting and that no one found it to be so; it might also have been the case that I hadn't intended it to be comforting but that it *was*. That's the extraordinary thing about music: its effect is unpredictable. It may make people feel more whole in their experience of life, it may address a spiritual need of some kind, it may help people to root themselves to their background and it may relate to their place in society or their self-determination. But I think it's unwise for the composer to assume that it'll have any effect at all. That's up to the listener, not the creator.

I also think that composers are the *worst* people to describe their own music. I can say what I think are the primary ingredients of the recipe for mine – for example, I believe that Kurt Weill has been a big influence on my musical theatre work – but they might not be identifiable to anybody else who tastes the finished cake. I suppose that if I were to describe my music in crude terms, I'd say that it's usually very (diatonically) melodic but that my harmonic language can be a little more complex than a lot of the music into which category I might be put. So while my choral music could be put into a broad category alongside, say, Lauridsen, Whitacre and Rutter, I'd tentatively suggest that mine is slightly less harmonically *calm* than theirs can be. When I'm writing a song I'm not content with a good tune; I'm thinking, 'Where can I go with this? What can I do to underpin the melody, change it, overlay it?' The grittiness and complexity of my musicals, if I can bracket them, is probably closer to an Anglo-version of Bernstein than to Rodgers and Hammerstein; so I don't quite fit in *there*, either. But I've inherited the building blocks of counterpoint and polyphony from my choral background and my classical training, and I can't *not* put them into my music.

You can probably detect an Englishness about it, although I think it's probably fairer to talk about an Anglo-Celtic flavour. Like a lot of British composers of my generation, I'm steeped in that. My favourite composer is probably Mahler, but I think it's quite hard to detect *his* influence on my music – although it could be in there somewhere. And I'm probably more interested in pop music than many of my classical counterparts are – I'm as likely to listen to hip-hop or Sting or Stevie Wonder in my car as to anything classical. I enjoy them all equally. So you see, I'm struggling a bit, because I'm trying to identify the ingredients of my music.

You mentioned the influence of minimalism in my suite *The Seasons*, which is a piece that originated on television. It's no coincidence, I think, that minimalism has arisen at a time when film and TV have become central to mainstream music-making. Since the 1970s the cutting and production of films has increasingly been determined by their pictorial rhythms – for which regular, repeated musical patterns are very useful. So while Philip Glass didn't start out by writing film scores, what he does in that context works well, partly because a composer can't be too proactive in a scene that contains action and dialogue. Film music is automatically self-limiting in content – if it's too busy it doesn't work because it requires too much concentration on itself. And a lot of film soundtracks have become little more than minimalism orchestrated on a large scale. Hans Zimmer, for example, does a Philip Glass kind of thing but with massive forces. The repetitive quality of minimalism is certainly in the DNA of the moment, and it will change, as all fashions do. But one reason why I sometimes stray into that territory is that it's very useful shorthand when writing film or TV music.

I've recently started to explore music for video games. And I'm interested to find that it's much more experimental than film music because its composers are allowed long periods of time in which to play around. In contrast, most decisions in the film music world are made by people who aren't musicians. To them, the status of the composer is relatively low, which is why a lot of mainstream film music can be limited in its scope.

Experience has shown me that you can never second-guess what listeners will like. If I write a musical of twenty songs I'll have my own two or three favourites but they're never the same two or three that the public prefers! And when you *think* you're composing The Great Tune, you're probably not; it could result simply from writing what feels right at that moment. However, I'm very rarely the only arbiter of the finished product because I work mostly in collaboration with other people. And where I differ from most composers who work in a more abstract classical genre is that when they finish a piece there's a sort of reverence about it being complete – it can't then be tweaked or changed, because that's *it*. In my world, it's never like that. I've always got to expect someone to say, 'That's lovely, but it's not really working for us; can you do something different?' Or even something as specific as 'It's four bars too long.' So I start where I have to start, and I write the piece I have to write; but if someone then asks me for an extra movement I'm perfectly at ease with discovering that it's *not* finished after all.

Much of my work also has a third-party element. It might be a story or a moving picture; it might be a conflict in a narrative; it might be a lyric or a text. And I rarely, if ever, sit down and think of music that's isolated from those ingredients. What normally happens is that the overall sound comes to me almost fully formed, and I'll break it down in order to create the piece's shape and form. Although I've never done any sculpture, I like the metaphor of chipping away to reveal what's inside the block of stone. And quite often I can endlessly chip away and replace the stone before going back to change the shape. All my big choral pieces – the Requiem and the King James Bible oratorio, *Every Purpose Under the Heaven*, for example – had major changes wrought because of the interaction with collaborating partners, and much of my work ends up as an amalgamation of my instinct and other people's instincts.

Usually, the problem is length – particularly in film and TV, where you might write a piece lasting for thirty-two seconds that has to go down to *twenty*-two. In such a short piece, that's a huge difference. And the process of honing down your material is very tough on your initial musical instinct, because you want a piece to unfold slowly and gradually, and there's almost *never* time for that. So you've always got to find a more economical way to achieve what you want to achieve. This is an everyday reality in my writing, which is why I don't recognise what some composers would call the 'winning moment'. Even if that's what it is, it's probably going to have to be half the length!

If you'd asked me at sixteen, when I started composing in earnest, what I really wanted to do professionally, it would have been to write pop songs and have a hit. But that didn't work out. It was eight years after I left college before I could support myself from composing, and if that hadn't happened soon afterwards I might have trained to become a music director in a school (I come from a family of teachers) in order to bring some stability to my life. In fact, not knowing what's going to happen next has been a norm for me, and it has been fine. At first I worked as a session player, a synthesiser programmer and anything and everything else that helped to make ends meet. And I think that's the deal, really. Anybody who can come straight out of college and be a professional composer is very unusual. I told myself that something would work out, and I hoped for the best.

In my mid-twenties I wrote and played music for comedy shows but I didn't envisage a point when I would actually be *making* TV programmes. I never would have guessed that that would interest me, even though I've always had a teacherly approach to music and have often felt that it isn't explained very well to music lovers who don't have a degree in the subject. What I like most about making my programmes is the research, and what I like least is actually filming them. But that's the gig, and if you don't have enthusiasm for your subject it's very hard to make anybody else love it. In the world of TV and film the way you communicate with colleagues is very important because a lot of your success depends on description, discussion and negotiation of your plans. But there are two sides to my character, and a lot of the time I'm in shut-down mode. When I'm composing I retreat into the music and I can't be too gregarious.

My favourite time to compose is around six o'clock in the morning when everything's completely still, and I'm usually here in the studio, working, by eight. I continue methodically through normal office hours and I try not to work in the evenings unless I absolutely have to. I also spend quite a lot of time in our house in France, where I have another studio and office. The animated films I'm doing at the moment require me to work here in London because I compose and record the music at the same time, using my virtual instruments. And it's a very slow process, working with the pictures in front of me and composing in real time, as it were, thirty seconds by thirty seconds. Most of my other music is written at all times of day and night – often in the night, actually, just lying in bed and manipulating the sounds that I'm imagining. I might sit at the piano and play a song through after I've thought of it, but this is only to make sure that it's singing well and to work out the accompaniment.

I used to compose at the piano, improvising and writing down something if I liked it, but in my thirties I taught myself to compose in my head. One reason is that the muscle memory in your hands makes them return to the same chords and the same progressions on the keyboard. There are piano-ish harmonies that are very difficult to avoid. Stephen Sondheim has said that *he* stopped writing at the piano because his right hand was much stronger than his left hand; the only way that he could avoid dissatisfaction with the bass lines of his work was to get away from the piano and the dominance of the right hand. If I hadn't taken this on board, a lot of the music I've written during the last twenty years would have been restricted by being written at the piano. *Bend It Like Beckham*, for example, has a piano accompaniment and a piano rehearsal score but a lot of its music is generated by instruments such as the *dhol* drum that you can't really 'do' on the piano; and if I hadn't written it in my head, it would have come out as too pianistic.

I can probably now get up to about forty-five minutes of music in my head while I'm working on a piece. That's the length of *Eternal Light: A Requiem*, all of which I kept in my head for about two months before putting it down on the page. And the odd thing is that once a piece is written down it clears itself from my mind, apart from the odd detail. So if I come back to it six months later it's like seeing a piece composed by someone else. Most peculiar feeling! And when I conduct one of my pieces I have to have the score in front of me.

A composer's career path is defined by setback as much as by success. You have to accept that you won't get certain jobs, that some things won't work out and that certain commissions won't lead to anything else. It's also important not to judge yourself by other people's successes; it's simply that they follow different paths. I think the only reason you continue working as a composer is that what you write is appreciated by the people who commissioned it. It's really as simple as that.

I also think it's a mistake to worry too much about originality, because you can't consciously be original; but you sort of *will* be, simply because you *are* original as a human being. Having said that, you have to go a long way to hear a new musical written in either Britain or America during the last twenty-five years that doesn't sound a little or a lot like Sondheim. His influence is so enormous. And in *that* context, being original means not sounding like Sondheim. But I don't think that the few composers who achieve it are thinking, 'I'm going to do something different.' It's just that something has triggered in them a response that moves in an unexpected (to the listener) direction.

Like all composers, I consciously try to avoid cliché and things that other people seem to do all the time. I think we're *all* slightly scared of writing a tune that we've heard before and which has entered the subconscious, and there are some very well-trodden paths in harmony that can easily sound samey. So I hope my *Bend It Like Beckham* will sound different, because I don't want to see another musical that's like all the others. But I may not achieve that. And, in any case, it's for listeners to decide. I don't think a composer can say, 'These two pieces of mine are completely different.' My attitude is that if a piece of mine works, and if people get a lot out of it, it probably doesn't matter how innovative it is. Someone saying, 'Gosh, how original – he's doing *this* ...' is a small kick; the much bigger kick is people finding your work a moving and touching experience.

As a composer, you do what you *can* do, and you end up getting the audiences that suit you. *Eternal Light: A Requiem* is approaching its four-hundredth live performance, and in Britten's centenary year it had more performances than his *War Requiem*; but it hasn't been done at the Proms, it's never broadcast on Radio 3 and it doesn't exist in the world of classical music reviewers. It has found the people – amateur choral societies and orchestras, for example, and their audiences – who enjoy it, and it's important for me not to worry about those for whom it would never be their favourite music. They've got other things to listen to. Besides, if you work in the commercial field, as I do much of the time, you're aware that music is a market and that there are loads of things in it to enjoy. Funnily enough, I sometimes speak to colleagues who write what you might call non-commercial music who would love to be able to support themselves better than they do from the odd commission here and there, and I have to remind myself that they're sometimes envious of my ability to write music that speaks to lots of people. In other words, each of us has our own role to play. And I'm not itching to be someone else.

I imagine that if I were hit by a bus tomorrow the obituary headline would read 'Composer of *Blackadder* theme dead' – which would be quite a harsh sentence, given all the other things I've written. But there are different publics, and I'm aware that I have a reputation in the TV world that's quite distinct from my reputation in music theatre. In terms of TV themes I'm seen as very mainstream, very straight-down-the-middle – you know, populist; whereas an expert on musical theatre will probably think of Howard Goodall as slightly left-field and *not* mainstream. Then there are people who know my work as a TV presenter but don't know my own music; and people who know my TV themes who don't know that I also make TV programmes *about* music, and who don't know that I write choral pieces. As I said earlier, my choral music is probably put into a category with that of John Rutter and similar composers. So I'd like to think that if I *were* hit by a bus, different groups of people would report my passing in different ways!

I certainly feel that my job is to fit into a number of different working set-ups. When I'm writing music for a *Mr Bean* cartoon I'm very much the servant of the comedy and part of a big team that includes fifty animators working around the clock, a group of directors, collaborators and writers, and Rowan Atkinson himself. I'm only one, tiny cog in that wheel. Whereas the composer of a West End musical has a very high status – I'm one of the three most important people in the room, alongside the writer and the director. But being a much bigger cog means greater risk and greater responsibility, because if a big theatre project's a disaster it's going to be worse for me than for most of the other people involved in it.

However, the divisions between the different areas of my work have become less clear over the course of my thirty or so years as a professional composer. For example, I wrote my first musical, *The Hired Man*,[3] in my early twenties as a deliberate change of mood from the satirical work I was doing to earn my living – writing songs for the TV series *Not the Nine O'Clock News* and touring with Rowan Atkinson. I wanted to clear my mind of all that and to write something with a very different point to it. And *The Hired Man* went completely against the tide of what mainstream musicals were thought to be. It's a tough story about working folk in Cumbria during the First World War and the growth of the early trade unions. But when I write musicals *now*, all the other things I've written – choral music, in particular, but also comedy songs – merge promiscuously into the mixture and I feel the weight of my whole background coming to bear.

What I know about music history is that if you try to predict where it's going – how it'll develop and what the Next Big Thing will be – you'll get it wrong. To take one example: the music of a man who lived in Leipzig three hundred years ago is now amongst the most listened to and performed, even in countries that have no cultural connection whatsoever with his. Yet in his lifetime Bach was a nonentity. Okay, a well-known organist in a few towns in north Germany, but by today's standards invisible. His influence on other composers was gradual and surreptitious, and it came to us most of all through the advocacy of Mendelssohn. In other words, he was discovered by a German composer when German music led the way. If he'd been discovered by a Russian or an Argentinian, even at the same juncture in history, the same thing might not have happened. And in the same way that you couldn't have predicted, even a century in advance, that Bach would become a massive figure, you couldn't have predicted the influence of Debussy. The fact that Stravinsky admired him was neither here nor there to normal people, because *they* didn't know who Debussy was.

All that's happening today, I think, is that music is in a period of

---

[3] Adapted from Melvyn Bragg's 1969 novel of the same name and first performed in 1984.

convergence – as it has been many times before, all over the world, when it has changed under a number of influences. But while, in Bach's time, there were only three or four big influences on music, there might be thirty now. In other words, it's the same process but on a bigger scale than before. And I think that composers worry too much about their place in it. It *may* be that Western classical music has had its period of pre-eminence and that it will fit into a wider network of musics – this may simply be what history does. And you can't stop that with public spending, by changing what people do in schools or by controlling the market in order to make people 'artistic'. Music will go in a direction that no-one can control. But why would one not be optimistic? All previous musical convergences have yielded things that we like, and it would be an odd convergence to create a future that was wholly unpleasant. That has never happened before.

Meanwhile, most of the sixty-five million people who live in the United Kingdom don't know who Sir Peter Maxwell Davies is. Despite being a huge figure in the culture of classical music he's not a big figure in the nation's popular culture. He's just another composer. So is Judith Weir, his successor as Master of the Queen's Music. In this sense they're no different from Bach – he was a jobbing composer of his time. And, lo and behold, it turns out that he was such a genius that for centuries his music has been loved by millions of people. That, to me, is both delightful and miraculous. And it doesn't matter how or why it happened!

Christopher Gunning

Christopher Gunning, Hertfordshire, September 2011

> ❛There's absolutely no point in writing a piece of music that doesn't have some sort of strong emotional feeling or intention behind it.❜

Christopher Gunning is known well to musician friends of mine and, like them, I've long admired his music for film and television. But my main reason for wanting to interview him was the emergence of his concert works from what I suspect he still feels is the shadow of his music for the screen. This is largely the result of a series of studio recordings in which he has conducted five of his seven symphonies (he was composing an eighth as this book went to print).

They confirm what he has always known: that his achievements as a film composer don't encourage him to merely dabble, dilettante-like, in symphonic music. He has explained in a number of other interviews that he could and perhaps should have been writing that kind of music from the beginning of his career, and *would* have written it then had it not been for his fears about financial security. Some of today's young composers may not have such fears, or may not have them to such a degree, but since all are at some point required to achieve a balance between artistic creativity and financial survival I thought it would be useful to record in this book the views of someone who followed a commercial path and was subsequently sidetracked professionally for nearly thirty years.

I also wanted to talk to him about his more general relationship to contemporary British music, some of which he believes has baffled and alienated concertgoers by its lack of discernible logic. 'At the same time', he has written,

> I have not relished the thought of being a fuddy-duddy composer writing in worn-out idioms. I suppose I was trying to define a way in which I could write music which communicates directly but is not so hopelessly predictable or slave to the various 'isms' which have cropped up over the past fifty years or so.[1]

[1] 'Symphony no 3, Symphony no 4, Concerto for Oboe and String Orchestra', www.christopher-gunning.co.uk/category/about-my-latest-works/

So I was pleased that in June 2011 he said he would be delighted to contribute to this book. Three months later I interviewed him at his home, a large, detached Edwardian house up a narrow, leafy lane on the outskirts of Watford, Hertfordshire. We talked in his spacious music room on the ground floor in the company of Sasha the border collie, who reluctantly lay down when told to stop distracting me with constant demands for fussing.

His practical, down-to-earth approach to work reminded me of Debbie Wiseman's, although they're very different people and she's never been a frustrated symphonist. Both of them know about the demands of the corporate world, whose preoccupations aren't necessarily artistic, and both are experienced orchestral conductors who I imagine are respected by musicians as team players. Unlike her, however, he now devotes most of his time to writing concert music and only occasionally accepts offers from the film industry. Were this not the case, it occurred to me on my way home after this encounter, I would probably have had to wait much longer to get an interview with him.

Before I left, over lunch prepared by his wife, conversation turned to the role that composers' spouses or partners play in the creative process, and to the notion that, without their practical and moral support, many great pieces of music wouldn't and couldn't have been written. But that'll have to be the subject of another book ...

The reason I'm a composer is that I can't do anything else! And I mean that more seriously than you might think. I seemed to be particularly hopeless at just about everything at school, and indeed was also decidedly average at various other aspects of music. The piano is my main instrument, and I can get around the keyboard, sort of; but I simply didn't think that, in comparison with people I saw around me, I was ever going to make the grade as a performer, at least not without a huge amount of stress. Apart from anything else, I'm far too impatient to sit practising the same blooming thing over and over again for six hours a day. I *hate* practising! The way a composer works, quietly beavering away at home, is much more my thing than going out and displaying myself in front of other people.

I didn't want to be a teacher, either. It had to do with the amount of time and energy that you have to expend in order to be an inspiration to your pupils: how much time is then likely to be left over for your own work? Some composers manage this sort of thing terribly well and enjoy lecturing or being head of a university department, but I wasn't at all sure that I was cut out for it, even though I've always had a strong academic side – in the sense of wanting to know all about the nuts and bolts and the history of music.

So music was really the only option, and composing became the only option within music. In fact, I'd always felt that I *was* a composer. I inherited, by some genetic accident, a very acute ear, which meant that if things were played to me at school I could usually go home and play them myself. And when I was very young I never had any difficulty inventing bits and pieces at the piano. So even when I was a child there was music going on in my head the whole time – and I've never been able to get rid of it!

Having made the decision to become a composer, you have to try to work out how on earth you're going to live in a fairly aggressive capitalist society that has no state subsidies for your work. When you're young with no independent means you have only two choices: one is to become a teacher and the other is to get involved in the media. These are the only ways to make a living as a composer.

I was interested in films and I imagined that I was going to be able to work rather like Richard Rodney Bennett, who became my teacher. I didn't think he was an exception in terms of his life as a composer, and so I imagined that I would work for six months of the year writing film scores when I felt like it (!) and for the other six months fulfil commissions from the London Symphony Orchestra. And that just shows the stupidity of youth, doesn't it? But I was worried sick about earning a living, and after I left college I concentrated on nothing else.

I went round all the London advertising agencies because I'd heard that there was good money to be earned composing for commercials. At the same time, other avenues began to open up as a result of composers putting jobs my way that they didn't want to do themselves. Some of the work was rather menial, but it was a start. Richard Rodney Bennett was particularly helpful because he suggested me for a documentary film, which I thoroughly enjoyed doing. What's more, five or six other documentaries came my way as a result. Richard also involved me in a couple of his own films by giving me arrangements that he didn't want to do. Dudley Moore did the same thing, and John Scott told me all about how the 'business' operated and how I could find work.

Throughout my twenties I continued with media work – commercials, some TV dramas, a few films and arrangements for pop singers. Yes, my symphonies and concertos were lurking in the background, but on the odd occasion that I took them out of the drawer I was too mentally exhausted to work on them. And there was always another 'commercial' job that had to be written for a looming deadline.

Did I want to express anything in particular in my music? Yes, I wanted to express all the things that I saw around me: painful things and beautiful things (by which I mean beauty in nature and beauty in people). But, little by little, I got more involved in the commercial side of composition, writing what began to be called 'applied music'. It seems to me a particularly horrible term, but there we are ...

There was another reason for my getting involved in 'media music,' and it had no bearing on earning a living. It was simply to do with the enjoyment of communicating through music that was performed while it was still hot off the press. I liked the immediacy of it. In a way, it was the modern-day equivalent of a new cantata every Sunday by J. S. Bach, or Haydn at Esterházy or Mozart's latest opera being performed and enjoyed immediately, although I'm not going to pretend for one minute that the music I produced was of anything like the same quality.

What I'm saying is that <u>communication</u> through music is all-important. It's everything. And although there are plenty of people who bullshit in the film business, there's one way in which the composer can't. Crucially, does the music *work*? Is it suitable for this particular scene or production? Does it have the right tone? Is it too depressing or too cheerful?

Now, I couldn't compose movie music in an idiom that wasn't readily understandable, and I've carried much the same thinking over to my serious music. A lot of composers write music that nobody seems to understand, not even the people playing it, and I don't know what to make of some of it. It's weird. People will go and hear a whole evening of what I think is complete tosh and then they'll write about it in the same glowing terms as something I think is wonderful.

When you look at the twelve-note system that Schoenberg invented, there isn't really very much to it. Basically, what you're doing is repeating a series of notes over and over again, manipulating them forwards, backwards or upside-down, and making chords out of them. But it seems to me that atonal music had one basic problem, which was largely unaddressed, and that was *harmony*. The plain fact of the matter is that we hear music vertically as well as horizontally, and so a lot of the music written using the twelve-tone technique without any real consideration of what was going on vertically simply doesn't work.

A friend of mine demonstrated this rather amusingly by playing three atonal pieces simultaneously. The result sounded just like a lot of contemporary works, which sort of proved that we listen to that kind of music in a particular way. And actually, when we've listened to it for a while we don't want to listen to it any more. This is a bit of a stupid generalisation, but if we think of the word 'atonal' we feel slightly seasick, don't we? Serialism is quite different: it's a method of *achieving* atonality when used in certain ways but which doesn't guarantee it. I think of serialism basically as a method of getting from the start of a piece to the end with some supposed intellectual rigour.

Look, if I've got to write a sequence for a film in which Granny's sitting in a rocking chair on a sunny terrace, am I going to use twelve-note technique? No, I'm going to write in E major or G major. But if there's an axe-murderer hiding round the corner and he's about to chop her head off, then I might well consider twelve-tone technique. And I've tried to develop this sort of duality in my concert music, because it *should* be possible to start in E major and finish with the most dreadful racket if your piece is about something terrible. Likewise, it should be possible to represent somebody being rescued from a shocking situation by starting atonally and finishing with a tonal resolution. I would have thought any idiot could see that.

In the early to mid-twentieth century, nationalism was quite important in music and there were definable trends in certain countries. I'm thinking, obviously, of Bartók and Kodály in Hungary; and in this country Elgar, to a certain extent (although his music is arguably quite Germanic), and Delius, whose music is of course partly French in idiom. It's epitomised above all by Vaughan Williams, who went back to English folk song in an attempt to create music that was specifically British. And, as with all trends, there were reactions against it. Incidentally, Britten was also a very British composer, partly because of his infatuation with the works of Purcell.

But I'm not sure whether the term 'British composer' means very much in my case – or indeed in present times generally, music being far more international than ever it's been in the past. As a composer I take my influences from here, there and everywhere – certainly from France (I'm a big lover of French music) and from Germany, Russia and the USA. I'm also much affected by the British countryside, and Wales in particular. Several of my works have been inspired by the Welsh hills and valleys.

Music is the perfect means of expressing emotion, but the composer can do this only in very general terms, not in specific ways. Quite often I just dive into a new piece without too much of a clue as to where I'm going. On other occasions, when a lot of thought has gone into a piece before I've actually started writing, I've spent time considering the emotional flavour of the piece rather than the specific notes. Possibly the shape and structure, too – it's important to me that I come up with material that contains a sense of the work's shape and span. Mind you, all the time everything has to be open to revision, and there comes a point when I have to exert authority over the piece.

When I've got no ideas, or so many ideas that I'm confused, one way out of the quagmire is to quite deliberately think of something visual. In fact I'm writing a piece at the moment which is really *very* representational. It's about a journey taken at night, through storms. The piece came about as a result of my watching a large grey freighter leaving the Mersey river one night and sailing off to a mysterious destination. It was a wonderful evening, and it was an inspiring sight to see this great ship chugging out, you know? And it got my juices flowing. The work will be called *Night Voyage*. But most of my music *isn't* pictorial, I think, not in the way that the Impressionists were. And if you're asking 'Do I see scenes?' with each successive section of a piece, the answer is no. In other words, the musical argument comes first.

While I was a student I had the awful experience of leaving a part-finished symphony on the London Underground. It was never found or handed in. I'd got a fair way with it, and I was so shattered by the loss that I just couldn't face writing the whole thing out again. I think I also felt that perhaps it was some sort of blessing in disguise: I'd been having some problems with it, and now I didn't have to carry on with it! Anyway, I hope I've since written much better symphonies, but it was only about fifteen years ago that I started writing concert music again. I just woke up to the fact that if I didn't do it then, I wasn't going to do it at all; and the awfulness of unfulfilled ambition was too much to bear.

The first piece I wrote was a saxophone concerto, which I sent to John Harle (whom I didn't then know). He wrote straight back and said, 'Chris, we must do it.' Very nice! Then I got to work on a piano concerto, tackled my First Symphony and other pieces, and began to feel that the mountains I'd encountered earlier were now not quite insurmountable. The twelve-note era had come to an end and it was now considered perfectly okay to write in any damned style you wanted; and this felt like a huge portcullis being lifted. Consequently, the first two or three pieces I wrote were rather tonal. And, lo and behold, I was writing concert music just for the hell of it, just for fun! I hadn't done that since I was twenty. I felt terribly optimistic! I'm now up to Symphony No. 7. I'm a bit embarrassed to hear No. 1 now, even though it was written only fifteen years ago, and I'm not sure about the Saxophone Concerto, either. But there we are ... They're out there.

Each of my symphonies has started off as a new beginning, but then it's emerged that there are threads between them all. What can I say about that? On the technical front, I'm very interested in one-movement form, which five of the seven symphonies have. I'm also interested in a piece of music being able to carry you for a certain amount of time because of a narrative running all the way through it. That strikes me as being virtually the summit of music, actually. Symphony No. 2, which lasts for forty-five minutes, has never been played, and I'm revising it at the moment. No. 3 took shape while I was going through a fairly tortured period, and that was one of the few times in my life when I actually used the composing of music for a personal purpose – you know, for getting 'stuff' out. So No. 3 is quite a tough one. Symphony No. 5 is my longest and most ambitious to date. At over fifty minutes, it traces a life from birth to death, and it's dedicated to the memory of my dear sister.

People keep telling me, 'Chris, don't write symphonies. Or call them something else, for God's sake.' But I call them by the general term 'symphony' in the hope that listeners will follow the musical arguments and also bring their own life experiences to bear on what they hear.

If you're writing a film or TV score you have a strict deadline, and so you just work all the time. I'm pretty well disciplined, actually, and one way and another I'll be working by about nine in the morning. And I'll carry on right through until lunchtime, whatever happens. Then I'll have a short break, and I'll go back and do some more work afterwards. Then I get very sleepy, so I either have forty winks on the bed or take the dog out for a walk. After that, I usually come back and work some more. But the afternoons are generally not the most fertile periods, so I return to work with a vengeance after supper. Sometimes I'll work through until one or two in the morning. I'm bloody antisocial, really!

I used to sit at a piano or at a desk, with a pencil and paper, and simply *write*. But now that some very good electronic samples are easily available it's terribly tempting to work with those instead. And if I'm working on a film score I definitely work with those, initially. I use Logic, one of the two main sequencing software programmes. One reason is that film producers know it enables you to create a mock-up of what you're going to record with an orchestra, and they expect to hear it before they pay out the money. That's a perfectly reasonable request. But of course they don't realise that getting a demo recording up to an acceptable standard sometimes involves a huge amount of work, so you can actually be doing the whole thing twice or even three times. People say, 'It must be so much quicker now that you work with a computer', but it isn't. I'm often on the point of throwing the computer out of the window and going back to the way I used to do it, but so far I've resisted the temptation!

Yes, I do have a sense of creating something which then takes on a life of its own, although this applies to my film scores more than to anything else I write. People write to me and say, 'This is the most beautiful music', and two people have commissioned me to write pieces because they've found some of my works incredibly emotional. Even my wife sometimes asks me, 'How did you write *that*?' Clearly, she's unable to reconcile what she thinks is a beautiful piece of music with the bastard who put it together! But the fact is that if a piece has a strong emotional feeling behind it, you feel it too while writing it. You *have* to. What's more, you're designing the notes in a way that will produce that effect, so you have to have felt the emotion. I don't think you can write music at times of *great* emotional turbulence, because you just can't get focussed enough, but you can do it afterwards. Yeah, I would say afterwards is a jolly good time to do it!

Can I just add something to that, because, you know, at the end of it all, what is the point of writing music? The point is to convey some sort of human emotion somewhere along the line, even if it's an intellectual exercise that you're involved in. Bach fugues: are they emotional? Well, yes, they are. And it's not just to do with the nature of the subject of the fugue. Sometimes there's great beauty attached to the actual working out of the music. So I would go as far as to say that there's absolutely no point in writing a piece of music that doesn't have some sort of strong emotional feeling or intention behind it.

However, I'm really not interested in music that has only an immediate impact, and which my mind can't exercise itself with afterwards. There's a quotation lurking here, isn't there? 'A heart that thinks and a mind that feels …' I just believe that mind and heart in music are inseparable, and that the secret of success for the composer is in managing to satisfy both requirements.

You ask how much time I spend not composing but doing things associated with being a composer. For fourteen years I was a director of the Performing Right Society and that involved me in one great long meeting every month. But then there were all the sub-committees to attend as well, so in fact I'd be going there every week for one reason or another. I was also involved in the setting up and running of the Association of Professional Composers (before it was merged with the British Academy) and I put a huge amount of work into that. Five years ago I decided not to do any more of that work. I've done enough, and paid my dues!

What else do I do? Well, keeping tabs on royalties is a nightmare. You can find yourself being ripped off all the time, so it pays to be vigilant in this area. Apart from that, most of what I do is answering correspondence. I get requests for my music from time to time, and I have conversations with people about any recordings that are likely to happen. So there's a fair amount of admin involved, and it's nice when my wife does some of it for me.

Yes, it's true that a composer can get typecast because of a particular work that's been successful. In my case it's *Poirot*. In some people's minds that's all I do, and so that's all I'm allowed to do. The fact is that it's simply become very well known. It accounts for probably 75 per cent of the requests I get, in one form or another – there have been umpteen different arrangements of it. And before *Poirot* it was a commercial: I tended not to be offered BBC classic dramas because I'd done the Martini ad …

And yes, I *have* been surprised by what performers have brought to my music – mostly by pieces being played at the wrong tempo! And it drives me completely mad, particularly when I've indicated what the tempo should be. Maybe they don't understand metronome marks, or maybe it's just interpretative licence. But it makes you realise the importance of a performer going back to the composer's own requests wherever possible. So yes, while I've had some lovely performances, others have been pretty dreadful.

I had a performance of an organ piece in which the organist was obviously having some sort of nervous breakdown and came onto the platform of the Queen Elizabeth Hall, sat down and played *anything* for about ten minutes. It was absolutely excruciating. And I then had to go and take a bow for this piece that I hadn't written! It was pure Monty Python. Oh … dreadful, dreadful!

In general, though, I don't have a problem with what you refer to as the public aspect of being a composer – because I'm not a public figure, really, am I? At least, I don't think it's very developed. I mean, if I had a team of reporters outside the house all the time I'd get extremely cross, but I don't have too many invasions of my privacy. I do get letters from complete strangers, and while some of them are flattering, others are mildly irritating!

And all sorts of odd things happen. Some time ago I learned of performances of my music that were going to take place in Russia 'in the presence of the composer', but nobody had actually told me about them. My wife happens to speak Russian and made further enquiries, but when she pressed the organisers after the concert she was told, 'Unfortunately there were visa problems, and he wasn't able to come.' What was all *that* about?

Going back to your question, I think there are composers who positively court publicity and others who prefer to be more private or even secretive. And I suppose I'm more like the second of those. I want to be judged by my music rather than by how much publicity I get.

Morgan Hayes

Morgan Hayes, London, March 2012

> **While we should celebrate difference, there's something about a *desire* to be different that can be irritating.**

Morgan Hayes is a composer about whom I kept hearing, at first in connection with the release by NMC of a CD of his music. And I grew curious about him when reading an interview that he gave to the pianist Jonathan Powell, published on the NMC website.[1] Although steeped in modernism he acknowledged a strong debt to music of the past and recalled his teenage interest in the 'mercurial, highly active' nature of Milton Babbitt's works, in which 'tonal references can shoot out of an atonal context'. He went on to acknowledge the importance of what he has learned from his principal teacher, Michael Finnissy, by referring to old-fashioned virtues such as practicality and unpretentiousness.

I was particularly struck by his response to Powell's suggestion that his musical style wasn't that of 'a posturing, crowd-pleasing post-modernist': he identified a turning point when hearing the pianist John Sweeney improvise for a ballet class (for which he himself was to become a regular accompanist) and for silent movies. He explained:

> It may not be the grandest form of music making but I noted that while the source material was identifiable (whether it was Chopin, Latin or Gibbons) the expression was entirely personal – it sounded bang up to date within its pastiche. I certainly preferred it to a lot of 'contemporary' music and Keith Jarrett improvisations. A more recent example was when I was listening 'blindfold' to an NMC sampler CD where the Robin Holloway Violin Concerto (with its explicit references to the past) leapt out as being every bit as fresh as the works it was flanked by.

All of this seemed to increase my uncertainty about the nature (or natures) of contemporary classical music. And I wasn't much wiser after listening to the pieces on his own CD. They sounded unquestionably 'contemporary', in the sense that I felt they couldn't have been written at any time other than now, but not overtly challenging in their modernity. I was

---

[1] www.nmcrec.co.uk/recording/violin-concerto-0#interview

interested to know whether they're typical of the work of a postmodern composer, if there is such a thing.

The following encounter took place in March 2012 at his home, a fourth-floor flat in a red-stuccoed mansion block in north-west London. He was softly spoken and a little reserved, perhaps closer in personality to the occasionally melancholy and romantic elements of his music than to the typically tense and turbulent ones. His wide range of cultural interests inevitably informed our conversation about his work, but because of my difficulty in locating him stylistically in relation to his contemporaries I began the interview by asking him whether he identifies trends in contemporary British music and, if so, how his own music relates to them.

Afterwards I wanted to photograph him outside on the small balcony overlooking the street, but because he had doubts about its stability we stayed inside. The photos I took probably make him appear more stern than he is, but we agreed that the one reproduced here is of a composer who looks as if he means business – 'which', he suggested, 'is no bad thing'.

I perceive a mainstream in terms of the kinds of composers who, for example, get programmed frequently at the Proms. And then there are others who are more wayward or quirky, such as Andrew Toovey. He's fifty this year, but there are no celebrations for him. He's the kind of composer who'd instead be advocated by someone like the conductor Ilan Volkov. In that sense, there are strands to the contemporary musical scene. But they may not be specific to British music.

Because it's easier to get an outsider's perspective, I once asked a German composer about this; and he told me that he perceived British music as not being edgy – whatever that means. Perhaps he was right. As to which strand I belong to, I don't consciously align myself to anything in particular. In general, composers seem to resist pigeonholes. But Arnold Whittall, in a very substantial article on my music in the *Musical Times*, described me as an Expressionist![2]

In 1988, when I was fifteen, I was drawn to Gerald Barry's *Chevaux de Frise* and Michael Finnissy's *Red Earth*, both of which were programmed in that year's Proms season. The Barry piece is march-like – everything is strong and rhythmical – and cast in variation form,

---

[2] Arnold Whittall, 'Distressed Surfaces: Morgan Hayes and 21st-Century Expressionism', *The Musical Times*, Autumn 2012.

while the Finnissy is in many ways diametrically opposed to that, with an absence of obvious pulse and a more organic structure. And at first I was slightly bewildered by both pieces. But both, in their different ways, had a startling impact on me – as did many other pieces, of course. Neither of those composers has since been commissioned by the Proms, which goes back to what I said about strands in contemporary music.[3]

I think there are still figures in contemporary British music who can be thought of as pivotal. For example, Tom Adès's new pieces are eagerly awaited, and I've never forgotten a magazine article by Richard Toop called 'Four Facets of the New Complexity' about James Dillon, Michael Finnissy, Richard Barrett and Chris Dench.[4] That had quite an impact on me. So did the 1986 Channel 4 TV series *Sinfonietta*, which opened my ears to the music of Berg, Schoenberg, Webern and many other composers. The now extinct British Music Information Centre was also a very valuable resource. But the important thing for a composer is to follow your own particular pathway rather than looking for iconic models to follow. What matters about other people's music is that it's important to *you*, not whether it has a mass following.

If I wanted to, I could write music in many different kinds of style, and I hope that I would somehow be able to inhabit each of them. But 'styles' aren't something that a composer chooses. Whatever you write has to come from some inner drive, otherwise composing is a vacuous exercise, I think. My music is making a gradual progression away from ideals about extreme density and complexity that I once held quite dear, and this is largely a result of some of the extra-curricular work I do.

I've ventured into dance accompanying more than teaching (which a lot of composers do) since being introduced to it while I was a student at the Guildhall, which had an affiliation with the London School of Contemporary Dance. And there was an important turning point when I began work as an accompanist with Millennium Dance – a performing arts school – and it was suggested that I go to hear the pianist John Sweeney play for one its classes. He improvised in a variety of styles, yet I felt that he inhabited everything he played in a very personal and unsentimental way. In fact, he transformed the atmosphere of the class with his inspiring playing. And I asked him

---

[3] Five months after this interview took place Finnissy's Piano Concerto No. 2 was given its first performance in the 2012 Proms season.
[4] Published in *Contact*, No. 32 (1988), 4–8.

if he would teach me. Spurred on by some of the things I learnt from him, I composed my piece *Opera* for violin and piano.

There's nothing wrong with extreme density and complexity, but as a composer you always have to be true to yourself. When I heard an angst-ridden and dissonant piece of mine played by Ixion at the Huddersfield Festival I thought, 'This really isn't me any more. I can't write another piece like that.' It was partly because the piece was a re-hash of some of the things I'd done earlier, but also because I felt I had to move on from that kind of style. This wasn't a desire to be more approachable or to reach out to an audience. *I'm* always the audience – multiples of me. No, it's a gradual evolution, not a sudden switch. It has taken place, bit by bit, over fifteen years as I've introduced new elements into my music. For example, my Violin Concerto begins with a key signature, which is something I probably wouldn't have been brave enough to do twenty years ago.

I write what I'm asked to write. Maybe that sounds terribly lacking in ambition, but in the case of the Violin Concerto I was asked for an eighteen-minute piece, so that's what I wrote. It was the same when I was asked to write a five-minute choral piece for the Aldeburgh Festival: I wrote what they wanted me to write. But I do enjoy writing in miniature forms, and I'm very attracted to composers like Granados and Scarlatti who wrote lots of shorter-scale pieces that aren't, as a result, any less good or less ambitious. I don't like music that sprawls, and if you can say what you want to say in ten minutes, there doesn't seem any point in writing something that lasts for thirty or forty. So when I'm editing my work I'm always inclined to cut things out rather than to add them in.

Having said that, when I look back at the Violin Concerto I see that I could have been slightly more resourceful if I'd had a more detached perspective. This is one of the great challenges of writing music, actually: although you have to be engaged with your material, you also need to be able to stand back from it – almost as if it's not your own – and to ask yourself questions such as 'What would happen if it were all played backwards, or if one part were transposed?' And then to see what would happen. The ability to do this comes with experience, I think. And without it, it's easy to become too precious about your material – and perhaps you then end up writing nothing *more* than a succession of miniatures. But then this is often what people want. In fact, my most recent commission is for just fifty bars of music, so that's a new departure!

What I want to express in my music varies from one piece to the next. Just thinking of a specific example, I wrote a seven-minute Piano Trio last year and its title is *Völklinger Hütte*, which is an ironworks – a UNESCO site – near Saarbrücken in Germany. And the piece is about the kind of impact that visiting a place like that has on you. There's only so far that I would be able to go in writing a travel guide or a poem about the sensations involved, so it's better for me to put that across in music. But not consciously – *Völklinger Hütte* could have been the title of many other pieces I've written. Only very occasionally do I encounter something that seems to summarise everything I've been preoccupied with creatively, and it could be in literature or the visual arts rather than in music. So in that sense, the titles of musical pieces are perhaps more interchangeable than one might think.

There are common threads running through a lot of my pieces, for example William Burroughs's novel *Cities of the Red Night* and my memories of visiting Tangiers. But they're not consciously applied to the music. Composing is more about recalling the sensations and the excitement of these things. So, in the case of the ironworks, I adopted a mechanistic kind of approach. More generally, I've rediscovered greater regularity of rhythm. That sounds a very dry thing to get excited about, but it's something that I would have scrupulously avoided (just like key signatures) ten years ago, even though it was the march-like rhythms that so impressed me in Gerald Barry's *Chevaux de Frise*. And octaves, too: they've been in music for centuries, but as they're something that I felt I should avoid, rediscovering them has been quite an exciting experience.

Why did I feel I should avoid them? I suppose because they were very much at odds with some of the more recent music I enjoyed listening to. Also, I dare say, because of what my composition teachers told me. But I think it's better to have something to react to, and to move away from, than nothing at all. And because you don't take these aspects of music for granted, you approach them with a sense of discovery. It seems to have taken me twenty years to properly come to terms with them in my own music, rather than simply copying them.

Japanese gagaku music is also an influence. In what I believe was my first composition lesson with him, Michael Finnissy suggested I listen to Sibelius's Seventh Symphony and some gagaku and then try to write something based on the latter.

There are certain musical ideas that I've always been attracted to. For example, I can get fired off by ground bass. A number of my pieces feature constancy in the bass, with different things going on over the top of it. This is very much at odds with the capricious, changeable aspects of music, and it roots them, in a way. (I find that a simple musical idea like that can also be helpful in getting you back into composition if you're slightly rusty.) But sometimes other people see my ways of working more clearly than I do. So while I don't see characteristics that are common to all my pieces, I've read about them!

The characteristics that I find easier to identify are in fact failings, not things that I've consciously done, and one of them is that some pieces terminate before they should. In one sense, I wish I'd had the confidence to pursue one section of the Violin Concerto more, in which case that piece would have been longer than it is. But the door seemed to slam shut on it. However, if I felt that I'd finally found *the* way of doing certain things, I probably wouldn't write another piece. What drives me on is not dissatisfaction, as such – that's too strong a word – but a sense that I can always do something better the next time.

I hope that there's a physical excitement about my music and that it has a visceral kind of impact on listeners. This is particularly important in a short piece, and I think it's related to my work in dance. In longer pieces that have larger spans, the energy of the music is sustained by juxtaposing different textures or presenting extreme contrasts; and weighing up these kinds of things is, for me, one of the most exciting aspects of composing. And of course they're not immediately apparent when I begin a piece. For example, the opening of my Violin Concerto was part of another piece that I wrote a long time before, and it was tagged on quite late in the composing process.

There's a lot of baggage around music, particularly in the way that it's written about, and it's easy to mistake that for the way the music actually *sounds*. Music operates on a number of levels, and you can speak in coldly analytical terms about a piece that has an enormous emotional impact. The technical apparatus can be quite cool and detached, while the impact of the music might be really passionate. Xenakis is a good case in point, and much of Milton Babbitt. And a Bach fugue, come to that. Which is why I hope my own music is physically exciting and has an emotional impact on listeners. But that's not something that I can consciously create. To try to do so would have the opposite effect, I think, because it would actually block the music instead of communicating through it. It's not that the emotional impact should be accidental, but that it should work in a way that's organic and uncontrived.

Of course, I acknowledge that my music isn't going to appeal to everybody. But it's very difficult to factor other people's sense of aesthetics or taste into the composition process. However, my engagement with the performers, if I've already worked with them a lot, influences the way I think about what I write. For example, if I were writing a piano piece for Jonathan Powell I might well have in mind some of the kind of music he's already associated with. Or if it were for Stephen Gutman I'd be thinking of Rameau. To that extent, it's nice to write with specific performers in mind.

I've never written a piece for theatre or film, which would be based on different criteria. Yes, I'd be writing something that *I* would be satisfied with, but at the same time it would be a much more collaborative process. I'd have to anticipate what the theatre director or the film director wanted. This isn't to say that the result would be more compromised; it's just that in the process I would have come up with something that I wouldn't otherwise have written.

Every aspect of my musical education, from brass lessons at school to music conservatoire and studying with Michael Finnissy, has been invaluable to me. My first piano lessons were very helpful because my teacher saw that I had an interest in composition and put me through all the music theory grades, for which I've always been grateful. From the age of ten, I think, I knew that I wanted to be a composer rather than a concert pianist. I also enjoyed drawing, but there were people at school who seemed to be more accomplished at it than I was; whereas there was no-one else at school composing music. So I just developed in my own way, writing piano sonatas and other very primitive stuff. And there was a gradual improvement in my work, helped by the music lessons.

Then I went to study at the Guildhall. I wasn't encouraged to do anything deliberately different or original there, and if I *have* arrived at my own way of doing things, it hasn't been by design. That's something that annoys me, actually: while, in many ways, we should celebrate difference, there's something about a *desire* to be different that can be irritating. The results can seem rather arch. And things that are superficially more conservative can sometimes be deeper!

What was also useful about being at the Guildhall was my contact with other students. It was very enriching, and I'm still professionally in contact with some of them: the violinist Darragh Morgan, the conductor Christopher Austin and the German composer Moritz Eggert.

And of course the simple fact of being in London, rather than Hastings, where I grew up, was tremendously important. But I had no real sense of what life as a composer would be like. I just knew that it was where I would always put most of my energy. Being a conductor, for example, just wasn't on my radar. It was inconceivable. Composition was the thing, but how I would manage a career as a composer wasn't obvious.

I was picked up by a music publisher much earlier than I'd anticipated. It wasn't something that I was looking for, because I was quite naïve about that side of the profession. And it seemed premature, actually. In the meantime I was doing all sorts of other work – catering, market research, playing the piano for ballet classes – so there were always two sides to my working life. But a composer's career isn't really planned. It just happens.

After I graduated from the Guildhall I got commissions and requests to write pieces, but I found it difficult to pursue them *and* to make a living from part-time work. So I moved back to Hastings for about six years in order to avoid the problem of paying rent in London, and this enabled me to write the compositions I was asked for and to take on a certain amount of part-time work locally. I was very fortunate to have that to fall back on. Then a one-year teaching post at the Purcell School came up, and the salary enabled me to move back to London. With the regular ballet work came a certain momentum, which I now see was essential, but I was still fairly clueless, really, about the life of a professional composer. Some do copying work, of course, or they write commercial music. In fact, I'm often asked why *I* don't write it. I would … but I'm not sure how good I would be at it.

A lot of my time – currently as much as 80 or 90 per cent, probably – is spent doing work that isn't actually composing. That's more than, say, five years ago, and it's simply in order to survive financially. I'm told that commissions are less widespread these days, and I've just completed a Sound and Music survey on the subject! But most of the work is associated with my composition in some way or other. For example, playing for dance classes has helped me to develop as a musician; and although an enormous amount of work went into getting the NMC CD of my music off the ground, it's a very useful promotional tool to have. Also, I revised and extended some of the pieces for the CD, and it was an interesting experience to revisit music that was maybe five or six years old. The piece called *Lute Stop* was previously four minutes long but is now something like double that, and I don't think the join between the music of the younger composer and the music of the older composer is obvious. (Of course, the temptation to tweak works annoys publishers!)

Composing usually involves conjuring up in your mind something that you want to write – perhaps a specific line or a texture – and then discovering, as soon as you try to find a way of putting that onto paper, that it evolves into something different. How you generate that picture material can vary. It could come from improvisation at the keyboard or from something quite random. But you need *something* to work with. This is part of the concept or narrative of a composition. I make a lot of handwritten sketches and then transfer them onto Sibelius before working with them, so I'm often leaping between the keyboard and the manuscript paper.

I started using Sibelius software in about 1999, so all my works from before then were sketched and then written up neatly by hand. And I took great trouble over the calligraphy – it was very important to me. When friends first offered me Sibelius I was quite reluctant to use it and I told them, 'It's very kind of you, but I need to write music by hand.' I gradually took to it, but sometimes it still feels strange because I used to be so fixated on the calligraphy side of writing music. Ultimately, the software has thrown up new possibilities, I think, and serendipity is one of them. In the early days of using Sibelius I made a mistake and mixed up the clefs in the piano part, but I ended up keeping the score that way because it actually sounded better than what I'd intended to write! And it leads me to believe that the copying process is sometimes part of composition technique. If nothing else, it can be important for a composer to just go with the flow of things.

Some of the music I enjoy listening to bears little obvious relationship to my preoccupations as a composer. It's all slightly confused by my work as a pianist, and I'm often thinking about what would function well in a ballet class. Poulenc, for example, I like a lot. And Reynaldo Hahn. They're both rather bitter-sweet and nostalgic.

What interests me about Poulenc is that his music couldn't be by anyone else. Take the slow movement of the Double Piano Concerto, which I've played several times for a dance class: when you hear it you don't think 'Oh, that's Mozart', even though Mozart is clearly the model. It can only be Poulenc, because his personality is so strong and imprints itself on the music. Boulez once noted that this was the wrong direction for French music to have taken, and Otto Klemperer took a very dim view of the Concerto, but I believe there's room for all kinds of music!

It's true: the composer *is* a public figure. Whether your 'public' is an audience or a small group of specialists in new music, you're performing to them. And you can feel quite exposed when attending a rehearsal and working with people you've never met before, particularly if they don't already know your music. Mine is quite demonstrative and strong – there's a kind of energy that has to get out – but what sometimes happens is that the playing is held back during the rehearsal. Even with years of experience I still think, 'Maybe there's a problem with the piece.' And then there's a sense of relief during the actual performance when the music takes on a different dimension and sounds so much stronger than it did in rehearsal.

And yes, performers do sometimes bring to my music things that I hadn't expected. The most obvious example may not be a very good one because it was actually in a composition lesson rather than a public performance, but I remember that, when I was studying at the Guildhall, Simon Bainbridge was rehearsing an early violin concerto of mine (not the one that's on my CD) and said about one section, 'Because there's so much going on here, it would be interesting to rehearse it twice: the first time with half the instrumental layer removed, and the second time as you've written it, as a *tutti*.' Hearing those two minutes of music doubled in length but repeated differently (the first time without percussion and woodwind, and the second time with), as if I'd added a repeat mark, was probably the most valuable lesson in composition I ever had. It involved a very simple revision, and listeners probably wouldn't think they were hearing the same section twice; but it was a kind of exposition that allowed the music to breathe. In that instant it became so clear to me, but I never would have thought of it myself.

Another example was when Darragh Morgan was playing a particular section of a violin solo that I'd written all in double stops, with a repeat mark. He suggested, 'Why don't you have just a single line the first time, and *then* double stops the second time?' Again, it was a brilliant idea because it allowed the material to breathe – and so I included it in the piece. That could only have come from collaborating with a musician whom I've worked with for years and whose musicality I trust.

Robin Holloway

Robin Holloway, London, March 2012

❛While I might not be hermetic, I'm not very worldly.❜

Robin Holloway's publishers e-mailed me to say that he was, in principle, interested in being interviewed for this book, and would I please call him to discuss it. I was nervous about doing so because, not having met him before, I'd formed a mental image of someone whose formidable intelligence might make him rather unapproachable. This wasn't entirely dispelled when, during the first of our phone conversations, he declared, 'The whole thing is pointless if you don't know my music or my writings' – in the circumstances, a perfectly reasonable remark.

In a sense, his writings made the interview unnecessary, for in his collections of articles, essays and reviews he'd already published his views on many of the issues I wanted to discuss with him. But I remained curious because, despite his speaking out against 'The uncertain idioms of "difficult" modern music, together with its palpable failure to gain popular acceptance',[1] only a handful of his two hundred works have been recorded and his name seems to crop up in concert listings only rarely. I wondered why, when he writes with such eloquence about the failure of some contemporary music to communicate to listeners, his own works have not gained greater popular acceptance.

One possible reason – that he taught composition at the University of Cambridge for thirty-two years and might therefore be associated with a concept of academia that's unworldly – he strongly refuted. Another might be that some listeners, aware of his frustration with some aspects of modernism, expect his music to be 'easier' than it is and are disappointed by its apparent complexity and dissonance. They'll be less surprised after reading his diagnosis of 'the malaise of music at large – the flight to the extremes that leaves the centre empty'.[2]

There's perhaps also a problem in that much of his literary work takes the form of criticism. Is he regarded as someone who's too easily unimpressed

---

[1] Robin Holloway, *On Music: Essays and Diversions 1963–2003*, op. cit., p. 198.
[2] *Ibid.*, p. 210.

and who can only find fault? He admitted to me that the compulsion to speak his mind has made him enemies within the musical establishment. But his writings reveal that his senses are orientated towards pleasure in musical sound and that he's as ready to express his delight in certain works as he is to dismiss others that repel him. 'The dissident doesn't *want* to be perverse', he has explained. 'He wants to enjoy the comfort of shared convictions rather than the vulnerability and paranoia of being out in the cold.'[3]

As an emeritus professor he retains a home at the University of Cambridge, but we met in north London in the tall Edwardian terraced house that he shares with an art historian and a composer/conductor who, like him, come and go in bohemian fashion. He was welcoming, relaxed and often humorous, but I was struck by the extent to which my experience of interviewing him resembled that described by Paul Griffiths nearly thirty years earlier: 'the atmosphere of a tutorial is rapidly reversed; he sits on a low chair, speaking quietly towards his shoes, and I feel myself put in the role of confessor'.[4] Whether it was the same chair, I don't know, but the family heirloom on which he sat was indeed low, and on a swivel base that encouraged him to swing from side to side as he talked and while I tried to photograph him.

You're suggesting that it doesn't add up, somehow. And it's true: I don't have many performances, and I don't have much music on record. At best, I acquiesce in this; at worst, I feel bitter and rancorous, or disappointed or jealous – all the human things that you'd expect. And what joins these feelings is puzzlement, because I think my music is an attractive and communicating product. I'm surprised and sometimes distressed that it's not so widely received as that of many of my peers or contemporaries. A performance seems to work whenever it happens – for example, my Fifth Concerto for Orchestra had a very good launch at last summer's Proms and couldn't have been more warmly received. You can't mistake that at a Prom, when feelings are so close to the surface. But one thing doesn't lead to another – such as a second performance. This has happened again and again, and I think it must be because there's no perception of my music having a central identity.

You can tell from reading my essays that my tastes are very eclectic.

---

[3] *Ibid.*, p. 297.
[4] Paul Griffiths, *New Sounds, New Personalities: British Composers of the 1980s, op.cit.*, p. 113.

My private passions, to coin a phrase, are extensive. I'm extremely open to influences, and will turn in this direction or that as I'm attracted or stimulated (not necessarily with delight) by some new thing. It's impulsive and intuitive, and it results in a great diversification of styles, a lot of references and a lot of dips into the past, visiting Bach or Wagner or Schumann (to name but three) in a piece. My musical language can't be called just neo-Romantic or neo-classical, because it's got a lot of both. It's also got old-style, gritty modernism and mid-to-late-twentieth-century constructivism, with Schoenberg and Bartók behind it. It's got time travel in it, and play with the past; and you might relate that to the sense that the available present has never been wider. So there is a completely private and non-programmatic sort of synthesising going on in my music, which I think makes me hard to categorise as a composer. And this perhaps contributes to people's sense that they can't get their arms around my work because it resists being comprehended in a simple way.

As for being remote and academic, that used to be an accusation against me in the early days, and it was like a curse. People said, 'He's in an academic post at a university; therefore he writes academic music.' It was *that* thoughtless. I no longer get that, because, as you rightly say, my music is so obviously non-academic. If I write a homage to Bach, it's not pastiche or 'correct' in an academic sense. It never was. What's more, my academic work has involved teaching lots of young students, generation after generation, year by year, all of whom I've lectured to in large groups of seventy or so, and many of whom I've taught in groups of three, four or five for historical subjects, and many of whom I've taught one-to-one for composition. That's not remote. There's nothing hermetic or hidden away about that. People are always coming up to me at concerts and saying things like, 'You won't remember me, but I was in the back row of your lectures in the 1970s; and it's influenced the way I've thought about music ever since.'

I think my chief impulse in life is a mixture of the ecstatic and the didactic. I respond very, very strongly to stimuli of all kinds, not just musical, and I want to express them in whatever way I can so that people feel them as strongly as I do. I want to communicate pleasure, delight, interest, curiosity – in the form of music, in the form of words, in the form of friendship or in my attitude towards life in general. I go around with my senses tingling and alert, and I want to express this in whatever ways I can. That might sound a bit gormless, but, as I said, the other side of it is didactic – I want to teach people that everything has meaning and value.

My work with students has involved introducing them to music by saying something like: 'Open Sesame! Here is a cave of *endless* richness, and I can perhaps help in the initial stages of exploring it. For example, here is Schumann, and the pieces you really should know – because they're marvellous – are this or that song cycle, this or that piano cycle; *possibly* try the Symphonies (some problems there), try the chamber music (some problems there, too), the late music (a lot of problems there) … This is the shape of the life; this is the shape of the oeuvre. It's at your feet. It's yours. Enjoy!'

As to how 'difficult' I feel my own music is in relation to that of my contemporaries, I'd have to say that I can't conceive of *any* composer not wanting to be understood. Yes, at one time the attitude was anti-communicative – experimental and quasi-scientific. Ivory tower, if you like. But music is music and the best of it does reach out. Of course, pleasure in music takes many forms. It can include the frightful, the painful, the brutal and the ugly, when legitimised by the expression of very strong feelings. That's not pleasure as hedonism, but it's a real part of the range of what art can give you.

We can appreciate a complex, cerebral construction, as in *The Art of Fugue*, through which beauty of proportions, beauty of workings and intense expressivity can come into being. And we can take just as much pleasure in purely sensuous beauty that seems completely brainless, like Takemitsu or some of the Szymanowski First Violin Concerto, which is a hedonistic swoon. Those might be extremes, but most music is between them, with an admixture of both. If it's all swoony it won't work so well because you won't retain it, so there's got to be an appropriate structure, an appropriate form, even for a total drench of musical perfume. Similarly, something cerebral that's dried out won't reveal its construction with force and persuasiveness if the polyphonic combinations aren't expressive.

To give you an example from one of my own works, the second movement of my Third Concerto for Orchestra is a passacaglia but its form isn't audible like that of the final passacaglia of the Brahms *St Anthony Variations*. It's a succession of musical objects that recur some forty times and that build from a very soft beginning towards a grand-slam climax. Communication here is at once cerebral, physical and sonorous and expressive.

Some music you listen to by lying back and letting it wash over you, or letting it sweep you off your feet. Other music is more rarefied, perhaps almost secret. It doesn't scream at you to be excited or carried away, and the composer might appear to be talking to himself. And these very different forms of musical communication can occur next to each other in the same work. The last movement of Mahler's Ninth, for instance: some of it is right in your face, some of it you have to crane forward to overhear. I myself favour communication as direct as possible. Wagner's *leitmotifs* are not an arcane language; they are, on the contrary, the means of clarifying his purpose. Yes, they're instructive and didactic, but they're also highly expressive. No secrets. I prefer music with no secrets over the self-reflexive world of Berg's *Lulu*, for example, with its private and perhaps fetishistic ciphers and games. Of course, *Lulu* communicates unambiguously, with very great and direct emotional power; but this is despite, not because of, its elaborate workings.

How do I discover my music? By writing it, by trying things out – fingers on the piano, actual sounds. Stravinsky said, 'I compose *avec la gomme*' (with the eraser), and I do the same: piano, pencil and paper, and eraser. This doesn't mean that I'm not thinking of the music as I walk around or as I drift off to sleep or as I wake up. When in progress, it's always present – I'm living it and I take it everywhere. I usually have a little sketchpad to hand and I doodle shapes – not musical shapes but physical doodles, patterns or textures, which sometimes develop into scribbling a stave and jotting down musical notes. Long journeys are therefore very exciting, yet boring meetings, too, can be quite stimulating; you've got to do *something* in boring meetings, and most of my professional life has involved a lot of them. Sometimes these ideas are turned into pieces, or bits of pieces, but mostly they're not.

Having a new piece in your mind can influence mood and behaviour. If the piece is dark, your mood is dark; and your days and nights can be full of tension and struggle until it's finished. I usually write very fast once I've got going, unless there's a problem, because I find the pressure unbearable. I'm carrying a very heavy weight and I need to put it down as quickly as possible to rid myself of that stress. Last summer I wrote a Trio for Oboe, Violin and Piano (a lovely texture that I'd wanted to explore for years, and at last I had a commission) in just four days. Four movements, one movement per day. Then I was so much in the mood that I wrote a new string quartet (not commissioned): five movements, five days. I was in a very happy vein. But it isn't always like that. My Third Concerto for Orchestra took me eleven years, on and off, to write. I'd leave it and do something else, and return to it and get nowhere, or get only a little way with it. And I carried it throughout my waking and sleeping hours, so anything else that could be finished and have a double bar put to it during that period was a relief.

I'm very conscious of the discipline required of the composer. And this is partly because I'm a nervous creature – like Berg, I always arrive in time for the train before! I've only twice flunked a deadline, and usually I'm a very good boy who hands in his finished work extremely early. But I have a lot of composer friends who have failed deadline after deadline. Then there are others for whom it can be very touch and go. I don't understand that, unless there's a bad creative block, a depression or some other circumstance that makes it impossible. I'm not a control freak – my work isn't precisely planned out – but as a composer you know what you've got to do, and you've got the dates, so you focus on it. The main part of being a composer is that you compose – it's as simple as that.

But while I might not be hermetic, I'm not very worldly, and I don't know how to promote my interests. And when I try to, I know that I'm doing it badly. I feel like a whore. Some people do it very well and therefore for them it's not whore-ish. It's natural to network and to fraternise, and then people remember and say, 'Yes, of course, we met … It was so nice…' And the commissions and performances follow. That's the way of the world. But I can't do it. When I try to, I feel uncomfortable and ill at ease; so it's ineffective and then I feel I've betrayed myself. Or that I've sold myself, to no effect. A *failed* whore – what's the point of that?

You asked whether there's camaraderie between composers, and I would describe it more as a strong sense of fraternity. In my case, it's grown over the years. I knew virtually no-one when I was beginning to get going as a composer in my teens and early twenties, and I felt alienated and out on a limb – *contra mundum*. Also shy and very embarrassed – which was a personality thing, not an attitude. I was brought into the fold by getting to know Olly Knussen, who was marvellous at calming me down and opening me up in those early days. Through him I began to meet people of my age or his age – such as the Matthews brothers. One thing led to another, and after a while I didn't feel so left out and I wasn't so farouche and terrified. Today there are very strong friendships, and we're in it together.

There are also cabals and cliques and enmities, of course. Well, not really enmities – it's not polemical or personal, more a case of two or three gathering together and discussing, among other things, how awful so-and-so's music is. It's not about his or her success; it's about the quality of the work. Music that I deplore is often *very* successful; I hate it not because it's successful but because I think it's cheap, meretricious or whatever, in its own terms. That it's successful just adds gall to the pearl!

I'm not so keen a follower of new music as I used to be. I'm less interested, actually. I'm less enthused. As you get older you tend to feel 'I've seen it all', and you *have*, to an extent. Those who are ignorant of history are doomed to repeat it and I *do* see the same things coming round again and again – like New Simplicity(!) or neo-Romanticism, or whatever. So I'm less than thrilled by our bright young hopes because the musical climate is much the same as it was thirty, forty, fifty years ago. It's about my response to the product, and I want something different. So if someone's music makes me tingle, I immediately want to meet him or her and to explore further.

I feel very strongly English, but I can't define it. It's not my musical idiom, exactly, although composer friends will sometimes say to me, affectionately and slightly teasing, 'That's one of your English pieces.' Other countries are more militant in their ethnicities, in a sense. James MacMillan is known as a fighting Scot and has a pronounced nationalism that I don't have. A subtler version, but one that has certainly not hindered her, is Judith Weir's Scottishness, which defines important aspects of what her music's like even though she doesn't proclaim it from the rooftops. And Welshness was a very important ingredient in the success of William Mathias and Alun Hoddinott. Irishness is not so clear. But Englishness isn't clear at all, and yet I feel it, with passion.

My musical loves are all German or Austrian, except that I also adore French music and American music and a lot of Russian music! And then there's Sibelius ... But in the middle of that eclecticism, that cosmopolitanism and that time travelling is an English person who is unified and of the time in which I live, however much I might dislike aspects of it. However, that Englishness in me is probably seen more clearly by someone else. I'm too busy writing the music.

I wrote a sort of concert opera (which hasn't been performed) on Ibsen's *Brand*, which is set in Norway in the 1850s but which for me was about Albion in the 1980s: although I'm a very un-political person, it was about the state of my beloved land as I perceived it under Thatcherism, becoming greasy with corruption and greed, but oblique – no slogans and no comparisons. Another of my unperformed works is a farcical comic opera based on the life of Cynthia Payne; remember her? – the Robin Hood of sex. That, clearly, has got a very English setting. And behind it was a very strongly held yet undefined reaction to the state of my nation as seen through aspects of her marvellous career(!) – wry, ribald and sarcastic comments from the side upon the corrupt centre. Again, there was no ideological or *engagé* political content – that's not my thing at all. I couldn't get up on a soapbox as an artist.

My experience of hearing a new piece of my own for the first time? Well, some performers tell the composer not to attend the first rehearsal because they don't want him there. There's a lot to sort out, and the initial play-through might be crude and disconcerting. I think singers, especially, need to have note-bashing that they don't want anyone else to hear. Of course, the performers are going to find mistakes or ambiguities that the composer will have to resolve, if not necessarily at that stage. Sometimes I *have* been present from the very start, and ... well, I learn from everything – from what goes right, from what goes wrong, from what the performers find difficult. I've got to get to know my own piece – to learn my way around what I've done – and so the aural experience is absolutely paramount. And, although I might think that I know these sounds intimately from having hammered them out at the piano and tried them this way and that, it's very strange how different they sound when played in real time by a string quartet, let alone a big orchestra. It's certainly what I meant, but it's still full of surprises.

Revision is pretty immediate after, or even during, the first rehearsal. Things that I might have slaved over to get right aren't right after all, and I notice this the moment I hear them. Often it's a matter of dynamics or speeds. But sometimes it's a matter of notes or proportions, in which case I try to alter them on the spot, or very soon afterwards. And sometimes I realise that I should just leave something out completely.

In general, I'd rather move on to a new work than revise an old one. But I've recently revised my First Concerto for Orchestra. This was at Julian Anderson's suggestion. It's a work from my early twenties, when I was totally inexperienced, and the notation was monstrously impractical. It was one of those all-or-nothing pieces. Julian said, 'It's not very nice. It's ugly. But it's authentic, and you mustn't disown this ferocious child! You must love it, and save it.' Which meant, in addition to cleaning up the notation, a lot of cutting and a lot of rewriting. It was strange, coming back forty years on (like the Alan Bennett play!) to my youthful self. I've since moved into such different places that it felt like working on someone else's piece. But it *was* mine: in the end, I acknowledged and acquiesced. And in the process I learned a great deal.

Once a work is finished and launched, it's no longer your property, in some ways. I remember that remark of Schoenberg: 'I'd like to be whistled in the street by the errand boys'. He then added something that I can't forgive him for: 'like a better kind of Tchaikovsky'! Of course, a composer *longs* for his work to be loved outside himself. That's part of succeeding, which I feel my music could do, given the chance.

A composer aims to be understood, but not in technical terms. An audience isn't going to say something technical to you, like 'I was really impressed by that change of harmony in bar 43', but they might say something personal that expresses how that change of harmony touched them. They notice the change in bar 43 through all the ways that perception can happen – some of which might be technically informed, some of which might not. And what's important to the composer is the audience's appreciation of his music, not the vocabulary that's appropriate to explaining it.

What does a composer most want to hear from someone who loves his music? 'It was great!' 'It was gorgeous, we loved it!' Simple expressions of that kind come direct from the heart and they reach the heart. I had just such an experience in San Francisco when my Third Concerto for Orchestra, which is one of the knottiest and most difficult of all my works, was performed there. Michael Tilson Thomas introduced it with evocative imagery and context: he said, 'The composer was inspired by a visit to South America, and this and that sight.' Those few minutes of verbal introduction put the audience in the right mood, and it set up a certain expectation that he could then build on during the unfamiliar, demanding and long span of the piece. It was cordially received and, after each of the three performances, members of the San Francisco audience came up and talked to me – unlike the English, who blench, as if composers have got leprosy! One young couple said to me, 'Oh, we just *loved* the bit with the alligators!' This was utterly naïve, clearly genuine, completely lovable. Perhaps an alligator *was* mentioned beforehand – I can't remember – or maybe a bit of music snapped its jaws at one point. Anyway, that comment delighted me.

Oliver Knussen

Oliver Knussen, London, May 2000

> **The worst imaginable narcissism would be to try to write what you think your music ought to be like.**

If any readers who previously knew nothing about contemporary British music are working their way alphabetically through the encounters in this book, they'll already be aware of the high regard in which Oliver Knussen is held by his fellow composers. But I wanted my interview with him to focus on his own music rather than the support, both personal and professional, that he has given to colleagues over the last thirty years. First I had to make contact with him, and this took longer than I'd expected. Even allowing for the fact that he spends a lot of his time away from home, conducting, I began to wonder whether he'd become slightly reclusive.

But one evening in November 2013 he telephoned me from his home in Suffolk. Sounding informal and relaxed, he said that he'd received from his manager the list of questions I wanted to ask him and was pleased to see that they addressed important issues. In fact, he wanted to respond to them straight away, so he had a proposal to make: that he answer the questions by e-mail (this would enable him to respond while he was away conducting) and that we meet at some point in the future if this was still necessary.

My heart sank a little because I feared that an e-mail exchange would have none of the personal immediacy of a face-to-face conversation. But he went on to explain that he communicates more naturally and spontaneously in writing than he does in person because he doesn't feel under pressure to give an immediate and perhaps insufficiently considered response. Had I read his recent question-and-answer piece for the *Guardian* (described by the paper as a rare interview with him) in which he talked about his first meeting and ongoing friendship with Britten?[1] Indeed I had. Well, he told me, it had been submitted to the paper by e-mail. I wouldn't have guessed, and so I agreed readily to his proposal and looked forward to his first e-mail. It arrived a few days later, and my subsequent questions

---

[1] The Arts Interview with Fiona Maddocks, *The Guardian*, 15 November 2013; also published in the programme book of Aldeburgh Music's Britten Centenary Weekend.

and queries were answered similarly promptly, often with a greeting such as, 'Here's some more, as requested. Hope it hits the spot.' Furthermore, the tone of his written comments was informative but informal, as if we were chatting in person rather than by correspondence.

Some readers will know that as a fifteen-year-old he conducted the London Symphony Orchestra in the premiere of his First Symphony (a work that he has since withdrawn). The memory of that event appears to cause him some discomfort, if not exactly embarrassment, and in our e-mail exchange he made more than one reference to what he described as the 'shenanigans' surrounding it. It's likely, I suppose, that the high-profile performance of a large-scale work by *any* composer so young will attract as much attention to his or her precocity as to the music, and Knussen's current ambivalence about the premiere of the Symphony is understandable given his self-effacing approach to his work. Anyone who has seen him conduct or heard him being interviewed will know that he's personable but unshowy.

Unfortunately my face-to-face encounter with him didn't happen, hence the inclusion here of a decidedly substandard photograph of him. It was taken in the Queen Elizabeth Hall in London in May 2000 while he was rehearsing the London Sinfonietta for the first British performance of Elliott Carter's ASKO Concerto – in typically straightforward, businesslike manner.

If you'd asked me when I was twenty what the term 'British composer' meant to me, I would probably have answered 'Not much'. At that time, the music that most immediately affected my own was anything *but* British: Carter, Ligeti and Takemitsu, for instance, though I was also eagerly following what Birtwistle, Maxwell Davies and Goehr were doing. But several summers at Tanglewood, where I worked primarily with Gunther Schuller and where I also attended classes given by Maderna, Ligeti and Messiaen (to name just a few!), gave me a sense of being involved in a much bigger picture. I was attracted to the USA partly for family reasons (I'm half-American on my mother's side) and also because of the amazing musical time bombs that came across the Atlantic on records during the Sixties – the Ives Fourth Symphony and Varèse's *Amériques*, for example; and, in quite another sense, the Berio Sinfonia.

When you think about it, Berio had spent much of the 1960s in New York, Boulez was at the BBC and Henze was everywhere – there was a tremendous sense of there being a shared international new-music culture (Lukas Foss used to refer to it as 'a sort of invisible cathedral that we're all building'). In this country the BBC Proms and the brand-new London Sinfonietta were firmly international in outlook, and the 1971 ISCM [International Society for Contemporary Music] Festival in London had made a big impression on me. My first practical connection to new music in this country was through Peter Maxwell Davies, who was very encouraging, and for whom I sometimes used to do musical odd-jobs as well as attending his classes in Dartington in 1974. He was also a most creative and articulate part of this strong movement against insular attitudes. I feel very lucky to have grown up during such an enormously rich era, at a time when London really was a major international centre for new music – on a level with Paris, Cologne, New York and so on. It's hardly surprising that I might have been a bit snooty about being labelled a 'British composer' at that time.

Nowadays things are very different, it seems to me. When I'm abroad, in Europe particularly, I'm acutely aware of being thought of as a very British composer and that, for instance, the presence of Britten or Tippett in my musical make-up can't really be shared with most composers from elsewhere. The most cosmopolitan of composers younger than me – Benjamin, Turnage, Anderson and Adès, for example – seem also to be perceived abroad as quintessentially 'British', even though the roots of their music couldn't be less insular, nor less individual. Perhaps growing up open to a multiplicity of stimuli in a poly-stylistic environment less doctrinaire than many European new music festivals exhibit has something to do with it. This notion is perhaps confirmed by the fact that similarly 'British' attitudes can be found in composers from Holland, Denmark and Finland – which likewise experienced big creative renaissances in the 1960s and 1970s.

Now you mention it, I suppose you're right about the term 'avant-garde' not being used much today. After all, several works which defined that label, like *Le Marteau* and *Gruppen*, have by now entered some sort of mainstream repertory. So I suppose that eventually 'avant-garde' will be simply a style-and-time-defining tag, like art nouveau, if it isn't already. I also feel that what was left of the 'avant-garde' in the 1970s – the 'new complexity' movement, for instance – has remained curiously frozen for the past forty-odd years: a long stasis compared to virtually any period in musical history, it occurs to me, particularly when you think of the frequency of seismic upheavals during the first half of the twentieth century.

But with 'serial' versus 'non-serial' we're talking about technique, not style. And the term 'Serial' with a capital S is misused terribly at the moment as a synonym for 'atonal' in populist musical journalism. This is something that bothers me a lot, because, although much of my music sounds, or is supposed to sound, pretty euphonious, a big part of why the notes are as they are derives from serial thinking. So the term 'serial' isn't redundant; it's just widely misunderstood. Serialism was and is an extraordinarily flexible way of thinking about music that can produce wildly different results, from Babbitt to Britten and *Lulu* to *Licht*!

At the moment we're definitely going through a phase when 'anything goes'. This is partly because of half-baked attempts at 'crossover', which are a pretty unsavoury (to me) compromise with commerce. And because it's easy now for anyone who writes music to instantly 'put themselves out there' with websites or whatever, the half-baked is much more publicly visible than it was. But surely there will always be strong, original personalities – in all areas of music – who find their own path, taking what they need from the world around them and transforming it in a way that enriches the whole picture. I know it's a cliché, but Mozart's a pretty amazing example. Or Berg – he's another example of a real original who was also in another sense an eclectic (or 'synthetic', as Stravinsky put it). In fact there are very few great composers whose musical speech didn't develop in this way.

I like to think that the many different styles and forms of good music today should be able to peacefully co-exist in a mutually enriching landscape, rather in the way that innumerable past styles and forms co-exist happily in our memory of listening experience. The criteria of what is good music and what isn't remain, ultimately, mysterious. For me, it's perhaps a sense of something exceptionally beautiful and full of meaning being communicated in such a precise, natural way that I don't need to be immediately aware of the means – it's so much easier to explain technically why something *isn't* good music.

I don't have any particular philosophy about what my music is or isn't. I certainly don't set out to express myself, and I find that idea repellent, actually. I only write what I feel compelled to write at the time, and sometimes that means: nothing. I start to compose because something new or odd occurs to me that I want to explore, or because I've come across a text that suggests music to me, or alternatively because I want to commemorate something or someone. Of course, I hope that the resulting music is expressive, but that's something that should happen of its own accord. I'm most often consciously communicating with a specific person – a singer or a player or a colleague.

I like to make things that will stimulate them and that will also take their characteristics into account.

Personally, I can't make much of a distinction between the responses of 'heart' and 'mind'. When I'm listening to a piece of music for the first time I want initially to be captivated by the sound of it – otherwise, why bother? But at the same time I'm involuntarily working out what's going on, and how it's made and why. Similarly, although I want my own music to make sense purely as sound, matters of function, balance and proportion preoccupy me very much.

Ideas can make themselves apparent in an infinite number of ways, really. The sudden apprehension of a single idea containing the whole piece doesn't happen to me much; more often these days it's a sense of being intrigued by the notion of connecting disparate things which are already there, in order to make something that *isn't* there. For example, what would happen if such-and-such a shape were imposed on such-and-such an object? This could be purely musical, visual or poetic – it could be anything. What would happen if a particular instrument or performer were to be put into a context one hadn't thought of them inhabiting before? That sort of thing. These juxtapositions, when potent, create a sort of grit-in-the-oyster situation which gives a context or stimulus to begin.

Perhaps the easiest example for me to describe is that of *Flourish with Fireworks*, because it resulted from a number of such juxtapositions. First, I wanted to write a concert-opener of four minutes' duration. What's my favourite piece of this kind? Answer: Stravinsky's *Fireworks* (1908) – also a favourite of Michael Tilson Thomas, for whom I was writing the piece. A very different but equally concentrated masterpiece by Stravinsky is the *Huxley Variations* (1964), the first piece I ever heard Michael conduct. And I wondered what might have happened if Stravinsky had composed *Fireworks* with the technical means he used in the *Huxley Variations* half a century later? Second, there was a painting, *The Fairy Feller's Master Stroke* by Richard Dadd, which I had on my wall at the time; it has multiple levels of crazy detail in a confined space. And third, the note-names of Mi, Ti, Ti and La, eS, sOl for the conductor and the London Symphony Orchestra, who were going to play the piece.

The composition was set in motion by the inter-reaction of all these notions, and although the result owes most to *Fireworks* and the note-names, it wouldn't be as it is without *all* of them. That's pretty representative of how my mind works: setting up a sort of impossibly tangled net of notions, then working my way out of it, Houdini-style, and – with luck – making something intriguing in its own right en route.

Regrettably, I don't have much of a working routine as a composer. What with all the learning of scores, conducting them and touring, my life is too irregular. What tends to happen is that when I've finally committed to realising an idea (I carry around many fragmentary pieces, some in my head and some on paper, that I've thought long about, often for years) and I have a decent stretch of time ahead, I start to tinker with it for a few hours every day or two; then one day it assumes a life of its own and gives me no peace. And at that point I start to work like a lunatic all day, every day, until it's either finished or abandoned. At that stage there's always something to be done somewhere in the piece, even if one bit of it gets stuck for a while. Then I usually get ill immediately afterwards – so much for reward psychology!

I had a quite peculiar history. You see, I didn't really have that much of what passes for a conventional musical education. I'd been composing since I could read music, when I was six or seven. I did this all by myself for quite a long while, and then had harmony and counterpoint lessons with John Lambert, starting when I was about eleven; and thinking-in-counterpoint certainly stuck, even though I was a terrible student and didn't advance beyond two moving parts over a *cantus firmus*. I was too busy writing music by the yard – a new piece virtually every week, which John would look at if I'd done my exercises. What he had to say about them was often very critical, specific and to the point, so that taught me a lot, although rather than rewrite things I'd usually just do another one. Sometimes we looked at scores together in some detail, too (I remember the Boulez Second Mallarmé Improvisation particularly). Then all the shenanigans around the Symphony I wrote when I was fifteen happened, and suddenly I was in the profession already.

Much more immediate in its effect was my *informal* musical education, at home with records and scores and at countless rehearsals of the LSO, where my Dad was principal double bass. He also played for the English Opera Group, so I sometimes went up to Aldeburgh with him and met Britten, who was very encouraging indeed. Later on, at Tanglewood and in Boston, Schuller was also most encouraging (which I badly needed then, having lost a lot of confidence following the aforementioned public shenanigans) and very inspiring to watch at rehearsals, but he didn't let me get away with easy solutions. The last summer I was at Tanglewood he had me work with Donald Martino – a very underrated composer who inhabits a sound-world somewhere between Dallapiccola and Babbitt – who, I now realise, made me appreciate properly for the first time that God really is in the details.

As a youngster I thought I had a very clear idea, from reading about Stravinsky and Britten, of what the life of a composer would be like; it never occurred to me that they were very exceptional figures and that most composers have to make a living by other means. I favoured conducting over teaching as my 'day job' because (1) my Dad always wanted me to be a conductor anyway and (2) I found that teaching composition tends to use the same part of the mind as actually composing, whereas rehearsing and performing is, for me, something psychologically quite different. With the best will in the world, and much respect for those who disagree, I don't feel that conducting is creative work – certainly not as I practise it. It's a most rewarding form of *re*-creation – particularly the preparation of new works, discovering character and form from the printed page and projecting it to the listener, a process which I always find fascinating and from which I've learned a huge amount.

Even so, the balancing act has become more difficult as I've gotten older, and I now need much more time to recover from performing than I used to – from 'ear-worms' and sheer exhaustion. For thirty years, until very recently, at least 60 per cent of my time was spent doing things other than composing – I had very active careers as a touring guest-conductor, festival director and my own record-producer – but in future (all being well) I hope to spend much more time actually writing. I do teach now a bit more than I did, but I don't find it as draining as I used to. Maybe I've got more to say these days!

I think my music became much more focussed and more concentrated when I was in my mid-thirties, which was the beginning of a very good time for me compositionally. I really felt I knew why every note had to be where I'd put it, and I liked the results much more (and still do). In the last decade I've had a lot more difficulty, partly because of composing more away from the piano and partly because of various crises; but the pieces that have come out (the Violin Concerto, *Requiem – Songs for Sue*, *Ophelia's Last Dance* and a few other biggish things that aren't ready yet) have surprised me both by their gentleness and by the way that they flow. They're quite different from my former sense of who I was.

Perhaps that comes from doing so much more of the work in my head than I used to – as much as possible, actually, since I've developed a real aversion to bashing bits out over and over at the piano. That has to be done at some stage, of course, but I try to put it off as long as possible and then use the keyboard mainly to correct things I've misheard at the table. A wrong turn is usually pretty clear early on in any creative endeavour, although quite recently I had the experience of writing two-thirds of a big work for large orchestra which I eventually realised I'd approached from quite the wrong angle and withdrew before it was finished. (I hope to salvage what's good in it and get it right before too long.) And sometimes there are good surprises that set me off in a direction I hadn't thought of when I initially wrote things down 'wrong'.

I cover a surprisingly small amount of paper in the whole journey of writing down music, though the pages are often worked over and over until I can hardly see what I originally meant. For me, composing is a process of imagining, physically writing something down and then responding to what I see – a dialogue between inner ear, hand, eye and a sort of spatial awareness of the form. I'm sure that if something physically catastrophic happened to prevent me from doing this I'd find a new way of working, but after fifty years of composing I can't really imagine it!

Why are most of my pieces short? Natural concision, in the main – though some of them would certainly have been longer had I not been working against a deadline. As a result, some of them will always be a bit lopsided for me. And that's surely why I'm pathologically resistant to deadlines now.

If you carry ideas over a long period of time, as I do, most requests can be fulfilled from pieces that you already want to write. I think the last piece I wrote out of the blue was *Two Organa*, which fell into place by accident, almost. I'd been asked to compose a short piece for a Dutch project involving a two-octave musical box mechanism which involved only white notes, and I'd almost forgotten about this when I got a phone call to say that the deadline was the following day! I'd just been looking at a new edition of the *Magnus Liber Organi*, so this was fresh in my mind. I invented a bit of cod plainchant and wrote canons on it, using varied intervallic doublings to clarify the criss-crossing parts and the 3/8 metre that's characteristic of the Notre Dame *organa*. End of story, or so I thought.

A month or so later I decided I wanted to write a piece to commemorate the twentieth anniversary of Reinbert de Leeuw's Schönberg Ensemble using restrictive tactics that included the number twenty and the musical letters of Reinbert's name. I wrote the whole thing against a very slow projection of the letters of Schönberg's name as found in Berg's Chamber Concerto, and then realised that this was similar to the way in which Pérotin used the syllables of the plainchant held for long time spans in the famous four-part *organa*. When it was finished and I heard the result I was happy with it, but the piece became multi-planed so early on that I felt it needed a small upbeat of some kind in order to prepare the listener's ear for the jungle to follow. At first I thought of playing one or two strata in isolation beforehand, but then it occurred to me that the little musical box piece, which shares the plainchant idea with the later one but sounds utterly different and toyshop-like by comparison, would do just as well. So I orchestrated it in one night in a hotel room in Eindhoven (while trying to watch Abel Gance's *Napoléon* on television, by the way – thank goodness it's a silent film!) and, lo and behold, the next morning *Two Organa* had emerged as it now stands, an unplanned and spontaneous 'unity'.

How do I think of my music? Simultaneously of the sound it makes and a 'spatial' sense of the shape and dimensions; unfortunately also, sometimes, a sense of what it was supposed to be as opposed to how it actually turned out. I like the sound of some of my pieces very much, and also sometimes have enjoyed how such-and-such a difficult corner has been turned. And there's no greater satisfaction than hearing a performance of a piece that 'talks back' to you and reminds you of why you wanted to write it in the first place. More often, though, I'm frustrated at how much less good it is than the one I'd meant it to be or it could have been. And very often, hearing early pieces is terribly embarrassing.

Sometimes I've been pleasantly surprised by what performers have brought to my music – a fresh characterisation can catch one off-guard in a very nice way. But my favourite performances tend to be those that come closest to my present intentions, which isn't fair as they do change and not all performers are mind-readers (though some are!). My way of coping with this syndrome has been to put a good deal of effort into ensuring that there are good recordings of my works as I want them to sound. After that, I pretty much stop worrying about what happens to them.

For the last twenty-five years or so I've conducted most of my own first performances, not from any particularly control-freaky tendency (though I'm told I am one) but because I've been asked to. My experience of working with orchestras has certainly influenced the way I write for them. My orchestration may not always immediately sound 100 per cent the way I imagined it (there are too many variables involved), but it does usually 'sound', particularly in live performance, and I'm proud of that (I'm acutely aware of the physical disposition of the orchestra and of the location of sounds in space when I'm composing). Also, these days I try to notate my scores in such a way that the music can be played straight off with a minimum of explanation from the podium – this doesn't mean that I've simplified my rhythmic language drastically, merely considered extra-carefully the way that it's barred out. I also try to be aware of each instrumental part from the point of view of the player reading it in isolation.

Touch wood, maintaining my own voice as a composer while conducting works by many of my contemporaries hasn't been a problem for me. I'm not concerned with maintaining an individual voice, anyway, because that's surely as personal and automatic as handwriting. Sure, one absorbs musical (and other) stimuli all the time, and they're bound to feed into what you do; but that's a natural process and an enriching one, too. Sometimes I've felt the need to start from a completely fresh technical point of view, and I'm always flummoxed to observe that the music seems to come out curiously the same, whatever I do ... I really believe that the worst imaginable narcissism would be to try to write what you *think* your music ought to be like – surely that would be a recipe for redundancy. So if I find myself starting, out of habit, to do things I've done before, I'm immediately on guard and try to undermine the pattern.

As a performer, I've had to learn how to cope with being a public person – not at all easy, as I'm fundamentally a rather shy person, although I can be very sociable indeed with people I know well and with whom I'm comfortable. The days preceding the first meeting with an orchestra I haven't met before are not unlike a nightmare combination of the first day at a new school and simultaneously being tortured (I imagine). It takes years to realise that the best way is to be comfortable with being yourself on the podium, that's all. But relatively recently I've realised that it is only as a composer that I can be as private as I like. At my stage of life I don't worry about 'career'; I just need to have the peace of mind to be able to get on with it. Harder than you'd think with a mortgage to pay, of course.

If it's true that I've been reticent about giving interviews (and I'm not sure that it is, as it seems to me I've done rather a lot, particularly on radio), it surely stems from my teenage experiences, which certainly made me very cautious later on. Even so, I've occasionally been burnt since. I can well understand that Britten, for example, found it impossible to continue with operatic subjects if they were prematurely 'leaked'. My situation is very different, of course, but I tend to freeze if I read the announcement of a Knussen piece that isn't yet written. I really can't bear the sense of someone looking over my shoulder, though there are a very few close friends with whom I do share work-in-progress.

The composing process is a very acute and personal one, and – in my experience – extremely demanding on the nervous system. When I'm deeply involved in a piece I become hypersensitive, with my sensory antennae working flat out; over a relatively long period of time this isn't a pleasant sensation, and I'm often not as nice to be around as I'd like to be. The physical act of writing the music out in fair copy acts as a relief – the 'raw' bit can be put on hold for a few hours a day while one takes care of the notational mechanics. I always do this as I go along, rather than saving it for the end.

I find that the actual work of composing becomes more demanding with age and experience. I can't tell you why – except that I've become more choosy as I've gotten older and, as I mentioned earlier, I don't want to do the same things, or do things in the same way, again. Of course, you have more technical means at your disposal than thirty or forty years ago, but you really should be on guard against falling back on them for safety. As to whether there's a great personal cost to being a composer, I can't really say; mine is the only reality I know first-hand, and I can't imagine myself functioning otherwise. For me, music is the most important thing in life, that's all.

John McCabe

John McCabe, Kent, August 2012

> **I expect the listener to meet me halfway and think, "Okay, let's see what he's got to say."**

I'd interviewed John McCabe once before – only briefly, many years earlier – and from time to time had bumped into him at concerts. So when I started to compile this book I hoped that he would contribute to it because I was looking forward to a good, long chat with him. I knew that conversation would flow easily, not only because he was relaxed and affable but also because of his wide knowledge of music – it was difficult to talk about pieces, however obscure they might seem, that he didn't know. Given that he combined composing (in all genres except grand opera) with a distinguished career as a concert pianist, teacher and writer, I often wondered where he found time to listen to so much music.

I was therefore pleased when in May 2011 he wrote to me, 'Your project sounds excellent. Indeed, I've thought we need another book of this kind, since it is a long time since the last one.' When I went to interview him at his home in Kent just over a year later he added that he'd once had the idea of compiling such a book himself; the reason he hadn't pursued it, he joked, was that he would have been unable to be included in it.

As I'd expected, this was one of the longer interviews for this collection because conversation was so effortless. In response to my first question – about the relationship, if any, that he saw between his nationality and his music – he said, 'Well, we can talk about that for three hours, really, or two minutes!' Sure enough, conversation also left the main roads of music and meandered onto the byways: he illustrated points by referring to Hindemith's Mass, John Williams's film music and Howells's *Missa Sabrinensis* rather than the late Beethoven String Quartets or Mahler Symphonies. (I felt slight one-upmanship when discovering that he didn't know John Williams's Cello Concerto, which I'd been listening to in the car on my way to the interview.)

As we talked I was reminded of how extraordinarily wide his musical tastes were. Enthusiasms that arose spontaneously included Korngold's Symphony ('a magnificent piece in which he suddenly relit the fuse of his imagination in a way that he wasn't able to do in other, film-connected pieces'), the passacaglia from Jerry Goldsmith's score for the film *Papillon* ('a wonderful piece of music, by any standard'), Malcolm Arnold's overture to *The Roots of Heaven* ('I think it's terrible, actually, a dreadful mish-mash, but I *love* it'), Roberto Gerhard ('I'm a great Gerhard fan'), Rawsthorne's Third Symphony ('wonderful piece'), some American composers ('Schuman, particularly, and Piston, and to some extent Roy Harris, wrote wonderful works with great guts and determination and *character*') and Webern ('I actually enjoy Webern and play it for pleasure, which I think would horrify some people').

So for me, at least, this encounter was pure enjoyment, even (or especially) when it wandered off track. At one point when I said I should apologise for the fact that we were discussing other composers rather than him, he laughed and replied, 'Well, I like talking about music, you see …'

―――

My mother was German, with some Finnish, and she used to sing Schubert songs and German folk songs. She was also a good amateur violinist, and played in orchestras and string quartets. And the basic trend of my parents' record library, too, was towards the German classics: Beethoven, Brahms symphonies and concertos, and lots of extracts of Wagner (which I still prefer to the complete operas!). But I've always had an interest in exploring other repertoires. Because of illness I didn't go to school until I was eleven, so I was at home with my parents' record collection and music on the radio, and with my own interest in exploring on the piano what was available to me. By the time I was eleven I knew most of the Beethoven sonatas – including the *Hammerklavier*, which I merely stumbled through and still can't play. And I knew the Mozart sonatas and Schubert sonatas and a lot of Chopin.

I was particularly fascinated with orchestral music and explored pieces such as Kalinnikov's First Symphony, which I still love, and Balakirev's First. I loved Russian music. I heard Copland's *Rodeo* and loved *that*, and of course I was interested in what was then new British music. I listened on the radio to the first performance of Vaughan Williams's Sixth Symphony and I got to know Alan Rawsthorne's music very well, *very* early. I got to know *him* quite early, too. And when I was still a kid I bought Bax's Third Symphony on 78s, having heard a broadcast of it – it was Barbirolli's recording. And I was hooked by that piece. So it's no surprise that I have this wide range of references.

When I was very young the basic language of most music colleges and universities was post-Stanford – very conservative and tonal. Then of course we got the great serial revolution, after which it was *only* acceptable to write in a post-Schoenberg style. I remember that in the early 1980s I gave a composition lecture to Vincent Persichetti's class at the Juilliard School in New York, and as I walked into the room I could see the serialists over *here*, the minimalists over *there* and another group at the front who were clearly tonal – it was obvious just by looking at them! But today, as you say, the distinction between serial and non-serial is largely redundant. Pockets of post-Schoenbergian resistance are still being flushed out but they're few and far between, I think.

I never had a problem with Stanford's music but I didn't want to write in that style. I wanted to be more contemporary. If I'd studied with post-Schoenbergians I would never have got very far with *them* – I would just have taken what I wanted from the lessons and written my own music – but it would also have given me something to react against. And young composers need that in order to define themselves with reasonable certitude and at a reasonable pace. If you're reacting *against* the official party line you find other composers you can imitate and learn from; and if you go *with* the party line you emulate the composers who write in that way. But when the field is wide open, and you can do anything you want, it's much more difficult for young composers to find out who they are.

I'd say that my music is contemporary – of course. But one of my problems as a composer is that I'm perceived as being neither far-out modernist nor far-out conservative. I fall into that group in the middle who don't appear to represent an extreme. And extremes are always easier to pigeonhole than the area in the middle. Nicholas Maw was another one. Tony Payne's a little more modernist than me but he'd also fit into that very large area, which is in fact most music, I think.

I write the kind of music that I'd like somebody to be writing for me to listen to – which doesn't mean anything at all(!) but does define, in a sense, where I'm coming from. I don't have anybody else in mind, and I don't actually consider the audience at all. I *hope* that what I'm doing will connect with them, because that's what it's all about; but I think it's very dangerous to write *for* an audience because then you're almost always going to be writing *down*. 'Accessible' is one of the dirtiest words in the English language – because of its misuse. Verdi had a sign on his wall saying 'Remember the audience', and although he was one of the great composers I think that's dangerous – a two-edged sword, really.

My music, it seems to me, and of course I *would* say this, seems fairly direct and relatively simple to follow, and the style isn't outrageously modern. But many years ago somebody did an analysis of my Oboe Quartet at the same time as doing an analysis of Roberto Gerhard's incredibly complex Concerto for Orchestra, which I happen to think is a wonderful piece – I'm a great Gerhard fan. And she discovered that we were using exactly the same procedures. I was aware that my Oboe Quartet is a *sort* of serial piece, but I wasn't aware of some of the complexities she found in it. They were purely subconscious, I think. I believe that *most* composing is a subconscious process and that the expressiveness of music comes from making it in a particular way.

I can't identify the moment when I found my own voice as a composer, because there isn't really such a moment. Or rather, I think that you see it only in retrospect. And I suppose that, looking back (a long time – nearly fifty years ago now), my *Variations on a Theme of Karl Amadeus Hartmann* is probably the piece in which I found my voice. I was ill at the time but I had an enormous excitement writing the piece because I felt I was discovering something. I think I was discovering *myself*. I remember thinking, 'This is exciting and *new*', but there was nothing new in the piece, even though it contains things that nobody else would have done. It's quite derivative. But I'm not concerned with originality at all.

You know what Honegger said about this? 'There's no such thing as complete originality.' Absolutely right. So when young composers tell me, 'I don't think I'm very original', I reply, 'Don't worry about it. Nobody is. Just get on with doing your own thing.' You learn more from other composers than you do from direct tuition, I think. Direct tuition should merely create a strong basic framework within which you can then assimilate other ideas.

I compose music because I have to. It's not exactly a compulsion, and I don't compose every day because I've got to compose *something*. I compose because I have to compose the particular piece I'm working on at any given moment. And I don't think I compose in order to express any particular thing. Stravinsky said that music can't express anything other than itself, and I think he was absolutely right. His point was that you can't sit down and decide to write a piece about, say, a battle – unless it's a purely illustrative piece, which most aren't. My piano piece *Tenebrae* and ballet *Edward II* are angry pieces – I was furious when I wrote them – but I didn't sit down and say, 'Right, I'm going to write angry music.' I mean, it took me eighteen months to write *Edward II*. Was I supposed to stay in a state of absolute fury for eighteen months? You can't artificially maintain a particular emotion in order to write a piece about it. It's just something that's in the air at the time.

When I write music I'm trying to say something that can be said only through music, in the hope that people will respond to it. And I expect the listener to meet me halfway and think, 'Okay, let's see what he's got to say', not to start off by saying, 'I know I'm going to hate this piece.' This is one of the main problems of contemporary music: people have been brainwashed into expecting not to like it, and there's an unwillingness to work at listening. It's an attitude that has become established over the last forty years, and quite what we do about it I don't know.

The same thing has happened in choral societies. Choral singing in this country has deteriorated since choirs have sung more and more pieces that are derivative of some mainstream twentieth-century music but easier (and also, by the way, not as good as the original). Choirs think they're being up to date, but because the music isn't terribly demanding it doesn't stretch them much. So when they come to do *Belshazzar's Feast* they suddenly find it more difficult than it was thirty years ago – which is the wrong way round. If you stop being challenged, it does you harm, culturally. And you miss out. I believe that people actually *respond* to being made to work.

I remember that in the 1950s Peter Racine Fricker was called in *this* country a European-style composer and in Europe a British-style composer. I've been described – it was in Germany, I think – as a typically English composer, but I had no idea what they meant by that and I still don't know. I don't really understand these labels. I don't feel that I'm a British composer except by dint of being born here and being of substantially British extraction – 50 per cent British, I suppose.

But I do think that there's a British ethos, a British expression, which comes out in music. The English character is perceived as a little reserved, a bit private, rather unemotional; but listen to Herbert Howells's *Missa Sabrinensis*, which is one of the greatest outpourings of ecstasy in *any* music, it seems to me. It's *very* un-British but in a style that's recognisably from this country. That alchemy works, but I have no idea how.

Sometimes inspiration comes to me while I'm walking or doing something else outdoors. I should walk through the woods with my hands clasped behind my back, shouldn't I? And with a notebook in my pocket. But I don't carry one around with me because I always reckon that if I think of an idea that's good enough I'll remember it. Which is not necessarily true, unfortunately.

I do write some ideas down but I don't plan out a complete piece in sketches. I write little bits and just knit them together, really – it's musical knitting. And sometimes I do the sleeves before the body, because I can't work from A to Z in a straight line. But I do have the whole piece in my mind. I know, either absolutely or pretty much, how it's going to begin and how it's going to end. I'm very conscious of the line through the music, and in order to achieve that I've got to write all these bits around it and gradually fill them in. Writing the music down is, it seems to me, a purely intellectual process, because the only way you can express what you have to express is by getting the nuts and bolts of its scaffolding correct. So you're concentrating on structure, thematic relationships and tonal schemes – in other words, the blueprint, the details through which this building in sound is created.

Most of this work is done on computer, and there'll come a point when I've got enough of the piece to say to myself, 'Right, I can write them all in, in order.' Then I'll either print out the result so that I can scrawl all over it and add things, or start working on different bits. And then I'll print *that* out. I print out a lot of drafts, which means I can keep a check on the structure of the piece. But, despite the technology, all this work doesn't take me any less time than writing by hand used to.

As a composer I've progressed through a stage of using serial technique – in my own, flexible way – to using many, more varied elements. These include simple tonality and avant-garde techniques such as note clusters and arithmetical progressions of rhythms that squeeze a rhythm in order to create excitement as chords become quicker and quicker. I did that in *The Chagall Windows*, for instance. Being a performer is helpful in this because – hopefully – it makes me very practical in the way that I write out the music. When I play other people's music I see the problems *they* have in writing it down for me, the performer.

I like to be fairly precise in my directions in scores, and in instrumental parts I'm quite obsessive about markings. For instance, I prefer to write a whole row of *staccato* dots rather than the word '*staccato*'. Then copyists come along and write one bar of *staccato* dots followed by the word '*staccato*' – which I do understand. The only area that I *don't* mark up well – and this is a technical failing – is vocal music. I'm told I write well for the voice, but I don't really understand it (I really can't sing). So I hope the singer will bring to the music things that I'm not sure about and can't write down. In any case, the music follows the sense of the words.

I very seldom revisit earlier works. I'd rather go on to something new. But, of course, after a piece has been given its first performance I go through it very carefully and make slight adjustments to things like balance. Very, very seldom do I cut pieces after performance because usually I've cut them before they were completed. In fact I've quite often cut as much as 50 per cent of a piece – and often the bits I liked best because they impeded the progress of the piece.

I don't particularly like giving pre-concert talks because I don't think they serve a very useful purpose. A talk *should* be useful – it should relate to something in people's experience or potential experience. And composers really don't know what to say that will be useful. The only answer is to turn up with a stack of CDs and ask, 'Right, what do you want to know?' And to hope that you can illustrate some points as you answer their questions. In any case, I don't like to give people too many clues about my music. I want them to respond to my music themselves rather than imposing their own version of my ideas on it. You see, I don't mind if they put their own pictures or story to my music. It shows that there's something in it that they respond to, and that they're being creative with it.

Performers have revealed things in my music that *I* wasn't aware of. For example, I've had quite a lot of wonderful performances of *Notturni ed Alba*, but when André Previn conducted it he played on the London Symphony Orchestra as if he were playing on a piano – he controlled the orchestra as if it were one instrument. The things he did, such as *tiny* bits of *rubato* that aren't in the score (if they *were* in the score, people would overdo them) were purely instinctive, but he revealed things about the colouring and even the structure of the piece that I hadn't noticed before. The same was true of *The Chagall Windows*: although it had had some wonderful performances, Bernard Haitink's was so visceral and exciting. I'd never realised there was quite that degree of dynamism in the piece.

But one of the worrying trends in music is that performers invite composers less often to go through the work with them before they give the premiere, or indeed any subsequent performance. In some cases I've been pretty sure that it was because they didn't actually know my piece well enough, because the performances then proved it! I would mistrust performers who didn't want input from the composer. On the whole, I've been lucky with performances of my music, but I remember some in which people played perfectly well but did either a gross misreading or a bit of 'interpretation' that wasn't acceptable. If they'd gone through the piece with me just once, I would have put that right. It worries me that they feel they know it all. They *don't*. Nobody does. But they can at least get a bit *nearer* to knowing it all.

The works that people associate most strongly with you aren't necessarily your best, though quite often they'll be among the better ones, simply because they'll have been performed more often. My *Cloudcatcher Fells* is part of the brass band repertoire, and *Scenes in America Deserta* is part of the vocal repertoire because the King's Singers do it all the time. And people know of *Edward II* and one or two of my other orchestral pieces. As long as the works that people remember represent you reasonably well, you can be very happy if people say things like, 'Oh yes, he wrote *The Chagall Windows*, didn't he?' That's not the piece I'd particularly choose to be remembered by, if I could pick just one piece (which I wouldn't), but that's irrelevant.

Everybody remembers *The Chagall Windows* and I think that's partly to do with the title – it's very important for a composer to have works whose titles people can identify with. Think of Birtwistle's *The Triumph of Time*, *Gawain's Journey* and *Earth Dances*: they're great titles for what I think are great works. But sometimes finding the right title is the most difficult thing about writing a piece. It's important to find the right one because then you stand a chance of getting people's attention, getting into their memory. I've written only one symphony – my No. 2 – that hasn't got a title or subtitle. And sometimes I compromise, as with *Symphony on a Pavane*. It *is* a symphony, I think, but it's important to me that a connection to audiences is made through the title. The same is true of my Symphony *Labyrinth*: it's essential to me that that work is perceived as both a symphony and a reflection of a labyrinthine situation.

Composing is a curiously introverted activity. And yet the composer is inevitably part of the community, regardless of whether he's an outgoing type. It's like having a split personality, really. Take David Matthews: like many of the composers I know, he's not introverted – he's quite accessible – but there's a certain hesitancy about him. And I think that comes from composers feeling that they want to say something in words to people but being unsure if they'll really be interested, or maybe worrying about picking the right words because they're actually much better at dealing with musical notation.

Despite the fact that you can't stop me talking, I'm actually very shy. I mean, having to telephone somebody I don't know makes me incredibly nervous and I'll put it off for as long as possible. But although I'm very shy I'm sufficiently confident about my role in life as a musician, and in my belief in music, to overcome that.

I respond absolutely emotionally to music. I'm concerned with heart and gut reaction. Parts of Tippett's *A Child Of Our Time*, for instance: I can feel a lump in my throat *now*, just talking about it without listening to it. And Nielsen's Fifth, when in the first movement the big tune comes bursting out in G major. The heart just leaps – *still*, after hearing it hundreds of times. So, yes, I listen to music just for pleasure. But having thousands of records is actually a drawback. I stand there in front of them (the CDs are all upstairs in the room above us, and may come through the ceiling at any moment) and think, 'What the hell am I going to listen to now?' I really need to have an idea before I go upstairs! But it usually ends up being Walton.

He was less innovative than Britten – one of my great musical heroes, who set out, more publicly than Vaughan Williams, to write music for amateurs. It was part of Britten's commitment to society, and a reflection of the place that he believed music should have in it. *Peter Grimes* is still my favourite opera and contains things that, again, bring a tear to my eye because they're so beautiful and so warm. I think it's the greatest opera ever written, really, for a number of reasons. And then there are his chamber operas. You might say that Britten invented, or *reinvented*, opera in this country. His introduction of the gamelan was also quite an innovation, and no other composer used the tritone with such concentration. It's the building block of the *War Requiem*, for instance.

Walton didn't do any of that. He just continued the previous traditions of concerto, symphony and so on, with enormous skill. I think his First Symphony is an absolutely phenomenal piece – the greatest symphony of the twentieth century, actually. I love Sibelius and Prokofiev and Nielsen and Vaughan Williams, but if I had to take one work that represents the symphony in the twentieth century, it would be Walton's First. Music isn't only about innovation. I mean, think of the lyricism of Walton's Cello Concerto! I'd give my right arm to have written that.

James MacMillan

Sir James MacMillan, London, June 2014

> **I write music in the hope that it communicates, but I know that in many cases it won't.**

Sir James MacMillan has sometimes struck me as a rather contrary figure. Although he claims to have been a late starter in comparison to his best-known contemporaries, he has had greater 'popular' success than any of them, beginning with *The Confession of Isobel Gowdie* at the Proms in 1990 and, two years later, the Percussion Concerto *Veni, Veni, Emmanuel* – whose five hundred performances at the time of writing make it one of the few contemporary works to have become a 'repertory piece'.

Also, as is well known, he holds strong views about politics, religion and nationalism – indivisible elements of his worldview which have inevitably made their way into his music. And sometimes his outspokenness on these issues has made him enemies, particularly at the 1999 Edinburgh Festival when he delivered a lecture entitled 'Scotland's Shame: Anti-Catholicism as a Barrier to Genuine Pluralism'. Nor does he hold back in his music, which is passionate and sometimes confrontational. Yet interviewers agree that in person he's calm, soft-spoken and courteous, and on every occasion that I've spoken to him he has been friendly and unassuming.

I first met him in May 2010 while reporting on the premiere of his Violin Concerto in London, and when I told him at that time of my intention to compile this book he agreed readily to contribute to it. But it was four years before the following encounter took place – again in London, on one of his frequent visits from his home in Glasgow, at the hotel in Waterloo where he was staying. He seemed pleased to see me again.

By then I'd come across an archive interview that suggested he would be in sympathy with at least some of the thinking behind the book. 'Music's not something which can just wash over us', he told *Classic CD* magazine in February 1999. 'It needs us to sacrifice something of ourselves to meet it, and it's very difficult sometimes to do that, especially the whole culture we're in. Sacrifice and self-sacrifice – certainly sacrificing your time – is not valued anymore.' He'd also become a grandfather, and I was reminded of another interviewer's comment that 'with his wave of grey hair and slightly portly demeanour he cuts a much softer figure than the gimlet-eyed young man of the 90s who glares challengingly from his early CDs'.

He has perhaps mellowed with age. But I imagine that he was occupied with, among other things, the issue of Scottish independence (the interview took place a few weeks after the Scottish government announced the date of the September 2014 referendum). As the topic seemed incidental to our conversation I avoided it, and I was interested to discover shortly afterwards that his advocacy of unionism made him more enemies in his own country. Interested, too, to learn during the interview that he thinks of himself as no more of a Scottish composer than a British one.

We talked in the foyer lounge of his hotel, whose loud piped music – of a distinctly non-MacMillanesque variety – we did our best to ignore. 'You can't go anywhere these days without this sort of thing', he sighed. 'We could ask them if they'd turn it down. If it was Maxwell Davies you were interviewing, he'd have caused a fuss already – he can't stand this. Well, nobody can, I suppose. But it might be alright ...' We chatted briefly about the fact that some composers are more comfortable than others with the increasingly public nature of their work, and then, determinedly ignoring the strains of Connie Francis's 'Vacation', I began the interview by asking him how often he visits London on business.

London is still really the musical centre of the UK, so I come here quite often. There are lots of things for me to do here. I had a meeting with my publishers this morning, and on this visit I'm working with the Genesis Foundation – which helps young artists at the beginning of their careers – and the choral group The Sixteen, as well as fitting in lots of new things. The other reason I come to London is to work as a conductor. I spend a lot of time doing that, although not as much as a 'real' conductor who does nothing else. I've always had a performer's instinct, and although I never made it as an instrumentalist I've always wanted to lead and organise performances in one way or another.

You're absolutely right that there's a wide range of difference in the way that composers interact with the public. I think most of them are shy – I've overcome a lot of shyness in order to be able to speak publicly or even perform – and I still have the composer's instinct which, as you rightly say, is solitary. By necessity, the composer operates in total silence and in solitary confinement, as it were. However, conducting allows me to get out of the house and to work with my fellow musicians, which I love doing. I've learned so much from watching them, talking with them and writing for them. They've helped me to be a composer, in fact.

It's no surprise to me that the two crafts of composing and conducting, which for a while became so separated, are coming back together again. Think of how many composers are also conductors: George Benjamin, Oliver Knussen, Thomas Adès, John Adams, Esa-Pekka Salonen ... Even so, I've been surprised by how much of my life has been taken up by conducting, and getting the correct balance, with composing as my main activity, is important. In the last few months I've been conducting in New Zealand, the States, Holland and India, which was very exciting; but, obviously, no music was written during that time because I was doing other things.

I've been composing since I was given a musical instrument (a recorder, though I very quickly moved on to trumpet, cornet and piano) when I was nine. But I had no idea what that would mean in terms of a career. As a child I was simply beguiled by the music of the great composers that I heard, and I was also interested in their lives, even though I realised that they were from different periods of history. So discovering that figures like Benjamin Britten, who was living and writing music a few hundred miles down the road, was a huge thing for me. As a teenager I began to understand what *his* life was like, but I never imagined that I could do anything similar. And I *don't* do anything similar, really – one has one's own trajectory, which is shaped by one's own circumstances.

After leaving university I didn't know how I was going to make a living. Academia was one route – I taught at universities for a while – but trying to establish a career involved trial and error, and I had no idea what was around the corner. There's still a bit of trial and error, in fact, and things are beginning to change again: I'm setting up a new music festival, The Cumnock Tryst, in the Ayrshire town where I was born and grew up.[1] This is a new artistic direction for me, and I don't know if I have a facility for it; but I have a great interest in inviting musicians to come and play at a special place. It's very exciting.

Mainland European musicians often detect lines and influences in British music that we don't, and they sometimes talk about a pastoralism that connects the likes of Birtwistle to Vaughan Williams. This isn't necessarily a pejorative thing, because the British musical soul has a facility for deep reflection, whether that's inspired by environment or

---

[1] 'Tryst' (pronounced to rhyme with 'heist') is an old Scots word for a meeting place, and also the name of a tune written by MacMillan and used in a number of his works.

countryside or whether it's simply in the nature of the British character. Outsiders can identify it. And when I'm able to stand back from my work I, too, see the influence of other British composers, most of them English: Britten, Tippett, Birtwistle and Maxwell Davies. We *can* talk about a recent British musical tradition in serious classical music, one that goes right back to Byrd, Gibbons, Purcell and Handel. And I feel very much part of it – I'm a British composer.

I'm also a Scottish composer, which is why I've always had an interest in the music of Scotland that *wasn't* part of the European mainstream. Because Scotland was always historically on the periphery of Europe and therefore not part of the great advances in music provision and patronage further south, we developed our own form of classical music – which, of course, is *pibroch* and the music associated with the pipes and the traditional clan system. So there's a parallel musical world that I, a Scottish composer, have to be aware of. And a different history – a pre-British history, sometimes. Robert Carver[2] predates the Reformation, the union of the crowns and the union of the parliaments; so that, too, is my tradition. It's a rich patchwork of elements that makes me the British and Scottish composer that I feel I am.

It's interesting that questions of orthodoxy and aesthetic straitjackets were very urgent in my mind some time ago but aren't as urgent now. The compulsion to feel that one had to stick to a certain direction laid out by avant-garde or modernist principles has dissipated somewhat, and I see younger composers who aren't so bothered about following the pathways that were laid out for us. My generation is an interim one, I think: we're between those who felt that they had to adhere strictly to something and others who have come to terms with the free-for-all. We're not completely comfortable with either approach. And I don't know who has it easier in the long run. Some composers feel liberated from what was confining in the 1950s and 1960s, but if there's a free-for-all, how do you give your music coherence? If everything's permissible, how do you decide what you're going to pursue with a degree of focus throughout your artistic life?

When I was young, my great discoveries were in the sphere of ethnomusicology – the music of exotic cultures such as Indonesia. Getting to grips with the gamelan for the first time and putting a suling (the small wooden flute from Java) in my mouth and playing it were fascinating experiences. But, as you suggest, the world has shrunk, and perhaps that sense of discovery isn't as exciting as it was even thirty

---

[2] A Scottish Renaissance monk and composer of polyphonic sacred music (c.1485–c.1570).

years ago. However, I think I've always been aware of the need to bring heart and head together in my music. In my view, music that's all heart on sleeve, with no rigorous technical control, is unbalanced.

Even the most powerful emotions can't be communicated well if they're not tightly controlled by a structure that's based on what the head does. I react to music in quite an emotional way, but I know that some of the subject matter I write about – whether it's sacred or secular – has an intensity that could swamp itself if there isn't a mind trying to shape it musically. On the other hand, some music is so brain-oriented that it's arid, and the human soul is left out of it. From my perspective, I see composers who've fallen one side of the balance or the other, and it's those who get the balance correct that I admire the most.

The other thing that's hugely important to me is musical structure. If I can get that right, other aspects of a piece take shape in such a way that I don't need to go back and tinker in a major way. So very early on in the composition process I try to think structurally, even as the notes begin to emerge. However, structure isn't necessarily noticeable to the listener. In fact, in many ways it should be hidden, or it should hide itself by projecting the compulsion and emotion of the music instead. One of the next things I do is establish – in my mind's eye, if not physically on paper – a visual image of the piece. This doesn't necessarily hem my ideas in, and the design can be changed as the piece develops, but doing this gives me objective control from the outset and enables me to say, 'That is my piece, or that is the likelihood of my piece.'

Like all musicians, I think, I take pride in the fact that music is an abstract form. It's *the* most abstract of the arts, probably. And it has self-sufficiency: it seems to communicate its completeness according to its own designs, without the need to be explained through words. Which is why some people argue that the most abstract forms of music – those that are 'purest' and most complete in themselves – trump all others. However, music also has a facility to be representational. It can paint pictures and tell stories. And we know that composers can be inspired by things outside the abstract box, things that can also inspire painters and writers.

My own music is becoming more and more abstract, and I'm writing pieces called 'Oboe Concerto' or 'Piano Trio No. 2' that have no programme or reason for existing other than what the music is. As a result, I'm writing programme notes very differently. I've just written one this morning, actually, for a new percussion concerto, and it's very factual. It just tells you, in as least boring a way as possible, what the music does, because I don't feel that I have anything else to say about it. But I've also written works like *The Confession of Isobel Gowdie* whose music wouldn't be what it is if it hadn't been for the very specific nature of its extra-musical inspiration – a story, a vision, an image, an event.

Beyond those of us who value the abstraction of music there's a huge mass of people who value its representational nature, and I find people saying, 'Oh, that bar, that passage sounds like *this* …' before giving a very graphic description of something. And I don't have a problem with that if it's what they see in their mind's eye when they hear the music. Whether it's a good thing or not, we live in a society that's dominated by the visual and the verbal, and people can sometimes be baffled when they confront something that can't be explained in visual or verbal ways. I don't know if other composers feel the same way, but I'm quite happy to live with a balance. Sometimes I need my work to be completely abstract, sometimes there has to be something else in it.

Every period in musical history seems to have had its own sense of fashion. I mean, Mozart was loved because it was fashionable. *Maybe* that meant 'new'. And then very quickly the new became baffling, or more and more baffling. Even going back to the mediaeval times, one wonders what it must have been like to be an ordinary person with no education, wandering into a cathedral and hearing an Ockeghem mass. How would you have made sense of those incredible musical structures unfolding, other than feeling as if you were walking onto the threshold of heaven? Maybe you'd have thought that this was what the divine's all about – which, of course, it is.

Beethoven's music could baffle an audience of its own period, and gradually the nineteenth century had to cope with this sense of mystery in music. It eventually led to the Second Viennese School, whose composers realised that they had to enter a kind of laboratory phase and perform music to themselves. Schoenberg established a society for the private performance of music because he knew that a group of aficionados would be able to appreciate it in a way that the general public wouldn't.

I'm aware that audiences very quickly settle into liking what they know and knowing what they like. So those who grow up with the classics have to be teased towards the notion that, while a museum culture is fine, tradition *lives* and is just as exciting in its modern garb. Some people are still baffled by *any* new music, while others who are more at ease with strong modernist terms might regard me as quite a conservative composer. I'm sometimes asked whether I write music with a particular audience in mind, and the answer is no. Every listener's response is different, so there's no point in my trying to second-guess what an audience will think of my music. And there's no point in trying to appeal to the uncurious. That would be soul-destroying. I write music in the hope that it communicates, but I know that in many cases it won't. I just have to take that on board.

But I do have an ideal listener in mind: someone who's thirsty for things they've not encountered before. And I suppose this is where a composer sounds arrogant, because that ideal listener is a bit like me. While I was still young I started listening to everything, including music from the other side of the world as well as the most experimental pieces of the 1960s and 1970s. In other words, my instincts were modernist – and I think they still are, even though the definition of modernism has become more diffuse. Most composers, in fact, are intellectually curious, and certainly curious about widening their musical horizons.

You raised the issue of spirituality, and I would say that music – certainly the music of the past – has had a kind of umbilical connection with religion. Musicians are the midwives of faith. So I don't see the dangers of a conflict between the sacred and the secular that some others might see. I like being part of a secular society, and I enjoy my music being played in secular situations to secular people. But I'm very much at ease with my Catholicism as well, and there was a point at which I realised I had to make that clear. There was a temptation to hide it, though, because British people are embarrassed about being publicly religious – for good reasons, sometimes. My instinct for many years was to keep it quiet, but there was really no point in doing that because it meant hiding an essential aspect of the kind of composer I am.

Over the last hundred and fifty years there has been a disruption between the worlds of faith (religion) and the arts, but in music this hasn't been so clear-cut. In fact, you could say that some of the major figures of music during this period were profoundly religious. Stravinsky was as conservative in his theology as he was revolutionary in his music-making, and he set the Psalms, the Mass, the Ave Maria and the Credo. He was a man of the world who was able to straddle both the sacred and the secular. Schoenberg, the other great pillar of modernism, converted to practising Judaism when he left Germany after the Holocaust, and some of his later work reflects Jewish culture and theology. It's no surprise to me that John Cage went to study with him, because he was as much a mystic as Cage was. Of course, Cage explored the religions and philosophies of the Far East, and I find it interesting that the original title of his most famous (or notorious) work, *4'33"*, was 'Silent Prayer'.

Then, of course, there's Messiaen, who was as much a theologian as a musician. And the major composers of the post-Shostakovich generation from behind the Iron Curtain – Schnittke, Gubaidulina, Górecki and Kancheli – are profoundly religious; while in this country we've had not only John Tavener and Jonathan Harvey but also Britten, in his own strange, labyrinthine way. So you could say that the search for the sacred has been part of the mainstream modernist aesthetic in music. For me, it's certainly not a cause for the anxious disruption that many people might associate with the divisions between the religious and the artistic.

There are what could be called 'conviction composers' – who include some of the ones I've just mentioned – and there are others who, like me, sometimes struggle with conviction. In fact, there are a lot of grey areas in the spectrum of belief, and I don't think that even the conventionally religious are necessarily in a position to explain the inexplicable.

Most of my composing work goes on away from the desk, in my head. It's like an iceberg, in the sense that most of it is hidden. And it can go on for years before coming out very quickly. I have an idea of the kind of pieces I want to write and I just have to wait until somebody asks for one of them. Or I can suggest that what I want to write will meet their specification for a new piece. This autumn I'm going to begin a piece that I've been thinking about for ten years. I haven't been working on it continuously, but it's been there in the background all the time, and I've gradually been devising it, shaping it and imagining its dimensions and its purpose.

I've just had to leave a piece in mid-flow to come down to London, and I found that a complete wrench because I'd got to the point where the climactic moment of the final movement was about to happen. But it doesn't matter, because I've been thinking it all through for a year. I often tell students who are worried about writer's block (or composer's block) that even though they're not physically writing, or the writing seems not to be flowing, the subconscious is working through the material, unperceived.

I write by hand because I'm not really computer-literate – it took me a while just to work out e-mails. Also, I feel that there's an important connection between what my hand is in relation to the rest of my body and how I approach the page with an implement like a pen. I find that notation is never completely adequate, so I use a lot of words to describe in a score how the music is to be played. I learned very early on, in fact, to give players as much information as possible about this and to use English as well as Italian words when notation itself can't communicate this.

A first performance can be quite tense and anxious while you're wondering if things are going to work out. But over the years you build up experience of composing that prepares you to make your connection with your material work better and better. In the early days, hearing my work at its first rehearsal was perhaps more of a discovery of myself, but now I can kind of second-guess what I'm going to hear. Maturity helps, I suppose. I'm less surprised – but no less delighted, I must say. I have in mind a kind of black-and-white spectral shape of the piece, but when I hear it in rehearsal or performance it's in full Technicolor. For that reason, the experience is always thrilling.

But you're right that composers talk about their own music in dispassionate terms. They have to, because they can't really predict its impact on listeners. Recently in Holland there was a performance of my *St Luke Passion*, which includes a passage in which Christ addresses the women of Jerusalem and talks about barrenness; and at that point in the piece I noticed a couple in the audience gripping each other very, very strongly, as if something had really touched them. Perhaps they couldn't have children themselves. I'd never thought about that before, and it reminded me that there are things in my work that have implications for people because of their own circumstances. I think a lot of composers get private approaches, either face to face or through correspondence, from people who've found a work particularly affecting. Usually, something serious has happened – death, probably, although it could be new life. Certainly, women have written to me about problem pregnancies that they were having and about listening to my music while thinking that the child wasn't going to survive. Do composers meet people from the audience? Sometimes, but perhaps not often enough. I usually find conversations after a performance very awkward, and receiving flattering comments is quite embarrassing, so I recoil a bit from that.

There's also the fact that my working life is very practical. It's only occasionally that I'm affected by emotion generally. Maybe I'm a cold fish. Maybe composers *are* – a lot of those whom I know are quite detached. Their work *isn't*, of course, and that's the point. Richard

Strauss said that a conductor should never sweat; it's the listeners who should do that. I sweat a lot when I conduct, but he never did. He was suspicious of performers who got passionately involved, whether physically or emotionally. He obviously had a detachment that allowed him to make sense of the distance between himself and his work, which I think is admirable.

The works of mine that are performed most often are *The Confession of Isobel Gowdie* and *Veni, Veni, Emmanuel*. They've sustained a life of twenty-five years, which is delightful, it's great. But I had no idea that that was going to happen. And that's the way I approach every new piece, because I don't know what's going to be performed years from now. Then there are what publishers call 'sleepers': works that just lie there, for one reason or another, waiting to find a life. One of mine is the Cello Concerto that I wrote for Rostropovich; it had a kind of flowering of performances but since then has sat back. Maybe it isn't a good enough piece, but I think the main reason is that the cello already has such a huge solo repertoire that new works don't really get a look-in. In contrast, *Veni, Veni, Emmanuel* has done very well, partly because there aren't many other percussion concertos.

I think one has to write for oneself, first and foremost. One simply has that instinct. But the instinct wouldn't be there if it weren't for other people, because it's feeling part of a shared, universal life that makes us the people we are and the artists we are, or aren't. I've always had a very wide interest in things other than music, and at one point I could have gone in different directions, professionally, if I hadn't made it as a composer. I remember sizing up, as a youngster, my options about politics – a topic that still fascinates me even though I've lost all my youthful certainties about it. In fact, I'm meeting a quite famous politician later today (I'm not going to tell you who it is!). I disagree with him about lots of things but I'll be fascinated just to engage him in conversation.

I'm also fascinated by writers, and I think this is because I've always envied artists who are able to encapsulate the world around them and who gain inspiration from the experiences of their fellows. One of my worries about music being an abstract form used to be that there was too much emotional detachment about it: you *could* write a piece of music without having any recourse to the world around you – or so it seemed. For that reason I've always wanted to reach out and find out what makes writers or film-makers tick, what makes them want to communicate. I think they've got a lot to tell composers about that.

So, in answer to your question, I'm sure music does have a purpose.

I don't know what it is, though! What I find so wonderful about music is its immateriality. You know, it's not a 'thing'. Okay, you could say that it's notes on the page, but when it comes alive in a performance you can't touch it physically. It's in the ether. It's the mysterious nature of music that's so wonderful and so baffling at the same time.

Colin Matthews

Colin Matthews, London, August 2011

❝Stravinsky's question "Who needs it?" should be on every composer's desk.❞

Colin Matthews is one of the first composers I thought of when planning this book, for he has been central to British musical life for the last thirty-five years. This is partly because his own music might be said to inhabit the middle ground between high modernism and tonal traditionalism, and so might be loosely classified as 'mainstream contemporary'; it's also because he's such an influential figure in the promotion of music by other British composers.

In comparison to most of their contemporaries, however, he and his older brother David (see next chapter) had an unconventional musical education. It began formally with piano lessons, encouraged by their parents but pursued with varying degrees of enthusiasm, and was fuelled by an absorbing interest in the symphonic music they heard on the radio rather than the performances of Gilbert and Sullivan operas to which their parents took them. Colin told Paul Griffiths,

> I think both of us have the same attitude – that if we're interested in something we have to follow it right through. ... Both of us felt that, if we were going to take an interest in music, then there was no point in doing anything else except write it.[1]

But they attended a school whose curriculum didn't include music, and so there was no music master to teach them when, still in their teens, they started to compose. For many years, in fact, they were each other's only composition teachers, and Colin had not yet left school when they helped the musicologist Deryck Cooke to realise his second and third performing editions of Mahler's Tenth Symphony (which Colin had privately transcribed, in full, from a copy borrowed from the BBC Library). He later worked as an assistant to Benjamin Britten and with Imogen Holst, and he maintains positions with the Britten estate, the Britten–Pears Foundation, the Aldeburgh Festival and the Royal Philharmonic Society. He also

---

[1] Paul Griffiths, *New Sounds, New Personalities: British Composers of the 1980s, op. cit.*, p. 100.

administers the Holst Foundation, with whose financial assistance he founded the recording label NMC in 1988.

He remains executive producer of NMC's recordings of new British music, which average one release per month, and one of my reasons for interviewing him was to find out how he combines what could be considered a full-time administrative career with the demands of composing. Another was to ask why he, like his brother, is so generous with his time in helping to promote other people's music. Does he, I wondered, consider this to be the public duty of the established composer? If so, it's one that not all of his colleagues fulfil with such commitment.

In May 2011 he replied to my request for an interview, 'I'd be very happy to be part of what sounds like a really worthwhile venture. You may know that Paul Griffiths did a similar thing in 1985 (it was actually at my suggestion), and I hoped that the Schafer book – which I grew up with – might be reprinted alongside it.' He asked to see my questions in advance as he preferred to answer some of them by e-mail, and three months later we met at his home in south-west London to discuss the remaining issues and to clarify some of his earlier comments.

This face-to-face encounter took place on the morning after the premiere at a Proms concert of his *No Man's Land*, a memorial to the fallen of the First World War. He apologised for being a little tired (and possibly, he joked, still slightly hungover), and it seemed natural to begin the conversation by asking him whether, after a high-profile Proms premiere, a composer is inevitably absorbed in a *post mortem* of the performance or whether he's already so involved with other professional commitments that he has no opportunity to bask in glory.

It's a question of putting it aside and getting on with the next thing. In fact, there's quite a sense of relief in having it out of the way. I've been working very hard on three pieces almost simultaneously, and this weekend I'm going to Leipzig, where I've got a new piece[2] being prepared by the Gewandhaus Orchestra. I left myself only two months to write it because of the pressure of deadlines and because when I was asked I couldn't possibly say no, even though I knew I was going to have very little time to do it. So last night will be put behind me fairly quickly!

In any case, a composer is always dealing with past music, as well as with scores that are in preparation – I spend quite a lot of time

[2] *Grand Barcarolle.*

answering questions like 'Is this note correct?' And most composers have to have another means of earning a living. I teach a certain amount at the Royal College of Music, I run a course at Aldeburgh every other year and I'm closely involved with the London Symphony Orchestra's composer schemes. But I've been very lucky in having administrative jobs rather than being committed to teaching. Being Chair of the Britten Estate and running the Holst Estate are activities that are obviously composer-related, and particularly with the Holst Foundation it's been wonderful to be able to give away money in the way that we have over the last twenty years.

I think it's the duty of a composer to become involved with musical trusts and committees. In that respect, I've been lucky in being able to channel funding into projects like NMC – to have been able to set up a record company through the benevolence of the Holst Foundation has been quite remarkable. In all honesty, I'm not sure that I'm any better at doing that sort of thing than anything else, but it does seem to be an obligation. And it puzzles me why other composers don't want to become more involved in such activities, even though there are fewer opportunities since the old Society for the Promotion of New Music went under. I think there's a lot of willingness, but composers tend to be focussed on their own concerns, which is no bad thing.

So I suppose my life is roughly half composing and half administration, and the two don't overlap much. In other words, composing is a separate activity that I have to find time for. I find it quite difficult to organise my time, in fact, but I have the benefit of not being tied down in any given period by the demands of a formal job.

When I started to write music I had no idea whatsoever of what the life of a composer would be like, because I had very little contact with any professional musicians. But I was very lucky in the people I met. The first real musician I came across was Deryck Cooke – I was still a schoolboy when I started working with him on Mahler Ten. I didn't have much contact with composers, though, and I didn't meet any of my contemporaries until much later on, so at first I had no idea what professional composing meant. I soon found out! It's rather remarkable that, although I had been studying with Nicholas Maw, the first composer I got to know well was Britten.

While I was learning my craft in the 1960s there was already a large range of musical choices available, and I was aware of, and open to, the influence of (to take a few extremes) Terry Riley, Milton Babbitt, John Cage and Cornelius Cardew. I also had a close interest in non-Western music. That all seems far away now, but it was beneficial, if only as something to react against. However, there are still some ways in which I feel I have yet to establish my identity as a composer. And this doesn't particularly concern me because I don't like the idea of feeling secure and knowing what I'm going to do next.

The term 'British composer' conjures up for me the image of the insular outlook that in the 1930s called Britten 'too clever by half' and later railed against William Glock's innovations at the BBC. I think virtually everyone working today is far too aware of what's going on elsewhere to be pigeonholed, although I suspect that British composers are regarded as relatively conservative by their European counterparts, which may or may not be fair. In France or Italy you're expected to have an aesthetic, a guiding principle, adherence to which can be more important than the music you write. If there's something that characterises British composers it's perhaps a slightly magpie-like tendency to take bits from everywhere rather than to follow a particular path.

I think one of the reasons that there isn't a pervasive musical language today is because of the ready availability of music of every kind. Until relatively recently there was only classical music and popular music (in the Western tradition, that is), and the two were closely related. And virtually all music was contemporary music. Nowadays we can very easily access all kinds and eras of music, so everyone's ears are much more open and there's no sense of a tradition that we have to follow. I'm not sure that music is going in radically different directions, though – I have the feeling that there's still a sort of current carrying everything with it. But we're too closely involved to see the bigger picture.

Does all this make composing easier? Not really, and there's no less need to acquire technical expertise. Other than in the world of 'sound art' there's no real musical equivalent to the kind of conceptual art that requires imagination but not necessarily technique (especially if you get someone else to do the actual work for you). Every composer I know still faces the same problems with a new piece, whatever style it's written in.

There's always a risk in aiming to compose something 'new' or 'different' that you embrace innovation for innovation's sake. After all, it was Schoenberg who said, 'There's plenty of good music to be written in C major' (not that his own late, tonal music is much to write home about). I'd add to that Boulez's 'Anyone who hasn't felt the necessity of serial language is useless' and suggest that the ideal path is to balance the two.

What I want to express in my music, as opposed to addressing the technical challenges of composing it, is a tougher question. I want listeners to be challenged, involved and perhaps moved, but all I can do is to try to write the best music I can, in the hope that the rest will follow. To me, the most important aspect of my music is its structure. The sound world follows on from that. One could use the analogy of the visual arts, in the sense that colour is usually of secondary importance to the way a painting is put together – although of course that's not always the case, and similarly some music can be structured around its sound. In an ideal world, the mind's eye and ear work together. I think it was Stockhausen who said that he had little time for composers who didn't conceive their notes with the precise sound (dynamics, pitch, timbre) in mind. But in his case that led, I think, to over-schematisation.

One of my musical shortcomings is that I can't think through my abstract or pattern ideas so that they transfer automatically into notes. Also, when things happen in my head they often do so subconsciously – as when you have a problem that solves itself overnight if you sleep on it. So, for me, composition is very much an act of writing down the music, and in general I need a pencil and paper in order to get it down. While I'm doing this I always have in mind the sound that I want to create, but the precise working out of detail is a separate process.

I started to use computer notation a long while ago, in the early days of the Sibelius programme. But I've become a bit of a Luddite because I still use the original Acorn version, which was remarkably sophisticated and wonderfully intuitive. Acorn machines (the platform is still developed and looked after) are exceptionally reliable. I use the Mac version of Sibelius as well, but I automatically go back to the Acorn because it seems to give you more control and less ability to fake – the cutting and pasting option is dangerous, I think, and I can see it in the way that other people compose! It worries me, in fact, that a lot of people now learn notation through a computer rather than as part of the broad music-writing process. For me, the main benefit is that it saves time. I've always enjoyed writing by hand, but it seems pointless to produce a beautiful, handwritten full score when it's going to have to be computerised in order for the parts to be supplied. And I would rather have control of *that* process than hand it over to somebody else to computerise, because I think you can be almost as individual in using a computer as you can be in writing by hand.

Most of the compositional work is done before I start work on the computer, but there are lots of shortcuts that are very handy, particularly when creating a full score. Once the sketch of a work is complete, I will probably put it onto the computer so that I have it there as a guide at the top of each page of full score. This helps in doing the physical scoring by hand, and it also helps when I come to computerising it because I can copy from the sketch onto each page.

Unlike the act of painting, there's no way to compose and complete a work at speed. Imagine being able to create the musical equivalent of one of Van Gogh's late landscapes in a single day! But in other respects, composing isn't so different from making other forms of art. You often read of novelists finding their characters taking over, and while I find that hard to comprehend because words are so tangible, it's certainly true that music, however pre-planned, can head off in its own direction. I sometimes use the analogy of a sculptor chipping away at a block of marble to find what's inside.

What preoccupies me when I'm composing is the temporal aspect of music in live performance: unlike a painting or a book, you can't put it down and come back to it later. I think this is at the root of the problem that some people have with new music. They're trapped with something unfamiliar and can't get away, and they don't want to respond to the challenge. (Of course, recordings are an answer to this, but there's no substitute for live performance.) However, as a composer you take this restriction on board with the job, so you can't really complain about it!

Of course, I want to communicate, and it's very rewarding when somebody understands what I'm trying to do. But I can't put 'communication' first. Like it or not, composers are saddled with very difficult questions of language – we've moved away from the vernacular and can only move back towards it in a way that puts the language in quotes, or which is ironic (postmodernism, I suppose). I can't see any point in writing serious music that's just simple and melodic, because there's more than enough of that already. As I said earlier, we're surrounded – like no other generation before – by music of all types and periods. Stravinsky's question 'Who needs it?' should be on every composer's desk.

That's not to say that 'occasional' pieces can't serve a purpose, and I've written – particularly for children – music that's tuneful and uncomplicated, although always (I hope) contradicting expectations. But that's a kind of sideline, and plenty of other composers can do it as well or better than I. My main job is to write music that makes people think. Whether it needs a level of understanding is a different matter. I don't think it should, because my preoccupations shouldn't be a concern for the listener. Can I add another quotation? 'The man who is misguided enough to compose in the hope of pleasing others generally ends by pleasing neither them nor himself' (Percy Grainger).

I'm aware that something I create in a completely dispassionate way can have an emotional impact on listeners, and that's as it should be. But if the work doesn't have intellectual credibility (whether or not the listener recognises this), it doesn't *deserve* to evoke emotion. Birtwistle once said something on the lines of 'a badly designed building will fall down; the same should apply to music'.

However, there are different approaches to emotion in music. I'd said in a radio interview before the performance that *No Man's Land* is in one sense objective and understated, and my wife, who was very affected by the piece, said, 'It's nothing of the sort.' Whether there's an embarrassment about admitting that you've achieved something that has an effect on people, I don't know. It's very heart-warming if somebody does react in that way to a piece of your music, and it's happened to me a few times; but emotion has to be kept in a separate compartment. I had to be very careful not to get emotionally involved when writing *No Man's Land*, because technique flies out of the window if that happens.

This is why I see my music in a different way from that of the listener, and why I prefer to talk about *how* I wrote it. I know from previous experience that music which is very dark or even violent can be written in absolute calm because it's being worked out carefully. There's a nice comment that I think Tchaikovsky wrote to his patron, Nadezhda von Meck: 'Often I'll find that my most emotional music is written in my calmest states.' I think I might say about *No Man's Land* that the simplicity of the way I've written some of it is an aspect that I myself find quite moving. I've achieved something that I probably haven't done before.

Tippett was somebody who could get very carried away by his own music. His response was very honest: he found his music beautiful. But few of us are like that. It's one of the big drawbacks of being a composer. It's very difficult for me to throw off the technical aspects of music, and so I'm very glad when I can just be directly moved by it without thinking about the nuts and bolts. Self-indulgent, pure pleasure listening would probably be headed by Richard Strauss and, because I like to listen to them without concerning myself too much with how they work, Ravel and Debussy. I prefer to restrict my listening so that it can be something special, but I listen to a lot of contemporary music as part of my job at NMC and record-producing has opened my ears to a lot of music that I would not otherwise have heard.

Some of my works have been written without commissions, and these days I certainly don't accept them unless they're for things that I want to do. Having said that, there's nothing like the offer of a commission for setting up a chain of thoughts. The terms of the commission become the parameters around which you work, but commissioners generally are very open-minded: they'll give you the forces and an approximate duration but, within that, you're on your own. And that's a very good thing. I can't think of any commission where there's been pressure on me to write in a particular way or to do something specific that wasn't what I already wanted to do. Of course, it *becomes* what you want to do, even when you're a little dubious about accepting the commission. Obviously, there are some things that I wouldn't want to do. I often feel under pressure when I meet an organist who says, 'You must write me an organ piece', but I'm afraid I'm not going to do that because, apart from being scared of the instrument, I don't find there's anything that I want to say through it.

Very few of my works have entered the repertoire. Strangely, they include some of the tougher pieces, like the one I wrote for the London Sinfonietta, *Suns Dance*, which has been played a huge number of times even though it's horrendously difficult technically. *Hidden Variables* has also been played a lot. But they're not entirely representative. It's a worry that people hear one of your pieces and then think that it's *you*. As far as I'm concerned, it's only a *bit* of me.

There's something of a problem – and it shouldn't be one – in the fact that pieces I've orchestrated, such as the Debussy Preludes, are the ones that are getting played. I'm known mostly for those and for *Pluto*.[3] I got upset, in fact, when a journalist in the *Musical Times* not so long ago asked why composers are always revisiting the past – pointing to Max's *Antarctic* Symphony, Tony Payne doing Elgar Three and me doing *Pluto*. I sort of put up my hands and said, '*Pluto* lasts about seven minutes, and I've actually written rather a lot of other pieces besides that! Don't typecast me because I like doing things that are useful.' Besides, I was almost corralled into doing that piece because I knew that if I didn't, they'd ask somebody else, and I rather arrogantly thought I could probably do it better.

[3] Composed in 2000 at the invitation of the Hallé Orchestra to complete Holst's suite *The Planets*.

Consequently I have slightly mixed feelings about the Debussy Preludes. I know that they get programmed because people think of them as new music that isn't dangerous, and I can't fool myself that the musicians would be playing something else of mine if they weren't doing the Debussy. But I certainly stand by what I did with those Preludes, and it's good that they're getting around.

I don't follow my own music around after the first performance, partly because of lack of time and partly because the public aspect of being a composer is not something I feel at all comfortable with. I'm happy working with the musicians in rehearsals, and in some ways I'd almost rather hand it over to them and not be there for the performance, where I always feel slightly uncomfortable. But I recognise that it goes with the job. With today's cult of personality, everybody is expected to be a public 'face'.

In the early days, to give a pre-concert talk was sort of torture for me, whereas now I feel that I've lost an opportunity if I *don't* do that. But it still doesn't come naturally to me. It's like putting on a false moustache. And I can't *really* say what I think about my music, either. My publishers think that I tend to be a little negative about my pieces, and so, as everybody wants a happy story, it's a question of putting on a brave smile and looking confident. We have to recognise that ours is a tiny niche market compared with the pop world. If we sell a thousand CDs, that's terrific; a pop record that sells only a *million* is a failure.

I don't think I've ever been surprised by performers' interpretations of my music because I try to be very precise in the way I notate so that if I'm not there the performance shouldn't go wrong. I'm more moved by the intensity of musicians. Like last night: to have Ian Bostridge and Roderick Williams singing their hearts out was extraordinary, even though *No Man's Land* was written with their voices very much in mind.

It was the same with my Violin Concerto. I worked quite closely with the soloist, Leila Josefowicz, beforehand but I don't think I was prepared for the extraordinary ability she has to project, particularly as she learned the piece and played it from memory for the first performance, which was astonishing. When performers give that sort of commitment I realise that it's way beyond anything I thought was possible.

David Matthews

David Matthews, Suffolk, October 2011

> **What the musical world seems to want is an endless succession of new pieces that are played once and then forgotten.**

Much has been written about the differences between the Matthews brothers in both their personalities and their music. In my experience Colin is more relaxed, urbane and casually assured and David more diffident and self-effacing. And although both of them read classics at the University of Nottingham, worked as assistants to Britten at Aldeburgh, helped Deryck Cooke with his performing version of Mahler's Tenth Symphony and became house composers for Faber Music, they've pursued quite different artistic paths.

Colin was a later and more tentative developer because, he admits, he floundered stylistically. But in the early 1970s he embraced modernism – and even minimalism in his Fourth Sonata – and so his music was in keeping with the spirit of the time. Winning prestigious competitions and attracting high-profile performances and recordings, he became an establishment figure earlier than his brother did. In contrast, David began composing earlier and with greater proficiency, confidence and stylistic assurance. But from the outset he was committed to maintaining a fundamental, if sometimes unorthodox, link with tonality, and this was somewhat at odds with the prevailing tide of musical opinion in the 1960s and 1970s. So, perhaps, was the strong sense of the pictorial – drawn from nature, poetry and the visual arts – in his music.

He has always written symphonic works that he calls symphonies, concertante works that he calls concertos, and works for string quartet that he calls string quartets because he believes that there's good reason to renew and regenerate these traditional forms. And by the turn of the century musical fashions had changed sufficiently for this evolutionary approach to be welcomed. He and his brother are now recognised as equally important figures in British music, and in a joint interview for BBC Radio 3 he told Colin that 'Sibling rivalry, if it exists, is something to do with the fact that when I hear a piece of yours I think, "Gosh, this is really good. I must try to improve!"'[1]

[1] *Music Matters*, 18 October 2014.

Having known him for some years before interviewing him for this book, I was often intrigued by two particular aspects of his personality. First, while he's always approachable and friendly he sometimes appears slightly distracted, as if part of his attention is elsewhere – which it probably is, since most composers are composing all the time even if they're not writing anything down. Second, whenever I've told him how much I've enjoyed a piece of his music he has appeared unsure how to respond except to look pleased. It was, in part, the nature of his response that encouraged me to ask many of the contributors to this book why composers sometimes decribe their music in ways that make it sound less appealing to the average listener than it might.

He has homes in north London and on the Kent coast, but as both of us had a spare Saturday afternoon during the inaugural William Alwyn Festival in Suffolk in October 2011 he suggested that I interview him at his hotel in Southwold. Our discussion was at first accompanied by the sound of talk and laughter from the bar below and later by something uncharacteristic and sinister: a seemingly endless series of sirens and blue flashing lights rushing past the window. Later that day we learned of a tragedy at the town's harbour involving the death of an elderly motorist. The sound of those sirens was of course recorded along with our conversation and made its transcription a rather somber task.

I don't really like the idea of music without national characteristics. It's a bit like modern architecture being indistinguishable all over the world. I much prefer that each country's architecture should be individual, and I think *music* should also be different in each country. To me, Beethoven sounds German, Debussy French, Sibelius Finnish and so on – and I think that's a good thing.

When I first started composing, my models were European and I didn't especially warm to British music. I liked Vaughan Williams and Elgar but not as much as I liked Mahler and Bartók. But I increasingly feel distinctively English – English rather than British – and I can see that my music belongs to the English tradition that goes from Elgar through Holst and Vaughan Williams to Walton, Tippett and Britten. I think there's something very positive about that. And in a more general way it's also helpful to listeners that, if I'm writing a symphony or a string quartet, they can place my music in the context of history and compare it with the past. Certainly, when I write a string quartet I'm thinking about the classical quartet form and trying to do new things within it. And I make this plain by calling a piece a string quartet rather than giving it a poetic title.

I think of music as a language of the emotions, and I believe I'm expressing my deepest feelings about life in my music. I often have what might be called an ecstatic reaction to the world – I get incredibly elated – and it's in such moods that musical ideas come most often. I feel it's not enough to be amazed by the world and the extraordinary fact that here I am, alive in it; I want to do something about it, and doing something about it means trying to put down in musical notes what I experience.

If I'd lived in the past I'd probably have been much more of a religious person than I am. I have a very puzzled reaction to the world, religiously. In my youth I was a Catholic convert, but I'm no longer a Christian because I can't believe in Christian doctrine. Nonetheless I think I have a religious temperament, and I'm continually in a state of wonder about the world. The fact that it exists doesn't seem completely meaningless. A lot of twentieth-century art has been very negative in the sense that it has rejected any sense of purpose in the world, which is why it's so dark and tragic; but I can't really feel that. So my music probably does have a kind of optimism, ultimately.

I don't expect it to be understood by everybody, though. I recognise the limitations of people in regard to new music, because even *my* sort of music, which isn't all that difficult, is difficult to *some*, I realise. Nonetheless, I often wish people would make more effort to listen to new music. I think they're getting lazier, actually. They have short attention spans and they want instant gratification. And a lot of new music doesn't offer this. Its language is tough and hard for people to take. Therefore they react to it, if they react at all, either negatively or intellectually rather than emotionally. And for their emotional satisfaction they increasingly turn to pop music. I can understand getting *some* emotional satisfaction from pop music, but it's a very limited sort of satisfaction, I think, because both the language of pop and the forms it uses are simplistic.

Emotion, I suppose, is what gives the composer inspiration. I'd certainly be very unhappy with a purely intellectual response to my music. But while I'm writing it I'm not thinking 'Am I consciously expressing myself?' because I *know* I am. I'm concerned only with the order of the notes and the techniques that I'm using. So I don't think of my audience when I'm writing, although I'd be disappointed if I failed to communicate anything at all and had a completely stony reaction. If that happened over and over again it would imply that I'm very solipsistic and have nothing to communicate other than things that matter only to me.

When I first started writing pieces that I thought were any good they were more closely related to German expressionism – Berg and Schoenberg – and to Bartók, that kind of world, than my recent pieces are. My musical language has become more diatonic and more obviously tonal. There's also been an evolution of technique, and my music is better written than it used to be. My early music, I now realise, was really quite awkwardly written for the instruments and this resulted in some rather poor performances. Nowadays I think more about the musicians. After all, they're doing me the great service of bothering to learn my music, so I want to give them something worth playing. Also, musicians play better when you give them interesting parts.

I think my pieces are probably better written since I've used the computer as part of the composition process. But I use it only in the final stages. I do my composing in the old-fashioned way of making sketches and then a draft, and even if I'm writing a large-scale piece I'll write out a full score in pencil; I couldn't think of *not* doing that. Then, instead of making the fair copy in ink, as I used to do, I put it on the computer. I think it's rather sad if in the future there aren't going to be composers' manuscripts anymore, because they're just so eloquent, whereas a computer score has no personality.

I still use the old Acorn Sibelius programme, so I can't make sound files of orchestral pieces. But to me they sound rather horrible anyway, and I'm happy to play a piece back from the computer to an electronic piano to check whether I've got the structure right. I'll often adjust the speeds, and quite often I'll find I have to make cuts or additions, mostly small ones. Sometimes I regret that I wasn't able to do this in the past, and I wonder whether I would have written more tightly then as a result. An example is *A Vision and a Journey*, the fourth of a series of what might be called symphonic poems. The first performance disappointed me and I realised I'd got something seriously wrong with the structure. This was before computers, so I couldn't hear it until it was performed. Afterwards I went back and revised it extensively.

I'm concerned with the interrelation of musical motifs, but in my pieces they're not constructed in any particular way. I've never written serial music, as such. I can see that there's some satisfaction in using all the twelve notes of the scale in a melody, but that's as far as I would go. I don't know that anyone writes twelve-note music – the

Schoenberg system – any more. Schoenberg said it was going to prove the superiority of German music for the next hundred years, didn't he? But it hasn't lasted.

Before serial music became popular in this country it was considered a very un-English thing. And so composers like Elisabeth Lutyens and Humphrey Searle were thought of as freakish. One wonders what would have happened if Britten had gone to study with Berg, but I don't think he would have turned into a twelve-note composer. I think he would have found it too restricting. Although Berg, of course, managed very cleverly to get out of the restrictions of the technique, and that's one reason why his music is so successful.

I didn't have a formal musical education, really. For a start, I didn't learn music at school – there was no one there to teach me – and I had piano lessons only up to the age of thirteen. I didn't start composing till I was sixteen, and then I taught myself; or rather, Colin and I taught each other. As soon as I started writing music I just knew that I wanted to be a composer – suddenly it seemed to be an essential part of life, which it hadn't been before. But I didn't know how on earth I was going to be one, especially as I wasn't going to go to music college. All I was concerned with was writing music, and I started, rather impractically, by writing two symphonies. I didn't even *think* of having them performed.

It was very helpful having Colin because I didn't know anybody else who was a composer. But eventually I thought, 'I'd better try to get a teacher.' I would have liked to study with Tippett, but he didn't take pupils; but on his recommendation I went to Anthony Milner. When I worked with Britten I didn't *dare* show him my music because I thought he wouldn't like it. I was writing sort of Mahlerian symphonies – so different from what *he* was doing. I knew *he* didn't teach, either, but I now think he would actually have been interested in my music, and I regret not showing it to him.

When I met Nicholas Maw in 1968 I showed him my music and he gave me unofficial lessons. He was extremely helpful. Later on Peter Sculthorpe really grilled me about what I was trying to do, and I think he was extremely useful in re-orientating me. You see, when I went to Australia for the first time (I was thirty-one), I started thinking of music in a different way. I was looking at Europe from a distance and realising that it was only a small part of the world, and that therefore one didn't necessarily have to follow the dictates of, for example, Boulez, who was presenting a central European point of view. Peter used to say that world music was largely tonal and that therefore there was no reason why you should give up tonality. And I agreed with him. This strengthened my confidence, I think.

Sometimes I regret not having gone to music college, because it would have been very useful to meet other musicians there and get my music played. It's essential, obviously, to hear one's music, and for a long time I didn't hear any of mine. But when I was about twenty-two I was lucky in sending a string quartet to the BBC, who at that time had a reading panel that passed the piece, which led to a performance and a broadcast. You couldn't do that now. I also had some orchestral songs workshopped by the Society for the Promotion of New Music – again, incredibly useful.

When I was nineteen I destroyed almost everything I'd written. I can't remember now what all the pieces were, or how many there were. At that time I was writing my Second Symphony, and that's the earliest piece of mine that I've still got. One of the pieces I destroyed was a very large First Symphony. I'm curious now to know what it was like, and disappointed that I don't have it any more. All I can remember is the first page, which was a bit like the end of Holst's 'Uranus', and the fact that at one point the strings played a sixty-four-note cluster passage which I wrote on three pages sellotaped together.

On the other hand, while I don't know whether anyone will be interested in looking at my early stuff after I'm dead, there can be a problem with people wanting to perform pieces or early versions of pieces that a composer has discarded. How much of Britten's huge output before his official Opus 1 should be played, for instance? Having said that, it's rather astonishing that he wasn't at all interested in hearing some of his later pieces again just because they got one bad performance or one bad review.

I often dream music, and I had an interesting experience the other night. I woke up having watched somebody (it wasn't me) play a phrase on the piano, and I could remember what the notes were, so I wrote them down. When I mentioned this to Gordon Crosse, he said it's like playwrights who dream the perfect plot and write it down; and when they get up the next morning they see that they've written, 'Boy meets girl'! So my phrase might not be of any use, but it would be nice if it were, because the dream was *so* vivid.

I think almost every composer finds the beginning of a new piece difficult, and I often make many drafts of the opening. I usually have a fair idea about what the shape's going to be, but not always – sometimes I proceed not really knowing where it's going, until at a certain point it suddenly becomes clear. This has just happened, actually, with the choral piece I'm writing. I'd been struggling with trying to decide what would be the overall form, and in fact I'd stopped writing it for a month. Then, two weeks ago, I heard a performance of Britten's Third Canticle, *Still Falls the Rain*, which keeps returning to the same opening phrase but leads each time to a different conclusion. The text of my piece divides into five parts, and it occurred to me that I could do something similar to the Britten canticle: three variations of the first section, and the last part an extended coda. So I'm relieved, because I now know exactly what I'm going to do.

The physical work of composing is exhausting. I have quite a strict routine of working in the mornings, from after breakfast till lunch. I've always found that's the best time to compose, when you're not too far from sleep, because the best music seems to come where you're in a kind of semi-trance-like state, where you're not distracted by other concerns, and certainly where you're not too self-conscious. I think the subconscious must be allowed to be free.

I often find that by lunchtime I've had enough and that if I go on after that I might not be working at my best. I need to work at my full capacity, to be absolutely in control of what I'm doing and not taking short cuts, so I tend to restrict myself. But it's good to work every day if I can.

Composing is a lonely business, so it's nice occasionally to appear in public. I don't mind speaking, introducing my pieces or giving interviews. And, of course, having one's pieces played in public can be a very gratifying experience. First of all, you've got all these musicians working on your behalf. With an orchestra you've got nearly a hundred of them, and if you have a piece played at the Proms you get applauded by five thousand people. I imagine any composer would enjoy that! No matter how many pieces you've written, to hear an orchestra play your music is still the most exciting thing ever. That thrill has never left me.

Writing music is also a form of self-exposure, but it's not a painful one. Obviously, some composers are more autobiographical than others. I don't mind expressing very personal things in my music, though I suspect that most people don't quite get what a composer is saying. They relate to you in a rather general way, I think, because you're not telling them anything in words. And also because they don't know enough about *you*. Or they relate the emotional content of your music to their own experience. But I don't actually *know*, because I have no idea how other people hear my music – which in itself is interesting.

I've never had a regular job and I've never taught, except privately, because I've always needed to give myself as much time to compose as I could. But I've tried to find other freelance work associated with music. At the moment I'm preparing new editions of the Vaughan Williams Symphonies for Oxford University Press. And I've always written words as well as music. When I first started work I thought I'd become a music critic (goodness knows why, and I soon gave it up!) but I've written numerous articles and reviews and programme notes. Two small books, too, on Tippett and Britten. So quite a lot of my time is spent *not* composing. I don't know how many composers earn their living just from writing music, actually. Hardly anybody, probably. Even Britten didn't – he played and conducted, too.

It wasn't really until I was about forty that I was in a position to get regular commissions. Most of my large pieces up till then, including several symphonies and a violin concerto, were written without them. Since then all of my orchestral music, with the exception of my most recent piece, has been commissioned. But I don't write everything I'm asked to write. I mean, there are some instruments that I'm not especially attracted to. For example, if someone asked me to write a harp concerto I think I wouldn't because I don't really know how to. I've been asked to write a guitar concerto but I don't feel confident about writing for the guitar, either. I haven't written very much piano music because I feel I'm limited by my technique; though I'm *not* limited at all when writing for strings, which I barely play – I can just about pick up a violin and produce a few notes.

More generally, it's a rather frightening thought that what the musical world seems to want is an endless succession of new pieces that are played once and then forgotten. And there are so many composers now, so that there's competition all the time for performances and no room, really, to establish a contemporary repertoire. When you think of Vaughan Williams's Sixth Symphony, which was played something like eighty times in its first year ... That would be impossible today. James MacMillan's *Veni, Veni, Emmanuel* has been played a lot, and a few pieces by John Adams, but that's a real exception for contemporary orchestral music.

No composers today enjoy the wide public that Britten and Shostakovich had fifty years ago. They were mainstream composers, and there isn't a comparable figure today. Composers like Arvo Pärt are more restricted in their range of expression, I think. Also, a lot of the people who listened to Britten and Shostakovich read contemporary novels and looked at contemporary art, whereas the people who read contemporary novels and look at contemporary art today aren't necessarily going to listen to any contemporary music at all.

The first rehearsal of an orchestral piece can be very depressing for the composer, usually because the music sounds so awful. But then there's a moment – with British orchestras it's often during the second rehearsal, actually – when it suddenly becomes 100 per cent better, and you think, 'This really does sound rather good after all.' And sometimes my music sounds *better* than I'd imagined because it's being performed better than I'd thought it could be. This often happens with chamber music because you tend to hear it in a rather flat way in your mind – you don't hear all the expression that a performer can put into it. And, of course, that will change with every performance.

So yes, I'm surprised by what performers can bring to my music through their interpretation and I can't understand a composer wanting to fix every single detail so that the music can be played in only one way. You've got to leave a score in such a state that people can perform it more or less as you want it when you're no longer there, but you don't have to indicate absolutely everything. I also can't understand a composer who doesn't like something that's interestingly different from what he'd imagined. But, of course, if performers go completely against the spirit of your music it's your job to tell them.

I don't think many composers would want to give too much away about their music, and I certainly don't want to tell people how to react to mine. For example, I don't want to tell them that a piece is beautiful; I'd like them to *find* it beautiful, perhaps. (And I *am* often intending to create something of beauty. There's nothing wrong with that, although some people seem to think there is.) So if I'm writing a programme note I tend to just describe the structure of the piece. I don't usually talk about its autobiographical qualities, although in the booklet note for the CD of my Violin Concertos I did tell the personal story behind the First Concerto and how I've never composed, before or since, in such a Hollywood-ish way: it involved breaking up with a girlfriend, fantasising about throwing myself into the Thames and then dreaming the opening of the piece afterwards. That's probably how many people imagine composers work, of course. But they don't, usually!

There are many satisfying moments during the act of composition, and most of them result from solving a problem after a period of being stuck and getting things wrong. Yet still, at the beginning of every new piece, I wonder how I ever wrote any of my music. Whenever I start a piece, I think that I can't actually do it any more – I feel I really don't know how to compose. Only later, when the piece has got going, do I realise that I still can.

Peter Maxwell Davies

Sir Peter Maxwell Davies, London, March 2014

> **"Living with music in a creative way is for me almost a physical necessity."**

For a few years during the 1990s I was involved in the musical life of Nottingham by interviewing conductors or soloists, usually by telephone, shortly before they came to the city to perform in a concert. Each interview was then printed in the concert programme alongside the more formal note about the evening's concerto or symphonic work. In August 1996 Sir Peter Maxwell Davies visited Nottingham in his role as guest conductor of the Royal Philharmonic Orchestra to conduct a concert that included his Sixth Symphony, only recently premiered at the St Magnus Festival in Orkney and not yet heard in London, and because I'd already interviewed him about the Symphony I was asked to host his pre-concert talk. It was therefore essential that I attend the afternoon rehearsal of the Symphony.

He'd told me in the phone interview,

> I'm always very keen to conduct my pieces for audiences that possibly don't get much new music. It's very important that they have a chance to come to terms with an orchestra playing these works physically in front of them rather than listening to a CD. The experience is quite different.

And, for me, the experience of hearing the Sixth Symphony being rehearsed was challenging. I remember feeling bewildered by the first movement but greatly moved by the last, which had a remarkable sense of inevitability about it. I also remember that during the evening performance a number of people in the audience walked out at the end of the first movement, and that Sir Peter, hearing the disruption in the hall, turned around, folded his hands in front of him and smiled resignedly until the early leavers had gone.

Fast-forward to March 2014, shortly before my encounter with him for this book, when I listened to the Symphony for the first time in many years and discovered that most of my difficulties with it had evaporated. I was left wondering what my 'problem' had been. And I told him this when we met at the Royal Academy of Music in London – in a top-floor flat used by visiting professors, off a quiet side street at the back of the main building.

I also reminded him about the reception of his Symphony in Nottingham eighteen years earlier because it seemed relevant to a discussion about contemporary music in general and his music in particular. He's aware that some listeners have found his music difficult or unrewarding, and I wanted to know whether he has a sense of it now finding more favour with the 'average' audience member, whoever that might be. I also wanted to ask him how he has dealt with audience reactions like the one in Nottingham, given that it wasn't an isolated incident.

He, more than any other contributor to this book, is a public figure (when this encounter took place he was about to relinquish the role of Master of the Queen's Music), and he therefore needs little introduction. But although he retains his familiar, birdlike charm, cocking his head from side to side while thinking and then fixing you with a beady gaze while speaking, he was more subdued than I'd expected. I also noticed, as he walked into the kitchen to make us some tea, that he's now a little stooped physically. I had to remind myself that I was interviewing someone who was less than six months away from his eightieth birthday and who'd been coaching pupils at the Academy all morning. And I was delighted to see him looking so well – his mental energy and enthusiasm undiminished – after a very problematic few years overshadowed by health concerns and difficulties in his personal life.

Because he was the youngest contributor to Murray Schafer's book of interviews with British composers I asked him first to look back over the fifty years since it was published and to reflect on the direction that his own career has taken. Has it been a surprise to him, I wondered, or what he expected?

I couldn't have known then what trajectory my career would take. But I think I took it for granted, perhaps rather complacently, that the things that have since happened to me not *should* but *would* happen. I assumed that that was simply what happened to a composer. But I'm not complacent about them now. I just think I'm very, very fortunate, in my eightieth year, that the music I wrote in the 1960s, and some of the pieces that I wrote in the 1950s, are generally accepted and played.

For instance, my Sonata for Trumpet and Piano, written specially for John Ogdon and Elgar Howarth, was rejected in 1955 by the Society for the Promotion of New Music as impossible to play. Today, a number of students here at the Academy not only play it as part of their final recital; some of them use it as an audition piece when they apply to come here, aged sixteen! And it's wonderful that that's happened.

I don't think I ever wanted to be an *enfant terrible*. If I *was* one, it was despite trying to write music that I intended to be clear and transparent. It's true that when I was a student there was plenty for me to react against, but at the same time I was very pleased that I had to study harmony and counterpoint in an efficient and considered way. Those basic harmonic and contrapuntal skills aren't rules written in stone, and an understanding of them makes the work of composing a great deal easier, so I think it's a pity that they're not always taught. It's a bit like David Hockney complaining about artists not learning how to draw. Craft, whether it's being able to make a line work in art or two contrapuntal voices work together in music, stands you in very good stead; and I think my *Eight Songs for a Mad King* and *Miss Donnithorne's Maggot* have survived and are played a lot *because* they're built on very rigorous craftsmanship – despite what people saw (and still do see, to some extent) as ruthlessly new in terms of their spiritual, emotional and even purely musical content.

But I do remember when both *Eight Songs for a Mad King* and *Worldes Blis* had very bad audience reactions in 1969. It even made the BBC News: there was a kind of scandal when about a third of the audience at *Worldes Blis* walked out of the Royal Albert Hall. And I was really upset and depressed about it. Mass exits like that haven't happened to me for some time, but you'll always get *some* people walking out. Not so long ago in Los Angeles people walked out of Shostakovich – it was just too much for them.

I think people very often look to music as something that, on a superficial level, always has to be comforting – a balm. And it isn't. Sometimes it can be very dark and can go into extraordinarily tragic realms. Some of my pieces are very dark indeed, and I think people react to them rather like they reacted to Sibelius Four when *that* was new. I wouldn't ever claim to be a composer on that level, but you know what I mean. One goes right back to the theory of catharsis in drama, which I think applies equally to music. You come out of it purged, in a way, and feeling much better!

In general terms, I think, you've got no choice, as a composer, about what you say in your music. It's something that you simply *do*. And you have to do it as clearly and as competently as you can. Basically, you just want to express what it is to be alive as yourself, in relation to a particular past and with a hope for a future. I don't think that you can do any more than that. Obviously, you want people to react positively to your music, but you have to accept – as *I* do – that this won't always be possible because some of it will be very dark. Think of the black paintings from the end of Goya's life and the extraordinarily dark thinking behind those last engravings of war and *Los Caprichos* – which, of course, weren't printed in his lifetime. It took a long time before people could appreciate them. In the same way, the vocabulary of music has had to expand in order to cope with composers' need to express such things.

Recently there was a performance of the symphony you mentioned – my No. 6 – at the Cadogan Hall in London, given by the Royal Philharmonic and Martyn Brabbins, and I was very pleased that the hall was full and that there were a lot of young people in the audience. And I don't think they had any difficulty with the piece. Everybody listened. The eighteen years since I wrote the Symphony have changed people's response to it – even to the first movement, which is quite gritty and tough. What's happened, I think, is that the harmonic language has become familiar enough to register and make a positive impact. And I emphasise the harmonic language, because that's something that disappeared at the height of the avant-garde revolution of the late 1950s and early 1960s. I remember the pianist Aki Takahashi performing a Xenakis piece and shouting out in the middle of it, 'Harmony is dead!' Which was nonsense, of course – how *can* it be dead?

I find that listening to my own music can be a nostalgic experience because it seems so closely associated with the time in which I wrote it. Hearing it brings things back – including things that aren't pleasant. But sometimes I go back to listen to pieces that were dismissed at the time as purely eccentric and very difficult. For example, I didn't listen to my Fourth Symphony for years because the reaction to it had been absolutely and totally negative. And this had put me off the piece. But then a few years ago Olly Knussen did it in Glasgow and Edinburgh with the Scottish Chamber Orchestra, and all the hostility had gone. When I heard the piece again I thought, 'Yes, it *is* intense, and it *is* difficult – for the players, particularly. But it was a statement worth making.' And I began to take pleasure in it for the first time.

Although most people have learned that contemporary music doesn't bite as much as they thought it did, you can't expect them to understand every new piece immediately. After all, when you first hear a new piece, you know that there's more going on in it than you can possibly absorb in a single listening. But later, when you listen to it again, you hear more things happening. In the case of *my* music, my aim is that there'll be something that holds the attention over and over again. And, particularly in the big pieces, I hope listeners will realise that there's a constructive tension between form and architecture. What I mean is that the music isn't simply *in* a form, but that there are things happening in its architecture which sometimes agree with its form and sometimes vie with it. In other words, there are not only harmonic and rhythmic tensions but large-scale architectonic tensions. And my hope is that these will draw the listener further and further in towards the core of each of these big pieces.

I think of musical architecture as a living, evolving thing, not as scaffolding. Scaffolding would be taken down after the work was complete, and then you wouldn't know about it; but you do, I hope, know about architecture when you listen to my music. This is quite an elaborate subject, though, and I'm not going to go into all the details right now. The other thing to mention is that when you're in the heat of writing a piece you don't think about these things anyway. You simply get on and do it, because you really can't talk about the music you're writing. The music is itself. And ultimately I want my music to appeal to both heart *and* mind.

It's true that composers talk about the form or structure of their own music rather than what it's going to sound like, and that's because of their objectivity. They have an emotional distance from their work. Besides, it would be looked upon as rather presumptuous for me to say, for example, that a section of my music is beautiful, even if I hope that it *will* be considered beautiful. But when I write a programme note I try to be as honest as I can while not putting people off by talking about musical structures in a way that suggests that I'm manipulating a Meccano set! You have to be a little bit careful when writing about your own music, because you can sound big-headed – which is not the impression that you want to give. You don't want to suggest that the music is overly intellectual. But nor do you want to suggest that it's trying too hard to satisfy the emotions.

Of course, I've written 'light' pieces such as *Orkney Wedding* and *Farewell to Stromness*, which gets performed all the time. I enjoyed writing them tremendously, and they're *not* dark. They're very extrovert. And you might say that I was pandering to popular taste when I wrote them – I've certainly been accused of that. Oh no, I wasn't – I really meant it when I wrote them, and I still find *Farewell to Stromness* quite touching.

Yes, the term 'British composer' does mean something to me because I've conducted music by Vaughan Williams and Holst and a lot of more recent British composers across Europe, and I often feel that I'm doing so in territory that hasn't previously heard this music. I'm very conscious of bringing them something that they don't know.

For example, I've conducted Vaughan Williams's Sixth Symphony a lot, and although it's quite a tough piece it's gone across very well in Germany and other countries; but it's certainly not known there. Fortunately I can introduce a piece of music in German or Italian or French, so I'll talk to audiences about what they're going to hear so that they'll have a more sympathetic ear.

I feel that there has been a big prejudice against British composers, particularly in Germany. At least, there was when I was younger. And I think it stemmed from the First World War, when it was *de rigueur* for concerts in Germany and Austria to begin with that hymn of hate for the English (the English, not the British). In that climate it became second nature *not* to like composers such as Delius and Elgar, who were very popular there before the war. So all this has made me very conscious that British composers have a special niche that has to be promulgated because their music isn't well known abroad.

What I found even more astounding, when conducting various orchestras around Europe, was that they'd never before played Sibelius Two or Three, or Six or Seven. Never! And I realised that Finnish composers, too, are perhaps outside the European mainstream and therefore not taken seriously. This is rather a vexed problem, actually, because nationality in music can become aggressive. It did in Vaughan Williams, to the extent that he didn't even have the patience to take Beethoven's Ninth Symphony seriously. I think he was rather deafened to it by his nationalist preconceptions. And you can understand that, since he wrote some of his best-known works during the Second World War – I think his Fifth Symphony was a propaganda exercise against German music.

But I've been answering your question from the point of view of a conductor, because as a *composer* I don't really think about the issue of Britishness in relation to my music. I've always been conscious that Holst, Vaughan Williams and Britten were important figures whose music had a very individual sound, and although I wouldn't try to identify Ben's as something that's particularly English or British I value very much that it doesn't sound like anyone else's. But *my* music simply comes out, and that's how it is. If it sounds influenced by the folk music of the place I live in, that's fine, because it's all around me. I've worked with and written for the fiddle club in Orkney and other amateur groups on the island, and the local folk music is the music they know. When musicians can't read music terribly well it's important that you write something that they can grasp fairly quickly!

Incidentally, I'd say that conducting is almost essential for a composer – you learn so much from understanding how the members of an orchestra think and work together. You stand there, listening to sonorities reinforcing each other and overtones from one instrument affecting the sounds of another, and you get insights into orchestration that you can never get when you're away from the podium. My goodness, does it sharpen you up! My orchestral music improved no end after I'd been conducting regularly. Alright, it happened a bit late, and I don't dismiss my early symphonies and other orchestral music. They're not bad. But I can hear the difference between them and my more recent works.

A great deal of the work of composition goes on in my head, and I think about the music a lot before I write down a single note. This is why not much tweaking goes on afterwards. I don't always work from the beginning to the end of a piece, but I usually complete one section satisfactorily before moving on to another one.

I still write by hand, not least because when technology was changing so rapidly and computer notation was being introduced I was living in a house in Hoy, in Orkney, with no electricity! Besides, I find the action of the pencil on the paper very satisfying. I've watched composition students at the Academy working away on their computers, and to me it seems rather like playing that electronic piano behind you: it doesn't have the physical quality of playing a *real* piano.

There's another reason, too: you can tell when composition is going well because the manuscript is fairly tidy and in order, while it gets a bit cluttered if you're having difficulties. The look of the page reflects the state of mind of the composer, and I like that! Also, everybody's music looks the *same* when it's notated with a computer, which I think is an awful pity. I've kept diaries since 1948, most of which are already in the library along the road, although nobody's allowed to look at them until I'm dead, obviously. And I still write *them* by hand, too, with an old-fashioned fountain pen!

When I'm at home I start a normal work day with a long walk with the dog along the shore, and sometimes I keep going back to a particular spot because the distance between objects that I see there is associated in my mind with, for example, moving my music from one pitch to another, or with a certain kind of harmony. So I repeatedly walk the distance between this big rock here and that bank of sand over there because in my mind it involves a musical time span. And, in a very simple way, the objects that I see become chords or other musical elements in my imagination. There's also the fact that when you're working with complex systems such as magic squares[1] you have to have learned them by heart. You can't write fluently if you have to keep referring to charts on pages.

The piece I'm thinking of is my Sixth Symphony: I remember walking along the shore an awful lot with the music, particularly the final section, going through my head. Afterwards, coming home and writing it down was fairly straightforward. Sometimes I simply sit down and find that the whole piece is there, ready in my head. I don't have to change a note. But usually that's a short piece like *Farewell to Stromness*, which I wrote straight out without altering anything, or short sections of a bigger work like some of the pieces in my ballet *Caroline Mathilde*. But I think that this can only happen when you've got an awful lot of experience of composing.

Nor do I think I could have got through the vast amount of music that I've written had I not had a regular work routine. I used to start at nine o'clock in the morning, but now that I'm a bit older I take it more easily and start at around ten with a good, strong espresso. And I go on for as long as it takes, until I'm exhausted. That might be at six o'clock, in which case I'll take a break and have something very light to eat. Or it might be later. Of course, when I'm at home there are sometimes wonderful days – in spring, summer and even winter – when the weather is so lovely that I take the afternoon off and go for a walk, or sit in the garden in the sunshine with a nice glass of white wine. And I'm prepared to do that because, in general, I keep a very disciplined compositional existence – steadily going, every day.

It occurred to me the other day that I haven't had a proper holiday for about ten years, and so I'm thinking about going to stay with friends in Italy later this year. For a couple of weeks I'm just going to enjoy being there, and I won't do any work at all.

I'd say that, in general, my music hits the mark that I intended it to. But afterwards I think, 'Well, the mark should have been higher. You can do better in the next piece.' Particularly with my symphonies and the other big pieces like the string quartets and some of the concertos, I've felt at the time that I was going as far as I could with the material that I had and with the musical processes that I'd worked out. But I've also felt that I had to screw things that little bit tighter the next time.

---

[1] A square grid of distinct numbers (each used only once) arranged in such a way that in each row, in each column, and in both the forward and backward main diagonals they add up to the same number. Sir Peter's *Ave Maris Stella* and *A Mirror of Whitening Light* are examples of works whose pitches and their durations were determined mathematically with the use of magic squares.

I've become more ambitious, and I'm always raising the level of the bar.

It's very hard to explain in a few words how I do this, but in general I simply take on something that needs more elaborate and thorough thinking through. And I aim to create something that has more intensity. I think that in my later years, when I dare to believe that I'm a bit more mature, this process has become almost unconscious. I simply *do* it. With Symphony Ten, for instance, I set the bar much, much higher than before – which explains part of my struggle to write the piece and part of my insecurity about the result!

I've always got new ideas to explore in music, which is why I can't be bothered to revise my older pieces even though I know I should. I'd much rather go on to something new. And when it came to writing my Naxos Quartets I was helped by having a ground plan for all ten. In fact, I conceived them almost as the ten chapters of a single novel. But, of course, during the process of composition all this changed: I tried out different things in a variety of ways and ended up writing the quartets in a different order. Some of them were short, some were long; some were more tragic, some were even funny.

You're right that the public role of the composer is at odds with the very solitary, private act of composition. People appreciate a pre-concert talk, and talking about your music can open doors for their understanding, but when you're writing music you're not thinking about what you're going to say about it! So my answer to the question 'Is it helpful to a composer to be a little schizophrenic?' would be 'Absolutely!'

It's not in the gift of a lot of composers I know to be able to talk articulately about their work in public. And if they find it difficult, there's not much that can be done about it. I'm also a conductor, and a conductor is a performer, in a way. So I'm used to being on stage in front of people and, until you mentioned it, it had never occurred to me that other composers might dread having to go up to take a bow after a performance of their music. But, although it's very hard to see into the mind of a fellow creator, I think all of us have dreadful self-doubts.

The first performance of my Tenth Symphony at the Barbican went very, very well but beforehand I had very mixed feelings about the piece because I'd written it under extraordinary circumstances: mostly in a little hospital room, when I was not at all well, to put it mildly! First, I felt that composing the Symphony was going too well, because the music was simply tumbling out of me. And second, a lot of the musical ideas were unlike anything that I'd had before. I thought, 'Some of this music, particularly early on in the piece, is so strange.' But that wasn't surprising, really, given that I could have died. Twice, actually, I came within hours of dying. It was that close. And although going through that experience taught me something, I couldn't be confident about the music because I'd never written anything like it. So I was very relieved when Antonio Pappano, who was going to conduct the first performance, came to the hospital to look at what I'd written and said to me, 'I like the harmony!'

What was I writing about? I don't know. The inspiration for the Symphony was the architecture of Borromini, but this was translated into ideas that were purely musical. And I'd be very hard put to explain how something spatial, borrowed from Borromini, became aural. I think this process goes on underneath the threshold of your conscious understanding. But I do know that developing an architecture in the music created conflicts with its form that corresponded to Borromini's conflicts between architecture and form in seventeenth-century Rome. And this was a very positive and constructive thing in the music.

As I've just said, some of the sketches for the Symphony look like no others that I've made. I think I was simply responding to pressure. In other words, I just had to write the piece in the way that I did. But then living with music in a creative way is for me almost a physical necessity. And although, over the years, I haven't written as much music as I would have liked to write, I feel that what I *have* written has an intensity which validates, in a funny kind of way, the experiences of my life.

Thea Musgrave

Thea Musgrave, London, February 2014

❛I really write for the players, not for the audience.❜

I'd met Thea Musgrave once before, in Nottingham in January 2000, when I photographed her after a rehearsal of one of her pieces. She liked the results and explained that she looked relaxed in the photos because while I'd been pointing my camera at her she was still jetlagged (she has lived in the USA since marrying the American violist, conductor and opera administrator Peter Mark in 1971). When I read that she was going to be in London in February 2014 for a BBC 'Total Immersion' day of her music, I hoped that there would be a chance to meet her again and interview her for this book.

'Sure! I'd be glad to meet up', she e-mailed me. 'It's going to be a little crazy but we will find a time!' A few weeks later came another message: 'Andrew, I LOST your list of questions. Grrrrr! I am doing too many things all at once.' Her schedule in London was indeed a little crazy because of preparations for three concerts of her music – given by students from the Guildhall School of Music, the BBC Singers and the BBC Symphony Orchestra conducted by Martyn Brabbins – and, on the same day (a Saturday), two talks about the works that were programmed. The second of these was an onstage conversation with Tom Service, who also interviewed her for BBC Radio 3.

A few days after this Total Immersion I went to interview her at the hotel in Earls Court where she and her husband were staying. We'd agreed to meet in the small bar at the front of the building, and she walked in with the demeanour of someone much younger than eighty-five. This was partly because she no longer wears the spectacles that for decades were such a strong feature of her appearance but which seemed to age her prematurely.

This being a Thursday morning, the hotel was deserted apart from staff, and so we stayed in the bar and chatted there for nearly an hour. The only intrusion was the persistent and piercing chirrup of a caged bird, which eventually gave up and became silent again. We shared memories of Richard Rodney Bennett ('I still can't believe he's gone', she said sadly) and she enquired about a number of the contributors to this book – some are old friends or colleagues, and she was interested to hear what they're doing.

I observed steel behind her charm and could only admire the way in which she looked forwards to as yet unwritten works rather than backwards at past successes. 'I'm doing *new* things', she told Tom Service in her radio interview, 'so it's not easier. You have to say, "How the hell can I work this so that it will be interesting?" Everything is new.' After she'd answered my questions she e-mailed me reviews of the Total Immersion concerts from her new iPad; and, apart from a slight hardness of hearing for which she'd earlier apologised ('But let's not go there …'), it was difficult to believe that she was already halfway through her ninth decade.

If the previous Saturday's tribute seemed overdue this was perhaps not surprising given that she has lived half of her long life abroad. I was interested to know how much of an outsider's perspective she has on British music, but first I asked her for her experience of the recent *Musgravefest*.

Exhausting, but oh, absolutely extraordinary! I got to meet all sorts of people that I'd known about for a long time, starting with Tom Service. I've often read his blogs in *The Guardian*, and I actually met him the day after we arrived in London. He was just so well prepared and easy to talk to. So that was actually enjoyable! Then meeting Martyn Brabbins, whom I'd never worked with before and who was really fabulous at balancing detail and long-line shape and impact – all in efficiently run, compact rehearsals. And then the Horn Concerto soloist, Martin Owen: he's an absolutely extraordinary performer, like a great singer. And the choral conductor Paul Brough, also meticulous and extraordinary in preparing and performing so much of my choral music.

It didn't surprise me that the BBC Symphony Orchestra and the BBC Singers were wonderful, but what *did* surprise me was the group of Guildhall students who played in the first concert. I knew they'd be good, but they were much more than good – they were really excellent, and so well prepared. I was absolutely amazed. And thrilled. So it was a great celebration, and it's nice to know I'm not forgotten!

I do still feel a 'British composer' because this is where I grew up. I think it is where you are as a kid that is important: it is what informs the rest of your life. It helps to guide you in what you do and how you handle things. And I *am* British. But I'm also American now – I have dual nationality. And I live in America simply because I married an American.

The most obvious difference about musical life there – and perhaps it's so obvious that I don't need to say it – is the vastness of America. And there are pockets of musical activity, more in some places – New York, Los Angeles, San Francisco, Chicago, Boston and Houston, for example – than in others. Also, of course, there's no national state broadcaster like the BBC. This is an organisation that I appreciate more and more because of the quality of the music programmes such as Radio 3 and the BBC Proms. Also the number of orchestras it has. After all, it was the opportunity to compose a piece for the BBC Scottish, after I finished my studies in Paris with Nadia Boulanger, that taught me how to write for an orchestra. Certain things can be learned only through that kind of practical experience, and when I was teaching in America I wondered how to help my students get it. Young composers write music using Sibelius, Finale and so on, and I'm glad they can do that, but some things that can be done very easily on a computer aren't transferable to working directly with an orchestra. So how do they get that experience? It's very difficult. The BBC Scottish fulfilled that function for me, and I hope it still does for young composers. Of course, America has a lot of orchestras, but in the current economic climate they're hanging on by a thread. Even opera companies are going under.

The other big difference is in the funding of music in America. It's not split between Arts Council grant, local authority grant and box office, as it used to be in Britain and maybe still is. Instead you have a board of directors, who usually donate something annually in order to *be* on the board, and then you raise more money by contacting your rich philanthropists. But that's not really the end of the story, and the good thing is that the board also goes out to the community to organise local fundraising events. So it's a sort of grassroots affair, particularly in the cities that don't have big corporate donors like the ones in Chicago, New York or Los Angeles. So you bring in your community, and you educate them to support you. You also educate the next generation.

I didn't set out to be a composer. I actually started in medical school before going into music. And although I liked composing I had no idea that I'd become a professional composer. I don't know *what* I thought I was going to do, to tell you the truth, but I probably assumed that I'd become a teacher. And I didn't have any role models as a composer because I didn't know any apart from my teacher at the University of Edinburgh, Hans Gál.

When I started composing, my music was very conventional, and so I thought I should write something more original for the finals of my music degree. I did – and the university nearly failed me. In fact, they passed me because of what they'd seen of my earlier, more conventional music. What's funny is that when I went to Boulanger and showed her the conventional stuff she raised the proverbial eyebrow at it. I said, 'Well, I do have this other music', and tentatively showed it to her (I was *very* tentative in those days). And she said, 'Oh! I see, yes! You have ideas. Now you have to learn some technique …' So she saw what potential was there.

No, I can't tell you what it was that I showed her because I don't have it anymore. I don't remember what on earth it was, but I assume it was fresher and more adventurous than my earlier pieces. At that time I wasn't aware of the various schools of music because I'd been tucked away in Edinburgh, where we didn't hear many contemporary pieces. And because I was busy learning about harmony and counterpoint, orchestration and music history, and studying the piano, I didn't get out very often. But after four years in Paris I came back to London and was out almost every night, going to the opera, going to ballet, going to concerts. And that's when I began to meet other composers and to learn what was going on in the musical world. I met a lot of people through William Glock and by going to teach at Dartington Summer School, and then I met Richard Rodney Bennett, who became a lifelong friend. In fact I knew him from when he was seventeen until he died last year.

Yes, my music has changed over the years. I was briefly a twelve-tone composer – you have to go through that phase, and I'm glad I did because it offered me a way of handling musical material. But that lasted a very short time and I certainly don't do it anymore. I think I was crazier in the 1970s and I liked to experiment, writing things like *Rorate Coeli* and the Horn Concerto, which are fairly far-out. I don't seem to do that now, but who knows? Maybe I will in another piece!

What became more and more important to me was the *drama* in music, and so I started to engage the players in more dramatic ways. In fact, some of my pieces concern a single player within a group, or a group of players interacting. *Space Play*, for example, is for nine players who conduct themselves. There's a small group (the strings) in the middle, a horn, and then the four winds at the four corners of the ensemble. They dominate in turn – they come forward to play – and their cues, some of which are in measured time and some of which aren't, control how things happen. So the music becomes a drama because there's a relationship between the different instrumentalists.

Turbulent Landscapes, a fairly recent piece, is based on six Turner paintings. Each of the six movements represents a particular painting and has a solo player from the orchestra who stands up to play. I believe musicians play differently when they're standing – I'm convinced that they play with more energy and more expression, which I love. Before that piece was played here last week I said to the tuba player, who's the soloist in the first picture, 'Don't you dare stand up until after the music has actually started! People have to *see* you standing up and becoming the monster in the painting.' That visual aspect of performance is important to a number of my pieces, partly in order to reach out to the audience so that they feel engaged and partly to give an individual player within the group a moment in which to express himself or herself.

Even when I was writing twelve-tone music I wanted composing to be more than an intellectual exercise. The intellect comes into it, of course, because you have to make sure that the details of the music are practical and workable, but I always wanted my music to be expressive. What do I mean by that? I think it's quite simple: something that can reach an audience. Like me talking to you: we have a communication, and we listen, understand and (hopefully) enjoy.

If something grabs an audience you can make it quite complicated musically. And if you make concessions it's not because of the audience but in order to follow through your musical ideas – which you have to remain true to. I remember that when I was writing one of my operas I wanted the chorus to come on stage and sing immediately, but I didn't give them enough time. So I had to fix that by repeating eight bars of music while they came on. That was a concession, in a way, but not a concession to the audience. You see, I really write for the players, not for the audience. Yes, of course I want to reach listeners; but who are they? *I* don't know. So I write for the performers, who I hope will reach the audience through their playing. And *there* I make the concessions that are necessary to the functioning of the music.

I used to tell my students, 'If you write something very difficult or awkward in a piece of music you'll never get a performance, because it will take an endless amount of rehearsal time. Orchestras simply won't do that, these days. They can't. Your idea might be a great one, but now you have to learn a way of expressing it in some kind of notation that the orchestra can grasp quickly. Then they can concentrate on making it expressive rather than worrying about the practicality of the notation.' My idea is that even a work such as my Horn Concerto, which sounds very complicated, should be almost sight-readable, in terms of notation, by a really good orchestra. Then the rehearsal time can be spent on balance and detail.

I think there are two ways of creating the form of a piece of music. One is to start by writing something and then thinking, 'Well, what can I do next?' And then you add something to it. Then you say, 'I've done that and that, and so now I do *this*.' You go from moment to moment and eventually you finish the piece. The other way is to start off with a bird's-eye view of the whole thing. And then, as you get further into the piece, you work out the details. I prefer the second of these processes because I like to have a feeling for the whole piece (but not all of the detail) in my head before I start writing. After all, that's often the 'wow' idea that the piece starts from.

For example, my Horn Concerto was written for Barry Tuckwell, whom I knew quite well in the Sixties and Seventies. When he was touring he used to send me postcards from around the world, and one he sent me from Mexico was of a central monolith surrounded by others. And from that came the idea for a piece featuring a solo horn in a group of other horns. I thought that would be exciting, and not a novelty for its own sake. Then the issue for me was how to create a musical form that would realise my idea practically in performance. What happens is that in the middle of the piece three of the orchestral horns move out into the hall, so that the soloist is, in a sense, surrounded by his colleagues. The soloist, not the conductor, cues in the other horns as if they were playing a piece of chamber music with him. In fact, they didn't need those cues because his solo part is cued into their parts. But I said to Barry, as I said to Martin Owen the other day, 'Let's *see* you give them the signals, because then the audience will hear the music better.' That's another example of sight enhancing sound as part of the drama of the piece.

So, although I like to plan the form of a piece in advance, I sometimes start writing in the middle of it. For example, if I'm very clear that there's going to be a turning point in the music or the drama, and if I have ideas about that, I might as well write them down. And then I go forwards and backwards from that point. Sometimes I come to a roadblock, in which case I just jump over it and go somewhere else in the piece; and then I come back afterwards to work my way through the roadblock.

When I write an opera I plan the libretto myself, and usually each scene is some kind of confrontation. It has to have some particular purpose, and usually a predominant emotion of some sort. And there's a very simple reason why I write my own text: there can often be a conflict between a librettist and a composer. I don't think of myself as a great writer but I know the proportions of the opera and how much text each section of the music needs. And writers sometimes forget how much music can expand the timing – a slow aria, for example. So the composer may have to request the writer to *cut* some wonderful text. Very painful! I also know which words sound good on certain pitches, and which vowel sounds not to use. For example, you don't give a soprano an 'ee' vowel to sing on a high note because she'll have to change the vowel sound in order to produce the note.

Writing my own libretto also allows me to change the text right through the rehearsal period until the opera is actually on stage. If something doesn't sound good, or I don't hear the words clearly, I can ask a singer, 'What's uncomfortable there?' And if necessary I can change a word. You can't do that with a wonderful librettist whose writing is great but perhaps not suitable for the demands of the music.

I collaborated with Lilian Groag to make a Spanish version of my opera *Simón Bolívar* because I don't speak Spanish. And we quickly decided not to be too literal about the translation because that simply wouldn't have worked. For instance, the line 'Decisions made today cast a long shadow' doesn't really exist in Spanish. It became 'Las decisiones de hoy te seguirán mañana' ('today's decisions follow you tomorrow') – same thing, but not *exactly* the same thing. It was a very interesting process.

Some people compose all day long for three weeks and then don't compose for a month. I don't quite understand that, even though I know it works for some of them, because it wouldn't work for me. All through my life, with few exceptions, I've written music every day, even if only for a short time. It's like keeping in shape physically. Some days are better than others, of course, and sometimes I throw away what I've written, but I still need to do it every day. And always in the morning. I used to tell my students, 'It's very important to know whether you're an owl or a lark – a morning person or an evening person. It doesn't matter which you are, but you need to know because when you schedule your life around classes you either have to get up very early to do your composing beforehand or go home in the evening and compose at midnight.'

I still do it the old-fashioned way: pencil and paper. I used to say to my students, 'You guys have to learn Finale or Sibelius, but I'm too old.' Fortunately my publisher sends my music off to a wonderful man in Edinburgh (my home town) who inputs it onto the computer. And then I'm sent a PDF file, which comes to me by e-mail in less than a minute, so that I can correct it. Sometimes he asks me questions, such as, 'Last time this horn had an F sharp, but now it's an F natural. Which is correct?' And I reply, 'Oh my God, I forgot.' Or, 'No, the harmonies are different there, so it *is* an F natural. Maybe we should mark it in the score, just to be sure.' Wonderful! It's a sort of very acute eye looking at the score and hopefully making sure it's free of errors – almost impossible!

When I think about my music I don't see the way I wrote it on the page. Instead I hear the sounds and think about the drama of a piece, and how it would work in performance. How it looks on the page is simply notation for other people. When you hear in your head something that you want to be in a piece, you have to decide how to notate it so that it will sound the way you want it to. So you have to know about instruments, even if you don't play them yourself.

My husband used to be a violist, and he once advised me that a viola line I'd written in an orchestral piece needed to be bowed in a particular way. When he played it to show me what he meant, it looked weird, but he said, 'Don't worry. It'll work.' Sure enough, at the rehearsal nobody – not even the conductor – said anything because the passage came out as intended. Certainly, when I write a concerto I'm in close touch with the soloist and I take his or her suggestions about the solo part. And if something is awkward to play and interrupts the flow of the music I say, 'Let's change it.' Sometimes that's easy, sometimes it isn't. But I want the piece to lie comfortably under the players' hands, as far as that's possible. And I can only do that *with* them. I can't do it for myself.

I don't, on the whole, go back and revise works. But recently I made what we call a jewel-box version of *Simón Bolívar*, which was originally written for a big orchestra, chorus and soloists. I revised the libretto, took out the chorus and added a few supers,[1] and reduced an orchestra of forty or fifty down to ten. That was a very interesting process. It was not really revision; it was rewriting in another format. Something similar happened with my opera *Harriet, The Woman Called Moses*, which is about the extraordinary story of Harriet Tubman, well known in America but hardly so in Britain. It was written for a regular opera orchestra and chorus, and six years later I revised the libretto and vocal

---

[1] Supers (short for 'supernumerary actors') are non-singing actors in an opera – the equivalent of extras in a film.

score to make *The Story of Harriet* (Julian Grant reduced the full score because by that time I was busy doing something else).

I find it interesting that you can reduce works but can't go in the other direction and expand them – except that we did just that, earlier this week, during the Total Immersion day at the Barbican. Lisa Milne was supposed to sing my *Songs for a Winter's Evening* but she fell ill and had to cancel two days before the concert. So we had to think about what we could put on the programme instead. And certain works weren't possible because we would have needed a bigger orchestra, and at that point the necessary extra players weren't available. Finally I said, 'You know, I wrote a piece for twelve strings called *Green*, and I think it would sound quite good played by a larger string group.' And that's what we did. So that was an example of a piece going *up* in scale – which doesn't usually work, in my view.

I don't mind the public aspect of being a composer, particularly if it involves being interviewed by someone intelligent. Talking to Tom Service was fun – it was like having a chat. What you also sometimes have to do, as a composer, is to address an audience before a concert, or talk on air about a piece of your music that's going to be played. I'm used to doing that, and through teaching I learned how to not be afraid of addressing a group of people. What matters is that you do it directly and straightforwardly so that what you say has meaning for an audience listening to your music. Clarity is important, and I think that's the Scots in me: if you want to do something, you might as well be clear about it! So I try to think carefully about what I'm going to say in public, perhaps highlighting something for people to listen for so that they'll understand the music better.

You talked about the possibility of a piece of music being so important to someone that it becomes part of his or her life, and that's lovely. But as to the question of whether its composer can really understand that, I think the answer is probably no. It's true that the audience's response to music is more subjective than the composer's, but when I'm writing a piece I'm hearing it, in my head, at the same time as I'm working out the practical details of timing or whatever. And even if I'm less involved emotionally while doing this than a listener is when hearing the result, I *am* still emotionally involved. Otherwise I wouldn't write the music. But I don't think I can really answer your question, because I don't know how to talk about this. Sorry!

Do I *enjoy* my own music? It depends on the performance. I mean, listening to Martin Owen play the Horn Concerto the other day was extraordinary. And I loved how some of the young Guildhall students addressed the pieces they played. Their commitment to making it a real *performance* was great. Yes, I thoroughly enjoyed that. And of course I'm often surprised by what certain performers bring to my music. It's like the difference between a great actor reading a text and *me* reading it.

A live performance is never the same every time, thank goodness. Sometimes it doesn't work too well, but at other times there's a moment when something totally unexpected happens. And I don't know what it is, exactly. But *you* know what I mean: the moment suddenly comes alive in an unexpected way. It's like having a conversation with someone and not quite knowing what they're going to say; and, hopefully, you're surprised and interested. And that's wonderful. That's what it's all about, I think.

Roxanna Panufnik

Roxanna Panufnik, Rye, September 2011

❝ I definitely view myself as providing a service of some kind.❞

My encounter with Roxanna Panufnik was unusual in that it began with a series of photographs rather than an interview. When she learned that I would want to photograph her for this book she had an idea: since most of her official photos are formal studio portraits, why not try something more spontaneous? In a few weeks' time, she explained, she would be at St Mary's Church in Rye, East Sussex, for the final rehearsal of her *Cantator and Amanda*, to be premiered later that day by the bassoonist Julie Price and the Wihan String Quartet; and she suggested that I photograph her there while she was listening to the players and interview her after the rehearsal. Undaunted despite the fact that her mother, Lady Panufnik, is the photographer (and author) Camilla Jessel, I said yes and, in September 2011, duly turned up not knowing quite what to expect.

This being a Saturday afternoon during the town's annual Festival, the church was busy with tourists and sightseers, some of whom inevitably pointed their own cameras at the activity on the temporary stage that had been set up in the middle of the nave. But Panufnik appeared unfazed by it all. Snapping away at her while she listened to her new work and made occasional comments to the performers, I felt rather obtrusive, but she assured me that I wasn't distracting her. At one point she even grinned at me while the musicians were playing, as if to suggest that she found the experiment fun.

The resulting images were far from perfect, technically, because of the varying levels of light in the church, my need to work around pillars, the stage and members of the public, and Panufnik's movement around the nave as she listened to the balance of the music. But they're at least a record of a musical event, and the one reproduced here is that which both she and I like the most.

Afterwards there was no time for the interview, so what follows is drawn from conversations with her by e-mail and on the telephone. Unfortunately it was only as this book was nearing completion that I learned that she experiences synaesthesia and perceives letters, numbers and days of the week as colours (shortly afterwards I re-read David Matthews's booklet note for the recording of his *Concerto in Azzurro*, in which he explained that he associates the key of B flat with the colour blue). I wish I'd been aware of this at the time of the interviews because it would have been an interesting topic to explore – since awareness of synaesthetic perception is assumed to vary from individual to individual, the phenomenon may also affect other contributors to this book even if they're unaware of it.

I didn't ask about her father, the Polish composer Sir Andrej Panufnik (1914–1991), but she made a number of references to his music and career, and it's clear that he remains one of the most important influences on her, both personally and professionally. While I was photographing her in Rye I was too involved with technical matters to observe her responding to the rehearsal of her new piece, and so I began my subsequent questioning by asking her to explain her feelings when hearing for the first time something that she has worked on in private for many months.

It depends on how it's being played. I was quite relaxed in Rye because the musicians were wonderful and had either been involved from the start of the compositional process or had previously played other pieces of mine several times. But it's always scary when you're revealing your innermost thoughts and emotions to an audience of several hundred or more, whom you've never met. The worst-case scenario is that the performers play the music incorrectly, the audience finds it ugly or much more esoteric than it's meant to be, and then you, the composer, are inevitably considered to be to blame! Of course, I'd love to have as many happy listeners to my music as possible; but in the end, as a composer, I must be true to myself. Personally, I only want to write the kind of music I'd like to listen to and which performers will enjoy playing; and then if other people would also like to listen to it, all the better.

My music leans towards the emotional rather than the intellectual. But, even so, it's nice when my audiences appreciate the extent to which I've thought out my compositions. My father was much cleverer than I at finding an equal balance between heart and head. In fact, his whole life's work was a delicate balance: trying to be true to himself musically while having to humour the socialist realists he lived under in post-war Poland; then, once free in England, trying to balance an ethereal and cerebral world with domestic family life (I know all about that, too!) and trying to balance his interests in geometry and spirituality. There was a great dignity and reserve about him, whereas I'm less shy about expressing my feelings – in music, that is, not in any other context!

This may, of course, be a result of the different time that I'm living in. After all, it was the 1950s when he was the age I am now. He did hear my early compositions and was always very encouraging, although as a young whippersnapper I didn't appreciate any constructive comments he gave me and I tended to ignore them. I now regret that deeply.

I studied composition at the Royal Academy of Music (with harp as my second study) and my formal music education was very helpful from a technical point of view: for example, in teaching me how to orchestrate by learning how various instruments work individually or blend into an ensemble. My professors wanted me to be a lot more experimental than I was, and my graduation report said that my music was 'naïve' but that I had a 'gift for melody'. At the time I was a little annoyed by this and tried not to take much notice of it, but now I can look back and see that, in a way, my professors were right. I *did* need to experiment more. I don't think it would have made much difference in the end, though, because, as I said earlier, I've only ever been interested in writing the kind of music I want to listen to.

I feel I learned just as much, if not more, than I did at the Academy from going to work for the BBC for three years as a researcher for TV music programmes. This didn't teach me composition technique, but it did teach me more general, professional skills that I didn't learn at music college and which are absolutely vital to a composer: a coherent telephone manner, the ability to write well-structured letters, promotion, networking and so on. After all, much of what composers do is centred on knowing how the 'system' works and who works it!

There are a lot of commissioning bodies, institutions and performers who do excellent work, but you need to learn which of them are interested in particular styles of music. For example, some of them are only keen on the more intellectual and experimental 'cutting-edge' or avant-garde music, whereas others place more importance on 'aesthetic accessibility' for their respective audiences. Some lucky and/or clever composers, of course, fall into both these categories!

I very much think of myself as a composer who just happens to be a woman, rather than as a 'woman composer'. In fact I'd hate to be defined and assessed by my gender. But I remember hearing that during the rehearsals for the premiere of my *Westminster Mass* in 1998 one of the orchestral musicians said that she could tell that a woman had written the music. I believe she meant that there was a warmth of sonority or tonality which, to her, sounded 'feminine'; but I can't be sure about this because I never found out who it was, so I couldn't ask her.

As for the term 'British composer', it tends to make me think of composers who were strongly influenced by English folk culture and landscapes, like Vaughan Williams and Britten. And it's a tricky label to apply to composers living and working in the UK today, because so many of us have mixed roots. I get labelled by Radio 3 as 'Anglo-Polish', which I'm very happy with because being Anglo-Polish influences my music completely and utterly. It's a constant presence in my spirituality, both professionally and personally, and I'm often told that my music sounds Polish – although I haven't quite figured out what that means!

In any case, contemporary classical music has blossomed into multiple styles and moods, and there are very few composers who write in such a formulaic way as the serial composers of the previous century. It's almost impossible, I think, to be so black and white about techniques and influences today. And I'd say that this has made being a composer both easier *and* more difficult than it was. Easier because your personal style is much more likely to find an audience, however large or small; and harder because it means that more and more composers are competing for the same diminishing number of commissions or grants.

I think what changed the musical culture in this country by giving composers permission to write in styles that were less 'modernist' was the massive success of Górecki's Third Symphony and some of John Tavener's works in the early 1990s. They were very soothing pieces, and people needed to be soothed because the 1980s had in some ways been a brash and rather aggressive decade. This type of music also seemed appropriate to the emerging New Age movement of the late 1980s and early 1990s, when people were becoming much more aware of environmental issues. In other words, it fitted the mood of the times, and its success brought contemporary classical music back into the mainstream. By then I'd left the Academy and had decided that I was going to have a career in TV production, but that music made me think again. Maybe I *could* be a composer after all.

However, the beginning of my professional career was a difficult time for me emotionally because my father was terminally ill. A few days before he died we had an amazingly candid talk that made me decide that life was too short not to do what I really wanted to do. And because I felt tough and brave after surviving the subsequent bereavement (I was still in my early twenties), I just went for it without much thought of how things might be professionally five, ten or fifteen years down the line.

When I left the BBC in 1992 I decided that I was going to make my millions by being a film composer. And I was very lucky: I got a place at the wonderful National Film and Television School in Beaconsfield. But I very soon realised that my plan wasn't going to work, partly because I'm a complete technophobe – you have to be very technically minded to compose music for film or TV. You also have to be very versatile and to be able to write music in lots of different styles. And I could only really write in *my* style. But I did compose the music for a documentary film about Armenia and the theme music for a BBC2 series called *Summer Dance*. And some of my music was used in a documentary about Cardinal Basil Hume broadcast shortly after he died. So a few bits and pieces of my screen music are out there.

I would love people to be soothed by *my* music, particularly the spiritual pieces. Over the last ten years I've spent a lot of time studying music of the three monotheistic faiths (Christianity, Judaism and Islam), inspired by the notion that we all believe in the same one God. I'm fascinated by different chant traditions and by the rhythms and modes of the countries those chants come from. I'm also greatly inspired by the church acoustic – its reverberation complements the natural bitonality of my music (I find myself automatically combining major and minor harmonies). I have no illusions as to whether the results of my work might deter any potentially dangerous fundamentalism, but if it reminds people of their similarities to each other, that's surely a bonus.

Although I feel it's my mission to build musical bridges between faiths, I sometimes use elements of world music simply to create an atmosphere that brings the listener to a particular part of the world. For example, I've used tabla rhythms in Indian-influenced music, and Sufi rhythms and modes in my settings of texts by the Indian poet Rumi. And I like to explore the ways in which different countries use different types of musical ornamentation.

Many of my pieces have a story behind them that has required a considerable amount of research. Sometimes this has involved my finding experts on a particular type of music or literature and then quizzing them on the nitty-gritty of it. I also use the Internet for musical research – Wikipedia and YouTube have been known to provide me with the thematic foundations of many a piece.

While I'm doing this preparatory work, musical atmospheres start to form, often quite slowly, in my head. And this type of musical feeling or mood is usually based on a very simple fragment such as a short melody, a rhythm or a basic harmony. Harmony is my first and foremost love, actually, and quite often when I start a piece the first thing I create is a harmonic progression. Melody also plays a huge part, but composing is for me as much about the harmonic implications of melody – that is, how melody works around the harmonies I've created – as about the tune itself. Anyway, these musical feelings or moods blossom as I realise them on the piano, so that by the time I start to actually write the piece I've already got a good idea of what it'll sound like.

Settings of texts, too, usually begin with a sense of the atmosphere they evoke. For example, at the moment I'm setting a Shakespeare sonnet, and it's obvious that its mood changes in the middle before returning to the mood of the opening. So what I normally do first is to create a kind of mood map of the whole piece. Then I think about the kinds of harmony and texture that will best convey each of the moods, and the piece begins to build up from there. Relating text to vocal lines happens almost automatically once I've found the appropriate harmonies; the vocal line is set over the harmonies in a naturalistic way, by which I mean that it follows the rhythms and pitches of the spoken word.

Pretty much everything I've written in the last twenty years has been commissioned, and I definitely view myself as providing a service of some kind. This is incredibly important to me because I don't think I'd ever finish anything if I didn't have a real deadline. I've written a few short pieces as presents – a couple of birthday fanfares and a love song for a Valentine's Day – but everything I write I want to write anyway. I love the huge scope of projects that I have coming my way, and I know that I'll learn something from each of them. Apart from anything else, there are so many sides to my character! My spiritual side is best displayed in my larger choral works such as the *Westminster Mass* or the Estonian oratorio *Dance of Life*. But you can find my cheeky side in *Beastly Tales* for solo voices and orchestra, while chamber pieces such as *Olivia* or *Cantator and Amanda* show my more intensely emotional and theatrical side.

I wouldn't say that my music has changed greatly since I began composing, although it's probably simpler and more direct as a result of my becoming less self-conscious about saying the things I want to say in it. This is certainly true of my choral music. What's *completely* different now is the physical way in which I compose: with a computer. For one thing, the process is much faster. And being able to play back my rhythmic ideas on the computer helps to reassure me that I've notated them correctly, because I have a bizarre kind of rhythmic dyslexia. I can hear, imagine and feel rhythm but I can't perform it. In other words, I can't conduct, dance or play an instrument in time. I haven't always had this condition; it came on with severe self-consciousness during my late teens, which makes me think that it could be psychosomatic.

I'm a terrible control-freak and I put masses of written notes in my scores about how certain phrases or sections should be expressed, or even *acted*. On the other hand, I'm quite shy and I very much consider myself a 'behind-the-scenes' person. For example, I get far more nervous about a pre-concert talk than about the performance itself. Next week we have the press launch of my latest CD and I'm going to have to give a presentation to eighty or so journalists and representatives of the music industry; nothing fills me with as much fear as the thought of that, even though I'm sure I'll be fine once I've started talking.

My father absolutely hated any kind of public speaking, mostly because while he was living in Poland under the Communists they would record him speaking about something and then completely distort what he'd said, either by taking his words out of context or by physically altering the recording. It was horrendous, and after a while he came to the conclusion that he simply couldn't take the risk. From then on he just wanted to let his music do the talking. Things are very different for me, today, and I accept this more public aspect of the contemporary composer's role. It's a double-edged sword, really: while talking in public about my music can be the most terrifying thing, I want my music to communicate to its listeners. And I know that it'll be easier for them if they know something about the person who wrote it and the evolution of the piece they're about to hear. There's no argument, in my mind, that to have the opportunity to explain to people how a piece came about, why I wrote it in the way that I did, and what they can listen out for when they hear it for the first time, is a fantastic privilege.

Having said that I want my music to communicate, I must add that I don't think much about the audience while I'm composing. I'm certainly not aware of any concessions that I might (or might not) be making to them. And the reason is that they're only one part of the 'package'. When I'm commissioned to write something for a particular event, the package also includes the musicians who are going to play the piece and the occasion itself, and so I'm aiming to fulfil the commission on *all* of those levels. As I've already said, I have to write what I like the sound of, musically; and if it happens to be something that the audience also likes, then that's fantastic.

It's rare that I make a false start and reject a piece early on in the composition process. And I'm more likely to move on to a new work than spend time revising an old one. But if somebody wanted to perform a work of mine that I hadn't looked at for several years, I'd want to make sure that I was still happy with it before agreeing to the performance. People often ask me to re-arrange pieces for different instrumental combinations, and I'm usually very happy to do that, especially as it extends the shelf life of a piece and gives me a chance to reassess it.

Minor revisions after a premiere or even during the rehearsals are more routine, and I often make small adjustments to new pieces. Maybe I've tried a little experiment that didn't quite work; maybe one section should be longer or maybe it's too long and needs to be condensed. More often, the dynamics aren't exactly right – perhaps there's a texture that's a little too dense. I find balance very hard to judge in my shed at the bottom of my garden where I write my music, so it's impossible for me to be 100 per cent sure about it until the players start rehearsing and I can hear all the parts performed together. Sometimes I may have made an informed guess while writing the piece, but just as often these minor details of balance and dynamics need to be addressed before or immediately after the first performance.

How much of my time is spent doing non-composing work? Too much! I seem to have piles and piles of admin. But I suppose it's split fifty–fifty between domestic and professional chores. The latter includes writing programme notes, attending rehearsals, getting new projects and ideas off the ground, and answering queries from potential performers and students (most of whom are writing theses on women composers!). I'd love to earn enough to be able to hire a personal assistant.

I have help with the children during the week, and I'm very strict about composing every morning whether I feel like it or not. But I really treasure the chance to switch from composer mode into mummy mode at the weekends, not least because this makes me feel fresher and more productive when I go back to my piano on Monday mornings. Of course, it's not always easy to mentally put aside the work that's been absorbing me, and I often have my latest composition on a loop in my head while I do my Saturday morning cycling, but it soon goes with the domestic distractions of the day.

Only time will tell whether the music I write is 'good'. It's impossible for me to be objective about it after I've been immersed in writing a piece for several months. I don't normally listen to critics (unless they're positive!) but on the one occasion when they were unanimously bad it did make me want to look again at the piece in question. More important to me are the reactions of the performers and audiences: if they're happy with my music, then so am I.

I never think logistics when I listen to other composers' work; it's always about how a piece of music makes me feel. But – egotistically, perhaps – my own music brings me intense pleasure. Because I'm shy and not good at expressing myself verbally, music seems to be the only way I can show everyone how profoundly I really feel. Could I have been anything other than a composer? Who can say ... except that I love cooking, so maybe I could have become a cook and poured all my emotions into food instead of music!

Anthony Payne

Anthony Payne, West Sussex, July 2012

> **❛ Don't study music expecting to learn its secrets so that you'll like it; just keep listening to it until the penny drops. ❜**

There was never any question in my mind about whether I should interview Anthony Payne for this book. Like most music lovers, I imagine, I have a sense of him being at the centre of British musical life: as a reviewer and critic for the *Daily Telegraph*, *The Independent* and *The Times*; as the author of a book about Frank Bridge; as a commentator for BBC radio and television; and as a contributor to film documentaries about Delius, Parry and Vaughan Williams. And of course he's known internationally for Elgar's Third Symphony, which he completed from the composer's sketches to create an 'elaboration' (the term required by the Elgar estate) that has been performed more than two hundred times. More recently he has completed Elgar's Pomp and Circumstance March No. 6 and has orchestrated Vaughan Williams's *Four Last Songs*. But it was only when I made contact with him to ask if he would contribute to this book that I realised how little of his own music I knew.

He and his wife, the soprano Jane Manning (whose contribution to British music as a performer is surely as significant as his as a commentator and arranger), have lived in north London for more than forty years. But at his suggestion I interviewed him at their second home, a small, terraced cottage up a village lane in West Sussex – not far from where Arnold Bax and John Ireland lived, I thought, as I drove there through leafy countryside in July 2012. The door was opened by his wife, who did most of the talking until 'Tony' (as he's known to almost everyone who meets him) took me upstairs, to the room that he uses as a studio, for the interview. Afterwards he moved to his work desk so that I could photograph him.

He was rather more solemn than I'd expected, and I was interested to read just over a year later an interview in which he told a journalist, 'I laugh, but I don't smile, so people often think I am a bit unfriendly.'[1] There was also something slightly anachronistic, if not exactly old-fashioned, about him: he referred to my list of questions by saying, 'That's what you

---
[1] *Time Out London,* 28 August 2013.

put on the screen' (he meant that I'd e-mailed them to him), and when recalling events he sometimes described himself as ten years younger than he actually was at the time. But he responded enthusiastically to my questions, and when I explained that they'd been compiled from the viewpoint of an amateur music lover I was pleased to hear him remark, 'Mmm, music lover of goodwill!'

This was a conversation in which one topic rolled satisfyingly into the next. But we kept returning to his development as a composer, which has been less straightforward than that of many of his contemporaries. He explained that he was a relatively late developer – not necessarily as a technician, although he had little formal music tuition and is virtually self-taught as a composer, but in terms of finding a mature compositional style. I subsequently wondered whether he feels that he has never caught up with contemporaries who hit the ground closer to running speed. At one time too, no doubt, his support of British music from an earlier era was considered unfashionable.

I began the interview by pointing out (with no disrespect implied and, I hoped, none inferred) his somewhat anomalous position in contemporary British music: that of the prominent figure who's nevertheless known for other people's music more than for his own.

I think that's very much the way things are. I've become known by those English music lovers who probably don't like modern music very much – they're a very conservative lot – and who kind of claim me for themselves. They love my Elgar but I doubt that they know a note I've written in my own, modern style. I'm also known to the sort of inner sanctum of modernist audiences, as I always would have been had I not written Elgar and expanded my audience hugely into *that* area. But the two groups don't meet very often, I'm afraid.

For my sins, I always wanted to promote turn-of-the-century, early modern and late Romantic English composers. The generation of Vaughan Williams, Delius, Elgar and Holst is very important to me, and I feel I belong there. But I also feel I belong to the post-Second World War avant-garde composers whose music was being played in the 1960s: Stockhausen, Boulez, Ligeti, Messiaen, Varèse, Gerhard and Lutosławski. They thrilled me. And I always wanted to espouse the two causes and somehow integrate them, which is what I hope my music does.

And now that you ask me, it really is extraordinary: I'm not entirely sure what it is about those two types of music that made me feel I belonged to them. My contemporaries – Sandy Goehr and Max and Harry and all those people – managed to cotton on to the avant-garde while they were still students, and so by the time they got to their mid-twenties they knew it all. Well, I didn't come to it until later, after I'd formed a composing style of my own and had written early juvenilia pieces in it. If I played you one of those pieces, you'd say, 'Oh, it sounds like 1930s English music.' You'd recognise Delius, probably, and odd references to the more modern Vaughan Williams, Bartók and Tippett. Not Britten, because he didn't appeal to me then. You might think it sounds a bit like Bridge – which is ironic, because I didn't know any Bridge at that time.

Then I went to university and was overwhelmed by hearing and learning about Schoenberg, Webern and Berg. To begin with, I didn't really take to them at all, but I was curious. What *was* there in that music that so many people were passionate about? I felt that I really must know. And so I listened and listened. At first nothing happened, but then, all of a sudden, I heard something – I forget what – that made me think, 'Yes! I seem to know it now.' But I can't really say why I fell in love with that kind of music, any more than I can say why I fell in love with Delius and VW when I heard them for the first time, in my teens; or, for that matter, why I *didn't* fall in love with Strauss, or indeed Mahler, which I heard at the same time.

When I went to university I dried up as a composer because I couldn't relate the new music I was hearing to what I'd been writing in my English, 1930s kind of style. I was fascinated by it, and knew instinctively that I somehow had to take it on board and feed it into my own musical language, but I got hopelessly stuck because I didn't know how to get down on paper the sounds I could hear in my head. After I graduated I didn't go and sit at the feet of Stockhausen et cetera, not because I didn't want to learn but because I didn't want to give myself away in front of other people. I never wanted to have my music discussed. I wanted to sort these things out myself.

The problem was solved some years later by a friend asking me, 'Weren't you a composer when you were at university? Would you like to write a setting of the Mass for my school choir?' I hadn't written anything for four years, but I thought I'd have a go at it. I started with something incredibly simple, almost like a painter beginning a picture by putting a splodge of paint in one corner of the canvas. Then I thought of something else to add, and somehow the piece began to work, and so the idea of writing a whole movement didn't seem so overwhelming. And after I took on board all the music I'd been fascinated by – Elliott Carter, for instance, and Varèse and stuff like that – I realised that I was composing music that sounded totally unlike what I'd been writing before.

For a long time I'd wondered what would happen if I took Delius, a composer from my past whom I'd been almost overwhelmed by, and translated his music into modern terms. It was a kind of folly, really, that I never intended to pursue. But when the conductor Mike Lankester asked me to write a piece (I forget what it was called[2]) for a classical orchestra of two trumpets, two horns, wind and strings, I thought, 'What say I try to do that now, just for a lark?' I didn't realise that the exercise was going to have enormous repercussions for my music. I'd repressed my love of Delius while I took off and became a modernist composer, but now I felt I could feed it back into my idiom. And I thought, 'It's as if my past is gradually joining hands with my present.' At last I was doing what had been at the back of my mind for ages: integrating the English Romantics with the modern avant-gardists.

The first three or four pieces written in what I consider to be my 'proper' style were broadcast by the BBC, and I was declaring 'This is me' comparatively late by the standards of my contemporaries. I felt way behind them, and it was a bit depressing because, although I was known as a music critic (I'd just finished my book about Schoenberg) and was promoting modern music, my contemporaries and friends barely knew that I was a composer. So for a while I felt lonely, because there seemed not to be many people in my generation who were particularly interested in Elgar and Delius and Vaughan Williams. The world I moved in was the world of modern composers: Nick Maw and Richard Rodney Bennett (we were friends) and Max and Harry. And there was always something fascinating on the radio to talk about. I remember Nick ringing me and asking, 'Did you hear the Boulez Third Piano Sonata last night?' It was all so exciting.

Then I got talking to Hugh Wood and discovered that he loved Elgar and liked Vaughan Williams. Nick Maw tended to be a bit sniffy about Elgar but loved Strauss, whereas I was sniffy about Strauss but loved Elgar! It later transpired that composers like Max and even Harry weren't anti-Vaughan Williams at all. They had quite a feeling for his music but were keeping quiet about it.

I absolutely love harmony, and I think there are a lot of composers today who don't give a toss about the vertical sounds of their music. They're going for other things – overlapping textures and ideas

[2] *Spring's Shining Wake* (1981).

crammed on top of each other – and they don't care what you get if you take a deep cut through a particular bar. You probably get about forty notes sounding, actually. I could never have that in my music.

At one stage I was fascinated by piled-up thirds and sixths that I haven't heard in any other composer's music, and I can always recognise a piece of mine because of its harmonic aura. As my style has developed I've realised that my melodies – and I do write what I call long 'tunes' – have become hidden or spread chords. I don't have tunes that are fitted with chords, like the accompaniment in classical and Romantic music; I have tunes which *are* chords. So my harmony and my melody are the same thing. To me it's almost mystical – you know, it's all just one great universe.

What attracts me very much to turn-of-the-twentieth-century composers – Delius and Debussy, for example – is the way in which they manage to hook you, sometimes with just one harmony. Or one little phrase will grab your attention and won't let you go. But it's no use having *only* that. You've got to have an engrossing structure as well. And I think this is the main problem in composition: inventing material with immediate impact that grabs the ear *and* intrigues the mind by following an argument or piecing out an architectural shape. You've got to be flexible enough to embrace both.

In the case of my *Time's Arrow*, it was structure that first grabbed me – the idea of a gigantic deceleration towards a static middle, then acceleration out to the end. Also mirror images of ideas, which are repeated in reverse order as the piece speeds up. I was always fascinated by the idea that we're rushing faster and faster away from the central Big Bang but are gradually getting slowed down by gravity so that we'll eventually get sucked back into it. Although this idea is now considered nonsense (apparently, we're going to go on and on forever, which is a rather horrifying thought), it was quite fashionable forty years ago and I thought it was a very good basis for a piece of music. And this occurred to me before I had a single individual sound to write down. The result is that *Time's Arrow* begins with a crash, and then a huge Allegro rushes out. It gets slower, and in the middle there's a stasis. Then the piece starts to build itself up and gets sucked back into the beginning.

Something else that fascinates me is the aftermath of disaster, and how you have to carry on regardless. An earlier piece of mine, *The Spirit's Harvest*, explored this autobiographically. Not wishing to be too corny, it was about the shattering experience of the young love affair that goes wrong and how you have to carry on after it. I suppose there's a sort of qualified optimism about the piece. I conceived it when I was still in my twenties, and I envisioned it up to the point where the disaster happened and everything ended in gloom, but at that time I didn't have the technique to carry through a big orchestral piece. Fifteen years later a Proms commission enabled me to write it. By then I was a different person and I could see things more broadly, and so I felt the piece had to end in a different way: with a rather ambivalent-sounding scherzo that goes along fast and light but with a strange lack of committed emotion. And that's what happens at the end of a disaster. There's still intellectual energy in everything, but your feelings have been smashed.

A lot of composers say that they cover their paper with sketches and then write the music out more neatly, but I can't work like that. I can't suggest a rough idea of what's going to happen over the next three minutes; I have to do it second by second, and get one bar right before I move on to the next one. It's the same with my literary writing: I can't trust one sentence as the basis for the next unless it's absolutely right.

You said that the score I showed you looks extremely neat, but it's actually only a rough copy. I love the visual aspect of doing things on paper, and I take pains to write music out slowly so that it looks good. If it's not neat it won't represent a good sound to me. And although I know it's blowing my own trumpet, I do have a good reputation in the profession for having a rather neat hand. Performers tell me that they'd much rather play from a score that's nicely handwritten than from one that's printed from a computer, because a printed score has got no personality at all – it looks like five hundred other scores.

In general, I don't discuss with many people what I'm working on. I don't even talk about it to Jane. I don't ask her what she's practising and she doesn't ask me, 'How did the composing go this morning?' Sometimes I'll tell her I've had a bad time, and she'll cluck sympathetically, but I don't think she knows what really goes on in my work room. She's just very interested in the end product, and fantastically supportive.

I find I have to stop working after a spell of about an hour and a half, and I'm envious of composers who can go on for long stretches. I find that if I'm stuck with an idea it's no use prodding about at the keyboard trying to work out what to do next. I'd just get utterly bogged down. So I've learned to have a certain amount of confidence to go away and do something else – gardening, going for a walk or watching rubbish television, anything to get me out of that mode. And the solution pops into the back of my head while I'm thinking about something else. In psychological terms, I have to trust my unconscious to feed me an answer to my problems. But sometimes this might take a few weeks, which is very painful.

I had a terrible time with the piece I'm writing at the moment. I think I was trying to slog away at it too consciously, and I got overtired and it just wouldn't work. A couple of months went by during which I was writing things down and not believing in them, but then all of a sudden a solution to the problem came into my head. It's a terrific relief when that happens. You think, 'Thank God! The old machine is still working.'

I'm never surprised by my music when I first hear it because it always turns out the way I intended it. (I know this sounds immodest.) But I *am* sometimes surprised by how important, and even striking, one section is compared to another. I'll remember the strain of getting one particular passage right, and I'll feel relieved and proud to have got it right, and then I'll sort of write off the next passage as being easy; but when it comes to the performance, the passage I took so much trouble over, and was so pleased to get right, goes by in a second while the other passage that I didn't set so much store by is like an explosion in the head. Something that required a lot of manipulation and knowledge and skill to get around a corner in a certain way goes fine, like a puff of wind, while the next bit is a magnificent, effulgent thing(!) that you wrote with little difficulty. In other words, the emphasis of those two passages is different from what you'd imagined, even though you got them both right. This is something I can't quite explain. My friend Justin Connolly says, 'We all aim for a target but hit something else!'

Sometimes I'll hear just a small detail that needs to be corrected. I remember having a run-through of my Wind Quintet by the Nash Ensemble and being quite disappointed by the piece. After about twenty bars I thought, 'Why does it sound so dull?' I thought about this and suddenly realised that, although all the counterpoint was beautifully done, the flute part was too low and didn't have a nice ring to it. I immediately saw what had to be done: raise the flute part in the texture and put the odd note up an octave so that the shapes go slightly differently. Then the whole thing came to life.

When I'm in the right frame of mind I do find my own music exciting, to the extent that if it were by another composer I'd think, 'What a jolly good piece!' But wild horses wouldn't drag a phrase like that out of me, especially if I were talking to one of my composer friends.

It's about not wanting to appear immodest, I think, because, although I know which bits of my music are meant to be exciting, which bits hypnotically still and so on, I can't actually say so. It would sound so pretentious. I don't think we do things like that in England!

I do feel British, but a British composer who's very interested in what's going on outside Britain. Vaughan Williams said that you get to know your roots and then look outwards; and my musical roots are definitely English ones. As to why that should be, I don't know. What's English about Elgar, for example? His music comes from Wagner and Schumann and French ballet. Perhaps we recognise that the temperament – the deep-seated melancholy – behind it is English.

I find that if I haven't listened to any CDs for a few weeks I begin to feel a bit lost. I like to keep a connection with the live sound of music, and listening to a piece that I know I like but haven't heard for some time recharges me. And that's another difference between me and some of my contemporaries: I think I've got wider tastes than many of them. I love most things except French music of the Twenties and Thirties (I'm not a Poulenc/Ibert-type person) and *bel canto* opera. I go off the boil immediately with Bellini and Donizetti, and then I come back with a bang with Puccini, which I really love.

It made me so angry fifty years ago when people were snobbish about Puccini being a 'popularist'. It was very artistically snobby in this country, I think, in the late Fifties and Sixties. A lot of people were going across to Darmstadt, mixing with the Europeans and taking on board all their attitudes, not wanting to seem 'small-time' by espousing English music. But we've always been like that in this country, haven't we? Not selling our own music. Today, there's a generation of composers young enough to be my children who don't care whether something's modern and chic and avant-garde and from the Continent. They'll listen to Ligeti and say it's wonderful, and they'll listen to Vaughan Williams and say *it's* wonderful. Thank God we don't have that snobbishness any more.

You can turn on the radio and hear Far Eastern music, classical music, Japanese music, Chinese music, folk music from the African continent – all types of modern music. And I think it must be a nightmare for a young composer to try to find his way among all these things. It doesn't make it more difficult for him to have his music heard, I don't think, but it might make it more difficult for him to find a serious style that represents him as he really is. That might not happen until he's in his forties.

Hans Keller once said to me, 'If Britten had lived two hundred years earlier than he did, he'd have written great works by the age of twelve.' What he meant was that, like Mozart, Britten would have had to learn only two types of music: Italian opera and north German contrapuntal music. And he could have taken those on board in a year. But in order to find your style as a composer today you have to take on board so many things that weren't happening even a hundred years ago. The other problem is that a young composer, perhaps only in his early twenties, may feel that he's in a kind of marketplace (young composers are *wanted*, after all, to win competitions and things like that) and so he may be forced to sell himself before he's really found himself.

Why am I a creative person? I think it all boils down to the fact that music made such a deep impression on me when I was a teenager. It absolutely took me over, and all I wanted to do after that was to have a similar effect on people by sharing my musical feelings with them. This will sound terribly egocentric, even though lots of other composers have said it, but you're writing for an audience of a hundred people like yourself, or a hundred yourselves, because you're the only person you know really well. You say the things that you yourself understand, and you hope that other people will understand them too. Which is why it's sometimes a bit of a shock when someone says of your music, 'I didn't get that.' You think, 'But it's obvious! *Why* didn't you get it?' And you hope they *will* get it after several listenings.

Do people want to use the verbal language of the Regency period? If not, why don't they want to listen to the music of their own time? I'm afraid I have to guard my tongue on this subject, because obscene phrases come to mind! A lot of people think that music should be entertaining and capable of being grasped at first hearing. They don't realise that hard work is involved in making some of it enjoyable. I freely admit that it's going to be difficult. The first time I played Webern, for instance, I found it very difficult indeed, and it was some time before it took on the shape of something natural. But it's only a piece of music, and a piece of music is like a person: you might not like them when they first poke their head round the front door, but in a year's time you suddenly realise that you know them. So don't study music expecting to learn its secrets so that you'll like it; just keep listening to it until the penny drops.

As for posterity, my music isn't performed much now, so I'm just hoping it will be done more after I'm dead! And I don't want to let myself down, so I have half an eye open for what people might say about me in the future. How would I like people to respond to my music? I think I'd like them to say something about it being like a page-turner of a book – that they had their attention grasped from the very beginning to the end – and that the piece made a great big overall shape. One of my aims is to *never* let up in my music; another is to never write a single weak bar, just as an author wouldn't write a single boring page in a book.

Elis Pehkonen

Elis Pehkonen, Suffolk, September 2011

> **I felt I had to write tougher, cutting-edge music because that's what everybody else was doing.**

It was inconceivable not to interview for this book as many of the 'big name' British composers as possible. But for each of them there are tens of others who are less well known and who persevere with their work unaided by publishers, managers, agents or recording companies. Together they form the majority of British composers – in numbers if not necessarily in influence – and because few are invited to talk publicly about their music I felt it important to interview some of them.

Elis Pehkonen (not to be confused, as he may sometime be, with Aulis Sallinen, Joonas Kokkonen or Jouni Kaipainen) agreed readily to my request – 'not for kudos', he explained, 'but because Murray Schafer has been a big influence on my thinking'. Nevertheless, he repeated a number of times his gratitude for being asked to contribute to this book. On each occasion I assured him that, although he may make few headlines, his contribution is valuable for a number of reasons, not the least of which is the fact that every composer is an individual in terms of outlook, experience and aims. And in his own case there's the important issue of localism.

For more than twenty-five years he has lived and worked in Suffolk and has developed a comprehensive knowledge and understanding of local musical life – much of which is non-professional despite the large number of performers and composers who live in the region. In practical terms it's strongly influenced by audience demographics, by the distance between concert venues (many of which are rural churches) and by the region's relative lack of public transport; and Pehkonen is clear about the need to programme events that local people will be prepared to attend rather than what might be thought good for them.

As if to illustrate this, visiting his home involves driving down a winding and apparently ever-narrowing lane deep in the Suffolk countryside and looking for what seems to be the last cottage in the village. When I went there to interview him in September 2011 his warm, chatty and hospitable wife led me through the garden, which contains palm trees and other exotic plants, to the enviably large wooden studio where he works. Inside were ordered rows of carefully filed scores, parts and recordings of his music. It was a tranquil and cosy space, part office and part archival library.

He's more reserved than his wife and apologised for not responding well to my questions. 'Hardly anybody interviews me', he explained. He's modest and unassuming, and I've observed that after a performance of his music he appears more comfortable bowing to the players than to the audience. But although he gives the impression of being unemotional, it's probably more accurate to say that his emotions aren't near the surface. For these reasons he was an interviewee from whom I sometimes had to coax responses and into whose mouth I had to be careful not to put words.

I wasn't surprised that when talking about his work he emphasised the importance of craftsmanship rather than self-expression. But he, more than any other contributor to this book, related his music to identifiable stages in his career, and he was the only interviewee who considered that he might have said all he wants to say in music.

My father was Finnish, hence my name, and I suspect that I sometimes get mistaken for other Finnish composers. But I was born in England and I can only think of myself as an English composer. I can't speak a single word of Finnish, and this has embarrassed me only once: when the British Council, assuming that I was a Finnish speaker, invited me to talk to a group of Finnish musicians, none of whom could speak a word of English. My roots are in East Anglia – in Norfolk, where I was born and brought up, and here in Suffolk, where I've lived for twenty-five years close to Minsmere Bird Reserve and the coast. Southwold, my favourite town, is twelve miles to the north and Aldeburgh eight miles to the south.

Do I feel in the shadow of Britten here? Not in the least. Once you know *Peter Grimes* there's obviously a naturalistic association with the area, but I don't think of *Grimes* every time I go into Aldeburgh! However, Britten was the first living composer whose music I encountered at school. I remember being bowled over by the *Serenade for Tenor, Horn and Strings* and having an immediate sense of what the music was doing, and why. I still regard it as his finest work, though this is possibly a personal prejudice because I know the piece so well. (I sometimes question its title, though, and wonder whether it should have been called the *Serenade for Horn, Strings and Tenor Solo* in order to avoid the allusion to the tenor horn of a brass band!)

I'd say that Britten seeped deep into my subconscious, and in fact my more recent pieces are rather similar to some of his early work. But it's important to emphasise that I write my *own* music. I certainly hope it doesn't come over as a pale imitation of Britten when it reaches the public ear. And I'd admit the influence of *all* the music I heard as a youth: my listening experiences revolved around Bartók, Tippett, Britten, Walton, Janáček and Stravinsky, among others.

As a student at the Royal College of Music I took part in performances of a lot of string quartets and got to know some of the repertoire that way; and it wasn't only classical quartets – we even played one by Roy Harris. In fact I could hardly avoid broadening my musical horizons while I was there, not least because of personal contact with my contemporaries. In particular, I much enjoyed Brian Dennis's systemic music, I admired Roger Smalley as a brilliant pianist and composer (and a Stockhausen enthusiast), and I attempted to tread in the imaginative footsteps of Martin Dalby.

I think this is how *all* composers work. The pieces they experience early in life work their way into the subconscious and come out later in many different ways. In my case it's certainly pieces from the more distant past that have been influential, and I don't feel that today's music affects what I write in any way at all. A composer can't help living in his own time, but I wonder whether some try to live ahead of theirs. Not that music is necessarily inferior if it's less accessible to the general public. Craftsmanship is more important than style.

One of my most satisfying creations is the selection of music (mostly chamber works) on a CD called *Turning World*, because it's very representative of my general stylistic position. As for my other music, my String Quartet No. 1 (a BBC commission) demonstrates a stylistic connection with Tippett and Britten; and a subsequent BBC commission, the Concerto for Two Pianos and Orchestra, shows my firm allegiance to the past with a series of references to Bartók, Britten, Janáček, Mahler, Rachmaninov, Steve Reich, Stravinsky and Wagner – all folded together into what I believe is a cohesive whole.

I think most composers regard themselves as self-taught – because, I suppose, it's impossible to teach somebody how to write music. They have to do it for themselves. But of course practical advice from other composers can be very fruitful. I've collected my fair share of names when seeking such advice, including Britten (people think that he never gave lessons, but I had two from him, the first when I was eighteen),

Lennox Berkeley, Alan Ridout and Richard Rodney Bennett. Richard was one of the best of that kind of teacher, and he actually broadcast a piano piece of mine, which he probably didn't enjoy playing.

Alan Ridout was my most sympathetic teacher – he was very good in that respect – but you need more than sympathy. You need a few kicks up the pants, really. Some of these teachers *were* quite critical and, although it was a shock to hear 'This is no good, you shouldn't be doing this', I could see immediately that they were right. I stopped having these lessons or consultations after asking a well-known BBC producer and composer if he'd like to appraise some of my work, and getting the answer, 'You don't need me to do that; you're your own best teacher!'

I identify four stages in my development as a composer. The first includes my youthful music, a series of short published pieces and some exploratory choral and orchestral works. After leaving the Royal College in 1964 I moved to Gloucestershire, where I met Laurie Lee and wrote my *Three Songs* to some of his poems – this was the first work of mine to be broadcast on Radio 3. And two years later, at Britten's recommendation, I got my first commission: the Incidental Music for *Everyman*, for the King's Lynn Festival.

This period of my career culminated in my *Missa Pro Defunctis* (1967), the first complete setting of the text of the Latin requiem. I still regard this as my best work, though few people know about it. It was written in a Handelian frenzy in just three months and was performed several times in the West Country between 1967 and 1974, while I was living in Cirencester. It has since undergone frequent revisions and the last performance was in Cheltenham in 1982, but there might be an opportunity for the latest version to be performed in the USA in 2017.

During the 1970s I felt I had to write tougher, cutting-edge music because that's what everybody else was doing. But it wasn't entirely successful. I'd like to think that people enjoy listening to my music but I know that in this second stage of my career I wrote pieces that weren't particularly enjoyable. Even *I* struggle to listen to the BBC recordings from that period, because they remind me of my painful efforts to keep up with fashion – not a good idea!

I regret writing some of the pieces that I wrote then, because I simply wasn't very good at writing that sort of music. And the reason that I tried to write it was that I was attempting to keep up with the Joneses rather than being true to myself. I often wonder why a lot of 'modern music' sounds much the same: tough, tuneless, intellectual, every effort a pale shadow of every other effort. (I call it 'Euro-Music' and hope the title doesn't offend too much!) Having said this, I recently encountered a marvellous piece by a young composer whose ethos is to write beautiful music.

I don't know if you've interviewed composers who felt they needed to make a fresh start, but it happened to me. I learned from making a lot of big mistakes after 1967 – overreaching myself, mistakes in timing, making pieces too long or too complicated – and in 1980 I thought, 'I'm going to try to start again.' And my third stage began with a commission from the Three Choirs Festival: *Buccinate Tuba* for choir and brass ensemble (with timpani and organ). By this time the musical climate was beginning to change, thanks partly to 'West Coast' American composers who were showing that there were ways of writing meaningful music without having to subscribe to post-Webernism or being carried away with the strictures of Boulez. I certainly found listening to Steve Reich very helpful and I started to write music that I once more felt was *me*. I've never felt comfortable in a trend-setting or cutting-edge position, and much of my recent music has been quite the reverse: very tonal.

A good example is *Amor Vincit Omnia* for Oboe d'amore and String Orchestra, which has been recorded by Jonathan Small and the Royal Liverpool Philharmonic Orchestra. Perhaps the best example of my work that blends tonality with mildly cutting-edge material is the *Russian Requiem*, commissioned by Jeremy Patterson and the Birmingham Festival Choral Society. It hasn't been performed much recently but it had a good innings starting in 1986 and including a wonderful performance at the Royal Festival Hall in London in 1993 that featured the London Bach Choir conducted by Sir David Willcocks. The last movement, the Agnus Dei, is purely tonal and at a recent performance it was reported that some members of the audience were moved to tears by it.

It might sound too casual to say this, but my current, fourth stage of development involves avoiding writing any music at all! And the reason is that I can't help feeling there's far too much of it out there already – too many young composers trying to make a name for themselves and too many middle-aged ones trying to earn an honest crust. I sometimes wonder whether composers should look at all their work, choose the ten best pieces, chuck the rest away and concentrate on getting people to listen to those ten rather than being burdened by the great backlog of music that's continually accumulating. That way, performances could be spread between more composers!

On the other hand, I feel a certain loyalty to the music I've written and to making sure that my two hundred or so scores are as good as they can be. So a lot of my time is now spent maintaining a library of my work: making minor revisions, tidying up manuscripts on the computer and producing short runs of decent-looking scores. If you look around this studio you'll see that it's in a fairly good degree of organisation – otherwise I'd never find anything.

By the way, this doesn't necessarily mean that there won't be a stage five. But it's looking unlikely because I suspect that I've said all I want to say, musically – not before time, some might suggest!

I have two working seasons. The first is from April to September, when I spend as much time as possible outdoors, gardening. As I'm currently Director of the William Alwyn Festival, which takes place every year in Suffolk in October, I also spend a lot of time during this working season planning and co-ordinating musical and literary events in the coastal towns and villages of Southwold, Blythburgh, Westleton, Aldeburgh and Orford. My second, 'quiet' season is from after the Festival until March, when the English climate forces me indoors to continue what I described earlier as my 'stage four'. Despite what I said about *not* composing I recently accepted (against my better judgement) two commissions, and I'm very much looking forward to the second of them, which is to compose a piece for the splendid new organ in Westleton church.

In fact I've never been without a commission of some sort, and that includes music written for performing colleagues. Sometimes they weren't really commissions: it was just that somebody asked me if I would write something for them, or that I said to a particular musician, 'I'd like to write a piece for you.' Not long ago I wrote a hymn tune, which I'd never done before, just because I wanted to and because I'd found some words that I wanted to use. In fact there could be lots of reasons why I write something. One reason might be that it's a good idea for me to write the piece. For example, somebody might suggest that I write a piano trio, which I've never done and which might exercise my brain in a new way.

I'm in the fortunate position of not having to earn a full living from writing music, so income from composition isn't that important to me. In that sense, I don't regard myself as a professional composer. Composing is very difficult and very discouraging if you're struggling financially, because you're not going to be writing good music if you're anxious about money. But although most composers struggle to earn a living, they carry on writing music anyway because it's what they want to do. Also, making a living from writing certain *types* of music

– commercial work, I mean – might discourage one from writing the things that one really wants to write.

Would I have been a better composer if I'd had to struggle more, financially? Of course, the creative urge is irrepressible, but if I'd fully understood how hard it is to make a living from composing I'd probably have given up altogether a long time ago.

I'd been composing for many years before I discovered the computerised score-writer. I currently use Sibelius 7 and it's a marvellous tool. Like many composers, I imagine, I wish I'd had it forty years ago. It helped me to make a fresh start at composing and I suspect that if I didn't have it I'd find great difficulty in writing any music at all. I have no wish to return to the physical labour of the pencil/paper/eraser process, which I haven't used for years. (I'm sure this is why some composers' scores were very sketchy: they didn't want to go through the laborious handwriting process. And maybe the very sketchy scores are the better ones?)

I used to find that producing sheet music without the luxury of a publisher (I publish my own work) was a struggle, not because I couldn't do it but because it took such a long time. Copying parts, in particular, was always a major task. Now, with Sibelius (and, indeed, the more sophisticated Finale programme), writing music is less of a struggle for me, and because the computerised process is quicker than handwriting I feel the music retains its freshness.

Then there's the fact that with the computer I get immediate visual contact with my music as it evolves. And of course I can create sound files of my work and hear it very quickly. So, with careful listening and planning, I can get the timings right and ensure that no section of a piece outstays its welcome. It's also easier to spot superfluous fermata: for example, the long crescendo followed by a pregnant pause! But, given that you have to be very careful when you're writing for performers, it's important not to misuse or overuse the score-writer by making your music unnecessarily difficult or complicated.

I don't *think* the results of writing music on the computer are any different from what I would have achieved with pencil and paper. I'm constantly revising on the computer pieces that I wrote using pencil and paper, and I find that it's easy to see ways of improving things such as timing because I can *hear* the music and make adjustments accordingly. But this raises an interesting question: if you were to write the same piece again in five years' time, would you do it differently? I don't think anybody's ever tried to do that, although most composers revise their work, to differing extents.

You'd think that amateur music organisations would sit down at committee meetings and say, 'Now, what should we do about composers living in our area who we know of? Let's find out what they're up to.' Not a bit of it. Amateur musicians are only interested in playing their instruments or singing, not in supporting local composers. And I believe they're doing a disservice to living composers by failing to at least acknowledge their existence and find out what they're doing. That's a bit of a generalisation, I know, but it's my experience. And I think there are a number of reasons for that.

Probably, inertia is one of them – they can't be bothered. Another is anti-localism – those in charge of the organisations prefer to get in people from outside the area. Also, probably, they think that all contemporary music is like Maxwell Davies or Birtwistle and so they believe they can't cope with it. To some extent it's understandable that professional musicians prefer to play pieces they're familiar and comfortable with, but with amateurs it's even more disappointing. They could be missing out on lots of rewarding musical experiences.

Of course, there's the problem of writing down to amateurs. One doesn't want to do that. But what about the good-quality, accessible contemporary music that amateur organisations could avail themselves of if they took the trouble to investigate it? I'm thinking of pieces like Jonathan Dove's *Seek Him that Maketh the Seven Stars* for choir and organ, which is terrific.

As long as I've done a good job on writing and producing the music, I'm quite happy for it to be in the public domain. Occasionally I write something very personal, but then I make sure I don't provide a very full programme note so that people don't know what the personal side of it is! Normally I prefer to concentrate on highlighting points in the music to listen for, and if one of them happened to be an emotional tune I'd probably use the word 'emotional' rather than 'beautiful' because it's less subjective.

Many works of art can make one tearful, but I shouldn't think there are many pieces of music that actually reduce people to tears. Of course, I don't deliberately write a piece of music in order to have that effect on people, but to know that it has given somebody great pleasure is amazing. *I've* often been moved by my music – maybe it's a narcissistic thing – and particularly by the *Missa Pro Defunctis*.

You asked me about the composer as a public figure, and I have to say that I don't feel important enough in the general scheme of things (I confess to being a part-time composer) to be of much more than minor interest. On the rare occasions that I get to hear a performance of my work I enjoy talking to people afterwards, and I hope that they mean it when they say they enjoyed it, rather than simply being polite. I don't know what people know about me and I've no idea whether I have any kudos anywhere. But I know what I'm writing and I know why I'm writing it. Although composing is probably, in my case, more emotional than intellectual, I know the craft and I could do a cerebral analysis of my most emotional piece.

The important thing is to write music that you hope will evoke a positive response from the performers. One always has to keep the public listener in mind. Like most composers, I also believe that in order to get a good performance you have to make sure your scores and your part-writing are as good as they possibly can be. But whether this means *interpretation*, in my case, I doubt very much. I haven't had the luxury of performers interpreting my music, because no single group of musicians has performed any one piece often enough to be able to play it in different ways.

However, I think I have the ability to communicate in the sort of way that Britten communicated, and so I *want* to communicate. And I wish that more people were familiar with my music. Does that sound immodest?

Joseph Phibbs

Joseph Phibbs, London, August 2011

> **I find it rather difficult that you have to tell people what a piece is about, rather than just letting it *be*.**

This encounter was atypical in that it was based on knowledge of only one work by its subject: *Lumina*, commissioned by the BBC Symphony Orchestra and first performed during the Last Night of the Proms in August 2003. Earlier that year Joseph Phibbs had been the subject of *Gramophone* magazine's regular 'One to Watch' interview feature and had explained that in responding to the BBC commission he'd wanted 'to present what I feel is my musical language at this stage of my life, in the clearest and simplest way possible'. When I watched the television broadcast of that Last Night his name was still new to me and I was more interested in other items on the programme, but *Lumina* was an enjoyable discovery. And because I videotaped the broadcast I was able to hear the work many times during the eight years before I asked him to contribute to this book.

His response to my request was to prove similarly serendipitous. 'I remember coming across Paul Griffiths's book in my school library when I was fourteen, and finding it very inspirational', he wrote, 'and I've felt for ages that an updated version of it is long overdue, so yours sounds like a wonderful idea.' What if the current book, I wondered, were also to find its way into school and college libraries and be read by aspiring young composers? What information in it would they find most useful? So was born the idea of inviting every contributor to offer his or her most important piece of advice (collected in the Appendix on pages 477–486) to a hypothetical young Phibbs of the future.

As for my encounter with the real one, I hope he won't mind me suggesting that it was memorable chiefly for the extraordinarily difficult journey to and from his home in north London. On that hot, sunny day in August 2011 a burst water main stopped all rail travel through south Croydon, and during both my journey to London and my return home after the interview I was stranded with hundreds of other passengers waiting for alternative transport or at least news of when train services might restart. On my way to London I felt lucky not to be one of the tourists who were about to miss their flights from Gatwick Airport, but I was still anxious about arriving late. Fortunately, Phibbs was at home all day and assured me on the phone that it wouldn't matter too much when I arrived. Sure enough, after a flustered half-run to his flat from the nearest Underground station I was welcomed into an oasis of coolness, calmness and courtesy.

He appears not to have inherited the more outgoing characteristics of his actor parents and he remains reserved and modest. Although a gifted pianist and cellist, he knew from his teenage years that he was temperamentally unsuited to the life of a performer: 'Because of my weak nerves', he explained in an interview for the Junges Beethovenfest in Bonn in October 2014, 'I think I wasn't meant to show off. I'm too nervous to play in front of people.'

Our conversation began with *Lumina*, which, at the time of writing, has still not been recorded commercially. I told him how much I enjoyed the piece when I first heard it and how it struck me as a work whose musical gestures don't need to be understood fully in order to be appreciated by what might be called the 'average musical listener'.

Well, thank you. I'm glad that *Lumina* communicates to you. Composing has to be about communication, even if you're really hoping to communicate to just a few people. And for me, at least, it's never been entirely about expressing what I want to express for my own good. But the difficulty about music is that it's an abstract art, and so it's impossible to pin down what it is you're expressing as a composer. You're expressing only the music, and the music has to follow its own path. And while there's a kind of joy in being able to communicate a certain feeling to a listener, it's impossible to know or to dictate what he or she should feel, and one wouldn't want to do that anyway. But it's very satisfying to feel that that's happened, when it *has* happened.

Lutosławski, who I think was a wonderful composer, used to describe himself as a 'soul-fisher': through writing music he aimed to catch the souls of his audience. It's perhaps surprising that this was what mattered to such a rational composer as him – that he was communicating first and foremost emotionally rather than intellectually. Britten once talked in an interview about trying to write in an idiom that the average listener might find a little challenging but wouldn't be completely confused by, and I think there's something to be admired in trying to reach an audience in that way. I mean, there's a generosity of spirit in doing that while remaining authentic – without writing down to listeners and without compromising what you want to write.

I remember that when I was writing *Lumina* I was strongly influenced by American landscapes, and so I tried to talk about them in my spoken introduction before the Proms premiere. I'd spent quite a lot of time in New York City and I wanted to evoke its frenetic quality (and, of course, its very particular quality of light), hence the work's fast, kind of jazzy section. And I thought it would be much more interesting in my talk to relate those environments to the musical line of the piece than to talk about its overall shape. After all, there's nothing particularly interesting about starting with a clarinet solo and ending with one, as I did in that work, although for some people that could be important.

Elliott Carter, whose music I immersed myself in a few years ago, talked a lot about analogies between music and literature, as well as the other arts, but I'm sometimes suspicious about analogies with *any* of the arts. Music is music, and it has its own way of working. You can't expect it to operate in the same way as another art form. Music unfolds, and is perceived, through time; so to link it, for example, to architecture and sculpture strikes me as being of limited value. Cinema and theatre, the other art forms that are to some extent fixed in time, seem to have the most plausible links with music.

The question of whether one writes a piece of music with a particular individual in mind is fascinating, and one that I've thought about a lot. Seeking a kind of mental approval from someone can be very dangerous because when you start thinking 'What would that composer think?' or 'Will that promoter or critic like it?' you immediately risk compromising your vision. So in general there's no-one in particular that I write for. But sometimes, when I've been working on a piece, I've thought about a good friend of mine who's older than me and who has loved music all his life. He's completely illiterate musically – he doesn't read music and he doesn't play an instrument – but he has a wide knowledge of music and he loves a lot of it. And I sometimes think, 'If *he* doesn't get what I'm doing, is it really what I want to do?' The answer, of course, isn't necessarily no! But it's still a question that I pose to myself. Is this music really comprehensible to me? Does it have emotional depth? Britten once said that as a composer you can only write the kind of music you love, that your heart is in.

In general, though, when I'm composing music I try to imagine myself as a first-time listener to it. It's probably rather lazy of me to quote other composers' comments about this, but I believe Stravinsky said he wrote music imagining that he was sort of multiplied several hundred times as the audience in a concert hall, so that he was listening to his own work in a mass of himself, as it were. And I try to write music that I would understand on first hearing. Actually, 'understand' isn't the best word; I mean music that I would *enjoy*. I suppose I'm never consciously aware of adapting my music for an audience other than myself, but if *I* don't get it first time, I'll think about writing it in a different way.

This means that I try to monitor the music quite carefully as I'm composing it. But that's not easy while you're in the middle of the actual process. As you spend time on a piece you get to know it *intimately* – you become so familiar with it that it becomes difficult to distance yourself from it as that first-time listener. And I think this is perhaps where a slight problem in communication has crept into the world of contemporary music. Maybe some composers have an unrealistically high expectation of the audience.

When I was very young, maybe thirteen or fourteen, I got into T. S. Eliot's *Four Quartets*. Of course, at that age I didn't understand them intellectually at all, but I just loved the beauty of the language; I absolutely adored them. And I think it's interesting that one can understand a great work of art like *Four Quartets* on a certain level at a particular age, and that one's appreciation then increases as one gets older or more advanced intellectually. However, there are very few pieces of music that I've grown to love that I didn't *like*, to a certain extent, when I first heard them. Even if my first impression was one of confusion, there was still something in the music that I liked and then liked more. But I'm very rarely conscious of responding to a piece of music intellectually. I may have discovered fascinating techniques in it after I've got into it on an aesthetic level, but it's never happened the other way round.

For example, Boulez's *Le marteau sans maître* is certainly a work that has incredible intellectual rigour, but I've only ever listened to it as wonderful music. There's something extraordinary about Stockhausen's *Gruppen*, too, but my reaction to it is entirely emotional – psychological, I suppose – and not intellectual. And so, although I would occasionally listen to Bach very analytically – following the fugal entries and so on – I'm aware that the music is functioning on a much deeper level than that. The technical ingenuity is one and the same with the expressive.

In relation to technique versus expression (or the rational versus the irrational), I try to apply the same set of criteria in my own work. I can only speak in terms of the music I enjoy listening to and which I therefore assume is the type of music that I would aspire, on an emotional level, to create. And the music that I love listening to is *only* music that I respond to emotionally. So I'm interested in exploring techniques only if they have some aesthetic or emotional or psychological meaning. In other words, I don't take any intrinsic pleasure from playing intellectual games, musically. For me, technique is a means to an end – in a way that I suspect it sometimes *wasn't* for Elliott Carter, some of whose music I nevertheless like very much. Throughout his life he took great delight in exploring highly intellectual processes. And there's nothing wrong with that; it's just a different way of looking at things.

When some people talk about new music, perhaps a piece they've just heard for the first time, they say, 'Well, it was a very interesting piece.' Or they ask, 'Did you find it interesting?' And I have a slight problem with that use of the word 'interesting'. It's sometimes clearly a backhanded compliment! But I often wonder whether it's almost a kind of excuse. I have to say that when I think about the music I really love – Bach, Schubert, Britten, Ravel, Bartók and Lutosławski, among many others – I don't actually find a lot of it interesting to listen to. I don't find Schubert lieder interesting; I find them beautiful, I find them exquisite, I find them ... remarkable! I don't listen with any intellectual interest to Schubert or to Britten or to a lot of the pieces I love, and so 'interesting' isn't a word I would use to describe them.

I love a lot of Lutosławski because, although it can be quite complex, there's always a logic and a clarity to it. There's a rhetoric, I suppose, a sense of direction and closure, and so on. What certainly *doesn't* fulfil me is music that sounds laboured. This may be one of the reasons why I love Britten's work: because it sounds effortless. He was sometimes criticised for that, actually, but of course his work involved a huge amount of effort. I mean, that's its beauty: it's the art that's covered the art. In contrast, although I like some of Tippett's works, I find that others sound too laboured, too struggled over. I don't want to hear the struggle, the pain, the months of effort. I like music to sound completely spontaneous, even inevitable. Of course, music *can* be 'interesting'. But it doesn't *have* to be, and I don't think it *should* be!

To be honest, the term 'British composer' doesn't mean much to me, and then only in a slightly pejorative sense! I think musical DNA is quite hard to trace anyway, just as Britishness in general is difficult to define. I suppose I have an image of it; but, frankly, one of the reasons why Britten is one of my favourite twentieth-century British composers is that, to me, he doesn't sound typically British! He's an interesting case, because at the time he was interviewed for Murray Schafer's book he was suffering from being too modern for the traditionalists and way too old-fashioned for the modernists.

For Boulez, who of course conducted the BBC Symphony Orchestra in the early 1970s, Britten simply didn't exist – he was just off the map. Walton even more so, probably. Looking back, it seems ludicrous that there should have been such a division, but it was a historical phenomenon that even Stravinsky got caught up in. There are some wonderful late works of Stravinsky's, but even *he* was saying, 'There's no way forward other than the twelve-note system.' Like any system, it can be used in very inventive or very dull ways.

My first composition teacher, Param Vir, was crucial to my training as a composer in encouraging me and teaching me a lot of basic technical knowledge as well as sixteenth-century counterpoint – which I suppose isn't something that you'd necessarily have got as a composition student, even at a university. And when I was at King's College London it taught Schenkerian analysis, which is becoming quite unfashionable now but which I found incredibly interesting and helpful. It's a way of unravelling various layers of music into foreground, middle ground and background. Foreground is the most elaborate, in that you're getting everything; middle ground is looser, the building blocks; and background could literally be just a few notes, or where the music's going.

This applies only to melody and harmony – it's not really a rhythmic system – and for Schenker it applied only to diatonic music (I think it was roughly from Bach to late Brahms). But I found this way of reducing music really useful in terms of analysing what's decorative and what's structural, and I still use it sometimes. For example, if I'm planning a long harmonic progression it's helpful in showing me where the sequence is going. Schoenberg's quip about his favourite bits of a sonata being left out of a Schenker diagram was a bit glib, because it's not, of course, about the decorative bits being less important aesthetically but about how they function structurally.

A fair amount of the work of composition goes on in my head before I write it down. I try to get the basic contour of the piece in my mind first, and if it's a piece for orchestra I'll try to identify the various sections, the kind of imagery (if there is any) and the emotional content of the piece. All of that is important. But invariably, when you actually get down to grappling with the notes, you find that things can change and the piece can go off at a tangent you hadn't quite expected. I think it's important to allow this to happen, so I try to prepare beforehand with the understanding that it might all collapse when I get to actually write the piece!

The difficulty with doing anything creative, I think, is that you can spend months on a very little amount of work, obsessing over things that aren't necessarily improving as a result. For the composer, this can mean becoming obsessed with the particular image or feeling you're trying to express. The problem – and I know it's not just *my* problem because I've heard other composers talk about it – is that, at the end of the day, music is both an abstract art and just sounds: noises, pitches, rhythms. And the danger is that you get so wrapped up in an expressive mindset that the music loses coherence. In other words, you can become more obsessed with the image outside the music than with the music itself. In fact, you can trap the music by preventing it doing what it wants to do. So you have to distance yourself from it and ask yourself, 'Objectively, is this music what I want? Does it have any objective beauty? Or coherence?'

For example, the last movement of my Clarinet Concerto is incredibly simple – it's probably the simplest thing I've ever written. But it took me quite a long time to decide to make it that simple. At first it seemed *too* simple, but eventually I realised that that was actually what I wanted.

Some of my pieces are scheduled for performance at a festival later this summer, and because they're quite old I've either had to revise them or have wanted to revise them. Of course, the performers want the updated scores and parts quickly, but it takes a lot of time to look back and reconsider something that you wrote so many years ago. This type of work – plus, of course, producing programme notes and so on – takes up quite a lot of a composer's time.

My ideal routine is to work very early in the morning – three or four hours of really solid work before noon – and then a bit more later on in the day. Over the last few years I've been fortunate in having quite a few commissions to work on, and when I *am* commissioned I tend to live in fear, I suppose, of not completing the work on time! This means that I tend to obsess over that one piece until it's finished. Whether that's a good thing or a bad thing, I'm not sure. I sometimes think it's good for a composer to have something outside of that process – an enforced distraction such as teaching or copying work – but I've never managed to do much of that. I usually teach one day a week, which is quite useful just in order to get out and talk to other people and also to see what younger composers are doing. It's fascinating to see what they're writing, in such a wide variety of styles. Some of them, you feel, are probably going to work in film music, on the commercial side of things, while others are wanting to pursue careers writing only concert music.

I remember Param Vir telling me, while I was studying with him in my mid-teens, 'Well, it's going to be a difficult life as a composer, but you can always do copying work.' This was in the pre-Sibelius years, and I came to the software only about ten years ago. I was trained in the old-fashioned pencil and paper, and I still write music that way. Although I use Sibelius to create a final score for my publisher, I always produce a fair copy by hand, which I prefer.

Five years ago I wrote *The Canticle of the Rose* – quite a long piece – for soprano and string quartet. For whatever reason, I simply felt that it was a good time for me to express what I was trying to express. And, despite all its imperfections, it's the piece that I probably feel closest to at this point in my career. The first performance was given by Lisa Milne, who's a wonderful singer, and I remember that at the rehearsal she sang one of the songs particularly beautifully. She asked me, 'I'm doing a tiny kind of *glissando* in this bit; do you mind?' I said, 'No, it's beautiful, absolutely lovely!' I hadn't specified any hook or *portamento* in the score; it was entirely her decision to sing it that way. She did it instinctively, and it was a wonderful example of a performer bringing to a piece her expertise – in this case with her own unique style of singing – where she felt it would work. It was a lovely thing, because that feeling of the elements coming together between the performer, the composer and the audience is so hard to define. It will be fascinating to hear how other performers respond to the same piece.

I know that some composers prefer to have complete control over how a piece should be played, with every possible nuance indicated in the notation – in an almost mechanical way. Well, that's not an invalid idea, but I think you're missing out on a huge amount of subtlety if you don't allow performers to bring their decades of training and expertise into the mix.

Some of what I suppose are my strongest pieces have been performed only a few times, and I sometimes feel that's a bit of a shame. And then there are others that I don't regard as my most serious pieces which, for whatever reason, have been performed more. It's true that music is ephemeral, in the sense that it doesn't fully exist until the moment of performance; but in this respect I think composers are luckier than theatre directors and actors who spend months – or weeks, at least

– working on a wonderful production which can then disappear *completely* if it's not filmed.

As a composer you have to defend what you've written, to some extent. This goes with the territory. Either you're willing to have a piece performed publicly, and so you defend it, or you refuse to have it played. Sorry to go back again to what we were discussing earlier, but people often want to know what a piece is *about*, and that's quite understandable. But in certain cases a piece can be about nothing(!) even though it's actually a wonderful piece. And I find it rather difficult that you have to tell people what a piece is about, rather than just letting it *be*. I mean, if they had the opportunity to go back to Mozart's time and to pick one of his symphonies at random and ask him what it was about, how would he respond? They might be intrigued to know what he was expressing, assuming that he was conscious of expressing *anything*, but would he just tell them, 'It's a symphony in G minor'?

Gabriel Prokofiev

Gabriel Prokofiev, London, January 2015

> **Contemporary classical music shouldn't be only for initiates, for people who are fortunate enough to already know about it.**

It was of course a thrill to meet a descendant of such a famous composer – Gabriel Prokofiev's father, the artist and poet Oleg Prokofiev (1928–98), was Sergei Prokofiev's second son. But I had a more serious reason for asking him to be interviewed for this book: I wanted to acknowledge the phenomenon of the pop-star-turned-classical-composer and I thought he would be the ideal person with whom to discuss it.

His own background is in electro-acoustic composition and he currently works not only as a composer of classical concert music but also as a producer of electro, hip-hop and grime records and as a DJ. In addition he is the founder of the Nonclassical record label and club nights at which contemporary classical music is performed in unconventional venues. I therefore knew that this would be an atypical interview, one that would be based on few of the questions I asked the other contributors.

I'd decided before we met that I wasn't going to ask him about his family connection because I wasn't sure of its relevance to our conversation. After all, he was born more than twenty years after his famous grandfather died. But it was one of the first things he spoke about when describing the unusual path that his career has taken. He was open, friendly and talkative ('Stop me at any time – I can keep chatting away', he warned me) and this was an interview of the most enjoyable kind, the sort that's essentially a spontaneous sharing of ideas and a stimulating discussion of them.

It took place in January 2015 in his studio on the top floor of a slightly run-down 1960s office block on a main street in east London. And it *is* a studio, not a study: approximately four metres by four metres, with a window running the full width of one wall, it was virtually filled with an enormous mixing desk, a variety of keyboards and consoles, microphone stands, speakers, racks of CDs and lamps. I also noticed, more incongruously, a solitary old-fashioned music stand, a trombone and, underneath the window, an old sofa barely visible beneath electrical cables and a pile of folders. Instead of negotiating my way towards it to photograph him after the interview, I suggested that we go outside the studio onto the internal staircase of the building instead.

Most of our conversation was about issues related to his involvement in the activities mentioned above. They included the identifiable areas of musical overlap between genres that appear to be very different from each other, the relative merits of different kinds of music and the different forms of pleasure that they bring to the listener, the need to promote contemporary classical music in ways other than the traditional concert hall experience, whose customs and protocol aren't being learned in the way that they once were, and the changing ways in which people listen to music and whether this does or should influence the ways in which it's written.

In order to establish some kind of context for the discussion, I began by suggesting that some readers will have grown up with a sense of an implicit hierarchy of musical genres, with 'classical' firmly at the top – not in terms of commercial popularity but in 'respectability' and perceived cultural value.

I'm totally aware of that because I grew up with it – my parents didn't listen to *any* pop music. My father hadn't had much access to it while growing up in Russia, and the nearest he got to it was jazz. There *was* one pop LP in the house: the Beatles' *The White Album*, which I think someone had left there by mistake, and which I listened to and liked when I was six or seven. But that sense of a hierarchy in music hasn't really gone away – I think I'm still haunted by it. There's also the weight of my family heritage. I guess every composer feels the weight of history and the great composers of the past – we're all in awe of Bach and Mozart – and I just have a little extra dose of that through having someone in the family who was so successful.

So in order to end up writing what I'd call contemporary classical music, my path as a composer has necessarily been a roundabout one. I discovered the joy of composing through making pop music rather than through writing classical music, and that was perhaps the only way in which I could have felt free from my ancestry to get into music-making in the most basic way. In other words, I think it released me from the pressure. I wouldn't say that I felt I had to compete, but I did feel intimidated by what I thought would be expected of me.

I was a very creative child and did lots of acting and drama, and when I was about seven I started playing the piano. Three years later I began learning the trumpet and started to write pop songs with a friend. We used to walk round the school playground at break time, making up songs and singing, and after we performed one in the school assembly everyone else was singing it too. That was when I discovered the buzz of creating music: one moment there's nothing and ten or twenty minutes or an hour later you've miraculously given birth to a piece of music. At first we were just playing around and didn't know what we were doing, but I became fascinated by creating interesting harmonic changes and other musical effects, and this got me hooked on the idea of composing.

By the time I was twelve I'd formed a band with other friends. We were called Syntax Error, which came from an error message on the BBC B computer we had at home. We organised a lot of concerts around south-east London, where we lived – even in Blackheath Concert Halls, funnily enough, where I've had a number of key concerts throughout my career. And we didn't only rehearse and perform the music; we made our own cassette albums and posters. It was a very creative and enjoyable experience.

At the same time I started to feel a real connection with classical music, particularly through my piano lessons. I was also going to a lot of concerts, particularly Prokofiev concerts, with my father. Whenever there was a decent performance of my grandfather's orchestral or ballet or opera music, he would take me with him, and sometimes we would meet the conductor or the soloist afterwards.

As I got into adolescence I became more self-conscious about being a Prokofiev. There was a self-consciousness about it in the whole house, actually – my father definitely had it. And I always felt I should be able to just sit down at the piano and play a piece brilliantly, first time. But, as we know, the greatest pianists practise six or eight hours a day, and I didn't practise much at all. When I was fourteen I wrote some piano pieces that impressed my teachers at school and got me really excited by the idea of composing classical music alongside the pop thing; but at the same time part of me thought, 'Maybe this isn't worthy.' It was that conflict again, and although I felt that I wanted to be a composer I was shy about announcing it. And when I went to the University of Birmingham I studied philosophy as well as music. So I was reticent and self-conscious about calling myself a composer, even though by my second year at university it was the main direction of my studies – I wasn't a performer and I wasn't going to be a musicologist. I did quite a lot of electro-acoustic composition, which opened me up to an amazing sound world: sonic art, poems with sound, and a freedom from worrying about harmony or tonality. I also played in a band called Spektrum that did a lot of work in the studio. So I became a studio composer/producer, really.

In my final year at Birmingham my instrumental piece *Journeys of a Cattle Herd* (influenced partly by Hukwe Zawose, a musician I'd worked with in Tanzania during my gap year) was performed at the end-of-year composers' concert. Judith Weir was the honorary guest and at the end of the concert she gave feedback about the pieces that had been played. She gave my piece a sort of commendation, pointing it out as something she'd liked and thought was particularly imaginative or whatever, and that was a really exciting moment for me. My father, too, was impressed, and I felt his acceptance and approval of me as a composer. It was the following year, when a piece of mine won the student prize at the Borges International Electroacoustic Competition, that he got really excited about my music, and that meant a lot for me. But he died just a few months later, and that's been a continuing sadness for me because I think he would have been a really supportive figure as my career developed.

My father was Russian – though his mother was half-Catalan, a quarter Polish-Lithuanian and a quarter French – and my mother is British. I was born in London and I've grown up in Britain, and I feel very British *because of* my rather mixed background, actually. Britain – and especially London – is becoming an international melting pot, and I really embrace its multiculturalism because I'm all for getting rid of barriers. And I believe this is one aspect of myself as a composer who's *very* British. Maybe, because of this cosmopolitan outlook and this openness to many influences, I should say that I'm a very *London* composer; but as a nation we do have a mixed background and our language has a number of different roots.

I also feel Russian, partly because of the family name and partly because I grew up listening to my grandfather's music, which is very Russian. But when I go to Russia people there regard me as equally British, and they see the British elements of some of my music: a strong interest in melody and certain types of phrases, which I believe comes from the song tradition and my interest in British popular music.

A lot of British composers have been strongly influenced by German and Austrian music of the twentieth century, and I often wonder why. I know the classical tradition is very European and that we're continually influenced by great composers whose nationality we sometimes don't think about, but why should a British composer want to follow a technique that was invented in Vienna for reasons that were part of central European history? Britten is one who didn't, but a lot of composers aren't following the direction that he took music in. There sometimes seems to be almost a rejection of what he was doing – as there is also of my grandfather's approach to composing.

I don't have a problem with the use of labels such as 'classical' and 'pop'. There are so many different types of music out there that we need some reference points. But I do have a problem with the idea held by some educated people that popular music has no integrity. I think there's a protective attitude in some areas of contemporary classical music that suggests, 'We're making high art that a lot of people probably can't even understand because it's beyond them, but one day they'll get it. Meanwhile pop music is for the masses.' In other words, some people emphasise an intellectual objectivity of classical music that can't be disproved, because this gives their work a kind of absoluteness as 'great art'. I find this patronising and not really fair to pop music, some of which has shown incredible innovation and longevity, and which therefore can't be belittled and put down in this way.

Yes, some popular music lacks intellectual depth and rigour because it's only about the immediate moment, and some songs are based on one simple idea that just goes round and round. In that sense, some pop music is throwaway. More generally, the big problem with popular music is that it's very fashion-conscious. Some new sound or approach will emerge in a natural, organic way but then, quite quickly, it becomes a commercialised trend. It's a contradictory situation, really: on one hand there's a kind of musical playfulness and freedom, but as soon as the magic happens people start to cash in on it.

What put me off working in that field is that you're continually faced with artistic restrictions because of the rigidly defined formats you're supposed to stick to if you want your music to be heard. This is one reason why people who don't know contemporary classical music need to hear it – it's exciting because it's *not* in a clear, repetitive format and because it *doesn't* follow a particular chain of events. But I think it's dangerous to focus too much on the formal aspects of music. We've all studied the brilliance of Bach (among other composers) and how his music is put together, but its driving force is its emotion and spirituality.

It seems to me that music has developed in opposing directions, and that there's now much less of it in the middle ground that satisfies both intellect and emotion. And as a result we're worse off. I also think we've tried to divide the musical world too much. Why, when there's exciting music outside the classical world, should composers be afraid to take inspiration from it, especially when composers of the past took inspiration from the interesting sounds *they* heard? Folk music – music of the people – has evolved a lot, especially in London, which has become so cosmopolitan and so mixed; and because it has absorbed all kinds of influences its evolution isn't clearly linear. But I'm interested in reconnecting with 'folk music' of our time, which is what I hear in the street or on the radio or coming from a bar or a car.

In the Nineties there was the so-called rave and electronic music explosion, and you heard on the radio a lot of strange, rhythmic, very driven electronic music that didn't have anyone singing on it. It didn't necessarily have a verse and a chorus; it sometimes wasn't even tonal. It didn't seem to care and it didn't really have any rules; it was all about a groove that felt good. Because of its energy it excited me, and I think a lot of composers who grew up at that time have something similar in their brain – Thomas Adès's *Asyla* has loud, banging beats at one point, and they're a clear reference to dance music.

It's important to bear in mind that a lot of what goes on in popular music happens in an instinctive and natural way. As I said, a new style or rhythm will emerge as a result of the social, geographical, political and cultural evolution in a city, not because someone has said, 'I want to make *this* kind of music.' For example, Jungle emerged in London – probably from Jamaican culture, because it's got a reggae-ish feel. Yet it often contains quite haunting minor chords, which I'd say comes from a British pop sensibility. But the main feature behind it was a result of new technology – the Akai Sampler – and the discovery of what happened to syncopated drum patterns when the tempo was doubled.

In other words, popular music evolves through a coming together of different cultures, often in a rather haphazard way. There's none of the self-consciousness or pre-planned intentionality that we sometimes find in contemporary classical music, the sort that makes us feel we have to theorise and justify what we've done in a clever programme note. And I think it's exciting for classical composers to take note of this and absorb it. But we have to be careful that this isn't done in a patronising and unnatural way, because this will stifle composers' creativity.

Of course, you're right: there *is* a fundamental difference between a late Mahler symphony, or Britten's *War Requiem*, and Jungle! And trying to compare them is probably pointless. But you can say that, in one sense, popular music is often a lot more functional – especially dance music, which is for dancing to. It *can* take you on an emotional journey, but there's much less inherent depth and complexity of emotion than in classical music because greater importance is attached to the delivery, and the personality of the performer, than to adherence to the score (which is usually very basic). The other, obvious, difference is that a symphony is much longer and therefore gives a composer the opportunity to develop his ideas in depth. And, of course, this is the appeal of classical music – it's a much more searching and intense experience.

I think this helps to answer your question about the different kinds of pleasure that classical music and popular music bring to the listener. But, although the impact of pop music is sometimes more immediate, a lot of great classical music also has magical moments that within the space of a few seconds elate you and excite you and mesmerise you. A lot of my grandfather's pieces had that effect on me – the Fifth and Sixth Symphonies, for example – when I first heard them as a teenager. I remember being really uplifted by them and also being taken on a journey.

Of course, when you're young that journey seems much longer because you're living at a faster and more energetic pace. And because the younger mind tends to wander more, it's harder to keep your focus. You're right to point out that part of the appeal of pop music is that it tends to come in bite-sized chunks, but I'm wary of making a complete generalisation about that because some concept albums are made up of small individual chunks – which some classical music can also be broken down into.

For me, the main appeal of pop was its physical element – its excitement and immediacy, which were important when I was growing up and getting rid of my energy. But I was listening to contemporary classical music as well, and I remember that my father had the complete vinyl of *Einstein on the Beach* and played it non-stop. The whole family was telling him to turn it off because we were going crazy with those never-ending Philip Glass loops! I also remember going to hear Stockhausen's *Stimmung* in Blackheath Concert Halls when I was about sixteen. I found it instantly gratifying, harmonically, but there were also those curious, unexpected, wild and spiritual aspects of the Stockhausen 'zone' that I found really creative and exciting.

As a composer you don't necessarily know whether you're writing good music or bad music. Sometimes when you think you're doing something really great it turns out to be not as good as something you wrote when you were fed up or in a bad mood. So my working method is to make sketch after sketch after sketch, and to then build on that.

I'm definitely a child of modern technology, and although I sometimes jot ideas down on the back of envelopes I usually input them straight into the computer. I'm not improvising or experimenting as I would at the piano; I'm using the keyboard simply to write ideas down, because that's the quickest way. And I can check and expand the ideas when I play them back.

For this part of the process I use Logic Audio because it shows the score in two ways: in normal notation and in graphic notation. The latter displays the music as coloured blocks of sound on different lines, so you see it much more in terms of proportions and shapes – which itself can be a creative stimulus. And in this form the elements are easier to move around, invert, transpose or whatever. Then I use Sibelius to create the finished score in normal notation. But standard notation often presents me with problems; and the way that more and more composers are having to write longer explanations at the beginning of their pieces of how they want the music to sound suggests that I'm not alone.

The issue for me is that my music has a lot of syncopated rhythms, which always look ugly in standard notation. You end up with lots of semiquavers or demisemiquavers, and rests in funny places because of all the off-beats; and when you look at the score you think, 'God, that's difficult.' When you hear it you realise that it's actually much easier – something like 'bam-bam-ba-*baam*, bam bam *bam-bam*, bam-bam-ba-*baam*, bam-*ba*-bam, bam-bam-ba-*baam*'. I know some composers are in love with the score and the processes that went into making it, but for me it's simply how you communicate the music to the performers.

You mentioned that it sounds as if I have quite a solitary existence as a composer, and it's true that studio composition is a lonely job. As an electro-acoustic composer, for example, you spends hours locked away on your own, just nudging filters and adjusting volume and balance. It's very intricate, time-consuming and tiring work. And you're right that mixing in the studio becomes the main part of the composition process. All composers tweak things, of course, particularly after a first rehearsal or a first performance. For example, my Concerto for Bass Drum's being performed again in a month's time and in the next couple of days I'm going to make some changes that I've been itching to make for ages. Studio work gives you even more opportunities to keep tweaking and editing.

On the other hand, I soon start to miss the human interpretation and interaction of composing for a live performance when I work in the studio for too long, and I love the feeling of liberation when I finish a score and hand it over. But I'm continuing to write electronic music and am about to start my third project with the British-Indian choreographer Shobana Jeyasingh: a contemporary dance piece whose music will be composed and recorded in the studio.

The way in which people listen to music today isn't at the top of most composers' list of priorities because, by and large, they compose music for concert performance. But I think it's an issue that they need to consider more than they do, especially if they realise that they're not reaching the majority of the public. There's a tendency for recordings of contemporary classical music to replicate the concert experience, and that's a valuable 'archive' approach; but I believe that an album that a lot of people will listen to needs to be produced in a different way. And that's a big challenge because of the issue of dynamic range and compression.

You can see that I record music in this studio, and in fact the Elysian Quartet was sitting right where we are now when they recorded my two String Quartets. When I composed them I was imagining them being played in a concert setting, but I wanted the recording to sound punchier and more immediate. So I made a couple of edits to the pieces and I changed some of the dynamics during the mixing process.

I think we've got to be practical and to take on these challenges, otherwise we risk letting down the public, who deserve access to a full range of music. Contemporary classical music shouldn't be only for initiates, for people who are fortunate enough to already know about it. The Nonclassical club nights that I've organised have shown that when people who didn't grow up with classical music are introduced to it, they really like it. It's about devising ways for them to hear it and getting them through the door.

For example, I wrote a nonet for nine cellos and later made a practical decision to make a version called *Cello Multitracks*, in which eight of the parts are pre-recorded by the cellist. Ideally, you have eight loudspeakers, one for each cello, and then the ninth part is played live. Because it's one cellist playing all nine parts the sound is slightly unreal, and the recorded sound is very close and dry. So that's an example of an acoustic piece that became a recorded, electronic piece. It has more of an 'age of the recording' sound than the original does, but I don't think I've compromised the music in any way.

Now I'm hoping to compose a stand-alone album (as opposed to a collection of short works) of contemporary classical music that people will be able to listen to in their car or on headphones. There's definitely room for composers to try things like this. It's almost like a new genre.

Also, taking inspiration from current electronic dance styles is, in a way, a return to the more traditional approach that drew on popular dance forms. The minuet was a popular dance and so was the waltz – which, because it enabled people to hold each other so closely, was considered a bit risqué until it was absorbed into society, partly through classical composers using that form. We lost that closer relationship between classical music and popular music when composers felt that they had to maintain more of a distance and write 'high art'; but maybe today we can write 'iPod suites' rather than dance suites?

John Rutter

John Rutter, Cambridgeshire, March 2012

> **You think you know what you're writing, but sometimes you're unleashing something that you don't understand.**

It took nearly a year to arrange the following encounter with John Rutter, but there was never any doubt that I wanted to include him in this book. He's a phenomenon: probably the most performed composer of all those whom I interviewed for this collection, yet the writer of the most conservative music. (I presumed that there was a connection.) My problem was that he's very busy, not just as a composer but also as a conductor – particularly of his own music, often in the USA – and as a record producer.

'Sorry not to have responded earlier to your invitation', he wrote to me in June 2011. 'It arrived while I was away in New York and I'm afraid it got submerged in the pile after my return ... At the moment I'm fully stretched, but hope to have some time probably in August.' August came and went ('Sorry my timetable is in such a state of flux, but I'm struggling with a major proof-reading commitment for my publishers, and other things have got bumped as a result') and it wasn't until the following March that I had the opportunity to interview him at his home in Cambridgeshire. It was a day on which I was able to interview *two* composers, and after driving to London to talk to Robin Holloway in the morning I got back in the car to drive north towards Cambridge.

It was an unexpectedly warm, sunny afternoon for the time of year, and as I approached the main door at the back of Rutter's cottage I found stuck to it a yellow Post-it note that read, 'Andrew Palmer – welcome, I'm in the office (behind you). John.' It seemed typical of the friendliness for which he's known. Turning round, I saw across the courtyard a large wooden building and found inside it his PA, who was working at a computer. Rutter emerged from a small side-office and suggested that we go back to the house for the interview, which was conducted across the kitchen table while we drank tea.

I'd wondered beforehand whether I would encounter behind the immediate charm of his music and personality a tougher side to his character, for the demands of his workload suggest that there has to be one. But he was as unassuming and likeable as I'd originally expected. At first, however, he seemed a little tense and spent a few minutes explaining how busy he was and how much he had to do. I got the impression that he interacts with everybody in much the same kind of way – he told me that everybody calls him John, and that he likes this – and that he takes on commitments, even when he's probably too busy, because he doesn't like to let people down or disappoint them.

Once his work was temporarily out of his mind he relaxed, and conversation started to flow easily. (It's always a good sign, I believe, when an interviewee asks me if I'd like another mug of tea and has one himself – it suggests that he's not desperate to get rid of me.) As we'd started to talk about the fact that his music obviously has an immediate appeal so to many people, my first formal question was whether he can identify factors that contribute to its success.

About three-quarters of my output, if not a bit more, is choral. And if you write for choirs, then by definition you're writing for a lot of people because the choral world is a huge one, particularly in America. Every high school there has several choirs, and every college and every church at least one. So having your work performed by amateurs results in a lot more performances than you get if your music is performable only by professionals. It's an interesting fact that if opera were performed mostly by amateurs, and choral music mostly by professionals, then *Tristan und Isolde* would probably be a lot easier and the Brahms *Requiem* a lot harder!

Totting up the number of performances doesn't really give a fair comparison with other types of music, because if you write avant-garde opera you're not going to get many performances – there aren't as many opera companies as there are choirs. But the statistics are astonishing. My American publisher told me that within six months of my *Requiem* being published in 1986, five hundred performances for which orchestral material had been rented had taken place in America alone. And that didn't include other performances with piano or organ accompaniment. He was as astounded as I was.

It's good to stretch a choir to its limits, but anyone who has to rehearse a church choir or an amateur choral society week by week would say that if you do that too much it just becomes disheartening. Or it takes up time in which other pieces could be rehearsed. So a lot of my music has been written within the constraints of the comfort zone of amateur or young performers. But you absolutely mustn't write down to them. You've got to write full on, but you've got to say whatever you have to say more simply. Schoenberg said, 'There's plenty of good music left in C major', and in a way I've tried to make it my task to see if I can add to it. I think it's actually harder to write a simple piece than it is to write a complex one. Quite often I begin with an idea that has layers of complexity that I realise aren't necessary, and so I'm paring them down in order to end up with something simpler.

Now, if I'd been composer in residence with the London Symphony Orchestra, there'd be no point in writing simply all the time because the players would say, 'Where's the challenge?' And such music as I've written for professional performers (there's not a great deal of it) *has* tended to be more challenging technically. Years ago I wrote music for a BBC television series about the archaeology of the Bible lands; I was given an ensemble of ten players and, my goodness me, I stretched them to their limits. They enjoyed it, I think – as did I, because it took me into new sound worlds. I don't *think* you'd recognise the music I wrote for that series as being by me.

What first got me excited about composing, while I was still a child, was an urge to create small pieces. I got more satisfaction from this than from playing what other people had written, perhaps because I didn't play their pieces terribly well. John Tavener was one of my closest friends at Highgate School (it was then a boys' school) and he was a most gifted pianist, so he would have got satisfaction from both performing and composing. As a composer you don't have to play any instrument (or be a wonderful singer) but you have to play them all in theory and know what they feel like; and I discovered quite early on that I could imagine the sound of an orchestra and what the players could do.

But even when I went to Cambridge I had no idea how to take the giant leap from writing small pieces to earning my living from composing. The catalyst was meeting Sir David Willcocks, who took a weekly class in harmony and counterpoint. In my second year he looked through the manuscripts of some Christmas carols that I'd just written for a concert in college and said, 'Would you be interested in these being published?' Had that particular door not opened, I'm not sure whether I'd be sitting here today and talking to you, because I don't think I'd have had the temerity to show my work to a publisher. But I didn't have to, that was the thing, because David Willcocks did it for me. Then commissions and requests and invitations began to flow in – when I was supposed to be working on my PhD, may I say! In fact, the PhD remains unfinished, and I don't think the world has really missed it.

I'd thought I might be an academic, but it seemed that I was floating away from that world and drifting towards the island of composition. And that's really where I've been ever since, though I've always done other things as well – not primarily to earn more money but just because they've captured my interest. I took a half-time lectureship at the Open University because I was interested in the use of music in education, and I started doing quite a lot of guest conducting – abroad, mainly. I also started my own record label, which continues to this day and which is another arm of myself, in a way, because when I write something I can find a channel for it to be heard in recorded form.

It may sound odd, but I realised that I needed a hobby, and it couldn't *not* be music. And so I've found a sideline in record production and sound engineering for other people. As a producer you have an important role as an enabler, trying to encourage the best possible performances in the available time from the musicians that you've got. I do about four or five recordings a year, so I still feel I'm being useful – or I hope I am. I'm also getting a window on the world of young musicians that I wouldn't otherwise have. This makes me feel that much more alive, and maybe even gives me a few ideas for the next piece of my own!

If somebody told me that I would never be allowed to compose again I might heave a sigh of relief and think, 'Good, that gets me off the hook.' But I would probably start to feel in some sense uneasy and wrong, and not at peace with myself. My mind is never free of music for very long, and I remember Professor Jack Westrup from Oxford coming to give a lecture at Cambridge and saying, 'If music isn't constantly going round your head, you probably shouldn't go into it for a living.' But I've never worked 365 days per year at composition. I think I lack the willpower, that's the truth of it.

I suppose there are two things that every composer would like inscribed on his tombstone. One is: 'He wrote like an angel.' We would all like to be admired for our professionalism of technique and our skill in writing. I would certainly be upset if even somebody who really disliked my music could say, 'It's badly written of its kind.' And the second thing is: 'He touched people's hearts'. For me, music is a communicative art. But it's also a constructive art, like architecture. And at the top of my tree of heroes I'd have to put (it's hardly original, this) Johann Sebastian Bach, because his mighty structures in sound go about as far as anyone's can go.

It's true that there's an English suspicion of wearing one's heart on one's sleeve. Harrison Birtwistle would probably say that to challenge people and to stretch their minds is more worthwhile, but I don't think that's what I was brought into the world to do. It doesn't mean that my admiration for those who *are* doing that is any less, and it's probably the case that the most enduring artists are those who challenge and explore new paths. And actually, if you come to understand the language, perhaps there *is* something in it to touch the heart. So I'm a bit cautious. I think, 'Is there something wrong with writing a little piece that might bring a tear to the eye?' *Then* I think, 'Well, if a politician started appealing to emotion I'd be suspicious.' Wouldn't you? Nobody understands the mechanism by which music touches people's hearts and makes strong men break down and weep, so it has to be used with care. I certainly have no wish to manipulate anyone's emotions.

I think there's less suspicion in America of art that wears its heart on its sleeve. A lot of (though by no means all) Americans would probably say that their emotions lie fairly close to the surface, and as audiences they're more spontaneous in their enthusiasm. Maybe that's why my music found an early welcome there and why so many opportunities have come my way from America. I'm proud and happy that that's been the case. It's probably been slightly to the exclusion of work that I might have done here at home, but any composer will tell you that you go where the opportunities are. The first piece I wrote specially for performance in America was my *Gloria*, in 1974, and it was an opportunity the like of which I hadn't had before. I seized it with both hands, and one thing led to another. Most people's career path in the arts starts by being local, then it spreads and becomes national, and then it becomes international; but for me, it's almost gone the opposite way, because my first widespread recognition was in America. It's a strange career trajectory and I can't explain it.

I was nurtured by the English musical (and particularly choral) tradition, and some people might say that my music is instantly recognisable as English. But I think all composers are magpies, really. It's good to be nurtured by the tradition you grew up in but it's also good to look beyond that. And I would put my hand up to all kinds of influences that aren't English. I have always loved American music, particularly Copland and Bernstein, and the great Broadway songwriters have been powerful influences in their own way.

Besides, I like to think that music transcends national boundaries and barriers. I get letters telling me about performances in many countries, and in Japan there's a choir that performs *only* my music – which is going a bit far, really! I don't know whether *they* would say, 'John Rutter's music is typically English.' However, choral music does have a national flavour because singing is not that far removed from speech. It's still the case – fortunately – that a Russian choir sounds completely different from an English choir or an Italian choir.

I can't imagine my music motoring far without melody. It *is* important to me. And I was lucky that nobody ever stopped me from writing it. Patrick Gowers, my composition teacher at Cambridge, wasn't a devout serialist (which most composers were starting to be in the 1960s) and he told me, 'Extend your technique but write whatever is in your heart.' I suppose my training enabled me to create extended structures, but something in me always wanted to write tunes. And I realise now that I'm probably as much, if not more, songwriter than composer. They're different skills, in a way.

Words come first, so if I need a text, the first stage of the composition process is to search for one. I've written my own words on a number of occasions, just because there wasn't anything to hand that suited. At the same time, I'm asking: how long a piece should it be? What kind of an occasion will it form part of? What are the available forces for it and what's their capability? What else will be on the programme? Then, when I've got as many of the pieces of the jigsaw puzzle as possible, it just remains to write the music. At that point I start doodling away at the piano and I find that the physical contact with it seems to help the flow of ideas. But any composer will tell you that the danger is that you start to write piano music transcribed for something else. Perhaps I'm helped by being such a terrible pianist – I don't think my fingers fall into pianistic patterns, particularly.

Unless I'm writing a very short piece I don't start at the beginning and work my way towards the end. I look for the landmarks while trying to see the piece as a whole. Writing a piece of music involves a certain amount of blundering around in the fog, and if any composer tells you that they never experience that, they're probably lying! I always say it's a bit like driving across the Cambridgeshire fens towards Ely Cathedral on a misty winter's day. The first thing you see is the big outline of the cathedral. You drive another half a mile and you start to see the shape; you drive closer and you start to see where the windows and the doors are. And finally you park in front of the south entrance, and you can see all the detail.

In general, I'm not a reviser. I take the view that what I've done I've done, and I hope that the lessons I might learn from the most recent piece will be put to good effect in the next one that I write. If somebody pointed out a glaring mistake I'd made, I might take that seriously, and occasionally I think, 'Why did I write that piece at all?' But I don't tinker with detail unless it's something basic like a wrong note in a published score. I've never put into print a revised version of anything I've written.

I knew William Walton, who was an inveterate tinkerer and therefore the despair of his publisher. He was a restless soul and a perfectionist, and he never quite felt that he'd got it right. And, quite honestly, all he did was make himself miserable. However, I don't bask in satisfaction of my work, and I don't listen to my own recordings unless I need to. I do have to confront my past music because I conduct it quite a bit, but I sort of dissociate from it. It becomes just a score on the stand and it doesn't make a lot of difference to me whether it's my *Magnificat* or Bach's. I'm simply trying to conduct the best performance I can. Otherwise it would be a bit like laughing at your own jokes, wouldn't it?

No, most of my musical pleasure is in other composers' work, and I enjoy listening to music even if I've been writing all day. But I think composers are always listening for how it's done, just as film directors who watch other people's films try to work out how many lights were used on that set, how many old cars they had to hire for that sequence, what the costumes cost, how they staged that car chase and so on. You can't completely switch off your professional knowledge when you listen. Although I like to think that my *pleasure* is pure and untainted – you know, the 'first day of spring' feeling – that happens less and less often because, let's be honest, anyone my age has just heard so much music. But I'm happy to be a member of an audience and to join in the corporate feeling of celebration that a great piece brings.

Composers receive letters, sometimes deeply personal ones, from members of the public. People tell *me* more than anything else how pieces that I've written have kept them going through harrowing experiences of bereavement or marital break-up or depression. You know, 'My beloved husband was wired up in intensive care, and we had to make the agonising decision whether to switch it off, and his last words were that he wanted to hear the Rutter *Requiem* …' Oh dear, oh dear! Musicologists and critics would sneer, very probably, and say, 'But that's not what music's for.' And I think I would agree that it *is* perhaps not what music's for. But if music has some therapeutic and healing effect, particularly during dark nights of the soul, then my goodness me, that's not to be sneered at. I take it seriously, and I try to reply to every letter that I receive from the public, even when I don't really know what to say.

I think it's possibly one of the highest privileges of being a composer that your music reaches people and that they're inspired to thank you for what's happened because of it. At that point you realise that you're not in control. You think you know what you're writing, but sometimes you're unleashing something that you don't understand. For example, I've been told that my *Gloria* has been used to encourage pushing in childbirth – apparently, it's recommended in one particular hospital for protracted labour! I never thought of it in that context. And I know that some yoga groups use my music in various meditative ways that were not quite what I had in mind.

The evoking of visual images has become an increasingly popular part of listening to music, possibly because people's imaginations have been conditioned so much by the cinema and television. I don't listen to music that way myself, but I don't have a problem with people wanting to do it with anything I've written. After all, a requiem is almost a two-way work, isn't it, because in so far as it deals with issues of life and death that are universal, everyone will feed their own experiences into the way they hear it, and they'll write their own narrative to it. For example, I've always loved the Fauré *Requiem*, and when I heard it for the first time I think I knew that it was going to be a companion on my life's journey. And as I return to it from time to time I hear it differently because *I've* changed.

I compartmentalise my life, I think. When I was in New York last week the performers stopped me for autographs and asked if they could have a photo taken with me (they got that in the lift, for goodness sake!). And in those circumstances you just have to accept that you're a piece of public property. I neither enjoy it nor don't enjoy it; it's just something that goes with the territory. I enjoy company – I'm quite sociable – but I like being private, too. And I think anybody who composes has to be comfortable spending a lot of time by themselves.

I don't believe that the private act of writing music is greatly at odds with the public face of the composer, because we want public appreciation for our work. Any composer who says they really don't care about that is an unusual one indeed, I think. Of course, the nature of some composers' work is that they're going to get appreciation from a small, committed elite of listeners. And, in a way, that can be the sweetest approbation of all. The applause of a huge crowd means less to most of us, I think, than a real word of appreciation from somebody important. On the other hand, without the applause of the crowd, where do we go next in our career? I think it's a question of saying, 'If I'm a challenging, complex, cerebral composer I have to accept that I'm not going to get the sort of audiences that Karl Jenkins does.' Composers mostly make their peace with this and are glad of the audience they've got, whether it be large or small. It's not a case of head-counting, really, and I certainly never think of myself as writing for a big audience. You just find the audience that you find.

This is why I think you have to have quite a strong degree of self-belief as a composer. We know that Tchaikovsky, despite being plagued by terrible self-doubts, was at his desk at seven o'clock every morning, getting on with it. And I remember talking to Christopher Palmer about Herbert Howells, who spent the second half of his career composing church music because he got a bad reception in the concert world: when I asked why he kept plugging on in the face of economic hardship, bad reviews and few doors opening to him, Christopher replied, 'Because he was a composer!'

Composing is a compulsion, and a compulsion doesn't necessarily make you happy. But it means that composers are driven, despite all the setbacks and discouragement. I can't think of many who gave up in the face of bad reviews. Most of them carry on regardless – because they're composers.

At one time I was rather typecast as a composer of Christmas carols, and I felt it was a bit of a millstone around my neck because it prevented people from seeing that there were other aspects to what I do. I've now got a rather more mellow attitude, and the way I look at it is that it's better for people to know you for some small proportion of what you've done than for *nothing* of what you've done. And Christmas carols are a way of making friends – in many cases, friends that you may never meet in the flesh. The funny thing is, so many people, wherever I go in the world, call me John straight away because they feel they know me. This used to puzzle me, but I suppose it's because they've known this or that little piece of mine for so many years.

I think what corrected the typecasting issue was writing my *Requiem* in 1985. It began to be very widely performed, and of course by its very nature it's more serious and reflective and substantial than a Christmas carol. Some of the people who know my 'All things bright and beautiful' and 'For the beauty of the earth' would be surprised to hear a more serious piece like the *Hymn to the Creator of Light* and would think, 'I didn't know he wrote that sort of thing', but I'm not going to complain. Any of us are lucky to have any of our works performed and known, and one should just count one's blessings!

Robert Saxton

Robert Saxton, London, December 2011

> **It's heartening to have one's work recognised, but seeking acclaim mustn't be on the agenda.**

Because Robert Saxton is the composer I knew best before compiling this book, the prospect of interviewing him for it was entirely pleasurable. There was no anxiety about meeting yet another composer for the first time and wondering what he or she would be like in person, only anticipation of chatting to a friend, albeit in more depth than usual.

The encounter took place in December 2011 at his home, a spacious Edwardian house in south-east London. The living room is an Aladdin's cave of books, magazines, scores, framed posters and other items to stimulate and distract, and after squeezing into a space at the end of the sofa for a preliminary cup of tea I was led upstairs to his study for the interview.

As always, he was concerned and needlessly apologetic, particularly about having had to postpone our meeting more than once because of the pressure of his work at the University of Oxford, where he's Professor of Composition and Tutorial Fellow in Music at Worcester College. Now that the interview was about to take place, was my chair comfortable? Was I warm enough? Was it too dark, and should he perhaps turn a light on? And later, during our conversation, did what he was saying make any sense? It did, of course, but it was only when I was transcribing our conversation that I understood the full relevance of some of his comments, which had come thick and fast while we were talking. And at that point I was faced with difficult decisions about what to omit from the published version.

Not long afterwards I re-read his interview in Paul Griffiths's *New Sounds, New Personalities* and began to worry. It was full of references to his music, including a description of how he conceives and develops a piece, and it made my conversation with him seem almost undisciplined. I'd found it fascinating, but perhaps I hadn't kept a sufficiently firm grip on its direction and hadn't asked enough of the right questions. Had we been strangers, would I have allowed myself to take my hands off the steering wheel in the way that I seemed to have done?

That question was partly answered by his subsequent request to make substantial changes to the edited interview. He did, however, give me permission to retain comments that I was reluctant to lose. 'And please', he urged, 'do revise my revisions.' The result has a little more technical detail than the first version and is even more colourfully illustrated with references to literature, the visual arts and philosophy. And it begins in the same place, with his response to my question about what he sees as the relationship between his nationality and his music.

―――――――

Some time ago I was invited to give a talk at the Liberal Jewish Synagogue in London, where I had Hebrew lessons as a boy. The theme of the day's events was what it means to be Jewish in Britain today, and I was asked to speak about what it means to me as a composer. The topic I chose addressed the journeys of Abr[ah]am and Jacob and the idea of wandering and return, and I spoke about my *Five Motets*, which I wrote for Edward Wickham's vocal ensemble The Clerks in 2002–03. For a variety of reasons, these use the 'In nomine' melodic line from John Taverner's early sixteenth-century *Gloria Tibi Trinitas* Mass (which has been a springboard for variations and transformations by British composers from Byrd to Maxwell Davies). In my talk I explained that certain aspects of my Jewish cultural heritage had come out in this setting of English and Latin texts for a group specialising in medieval music – a group which has since started to give cross-cultural concerts in conjunction with Arab musicians! And I mention this because I think it illustrates what it means for me to be both a British composer and a composer in Britain in the early twenty-first century.

Two factors in particular have influenced how I feel about this. First, my family are Jewish immigrants and I was brought up partly in the Anglo-Jewish community. My father's side of the family came from Lithuania and Russia, and my mother's from Poland and Holland; and because of the virulent anti-Semitism of the Baltic States, Russia and much of eastern Europe at that time, they fled at the close of the nineteenth century. And they found a home, for which they've remained eternally grateful, here in Britain. Second, my paternal grandmother came from a Church of England family and converted to Judaism (courageously, I imagine, since this was just after the First World War) in order to marry my grandfather; and as a child I spent a lot of time with them at their home in Norfolk.

Until I was thirteen there was synagogue on Saturdays and Church of England school assembly every morning at my day school (I still adore the great Vaughan Williams hymns we sang). Then I went to a boarding school whose single-sex community was racially and religiously mixed, ranging from Hindus and Buddhists from India and Thailand to Libyan Muslims and boys from other African countries. Culturally and spiritually I still feel close to many Jewish ideas, but I've always been interested in the entire Judaeo-Christian heritage – indeed, the Protestant Reformation was one of my topics in A- and S-level History. And with a background such as this, the issue of identity can be paradoxical. My late father, who was a British army officer during and for some time after the Second World War, visited Israel later in his life and remarked that he felt oddly 'foreign', even though he was a supporter of the Jewish State.

As I said, I grew up partly with my father's family in East Anglia, and between the ages of nine and sixteen I had regular contact with Britten, who lived only forty miles down the coast, in Suffolk. He was extraordinarily kind and generous to me, and also exacting when it came to professional standards, which is something I'm still deeply grateful for. Studying with my principal teacher, Elisabeth Lutyens, from my mid-teens onwards was also profoundly inspiring, and the intense rigour and strictness that she demanded (and expected) were what I needed. She often told me, 'I'm not interested in self-expression. What I want to know is: is that note in the right place? And if not, why not? You *must* know.'

When I look back at my early pieces I see that many of them were tips of icebergs, in the sense that what I was *really* doing was not writing 'works' but trying to work out how relationships between musical intervals in various contexts worked, both linearly and vertically. I could have filled whole books with musical exercises, and in fact Liz warned me, 'Don't do your workshop exercises in public. Don't publish things too early, because a lot of this stuff is private.' She was absolutely right.

Liz was professionally international in her attitude, and she passed this ideal on to her students, both aesthetically and technically – just as the Tudor and Stuart composers (from Tallis and Byrd via Gibbons to Purcell and, later, Elgar) used the *lingua franca* of their European colleagues. During my student years Maxwell Davies and Birtwistle were thought of as 'the British avant-garde' but I always sensed that there was more to them than that; and it's now apparent that they're in fact profoundly British composers in multi-layered ways, and without being parochial.

Two of the most 'avant-garde' composers (contextually) were Monteverdi and Haydn, but their technical armouries developed inventively at the service of their ideas and imagination because they had a lot to communicate as artists. This is quite different from a composer putting his or her head in the sand and producing received clichés; or, at the other end of the spectrum, working in a vacuum and trying to be original at all costs. The point is that when Dunstaple, Beethoven, Vaughan Williams, Bartók and Messiaen developed their compositional grammars they did so with an integrated process that offered a refreshed (and refreshing) perspective on both past and present. Tippett's *The Vision of St Augustine* does the same thing – it renews and enhances the English choral and orchestral tradition, with searing intensity and unforced originality.

Some people have commented that my music of the past fifteen years or so sounds different from my earlier works, and I find this interesting because I've always been concerned with cohesion across parameters. The fabric of my recent music is just as interwoven, and in fact I use ordered interval cycles to trace the path of the music at different structural levels to a *greater* extent than I did even in my older, totally chromatic music.

My students know that I'm dubious about labels and categories, and I encourage them to concentrate on the thought processes of composition rather than relatively superficial issues such as musical style and manner before they've got the basics under control. You could say that I try to act as a guide and magnet in relation to the ideas or concepts they want to explore in their work. I find teaching rewarding and stimulating but also increasingly complex, partly because, when I started teaching, my students were six or seven years younger than me, whereas now they're forty years younger. And when I work with them I have to bear in mind that for at least sixty years *all* musicians have been subject to musical experiences which at best have resulted in a vibrant plurality and which at worst have led to a kind of cultural amnesia.

Certain aspects of aesthetics and taste will (and must) always change. But what constitutes 'good composing', and taste or decorum in music, hasn't so much been challenged as *ignored* in some quarters. I suspect that this is in part an understandable reaction to the authoritarian 'elitism' of late modernism, much of which had noble aspirations and which is at present unfairly derided even though its worst manifestations (particularly in architecture) were, I accept, horrendous. I think it's also on account of modernism's 'counter-pole': the current obsession with 'easy' communication. What's rarely, if ever, addressed is the fact that it has been totalitarian regimes of both left and right that have fostered populism and mass culture, particularly during the twentieth century. In the process they've banned, denounced, imprisoned or murdered the perpetrators of what they considered to be 'outside the box'. Paradoxically, it's now the free-market economy which has resulted in the more recent phenomenon of instant accessibility, comprehensibility and financial viability, combined with a fear of 'elitism'.

As a composer, I *of course* want to communicate. Having shared my life with a professional soprano for thirty-six years has had an enormous influence on my attitude to, and my understanding of, performance and interpretation. And I still write for a variety of performers and organisations – including the Church. But in the wider world the pendulum swing between left and right often results in cultural blandness. And this isn't confined to classical music: senior voices in the rock music world say similar things about a lot of recent pop music and the industry that surrounds it.

It's this rich but sometimes perplexing artistic and cultural environment that composition students have inherited, and they have to come terms with it as artists and thinkers. But please note: I'm *not* advocating a return to past values at all costs. Much of what goes on in the so-called musical establishment is a daily round of retrospection – to the point of saturation with 'museum repertoire'.

In a sense, composers write for themselves. They're on a voyage of discovery, their appetites have been whetted and they just have to carry on. Of course, it's heartening to have one's work – rather than one's personality, as sometimes seems too frequent these days – recognised, but seeking acclaim mustn't be on the agenda.

Imagine you're the only person alive on a desert island (with no discs!). Some inner compulsion makes you want to express what you see and hear around you – and possibly beyond. You paint it (assuming that you have a twig and some dye from island fruits) or you write a poem (assuming that you have language). Why do you do this? Not because you want to be famous – there's nobody to admire you or your work. And not for financial gain, because money's irrelevant. Presumably you do it because something that might be termed spiritual (call it what you will) has impelled you to define or express a relationship of some sort between you and something that may be greater. Or perhaps you're concerned with light and shade, or the structural angles of trees in a landscape, and you want to investigate and interpret these things rather than address anything overtly metaphysical. Whether or not you choose to place your creation in a bottle (assuming that bottles exist in this hypothetical world) and send it out to sea so that another human (if there is one) might find it, is irrelevant.

It's true that the majority of historic art works that we consider important were produced at the behest of the Church or aristocratic patrons. But this doesn't necessarily mean that the artists weren't also working for *themselves* – in pursuit of their inner ideas, ideals and visions. In my experience, commissions don't so much require an artist to search for a new idea as bring into focus an idea that's already present in his creative imagination.

Composing isn't a job; it's a way of thinking and of perceiving the world (and beyond), and it's concerned with trying to understand and come to terms with this. So it's related to philosophical and spiritual matters as well as to human drama. Nobody captured this as well as Mozart and da Ponte did – their work encapsulates all human experience. Handel did it, too (in his operas, at least), as did Berlioz, Verdi and Berg, who couldn't have written *Benvenuto Cellini*, *Falstaff* and *Wozzeck* respectively without being acutely aware of the way in which the task had to be approached. For me, all three operas demonstrate an ideal conjunction between the conscious and the subconscious.

By the way, I'm not suggesting that composers shouldn't be paid for what they do! But inherent in what I've been saying is my belief that past and present combine and fuse, continually and 'naturally', in a creative mind. Which is why I'm not interested in *conscious* attempts to abandon the past or re-create it through pastiche. It seems to me that the most positive approach to composing is a professional, disciplined and empirical attitude, with ears, eyes and mind continually alert, both culturally and intellectually.

I've also long been convinced that originality or variety of subject matter is not *necessarily* a true element of creative 'need'. One of the most obvious examples, I suppose, is Cézanne and his *Mont St Victoire* paintings: approaching the same scene in different ways was in itself the fascination and the reward for him. I remember going to an exhibition of landscapes by David Hockney some time ago and being struck by the way in which he'd tackled the same tree or scene many times; it showed that idea, technique, ambition (in the best sense of the word) and personal vision can't be separated. What also interested me was that, while his paintings were realist – in the sense of not being abstract – there was no hint of anachronism in them. They were the work of an artist who'd obviously absorbed a vast range of technical matters and who'd produced his own work in an entirely natural manner – achieved, as we know, by means of endless questioning, *self*-questioning and sheer hard work.

I tend to spend ages thinking about a new piece, particularly if it's a large-scale one, and I usually begin with the aural conception or challenge. Then I move to the actual notes, which I write in different ways in order to try out various routes and strategies. And if needs be, I can write very quickly. When I took my BMus (a postgraduate degree at Oxford) in 1976 we not only had to submit portfolio composition; we also had to sit a six-hour exam (alongside about a hundred other candidates who were being examined in various disciplines), during which we had to complete an entire piece, from sketch to copied score. Tasks like that are excellent training, and this may explain why I have a strong memory, both aural and visual, of what my scores look like throughout the working process.

Computer technology doesn't influence the way I compose, for the simple reason that I use Sibelius only for notation of the final score after many highly detailed written drafts. But electro-acoustic technology can help to realise concepts such as canonic structures with microsecond time entries in vast numbers of parts or voices, which is part of the aural world that composers now work in. The stable door's open and the horse has bolted! It's exciting and creatively fascinating – you only have to observe what the French Spectralists have achieved in engaging with the nature of sound itself to hear what's possible both aesthetically and technically.

However, I discourage students (undergraduates in particular) from writing stylistic harmony and counterpoint – that is, sixteenth-century polyphony and Baroque fugue – at the computer because I want them to sense the lines and harmonic relationships of music in the way that Bach did: as a 'writing experience'. These days, students are expected to submit computer-set final versions of their work for exam portfolios, but working out a full-scale fugue in the Baroque style has to be done partly on paper, just as pure mathematicians tend to work initially with concepts 'on the back of an envelope'.

Drafting music can involve complicated notational issues, and I do this in my own personal ways, rather as a Renaissance fresco painter might have worked on a preparatory cartoon. And to set that up on a computer would waste time and be restrictive. I'm aware of different sketching methods because I'm interested in the relationship between ear and eye, and in how clearly things are heard in relation to the way they're written down. It may or may not be relevant that I read a good deal of philosophy and am, for example, interested in the approach of

Wittgenstein (and others) to the sign (signifier) on the page and its interpretation as meaning or sense. This doesn't necessarily have a direct relationship to musical notation and 'meaning' – there are, after all, a number of different views about whether notated music constitutes a language – but it's a fascinating aspect within my creative 'orbit'.

The first time I heard a note of my orchestral music was when the BBC Symphony Orchestra played it, and by then I was nearly thirty. In contrast, the university department I teach in regularly organises workshops, recordings and performances of students' music as part of the syllabus. And students don't seem particularly concerned about finding a publisher of their music because they can communicate with each other internationally and distribute scores and recordings as electronic files. Which begs the question, 'What is the future of music publishing in general?'

In other ways, though, being a young composer is more difficult than it was. First of all, it's not all that easy to define what a good piece *is*, even though as a composer you have a sense of whether something has technical, imaginative and aesthetic value. As a teacher, you're on more secure ground when teaching sixteenth-century polyphony or Baroque fugue because both instructor and student have models that are used as yardsticks. Teaching so-called 'free' composition involves a considerable amount of psychology because you have to enter into the student composer's head, conceptually and experientially, at many levels; this is worthwhile and exciting but I'm always aware of the vast responsibility involved.

Composers compose because they're fascinated with and obsessed by every aspect of their craft. But being a professional composer is about more than the notes (neither Bach nor Bartók was, in today's terms, a 'professional' composer, but both were composers of undoubted professional standard!). It's also about attracting funding, working in and with the media, communication and outreach work, and – at an advanced level, in academe – research. In the 1980s and early 1990s I did education outreach work for Glyndebourne and the London Sinfonietta, both in the UK and abroad, which was exhilarating but sometimes disappointing, particularly when I couldn't continue to monitor the results of a project after it was supposedly complete. I also introduced BBC TV4 Proms on live television for a few years and enjoyed doing that, although the lack of time and depth of discussion available were rather uncongenial. It was made clear to me that the less technical talk the better – a kind of inverted snobbery that I find unnecessary and unfruitful.

My students are encouraged by a number of organisations to engage in self- promotion and are given advice about it, but when I was a student that kind of 'obvious' self-marketing was considered rather bad form. Things were different then: BBC Radio 3 made it relatively easy for a student composer to consult a producer and have a serious discussion about his or her hopes and ideas, and its reading panel screened scores that were submitted for performance. What was then seen as 'quality control' might now be interpreted as a form of censorship, but I don't think today's approach is entirely satisfactory, either. I have no quibble with student composers learning how to market themselves, provided this doesn't detract from the value and quality of their work; but who makes judgements about these aesthetic and cultural issues is another matter!

Composing is a private activity whose results are eventually made public. In that sense it's rather like writing a play (but not necessarily poetry or novels). I don't want people *not* to play my music – I'm most grateful when they *do* play it – but the greatest satisfaction comes from bringing to fruition a piece that I've lived with for some time. In general, I work most successfully – by which I mean that I find the artistic results viable and profoundly satisfying – when writing relatively large-scale pieces for small groups of performers whom I know and who want to work with me. This avoids what I think of as the 'machinery' and politics of the orchestral and operatic worlds. During the last few years several younger performers have discovered or rediscovered my music – older pieces and more recent ones – and their attitude and abilities have been a revelation and a delight to me.

But these days I hardly ever attend concerts unless I'm supporting students. This doesn't reflect a loss of faith in music; quite the opposite, in fact. Music means so much to me that I find its manifestation in a public arena awkward, particularly if I'm surrounded by what I consider to be unreasonable, unsolicited opinions – in the way that it's distasteful for an off-duty doctor to have to experience amateur medical discussion! I prefer rehearsals and being with performing musicians. I also enjoy listening to music in a liturgical context, and I get great satisfaction – and indeed solace – from *writing* liturgical music to be heard by a congregation as part of an act of worship. That's a musical activity that doesn't entail selling one's wares to a paying audience, and so psychologically it's different from writing for the 'marketplace' of public concerts.

You're right to suggest that most composers talk about their own music in dispassionate terms, and I think it's the result of modest self-confidence rather than arrogance. After months or possibly years of intensive thought and work, no artist really wants to articulate the process that's involved, particularly as so much of it is intangible. Working *within* music is different from thinking or talking *about* it. On the other hand, composers can be defensive – without necessarily realising it – when they're questioned about their work, because writing music involves baring oneself. And one form of defence is to be dismissive. Henri Cartier-Bresson, for example, is supposed to have said about his photography, 'I just happened to be in the right place at the right time.'

Fortunately, I'm never stuck for ideas for my work. They're constantly with me and, in a sense, worrying me – as they must. In fact, I have so many that I don't expect I'll fulfil them all. There's a large-scale, musico-dramatic work that I've wanted to write since I was about twelve, and it may have to remain a dream. There's also a projected novel (for which I've written drafts) that comes out of my Anglo-Jewish experience. It's concerned with the very nature of writing, set against a background of what might be described as real and imagined outer and inner landscapes.

For me, the manner in which ideas are realised is paramount. So I'm very interested in technique. And not just that of music – when I go to an art gallery I want to know how pictures were painted. For example, how *do* you paint a fresco on wet plaster? As Hindemith made very clear in his writings, it's this kind of technical curiosity, combined with a determination not to be satisfied until one's 'inner vision' is realised, that impels and sustains artists of all disciplines – *and* philosophers and scientists.

My interest in the process of writing music rarely deserts me, but of course I can sometimes feel depressed and become despondent. And I've learned to acknowledge that this is part of a recurring pattern which, in my case, simply has to be gone through, and against which I brace myself. Whether it's some kind of hair-shirt mentality, I don't know, but I can make myself continue (though not always in a straight line!) by setting myself a technical task and not stopping work until I've gone some way towards finding a solution to it.

As I said, composing is a craft, and there's a sense in which you have to work continually at it in order to realise what's in the deepest recesses of your imagination. So you have to be vocationally obsessed; if you're not, it's too painful. I draft or sketch or write music everywhere, although the later stages of the process (editing and revising) obviously have to be completed 'in the studio'. I'm aware that Wagner criticised Brahms for writing every day, the implication presumably being that this led to lack of inspiration and was workmanlike in the worst sense. When Tchaikovsky was asked about the source of his inspiration he's supposed to have replied, 'I sit down at nine o'clock each morning, and Mademoiselle la Muse has learned to be on time for the rendezvous.'

John Tavener

Sir John Tavener, Dorset, October 2013

> **One of the functions of music is
> to help us to transcend suffering.**

The death of Sir John Tavener in November 2013 was headline news, in a way that the passing of no other contemporary British composer, however eminent and however important his or her contribution to music, would have been. This reflected not only Sir John's originality (and perhaps his personal eccentricity) but also the extraordinary success of his music – he has been described as the most popular British classical composer of the late twentieth and early twenty-first centuries.

This perhaps unlikely popularity was one of the things that I wanted to ask him about when I went to talk to him at his home in Dorset just five and a half weeks before his death. And I explained to him that although, as with the other interviews for this book, I would be asking a mixture of 'standard' and 'particular' questions, in his case there would probably be more of the latter as he was such a singular figure in British music. 'I suppose I am, yes', he agreed.

The encounter had been postponed because after returning from a holiday abroad he'd been unwell, and I knew that he was frail and in poor general health. Sure enough, he looked tired and drawn as he welcomed me into his home and showed me to the living room, and the famously plummy voice was weakened and hoarse. His wife was away for the day and he was alone in the house, but after about half an hour a carer let herself in through the front door and made us tea. For the duration of my visit Sir John sat on a sofa, moving only to periodically stretch out at right angles a long, spindly leg (the effort of doing this sometimes made him grimace), and I learned that this was where he spent most of his day, working, reading and thinking in an attempt to distract himself from constant physical pain.

This was not his final interview, because he gave a number of others in the weeks before his death. Plans for celebrations of his seventieth birthday in January 2014 were well advanced, and he was preparing for the first performance of his *Three Shakespeare Sonnets* in Southwark Cathedral (this took place, as planned, three days after his death). But it was one of the last that he gave. However, I'm not sure how revealing an encounter it was, since he mentioned in some of the other interviews a number of the topics that I discussed with him. (As they weren't all prompted, they must have been important to him.)

After we'd finished talking I suggested that he stand in his front doorway for the photo, but he said that he would prefer to remain where he was. By this time sunshine had broken through the morning's rain clouds, and I photographed him sitting on his sofa looking towards the window. It seemed appropriate at the time, and seems even more so in retrospect, that he was staring patiently and peacefully towards the light.

What I remember most strongly about my encounter with him is *his* interest in *me*. He asked a number of times whether I agreed with what he'd just said, and enquired similarly about my own musical tastes and spiritual experiences. As I got up to let myself out of the house and thanked him for his time, he said, 'See you again.' I would have liked that very much.

When I'm composing I'm not aware of what I'm actually doing it *for*. I'm aware of saying something that I feel I've got to say, but not aware of anything as practical as a function of my music. However, when I look back I can see that I've done something broadly similar in almost everything I've written. Normally there's been a connection to either a text or a metaphysical idea because I find it impossible to conceive of music minus the metaphysical dimension.

When I was fifteen and setting down sonnets I already found myself having preoccupations with metaphysical ideas. At that time it was death. And death has sort of been close to me ever since then, partly because I've been ill most of my life and partly because it's been something that I've felt compelled to write about. I had a deeply inspiring composition teacher, David Lumsden, who talked about the magic and mysterious sacred power of music but who also introduced me to modernism – we looked at scores by Ligeti, Schoenberg and Webern. Under his influence I wrote a piece called *Chamber Concerto*[1] which was highly serial and probably the only abstract music I've ever written.

I'd love to be able to write something as rhapsodic and wonderfully feminine as the Chopin Nocturnes, but I haven't yet been able to! And I don't know how much time I've got left now. At the moment I'm

---

[1] Now known as the Piano Concerto (1963).

working on a setting of Dante – I've been attempting this all my life, actually, because Dante is quite difficult to set to music.[2]

I'm moved to write my music, but the success it has had ... well, that has always staggered me, because when writing music I've never been aware of an audience, even in pieces like *Song for Athene* or *The Lamb*, which have enormous popular appeal. The fact is that I wrote those pieces for members of my family or in memory of a particular young person who died, and so I've always been surprised by the reaction that they've had from the public.

It may be the ecstatic element of my music that appeals to audiences, because I feel that however hard man tries he can't fall out of the transcendent. In a way, he's locked in it. Atheists can rage, and Nietzsche can say, 'God is dead', but to me this falls on deaf ears. I know, for instance, when I read Saint John of the Cross, Rumi, Shankara or any of the great mystics of *all* traditions, that they're right. I can't explain to you why; I just know.

Some pieces come to me almost fully born, though they're usually the shorter ones. Often they're born of certain events in life, like the sudden death of someone or a love affair. Some were born by falling in love with a poem or even falling in love with a language. I must have set twenty or thirty languages to music (more than any other composer, I would have thought), including Sanskrit, Arabic, Italian, German, Latin and Greek. While I was doing *The Beautiful Names*, a setting of the beautiful names in Arabic of God, I didn't exactly learn Arabic but somebody came here almost every day to teach me how the grammar works.

Other pieces take me forever, and when I start them I go through a process of thinking, 'Oh, I really don't want to have to do this.' And I agonise about them for a long time. But then the idea proliferates and comes to a point where I feel I'll burst if I *don't* do it; and then it's a relief to write it down. And the writing down of music always informs what emerges: what's happened in my head becomes much more interesting once I've put it onto paper.

Curiously enough, a piece that comes fully born doesn't necessarily seem more inspired than one that I agonise about. *The Lamb* came to me in my head while my mother was driving me from Cornwall back to London, and then all I needed to do was write it down. But other pieces, like *The Veil of the Temple*, take me forever. And there doesn't seem to be any rule to it – it's got nothing to do with the length of the piece.

[2] At the time of this interview Sir John was setting Dante's *Farewell to Beatrice* to music.

So composing is an adventure, and I never know exactly where it's going to go. It would be so boring if I wrote down just what was in my head, and nothing else happened. *The Veil of the Temple* was my biggest recent adventure, and I was actually asked for it – it wasn't my mad idea to write a piece that lasted all night. I thought I couldn't possibly write seven hours of music, but it just grew and grew and grew. I knew that was the goal I had to try and reach, and somehow I got there.

Because symmetry is terribly important to me I agonise over numbers and getting the formal structure of my music as mathematical as I can. I like to be able to explain every bar that I write. This is just to satisfy me, really – it's a private thing. But then, as you say, some people love Bach's music for its mathematical qualities. I can understand that. But is that why I love *The Art of Fugue*? No, I think *The Art of Fugue* is wonderful not because of its counterpoint but because of the harmony that comes out of it. Extraordinary piece.

I usually begin a piece with a text, which determines both the melodic line and the rhythm of the music. This is why I have to fall in love with the poem or the language (if it's not English). Then, in a strange way, I become sort of suffused in the spiritual and physical world of that language. For instance, when I set an Italian text I become very moved by all things Italian because I'm so deeply involved in that world. Does that make sense?

Sometimes my starting point is a metaphysical idea that's expressed in short phrases. For example, a recent piece called *Gnossis*, which has little bits in Arabic, little bits in Sanskrit, little bits in Latin and little bits in Greek, isn't a poem, as such, but a series of mystical utterances that I felt were best expressed in music. And sometimes I dream music. Only recently I dreamed that I had one foot stuck in Hell while my head was in Paradise, listening to Mozart. I don't know what it meant, but that's how it appeared to me. And the next day, when I looked at what I'd been writing, I saw that the melodic line was connected to Mozart, so I decided to end the whole piece with Mozart.

I always write by hand – with a pencil. I can type slowly to look things up on the Internet but I'd never be able to write music on the computer. I used to have a regular working routine and I worked all day when I wasn't sleeping or out walking. In fact, my wife thought I was overdoing it, working absurdly hard and writing *so* much. It may have partly brought on my illness, even though working involved periods of not being able to do anything, when an awful lot of time was spent staring at the ceiling. Or alternatively, in those days, going to Greece and swimming.

Since I've been ill I can only work for one or two hours a day, in the morning, otherwise I become breathless and exhausted because of the pressure on my heart. And I can't escape any more: I can't go to Greece, I can't drink wine and I can't eat very much. But I believe that all these things happen to us for a reason in life, and that they're not just arbitrary and nasty.

Incidentally, I'd like to go back and increase the *tempi* of a lot of the music from my middle period. My heart's been mucked around with by surgeons and now beats faster than it used to, and I'm absolutely certain that one composes to the speed of one's heartbeat!

Yes, I think you *could* say that because of the nature of the texts I set to music, my focus as a composer is a kind of vocation. And I'm aware that if I'd existed at the same time as Josquin des Prez or the Tudor English composers the Church would have been for me the wise patron that it no longer is.

When I was in my late teens I idolised Stravinsky and used to go to every concert he conducted in England, so I had some idea of what his life was like; but I didn't really have an idea of what the life of a composer would be like for *me*. As for making a living from writing music, I think that became important to me only when, very late in life, I finally decided to get married and have children. But that coincided with a period in my life when money seemed to be coming in anyway. Otherwise we wouldn't be living here! The idea of being a professional composer doesn't terribly interest me nowadays because I don't want to write film music or knock off short pieces for commercial purposes, even though I could.

I used to talk about wanting to be a conduit or vessel through which music flows, and about my desire to minimise, to some extent, the influence of my personality on what I wrote. Nowadays I feel more that my music has to undergo a kind of *transcendence* of my personality. I don't think Stravinsky's idea that music expresses nothing at all, and has nothing to do with the personality, is true. I mean, every note of Stravinsky looks like him and sounds like he looks. I'm thinking about what I've written recently: by setting the Tolstoy short story *The Death of Ivan Ilyich* I've actually been writing an autobiographical piece, but the music is ritualised and objectivised. I hope there's no self-indulgence in it. I don't like any kind of indulgent music.

I think the accusation of my pieces being over-simple is no longer applicable since I've felt the necessity to compress my musical thoughts.

Partly because I can't sit at a desk or at the piano, the music that I've written since I was ill in 2007 is much terser and rarely lasts more than twenty minutes. As a result, there's a kind of intensity about it. Everything is much more concentrated, and I don't think you could accuse my recent pieces of washing over the listener.

When I think about my music the phrases that come to mind are poetic, such as 'divine darkness'. My music has both raptness and darkness – a mixture of the two. There's a sort of not knowing – because, in a deep sense, my religious faith is based on not knowing. I grew up in the Presbyterian Church and I remember my pastor saying, 'Life is a creeping tragedy; that's why I must be cheerful.' I thought that expressed it wonderfully! (He used to break down in Easter sermons because he wasn't totally sure of his beliefs. And he wanted me to go through the experience of watching him – and his wife – die of cancer. He was an extraordinary man.)

I'd love to be able to communicate the kind of pain–pleasure that *The Marriage of Figaro* gives to me. I recently went with my family to see a performance of it at Glyndebourne and found that I was weeping all the way through it, but also absolutely delighted and laughing because it's so funny. It's got everything: sensuality, a sense of wonder, playfulness, compassion. And it never lets up in inspiration. I would say that it's the greatest work of Western art ever written. Do you agree? But I can also be deeply moved by what some people would say was third-rate art. For example, I adore hymns and can still get terribly moved by them, although I don't know why. My Presbyterian pastor used to say, 'The words of "When I survey the wondrous cross" – "His dying crimson like a robe / Spreads o'er His body on the tree" – are so intense that one almost can't sing them.' The words of some hymns *are* extraordinary.

Musicians who perform my music say that they recognise certain stylistic fingerprints on it, such as intervals that I often use. I'm not sure that I recognise them myself because I never listen to my music and I very rarely sit down and analyse it. The closest I get to doing that is when I work on it with my editor. Since I've been ill she has gone through my music with a toothcomb and asked, 'Are you sure you mean this? Are you sure you mean that?' Otherwise I don't think about it much. I enjoy the fact that it takes on a life of its own once I've let go of it, and I've rarely been upset by any direction that performers have taken it in.

But I'm fed up with hearing *Song for Athene* every time I turn on *Essential Classics* in the morning. They keep playing it. Why? It's not a piece to be listened to on the radio; it's a piece that I wrote for a friend and which then became very popular because it was performed at Princess Diana's funeral. It *belongs* to a funeral. I'm seventy next year and people are already talking about birthday concerts and how they want to include *Song for Athene*. But it wasn't written for a concert.

I've been wondering how to answer your question about the connection, if there is one, between my Britishness and my music. I certainly feel a very strong connection to Tudor music – Taverner, Tallis, Sheppard – which I think is some of the greatest Western music ever written. Although I greatly admire Britten and Elgar, in some ways I feel closer to Warlock, who had a very singular vision. The intensity of that vision moves me, although I'm not a miniaturist composer like he was.

Different places have also been important to me at different times in my life. I moved here to Dorset because it's a wonderful place for walking, and I used to have a big dog which I walked every day. The countryside around here is a congenial backdrop rather than an inspiration for my music, and I've been influenced more by Scotland (which I'd always avoided until recently) and Greece, where we have a small and increasingly dilapidated house. Since I've been ill I haven't been able to work very well in Scotland, and Greece has diminished in importance because I can't cope with the climate, but what inspires me in both places is their sense of timelessness. That's the dimension in which music – or at least the music I'm most interested in – exists.

When I was ill in 2007 (I nearly died) it was music that brought me back. I was in intensive care in Switzerland, and my wife was with me. She played some Mozart; and I, although still seemingly unconscious, started to conduct. Clearly, music exists in a dimension that's outside time. Later, when I was lying on a sofa in this room and trying to recover, I listened to late Beethoven. Before then I'd never enjoyed the sound of his music – the way he spaced chords bothered me, and still does, because it seems less musical than Mozart – but I was deeply moved by it, partly because it sounds absolutely newly minted and like nothing else that has ever been written, and partly because I felt that it was music that came out of deep suffering. I believe that suffering is part of life – we can't avoid it, even if we *can* avoid thinking about it – and that to transcend it is part of what we are here to do. So that's one of the functions of music: to help us to transcend suffering.

However, I don't understand the huge love of Mahler's music. I think his songs are wonderful but I find the Symphonies rather vulgar and bombastic. And self-pitying, to a degree. How much more wonderful are the Chopin Mazurkas and Preludes? Or Schumann ...

As to where contemporary music is going, I sometimes toy with the idea that it's like religion: both have become terribly diverse because we live in an age without absolutes, and so both are going in all sorts of directions. Maybe that's a good thing. But I also feel that, to a certain extent, religions have reached a form of senility, and that music, too, is suffering a kind of decay. On the other hand, a rediscovery of the sacred has begun to take place, I believe. My oldest daughter is studying Theology and Religious Studies at Cambridge, and that's a direction that I see a lot of young people going in. And while Stockhausen may have been a bit crass and New Age, he had an extraordinary vision and I believe that he was beginning to feel something deeply spiritual again.

I think what we're seeing in religion is a change in direction from the spoken and literal to the unspoken and symbolic. Science plays a part in this – I've recently read books by neurosurgeons who describe how near-death experiences keep cropping up with a certain regularity, which I feel is a hopeful sign. As for music, the fact that the twentieth century produced Stockhausen, Messiaen, Morton Feldman, Arvo Pärt and Stravinsky (who, in my opinion, wrote the most sacred music of all of them) suggests that there's a greater awareness of the sacred than there was in the nineteenth century, or perhaps even the eighteenth century. Not that I think the *quality* of the music is quite as high. Stockhausen was deeply interesting, but I don't think he was a great composer in the way that masters like Josquin and Mozart were great. And Stravinsky: I think you have to search quite wide to find anybody on his level. Do you agree with that?

Nowadays I'm very much within myself, and alone while my wife is away during the day, on and off – she's studying to be a doctor at King's in London. And because I can't work very much I listen to a lot more music than I used to. This includes contemporary music, which I used to be very critical of but which I now enjoy listening to because I'm very interested to know what other composers are writing.

In general, I listen to music without analysing it. I remember that when Harrison Birtwistle's Violin Concerto was played at the Proms last year Anthony Payne was interviewed about it and said that he could follow every single note, right from the beginning. Well, I've got perfect pitch, but to be able to follow the musical argument from the beginning to the end of a complex new piece by Birtwistle seems beyond my comprehension. Listening to it with that kind of analytical mind doesn't seem a possibility to me.

I've been influenced by a number of traditions, but only recently have I come to re-appreciate Western music and to love it. I don't like American minimalists – I get bored to tears by John Adams – but I greatly admire Arvo Pärt because I feel that there's a very good reason for his music being as it is. I'm also listening to more nineteenth-century music than I used to, and I've been particularly struck by Chopin. It's very easy to say that he's a sort of lounge composer, but he's much more than that. Do you like Chopin?

On the whole, I try to listen to as wide a spectrum of music as possible, and that might include Josquin, Mozart and Stockhausen all in one evening! What links those composers, for me, is the sacredness, the sense of play, the sense of wonder and the sense of the feminine that they have. They're all important aspects of music for me. Do you like early music? It seems to me a perfect mixture of mind and soul. That's why I love it so much. And do you like jazz? I love its wonderful improvisatory nature – its freedom within a discipline.

Quite a bit of my time is spent doing interviews like this one. This is partly because I feel I'm near the end of my life and so I spend a lot of time looking back on what I've done. And I like talking about it. Going through my pieces with my editor on the phone is very tiring but I enjoy that, too. I used to enjoy conducting when I was young, and I was a very good pianist – I studied with Solomon and could have been a concert soloist. I can't play anymore because while my left hand is not exactly paralysed it doesn't really move. I used to sing (I had a dreadful voice but could mimic all sorts of parts, including a soprano!) and I used to enjoy singing Mozart operas from beginning to end. I had nothing like the practical musicianship of Benjamin Britten but I did have a similar kind of talent for playing the piano, if not conducting.

Britten was the most amazing musician, wasn't he? Distant man, difficult man to get to know ... but I'm very grateful to him because it was because of his interest in what I was doing that Covent Garden commissioned me to write my opera *Thérèse*. So he was a great help to me in the early part of my career. Do you know the extraordinary story about Stravinsky asking him for scores? Peter Pears told me that, although Stravinsky could have gone to Boosey & Hawkes to get them, he wrote to Britten and asked, 'Will you send me the score of *Noye's Fludde*?' Then he composed *The Flood*. 'Will you send me the score of your *War Requiem*?' Then he wrote *Requiem Canticles*. And this went on and on: Britten's *Abraham and Isaac*, then he wrote his own *Abraham and Isaac*. Pears thought he had jealousy, deep jealousy, of Britten.

I find that the more worldly and political element of the music profession doesn't interest me very much, and so I try to avoid it. And I don't really mix with composers, although I live near Harrison Birtwistle and we did used to get drunk together at Dartington. I prefer to be in the company of writers or painters – creative people who exercise a discipline other than music – because I find that more stimulating. Cecil Collins[3] was a close friend – most of the pictures hanging in this room are by him.

I don't think of myself as a public figure, but I know that I became one – in a way that I now regret. I can't think why I allowed myself to be dressed up in cloaks and photographed with icons and candles in a ghastly, pious kind of way. I hate those photos. I didn't care enough, and I should have done. I feel the same way about those films of me made in the 1960s: I don't know why I behaved in a rather shocking way, except that I was slightly angry in those days and wanted to give the impression of being more of a pop-star figure – which I now think was just youthful and stupid.

I was angry because I hated the po-faced music that had been written in the 1950s by Birtwistle and Maxwell Davies and Goehr. I also felt that music in general had become serial to a ludicrous degree – it was a purely mathematical exercise and I simply had no time for it. The worst of the plink-plonk music is the meaningless plink-plonk, and I found a lot of it in British music of the 1950s and 1960s. (I don't find it in Webern, which I think is elegant and beautiful and deeply felt.) I never really loved pop music, either, and I think my connection with the Beatles is over-written-about. I felt that they were more talented than the po-faced serial composers of the time, and I wanted to say so, but I should have kept quiet and not allowed those films to be made.

I'm not someone who eschews beauty and I don't understand the curious element of contemporary culture that does. I think beauty is the ultimate aim in art, and I'm 'old school' in so far as I want my music to be as beautiful as I can possibly make it. But I wouldn't talk about it in those terms and I certainly wouldn't describe it as beautiful in a programme note. Good heavens, no. I'd talk about its structure. Why? Because I wouldn't assume that it *was* beautiful. If somebody else told me that it was, I'd be very happy. And I'm pleased to say that, quite often, people do.

---

[3] English artist (1908–89) originally associated with the Surrealist movement.

Judith Weir

Judith Weir, London, November 2011

> ❛Composition isn't about a
> person; it's about sound and
> music, whose magic is ephemeral
> in its effect on us.❜

In July 2014 it was announced that Judith Weir was to succeed Sir Peter Maxwell Davies as Master of the Queen's Music. Like him, she was to be appointed for a term of ten years, and much was made of the fact that she was to be the first female Master in the 388-year history of the role. An unassuming one, too: she told Tom Service

> The palace asked a lot of people who it should be, and I said Jonathan Dove would be the best person. But they took no notice of me, and a few weeks ago they told me they had had the most suggestions that it ought to be me – so 'well done'.[1]

Naturally, when I interviewed her for this book in November 2011 I had no idea that I was talking to the next Master (the role has no female title but at the time of the appointment a friend of hers suggested 'Mastress', which I imagine she liked). It was just one more encounter – an important but in some ways unremarkable one.

After walking for a few minutes from the local Underground station I found her house, a large end-of-terrace on a street corner close to an arterial road in south London, with plenty of time to spare, and so walked around the grey, damp streets for a quarter of an hour before knocking at her door at the agreed time. She welcomed me in, introduced me to her partner and their dog, who then went out for a walk, made us some tea and took me upstairs to the first-floor living room for the interview.

We sat around the coffee table to talk, and she leaned forward conscientiously while answering my questions, rather like a professor giving a one-to-one tutorial. She spoke softly and rather earnestly but not without humour, and I couldn't help noticing that her emphasis on the importance of clarity in her music was echoed in her speech, which was precise

---

[1] Tom Service, 'Judith Weir Prepares to Be a Radical Master of the Queen's Music', *The Guardian*, 21 July 2014.

and succinct. Afterwards, as the light was fading, she stood by one of the windows for a hasty photo session.

In short, this was a straightforward, businesslike encounter with a straightforward, businesslike person who nevertheless put me at my ease and engaged in discussion with gratifying seriousness. Some of her responses made clear that she'd spent time considering my list of questions beforehand; and I became aware when transcribing our conversation, even more than when we were actually having it, that the success of this interview was determined by what she said rather than how she said it.

In the light of her royal appointment I'm interested to see that she answered my question about the increasingly public role of the composer by saying that she strongly disliked this trend, and I wonder whether she would now answer it differently. But this was only one topic of our conversation, which began with recent developments in music and the suggestion that the term 'avant-garde' is now as redundant as the distinction between 'serial' and 'non-serial' that Murray Schafer explored in some of his interviews. I told her about Gordon Crosse's comment in his interview for this book that it's currently fashionable for a composer to be unfashionable, and I asked her whether she sees music following multiple paths rather than a single one.

Yes, I think that's what's happened. Even fifteen years ago it was easier to identify a very strong strand of new music among the many different things that composers were doing, and to say, 'This is the way it's going.' But now, it's impossible to ignore everything that's happening musically, particularly as the Internet allows us to hear so much, and impossible to say that there's only one form of progressive development in music. I would be cautious about describing the music scene as having 'fragmented', because that sounds negative. The composers who are doing their own, different things might well feel that they're actually *gaining* something from all the other music that's around them, and that music in general is therefore developing more strongly than it might otherwise do.

Gordon Crosse's comment is interesting, and I've heard people say that the only kind of success available to composers today is what in the past we would have called 'cult success' – the sort where you have a small group of adherents who are very devoted to what you do! But, again, it could actually be easier now that we've accepted that in 'contemporary serious composition' (I don't know what else to call it) everyone may plough their own furrow, and is probably doing so in his/her own mind. We tend to put certain composers – for example, those who are always writing tonal church music – together in a group, but they might not feel that they've got anything in common with each other. The same might be true of people who write maximal music for small instrumental ensembles: they might hate being put together in a supposed strand with composers who they actually don't feel a similarity to.

So I think the current musical scene allows composers much more freedom to develop what they want to write – and, we hope, for it to be heard, although the broadening of the scene may mean that small (and ever smaller) resources are spread more and more thinly. But all this is for people other than composers to comment on!

As for the term 'British composer', it may have meant something in the past – in the twentieth century, even – but I don't think that it's a very useful description nowadays apart from the obvious fact of living or having to work in Britain. And the reason is that music is so international. I don't even think of myself as a *Scottish* composer, because I never know where I'm from, really – I've lived in so many places. In that sense, 'British' actually suits me better, because it means partly from England and partly from Scotland.

Key to my motivation as a composer is the idea of my music being played – a group of people performing it and another group of people (which may not need to be a very large group at all) coming together to hear it. That live gathering together of people who have made a journey towards a performance in order to attend a particular piece, who have been brought together by it, is the best thing in music, I think. The rich atmosphere that results (and by that I don't mean that everyone has to love the piece) is what I look for in any performance.

Does this influence what I write? It could do. There's certainly a lot of consideration about how I'm going to make a piece of music work, by which I mean that I hope both the detail *and* the overall intention will be clear to listeners. And this could have some bearing on the forces involved. But I just write what I can. Most of the orchestras in this country devote disgracefully little time to playing new pieces, and this reduces the number of statements that composers might make in that medium. It's often said that it's as difficult to get a second performance as the first, and so it's perhaps wiser to take on projects that have more performances built in. The good thing about an opera is that no-one would *ever* put one on for just one evening; and it's in opera, I think, that I've made my biggest statements as a composer. In one sense, I've done that because I feel that it's the easiest thing for an audience to grasp. It's a way of making my ideas and thoughts very clear, because people receive them not just as sound but as visuals and as action on the stage.

I think there are many composers who would wish to make those big statements but who are simply being prevented from doing so; in which case, of course, it makes sense for them to write for smaller forces. In other words, they have purely practical reasons for doing this. I can't see anything in the current musical climate itself that's discouraging them from making large-scale statements.

The word 'communication', in relation to music, is difficult – in the sense of not being straightforward. Of course, it's been slightly foisted on us because it's seen by funding bodies – and indeed performers – as A Good Thing. But I'm not sure what is actually communicated to listeners. And the idea that I think of something which is then picked up by them, as if we were holding some kind of séance, seems odd to me. I much prefer to think in terms of 'expression' – stating my music with clarity. I'm dismayed when I hear music that seems indistinct in its detail, and there's a lot of that kind of music around. For me, clarity could mean simply that certain ways in which the composition is working become clear. A really well-structured, well-argued piece can bring a feeling of more than pleasure or repose; it can bring a sense of satisfaction, a feeling that everything's all right in the world because everything in the music has dropped into place.

The idea that I have a particular thing to say to listeners might be more appropriate in the case of opera, because it seems to me that you *must* want your audience to receive your story in such a way that they can take it away with them. But in the case of instrumental music my aim is that a piece will work in performance because people will be able to tell what's happening in it. And it's really up to them what they take from that experience. They might not want to try to understand my intentions when writing the piece; that's their choice. I probably do want them to receive something appreciable from hearing it, but of course I never know who 'they' are.

It's true that people can appropriate a piece of music to their own circumstances. And, in a sense, they have an absolute right to come along in a certain emotional state to meet my piece. Maybe that state is appropriate to what they think they're hearing, maybe it isn't. But, as I say, it's really none of my business, particularly as I can't guess who will be in the audience. And to think about these things at the point of composition would be impossible, really. People have said to me after performances of my music, 'That was really *you*.' And, when challenged as to what that actually means(!), they haven't been able to come up with anything that I can really relate to. I feel that when I'm composing I'm the furthest away from thinking about myself. And so I find it difficult to imagine a composer deciding, 'I'm going to tell the audience about *this* particular aspect of my personality.' Composing is an abstract act in the very best sense: your mind is absorbed with something that's *not* to do with you or with the here and now, and the best moments in composition are those probably quite brief ones in which you're not thinking about anything except the workings of the music. So, in answer to your question, self-expression is definitely an unconscious activity rather than a direct goal.

It's often not possible or even desirable to work for eight or ten hours a day at composition. Those long days come at some points in the process but not at others. And I don't have the kind of life in which I sit down to start work at nine o'clock and carry on until a certain time. My *pieces* don't have that kind of life, either: they begin with a lot of thinking and my not doing very much (it would seem). The process isn't just difficult to describe; it's difficult for me to *know*. It's almost as if the music creeps up on me. I notate things that might seem to be of no use at all, and so by the time I've *really* started to write the piece down – in lots of sketches and then in neater copy – I feel that I'm well into the process. In other words, I'm sometimes composing when I'm not aware of it. Or pondering questions that haven't yet been answered sufficiently for me to get going with the piece.

As I said earlier, the moments of absolutely, totally focussed composition come along rather rarely – they take up a very small percentage of my time. And I think a lot of other composers would say the same. Many of us teach, and at the moment I'm doing a lot of score-reading for people who have asked for my advice. When you first contacted me about this interview I was about to go to Austria, where my latest opera was being done, and because of other work associated with it I was away for about two and a half months, not composing at all but just waiting around at rehearsals to answer questions about what was going on. And being a public person, which I don't really like. The public role of the composer isn't as big as many others in the arts, but in my own case I'd be very happy to do away with most of it.

When I was growing up we very rarely heard statements from composers; we heard only their music. Britten was occasionally interviewed, I suppose, but never during a concert. Now, it's almost as if artists are expected to act out their work. And you're right to suggest that many composers are unsuited to that. As you say, so much of our work is done in private – not in the sense that we're keeping secrets to ourselves but in the months and months of solitary clerical work, as it were. Yet we're expected to then leap into the public gaze and be witty and amusing or exciting people. I'm not sure that this actually helps the public, who sometimes get a very wrong impression from the composers' explanations of their own work or what is assumed to be their personality when they're seen out in public.

The idea for a piece of music can, and often does, come in a moment. And then there's months of work, trying to recapture that moment which so many people describe as inspiration. You're getting down on paper, by a rather indirect method, something of an incredible surge of thought or magic that's come into your head; and to try to embody that, or to even talk about it, isn't really possible. So, although composers may appear to talk dispassionately about their music, I don't think they're dispassionate *people*. It's more that the act of composition involves (ideally) a transcendence of the self. Hence my disquiet about composers today being expected to personify their music for the public. Composition isn't about a person; it's about sound and music, whose magic is ephemeral in its effect on us. So for us to express the drama in our *behaviour* is not only difficult but wrong. It's for the music to do that.

I can bring into my mind's eye the opening page of a score as I've written it out, but my memory of the music is always a sound picture. And I feel very strongly that the score is just a blueprint, a set of working instructions on the way to the composition actually happening in terms of being performed. This could be at the point when the performers first rehearse it – when the physical sound of the piece is produced for the first time – but I could be more extreme and say that composition doesn't exist until the sound reaches the ears of a *listener*. However, the rehearsal is very important to me, and it's fantastic (usually) when I first hear the sound of my music. Maybe the performers have got nowhere near it, but the piece suddenly comes alive and feels so much *more* than I had imagined. There's a huge amount of added richness to it. And the piece is no longer a theory in my head but a fact. In the case of larger pieces, I can honestly say that my favourite moments are during the later rehearsals – or, in the case of an opera, during the dress rehearsal. There's something wonderful about being pretty much on my own in the auditorium – just me and the music.

When there are problems they're often to do with *tempi*. Because all composers are quite specific these days in indicating the speeds they want, I can be quite taken aback if somebody decides to play my music much faster or much slower than I expected. In a way, they have the right to try that out, and I'm often open to quite a lot of changes in that area; but I've sometimes been uneasy about what's happened when performers have played my music for the first time. They've obviously heard it in the way that they're playing it, and to them it sounds right. The difficult interactions that follow are always with conductors, and when you say, 'Oh, could it be a bit faster?' they get out their wretched little metronomes and conduct the piece *exactly* to tempo! *I* can get it wrong – there's a kind of disparity or inexactness between what music sounds like in your head and what the metronome tells you. And no ill is meant by the performers who misinterpret what you've written. But it's extraordinary how contentious an area this is!

My experience of composing is sometimes a great struggle just to get the notes down, and sometimes I don't at first see everything that's in the piece. So there have been occasions where I've re-composed earlier material, using notes or even complete sections from a piece and writing them in a different form or for different instruments. To me, this is a more exciting procedure than revision, which I see as a kind of neatening up of dynamics or other small details after a first performance.

My formal education in music took place a long time ago, when there was almost no composition teaching. In my final year at university I was very fortunate to have about ten composition lessons from Robin Holloway, a very fine composer and teacher, who happened to have just joined the staff there. But that was all the university composition teaching I got. What I *did* get was tons of harmony, counterpoint and other theory, which at the time seemed so boring to have to plod through. Forty years later I can see that it was helpful in teaching me fluency in handling notes. But I still learned a lot of my craft from practising it rather than studying it. Playing music was also very educational, as was meeting other composers of my age, or a bit older, and sharing experiences with them.

But I had no thoughts about becoming a professional composer. That wasn't the impulse in the very beginning. Of course, when I actually started writing music, in the late 1960s, my idea of the life of a professional composer was very different from what it is now. And you could say, 'The life of *which* professional composer?', because each of us is involved in a different mix of activities. The job has changed, even in my time, partly because, as we've already discussed, people now want the composer to be much more of a public figure. What concerns me very much at the moment is the change in funding of university degrees, because I fear that a subject such as music will be hard-hit. Most music students get into huge debt, particularly if they do postgraduate study, and very few of us composers go on to earn a lot. My pessimistic expectation is that there will be fewer opportunities to teach music at college or university level – in contrast to the high number of very, very good composers teaching in universities twenty years ago.

For *some* students – the chosen few – there seem to be a lot of high-profile opportunities in their first ten years. And that's great. It's what they need immediately after a period of training. But I wonder what's going to happen to them afterwards, when resources are thinly spread. I'm concerned that composers further along the line are not being heard so much, which is the result of increasing emphasis on youth rather than on the genuinely new.

It's difficult to know where to begin when trying to explain how my music has changed since I became a composer, because I wrote a lot of music in my teens that I don't have any more. If I could look at it I'd probably be able to give you a more interesting answer! But I think my work has become more fluid and more fluent, simply as a result of knowing more about what direction I want to go in, musically. On the other hand, when I hear my very early surviving pieces after a long interval I'm sometimes surprised by how much they resemble what I do now, if only in roundabout ways. So perhaps I've always had in my head the kind of musical shapes I'm trying to get on with today.

Sometimes I begin a piece with melody and derive other things (harmony, for example) out of it, but these days I increasingly ask myself, 'What will this piece be *like*?' I look for the particular animating feature of the music and start to work towards that, even though I know that the piece may end up very differently from how I first imagine it. It could be that the beginning and the end of the piece are going to make important musical gestures; or, in the simplest possible case, I might want to write a piece that starts off very thin and becomes richer and richer as the music piles up. In each case, it's the shape of the music that I usually think about first.

I'm glad to say that I still write by hand. I'm extremely fortunate in that my publisher still provides me with copyists who then do the computer side of things for me. As you'll have gathered, I'm part of a generation (the last one) for whom the process of writing by hand is too deeply ingrained to change; but one obvious benefit of computer scores is that they're much easier to revise.

Some people seem to think, 'Oh, these poor composers: they get commissions and have to sit down and write something for someone, like a tailor has to make a garment. If only they could write what they wanted to.' But for me, it's almost the other way round: nearly all of the commissions that I've undertaken have given me either quite a wide area in which to operate or have allowed me to do exactly the thing I wanted to do anyway. (I'm using the word 'commission' to mean not just something that is paid but something that has been suggested to me.) Having a commission allows a piece to exist, because it gives you a real reason for writing it: you know that people want to hear it.

And you're right: it's easier to compose to a particular specification than with a blank slate. A commission directs you in a certain area and may perhaps take you back to some ideas that you've had to lay aside. That's how I experience it, anyway. Or it can be welcome in making you think about writing for a particular group of instruments that you thought you didn't want to write for. For me, it's sometimes like being taken back to an area or a corridor that I'd temporarily moved out of but was thinking about.

I was interested that you wanted to talk about composers becoming known by a single work, or a small number of works, to the exclusion of everything else they've written, because I worry about this myself. I've written a very broad group of works in all sorts of media and of all sorts of lengths, difficulties and intentions. And I'm proud of many of them. But, naturally, the things that get played the most are the simplest, shortest works: for example, carols and small choral pieces. To me, they're lovely, and I don't disown them in the least, but it's possible for them to be the only pieces of mine that people know of. At the moment I'm being asked to write a number of short choral pieces, and I can tell that they're the ones that people are most likely to hear, enjoy and feel at home with. Whereas *I* think of myself as a composer who's done all sorts of things, including operas and big orchestral works.

I truly believe that in my older age I've gone beyond listening to music because of what might be in it for me – for example, in terms of helping my technique. I've also gone beyond the feeling that there's music I *ought* to like – or, more to the point, that I ought *not* to like! I'm quite a listener, and it's all about *pleasure* in listening, it truly is. There was a long period, I now see, when my listening habits were … I don't want to say 'infected', but listening to music was complicated by what I was looking for in it. Today, I simply let my curiosity lead me. I'm sure that the analytical part of listening is still there, which isn't surprising after a lifetime of serious music-making. It just happens. And, in a way, that's more of the pleasure for me: I can think, 'Ah yes, this is why the music has that effect on me …' With a less than good piece and, I'm afraid to say, a lot of the music by students that I hear, I can often predict quite quickly what's going to happen in the piece, just because I know what to expect from a lot of other music. Of course, I recognise that my perceptions depend on how I'm feeling, as well as what the music's like.

What would make me think 'That's a great piece'? It's terribly difficult to say. I think it would just come out of the composition. Something, or any number of things, could just grab me. At the beginning of this conversation I talked about clarity, and I do want to be able to see clearly what's happening in a piece of music. For me, a common problem among young composers is that they try to do everything at once in a piece; and I don't blame them for this, because many of them are studying for degrees and being asked to show their competence in every field. But I like to see that the composer has made some kind of choice in what the piece is like, and has rejected a lot of material before saying, 'I'm going to give you *this* rather than *that*.' That's a good start, I think.

Debbie Wiseman

Debbie Wiseman, London, July 2011

> **I love the fact that, whether people like or dislike the music, what I write will be performed and then heard.**

Debbie Wiseman is unarguably a specialist composer, known almost exclusively for her two-hundred-plus scores for film (*Arsène Lupin*, *Tom & Viv*, *Wilde*) and television (*Jackanory*, *Judge John Deed*, *The Promise*). Unlike her fellow film composer Christopher Gunning, for example, she has no parallel body of concert music that has been overshadowed by her work for the screen, and she's happy to be a leading fish in one of classical music's ponds rather than a minnow in the mainstream.

Because her pond is a commercial (and presumably competitive) one, she knows the importance of self-promotion, and so, although she doesn't – I imagine – seek publicity for its own sake, she has over the years agreed readily to my requests for photoshoots and interviews. I first photographed her in October 1999 at the CTS Studios in Wembley, where she was recording one of her film scores – for she's also an experienced orchestral conductor who's used to helping musicians bring her work to life. Rather to my annoyance, when I photographed her in July 2011 after the interview for this book she appeared to have aged barely a year during the intervening twelve. As on the other occasions when I've met her, she was immaculately presented – a fact that's significant only because it suggested that in her branch of composition, which has a strongly corporate element, good grooming can be part of professional presentation as well as personal taste.

I noticed that this impeccability extended to her working environment at home – a large, modern house in north London. Her studio, occupying one of the bright, spacious ground-floor rooms, was dominated by a grand piano, an even grander TV monitor and a bank of computers. In fact, there was little else in the room except a couple of office chairs, a modern, cuboid coffee table on wheels and bookshelves containing copies of her soundtrack CDs and DVDs. Framed certificates and posters promoting some of the films for which she has written music lined the walls. It was part composer's study, part recording studio and part film executive's office.

Her natural gifts as a communicator have recently been exploited in her presentation of radio documentaries, most of them about the process of composing music for the screen, and to these she has brought straightforwardness and authority. She has also released what she describes as the most personal of her recordings to date, a collection of solo piano music that includes a few short abstract compositions as well as themes for film and television productions (in the pre-orchestrated state in which she conceives them at the keyboard).

In person she's relaxed, hospitable and chatty, often emphasising points by saying the same thing in a number of ways. I detect beneath her warmth and charm a tough, businesslike pragmatism that would be more appropriate to the formality of a Deborah than to the informality of a Debbie, but the latter name suits well both her cheerful personality and the collaborative nature of realising a complex modern film score.

I've always felt that music should be useful and that it should serve a purpose. So the idea of sitting at the piano and writing something just for myself, which nobody else other than members of my family is going to hear, does not appeal to me in the slightest. I want the music that I write to be heard by an audience. So writing for film is very appealing to me because I know that there's a purpose for it: it's going to accompany a drama.

Also, I have the music performed by (usually) a world-class orchestra very soon afterwards – sometimes within six or eight weeks. The whole process is very exciting and adrenaline-filled. The best part, of course, is that the music ends up on the film and can reach an audience of millions very quickly. If it then goes to television it can reach another large audience. And I love the fact that, whether people like or dislike the music, what I write will be performed and then heard. For me, that's what drives me to put the notes on the page.

Many classical composers feel sad that something they've worked on for a couple of years gets a first performance and very rarely a second performance. Often, that's *it*, you know, or it may take months or years for anything else to happen with that piece. But a film has a life. Obviously, the success of your music is intrinsically linked to the success of the film, and if the movie does very well at the box office, the chances of people hearing your music are that bit greater. And then the chances of taking it into the concert hall are that bit greater still, because suddenly people are interested in hearing the music from the film that they enjoyed so much. It's something that *can* be taken aside from the film to stand on its own, and I enjoy knowing that it's going to be listened to by lots of people, not just me and my family and friends.

Almost all the music I've written has been commissioned for a film or a television project or a commercial, although occasionally I've been asked to write a string quartet or a choral piece for the concert hall. Very occasionally I'll wake up in the morning with a melody in my head, and I'll come to the piano and just write it down. It's not for a particular film and it hasn't been inspired by anything in particular; it's just something that was in my head that day. If I like it, I'll keep it and write something like 'Nice Theme' on the page.

But as we sit here now I can think of only one of those themes written in the morning or late at night that has ever found its way anywhere. I've never had a sort of bottom drawer that I go to for things that might work, and I've never managed to access anything from the past for use in the present, possibly because I feel that I'm always growing musically and I don't want to ever go back. I start every new project with a clean slate and a clean sheet of manuscript paper. I always want to push myself to try something new and to come up with something different.

You see, being trained in the classical music world forces you into perfectionism, or a desire for perfection, that you can never quite achieve. Occasionally you get a compliment, which is lovely, but in general you're being told what you need to improve. And I think that's embedded in you through your training. So when I was studying piano my teacher, quite rightly, would always pick up on what was wrong rather than what was right in my playing. And I find that the same thing applies in my composition: I'm always looking at what's wrong with it rather than what's right with it. And I can always find lots of things wrong with it. To look at it and say 'Yes, it's great' is very difficult, I think, for anybody who's got that sort of perfectionist streak.

So I know that if I didn't have a deadline for my work I would just revise and revise and revise. It might not even get any better as a result, but I'd still want to do it because I wouldn't be able to leave it alone. But if I know that an orchestra is booked for next Friday, say, and that I have to get the score ready and the parts have to be copied and everything has to be ready for ten o'clock that morning, I don't waffle and I don't go over things again and again. I finish the piece and give it to my music copyists, they prepare the parts and away we go.

When writing a particular melody or harmony I don't think, 'This needs to be understood' or 'This needs to be accessible', because at that stage there's nobody other than myself that I've got to please. It's an instinctive thing: I watch a particular scene from a film and then I write music that seems to work well for it. I don't know how that happens, because I try not to think about it too much in case whatever it is that makes it happen goes away! And, you know, I do have a client that I have to please, otherwise my music won't end up on the film and I'll be replaced by another composer. So there's no real sense of audience participation in this process at all. The purpose of composing is always to serve the film.

But I would say that, for me, writing music for films is about encouraging a heart response rather than a mind response. After all, what directors are after is the emotion that only music can bring to the film. Whether it's extra magic or drama or tension or pace, it brings something that can't be achieved with just the visual image and the dialogue. That's why music is such a powerful force in a film. So for me it's always about emotion.

However, with that comes the requirement for a certain technical proficiency. It's no good just saying, 'Oh yes, I'll write sweeping strings here, and I'll put the brass in there because it's supposed to sound powerful.' You have to have a technical understanding of the orchestra and the way it works, of how to judge a chord and how to balance particular instruments. And from that technical knowledge comes the ability to tease out the emotion of a scene.

So I'm very grateful to have come from a classical background and to have had a teacher like Buxton Orr who was very pedantic about composition technique – how you structured a score, how you wrote it on the page, how you put in the dynamics and phrasing for the individual instrumentalists. I don't know everything about them, of course, and I'm learning all the time, but I do have a technical grounding that helps me enormously in judging things and writing without having to *think* about the technique, most of the time.

I was never trained in any of the technology now used in film composition. A lot of it didn't exist when I was studying music at college. Programmes like Sibelius were just starting out, but they weren't everywhere like they are now. I entered the music industry writing music on manuscript paper with a pen, doing the old-fashioned thing of putting every dot on the page and giving it to a music copyist who would copy it out note by note, transcribe the score and prepare the parts for the orchestra. I've always orchestrated my music, and that used to be a laborious process.

I can't even remember how it happened, but I began to get

computers and software and they became part of my working life. I started to use software to do what are called mock-ups, or previews, of a score, so that directors could come and watch the picture while listening to the music before we got into the recording studio with the orchestra. That was the most amazing advance, because instead of me having to sit at the piano, play the chords and say, 'This is where the brass comes in, and this is the strings, this low bit's going to be on the bass drum', I could explain the music in a way that was much easier to understand. For directors it wasn't such a leap of faith, and they were more comfortable because they knew what they were going to get in the studio.

The job of transposing and preparing parts can now be done in a couple of days instead of a week, so technology has helped in ways that I could never have imagined when I started out. The downside is that some instruments don't sound that great when sampled, and so I find myself tempted towards using instruments that do. I've got very good strings, percussion, harp and piano samples, for example. Otherwise I have to say to the director, 'Don't worry. I know the saxophone sounds like a duck on the sample, but it'll be great on the day.' Fortunately, they usually understand.

I don't like the technology to dictate anything creative, because that's awful, but 85 per cent of the time I'm thankful for it. And one reason is that I usually have a very clear idea, before I go into the recording studio, how something's going to sound. There's very little element of surprise anymore, and that's sometimes actually a bit disappointing, because when I started out I used to like the magic of dots on the page being brought to life only when I was standing there in front of the orchestra. But occasionally I'm surprised by the level of excellence that the musicians bring.

And a performance can bring out something in a particular passage that I could never have imagined. I remember one particular moment at the very start of *Wilde* where I'd written a simple little tune for solo violin: the player gave it a kind of Irish twist that was just so lovely and very perfect for Oscar Wilde. You can't necessarily prepare for little things like that coming out in performance.

I do a lot of things other than just sitting at the piano and writing, and I think they're important to do. A composer's life is very internal and quite lonely, because you're always at the instrument where you write, or at your desk. If I didn't have another, outside life I would probably be here twenty-four hours a day and never move. So I give the occasional interview or talk at a school.

I don't actually teach, but I give masterclasses at the Royal College of Music a couple of times a year and look at what the students do. Often I set them a task where they all have to write music for the same scene of a film, and I enjoy watching how music completely transforms the picture, and how some of the students get it incredibly right and others get it horribly wrong. I learn as much from them, I think, as they do from me. So I force myself to do something more extrovert than writing music, and to be out in the wider musical world. Without the performance and the energy that that brings, music isn't alive. And music exists in order to be brought to life.

You're right – some composers do become known for just one piece that they've written, to the exclusion of their other music. And of course the person who immediately springs to mind is Michael Nyman. Mention his name to most people and they'll think, '*The Piano*'. But I don't know if he would want to be remembered only for that. A phenomenon like that is usually the result of the success of a particular project, which then has a knock-on effect on the directors, the editors, the composers, on everybody involved with it. And then, of course, it becomes a sort of iconic thing. So sometimes it's not your best work that gets that kind of recognition. It's simply a series of events, or timing or a piece of luck that causes it to happen. Boom! Suddenly there's a massively successful work that will define your career in a way that you could never have imagined it would.

You're also right that the names of film composers probably don't register with many people who go to the cinema. So some of them won't notice that the music they're hearing is by a composer called Debbie Wiseman. Obviously, there are fans who *do* notice because they love everything to do with film music. But the average audience member would go to a cinema simply to watch a film, not to listen to the music, and it's absolutely right that they should do that.

I'm a big fan of John Barry and Ennio Morricone and Jerry Goldsmith – I've loved their scores over the years. And I thought the scores for *The King's Speech* and *Atonement* were lovely. But I don't listen to much film music now, partly because of lack of time – unless, of course, there's something that everyone says, 'You must see.' It is a sad fact that when I go to see a film I'm more interested in the structure of the score, where it's falling in the picture and how it's working with the visual image.

I *should* be sitting there enjoying the whole thing and being transported into whatever world the director wanted the audience to be transported into, but I find I can't do that because I can't turn off the part of my brain that spends all day analysing a particular sequence of music. Very occasionally I'll get so blown away by a performance that I switch it off for maybe twenty minutes, and then I'll come out feeling absolutely elated because it's been so wonderful, but it takes something absolutely brilliant to do that.

The same is true when I go to concerts. I shouldn't be thinking, 'Is that out of tune? Are the cellos playing a little bit too loud there?' I should be just transported into the world of the music. But I find that I can't do that. I've lost the ability to go into a concert or a film and enjoy it as a normal member of the audience. But I wouldn't want to do anything else for a living, so ... it's horses for courses.

People often say to me, 'Oh, the film world is very male-dominated', which it is. 'How do you feel about working with so many men and so few women?' And my answer is that it doesn't really occur to me. The leader of the Royal Philharmonic Orchestra, which I work with a lot, is a woman (Clio Gould), and these days I also work with a lot of female directors and editors. Every composer has his or her own voice and that voice is a reflection of their personality and the way they hear their music. I don't think it's gender-based at all.

People have said to me, 'Gosh, I was listening to your music for *Arsène Lupin*' – which is a French action adventure film that has full-on, what you might term 'masculine' music – 'and I didn't know that a woman could *write* that sort of music.' That's quite an odd thing to say, because writing powerful music doesn't require any attributes of male physicality. It's just the way you put the music on the page and orchestrate it.

I was really interested by the question on your list about whether there's a piece of my work that I feel best sums me up as a composer. And the truthful answer is no, because I don't feel that I'm in a sum-uppable position, if you know what I mean. For me, being a composer is an ongoing process, and I don't feel that I'm anywhere near where I should be, or where I hopefully will end up, in terms of my development and ability. There are some scores of which I feel particularly proud; *Arsène Lupin* had two hours of music in it, in a fabulous array of styles – drama, comedy, action, romance and mystery. That was a huge challenge for me, and I was very thrilled that I managed to come out of it alive! But I feel that I have yet to write the single piece that is *it*, the piece that sums me up as a composer.

That's the wonderful thing about music. The greatest theme, the greatest piece of work, is just that tiny bit out of reach. It's that perfectionism thing again: will I ever get there? Will I write that one piece that makes me think, 'That's it, that's perfect'? I don't know!

Christopher Wright

Christopher Wright, Suffolk, March 2012

> **The purpose of composing isn't necessarily to please anyone, and it really *shouldn't* be.**

The first conversation in this book was with a composer who's firmly established as a leading figure in contemporary British music. This final one is with a composer whose name will be unknown to most readers unless they've read about the recordings of his music. Few, probably, will have heard those recordings and even fewer will have heard any of his music performed live. They may therefore wonder why I wanted to interview him for this book.

Apart from what I believe to be the quality of his music, there was the fact that his relative lack of success raises questions about the definition of a composer. Is this someone who makes money, if not necessarily a living, from writing music? Christopher Wright has received very few commissions, and during his professional life composing has effectively been his hobby – albeit one that he has taken very seriously. So is a composer simply someone whose music is performed in public? Wright's has had very few performances, and until the concert premiere of his Violin Concerto in 2012 most of these were of his smaller-scale, chamber or vocal works.

The Concerto is perhaps his biggest success to date, and its studio recording in 2011 was reviewed positively by *BBC Music Magazine*, *International Record Review* and *The Strad*. But recordings of contemporary music, and indeed of classical music from most periods, are no longer made unless the majority of the cost is met by sponsorship, often from the composer himself (or from his estate). So Wright isn't unusual in having to fund recordings of his own work. Where he differs from his contemporaries is that without these recordings he would never have heard most of his music.

'In August 2009, Christopher Wright lost his wife Ruth to cancer', Elis Pehkonen wrote in the booklet note for the Dutton recording of the Violin Concerto. 'His close friends were fearful that this loss would shatter his musical confidence.' It didn't, and he wrote the Concerto, subtitled *And then there was silence*, within a short space of time the following year. But Ruth still seemed present by her absence from his home when I interviewed him there in March 2012. Although unused (I imagine) to being interviewed about his music, he retained the authority of an experienced teacher and was thoughtful and articulate in his responses.

Eighteen months later he went through a difficult period, questioning the worth of a piece of his chamber music after hearing it performed and – not surprisingly – enduring anxiety about the recording of a large-scale orchestral work. For a while he even considered withdrawing his contribution to this book. I was pleased that he decided not to (after the recording session went very well), not least because the self-doubt he experienced is surely common to all composers, even if few admit to it.

Is a novelist any less of a writer if his novels remain unread by the public? Or a painter less of an artist if his canvases remain unseen? Christopher Wright has become no more of a composer since his music has been available on disc; what has changed is that he no longer communicates into a void, for the public can now hear what he wants to say. So I believe there's another reason why it's appropriate that this book ends with my encounter with him. Meeting him and his music has been a cause for not only gratitude but also wonder – at how many other Christopher Wrights may be out there and whose music I may never hear.

———

When I was a teenager it was wonderful to go to Aldeburgh and think, 'I'm walking on hallowed ground, almost – this is where Benjamin Britten lives.' It made me reflect on the two very different worlds of professional and amateur music-making, because at that time I very much belonged to the latter – and in fact I seem to have remained in it for most of my life.

My family wasn't musical in the accepted sense of the word, but they encouraged me a great deal in my musical interests. When I was eight I started to have piano lessons, only to give them up and then restart them during my teens; and at the age of eleven I taught myself to play the trombone. There wasn't much music at school, so I joined the local brass band and later a youth orchestra, and this both broadened my musical experience and helped me to decide that my real musical interest was composition. *That* was what I really wanted to do.

I went to study music at the Colchester Institute (it was then the North-East Essex Technical College), where I was delighted to receive formal music tuition for the first time in my life. What with learning about music history, studying harmony and counterpoint, the use of a well-stocked library and, of course, making lots of music ... oh, I was in my element! I later specialised in composition, had lessons with the late Richard (Tony) Arnell and took a degree. But I needed to earn a living, so I decided on a career in teaching.

At that time I had the rather naïve notion that a composer earned a living by selling scores to music shops, in rather the same way that an author sells books! Which was ridiculous, of course. Only later did I realise that a composer's income is from commissions and royalties, along with residencies, lectureships and publishers' retainers. That world seemed to me then a rather closed, exclusive one, and it still does.

As a composer you have a musical idea – a kind of aural picture in your mind – which you then try to make sense of on paper. And for me, this is the most difficult part of the process of composition. The other big problem is that music has to be *heard* in order to live. Composing should never be only an academic exercise, but until what you've written is actually performed it remains a series of graphic designs that are really quite meaningless. And, in my experience, finding performers is an enormous challenge. Many amateurs shy away from contemporary music, and professional performances, especially of orchestral music, are almost impossible to obtain. This is why I embarked on making professional recordings of my music in 2007, at the suggestion of my late wife. The idea was simply to find out what my music sounded like. Of course, it could have all been a humiliating flop, but it seems to have worked.

My first reaction to these recording sessions was amazement at how brilliantly the music was played. My second reaction was relief that the music worked, because until you hear your own music you can never be absolutely sure how it will turn out and whether you'll end up with egg on your face. After all, if there's a problem, it's usually considered to be the composer's fault! And I'd never previously been able to guarantee that what was written on the paper would be performed as it should be. I've never had the privilege of being a composer in residence to a professional orchestra (or to any group of musicians, come to that), which would have given me the opportunity to explore ideas and try them out. So I've always had to rely on imagination, basic knowledge and the limited experience gained from just a few performances in the past. I'm sure this is typical for many composers, actually, and it makes you very careful about how you write.

An interesting comment made by a performer in one of my recordings after she learned that I'd been a trombonist was that she felt that I'd probably be a good orchestrator. It's certainly true that a trombonist can spend a great deal of time counting rests, and I confess to missing the occasional cue because of being over-absorbed in what the rest of the orchestra was up to. So yes, listening and working from the inside, so to speak, has been a great help. It's all gone into the learning pot!

It's difficult to talk about influences on my music because there are so many of them. I'm not much of a pianist, so I've learned repertoire mostly by listening to other musicians performing and of course by studying scores. And most of this repertoire is orchestral music. The first scores I tried to follow were by Stravinsky, Tchaikovsky and Vaughan Williams because I just loved the sounds that these composers made. I didn't understand much of what I saw or heard, but it excited me.

By my mid-teens it was twentieth-century British music that generally captivated me, and Holst in particular that excited my imagination. Having heard *The Planets*, I wanted to explore everything Holstian, including his written essays about music. I was particularly fascinated by his *Terzetto* for Flute, Oboe and Viola and his wonderful setting of Henry Vaughn's poem 'The Evening Watch' for eight-part unaccompanied choir. Later on I moved from cerebral Holst to heart-rending Walton, whose deeply passionate and romantic music still enthrals me. (My *Spring Overture* is a consciously Waltonian piece.) Of course, there have been, and there still are, many other composers and influences that fascinate me: Bartók, Hindemith, Ravel and Debussy, for instance. The list is endless, actually. But my heart still lies very much on home territory.

I remember that when I was a student I was set an essay question on the lines of: which composer, Britten or Walton, will be heard more in thirty or forty years' time? The subject intrigued me, not only because I was a native of Suffolk – Britten's home – but also because of my adoration of Walton's music. Looking back with forty years' hindsight, I think I would answer the question now with less personal bias. There is, I think, a coldness – or perhaps a reserve – in Britten's music that can be attributed to the landscape that inspired him and which is also superficially present in the character of Suffolk people. There's also, in both Britten and Suffolk people generally, a great deal of practicality. We're very pragmatic folk! Passion is very much present, too, but it lies beneath the surface. Walton, on the other hand, seems to me to display his passion much more directly – there's no specific landscape driving his personality or his music. And because of this, I believe that Walton's music reaches out more readily – it's warmer. (All this is a very personal view, and undoubtedly at odds with what many other people think.)

The intervening years have answered that original essay question. And, thankfully, now that we live in a postmodern world there's equal room for both composers. In recent years there's been greater acceptance of emotional expression in music, not just of the cerebral or intellectual processes behind it, and I think that's a very good thing.

I start composing from what I hear in my mind, and that can cover quite a wide spectrum of sounds because I'm very 'schizophrenic', musically! Some of what I want to write verges on atonality, while some is purely tonal, or diatonic; and I liberally mix the two. My 'aural pictures' – the musical sounds imagined in my head – are essentially tonal in character, and I find that tonality still offers the most liberating way to express musical thought because of its intrinsic potential for variety, particularly when contrasted against the extreme chromaticism of atonality. (It's interesting that Schoenberg often described his music as 'pan-tonal' or polytonal – maybe a good precept!) But I'm not really concerned with musical 'systems'. For me, they're merely an aid to the composition process.

Nor am I concerned with fashion, and whether I'm doing what other composers are doing, or whether I'm doing what I *should* be doing. I need to be ... ruthless, I suppose, about it: I say, 'Well, if people don't like it, too bad.' For me, the purpose of composing isn't necessarily to please anyone, and it really *shouldn't* be – although sometimes there is a need to entertain. I compose in order to communicate something of myself. Music is my one vehicle for self-expression. I'm not a wordsmith, I don't paint and I'm not a hugely sociable person; so if people want to know me, they have to know my music. That's where I am.

When I begin a new piece I try to think broadly, in terms of its overall effect, structure and sound. And the type of piece I'm writing will determine the degree and extent of pre-planning. Detailed notes, yes – those will be thought through in my head first of all, then tried out on the piano and finally transcribed on the computer. There's always an element of ... not trial and error but of rethinking a phrase or chord if necessary. An intellectual process will guide the course of the music but, as I said earlier, composing is never a purely academic exercise. The music always goes where the ear takes it, and I find that quite often it doesn't take the most obvious or logical path.

As I also said, expressing the music in detailed notation is for me the most difficult part of this process, and it's made even more difficult by the number of false starts that can be involved. I often find myself returning to my original ideas or thoughts about the piece, perhaps because experience has made it easier for me to express what I want to say. I now have a better idea of what will or won't work, technically, and how far I can push the boat out, so to speak, or how far I should rein it in.

I tend to think primarily in terms of melody, although colour is also very important to me. I conceived my Oboe Concerto as pure melody from beginning to end, whereas my Violin Concerto explores it with an emphasis on texture and colour as well. Then there's my Wind Quintet, which is multi-faceted – and essentially atonal (but not serial). My four String Quartets show well how my music has progressed over the last forty years, since this is the single genre in which I've composed consistently. In other words, the four Quartets span my composing life.

A few years ago I composed an ensemble piece, *Munrow's Muse*, celebrating the life and work of the late David Munrow.[1] The work was to be recorded, so there was a cut-off date for completion. And I finished it with some three months to spare. But during that period I kept brooding on it – a bit too much – and changing little details, sometimes on a daily basis, until my wife told me to just leave it alone! The moral of this story is that a composer can sometimes have too much time, or at least can *spend* too much time, poring over a work and constantly revising it, possibly out of all recognition. This can become an obsession, in fact. So self-imposed limits can often be a helpful discipline for the composer, because they concentrate the mind.

Revisiting older works and completely revising them is something that I do rarely, unless it's to make an adaptation of some kind. Let's remember: when you compose a piece of music you're capturing the moment in time that you're at – which includes your environment, your knowledge and your experience. So I don't think you should go back to the music that you wrote, say, twenty years ago and alter it just because you don't compose like that any more. That would be like trying to rewrite history. On the other hand, I often adjust technical details of my music, particularly in early works that are being prepared for a first performance or a recording. Hearing my music has had an enormous impact on my technique because what I've learned as a result has enabled me to write more clearly and more succinctly, and I sometimes wonder whether I would have got to this point far sooner had things been otherwise. Sadly, this is something that I could change only if I were Doctor Who! You see, I still believe in craftsmanship: you learn your craft, *then* you practice your art.

---

[1] British musician and early music historian (1942–76).

Having said this, I'm now far less analytical when composing than I used to be, and instead of being overly cognitive I rely far more on my subconscious to do the work. I think that perhaps too much emphasis is placed on controlling music – by which I mean packaging the creative process rather than focussing on the end result and its substance and content. As I said earlier, composing is for me about the end, not the means.

You suggest that there was a period when some forms of tonal music were considered 'old hat' in this country. And you're probably right, in that this was the position held by many academics, promoters, critics and broadcasters. Some might say that these are the only people whose views on music count, but what about those of the musical public? I think it's possible to argue that one of the main reasons for the general decline of interest in contemporary 'art music' in the last half-century is that composers have been too 'cerebral' (intellectual or academic) in their approach to composing, and therefore too removed from their audiences. For a composer to write a tune, or a piece that could be enjoyed in simple terms, was and still is a mortal sin in some circles! (I expect to be committed to the musical Tower of London for making this statement.) There has been an explosion in popular culture that hasn't helped, because it has made what contemporary composers do seem more obscure or marginal; and we're *all* guilty, I think, of forgetting our audiences from time to time. But we're *not* all guilty of ... well, holding them in a kind of contempt!

Of course, the issues are more complex than I'm implying. I admit that. For example, I believe that the avant-garde has made a positive contribution in getting us to think afresh about the nature and purpose of contemporary music. But an unfortunate outcome has been the monopolisation of the musical establishment, to the detriment of what might be called mainstream music. And this has been particularly noticeable in composition study at university. Composition as a research subject has displaced composition as *music*, and this has resulted in the creation of contrived originality. Perhaps we're all now coming to our senses, because in recent years there's been a kind of realignment and a much greater tolerance of tonality. Composers are connecting far more with their public, and this bodes well for the survival of serious classical music. As to *why* this has happened ... well, there are probably multifarious reasons, some perhaps more cynical than others!

The differences in status between amateur and professional musicians are difficult to define. When we began this interview I suggested that the most obvious ones are between desire and outcome, by which I mean the opportunities that exist for one group but not for the other, particularly regarding remuneration (or the lack of it). But we shouldn't underestimate – nor overestimate, for that matter – the difference in the degrees of competence and awareness possessed by the two groups. Some professionals may be more competent technically, but some amateurs may have far greater musical awareness. And much of this is dependent on education, experience and preconditioning.

I believe Berg wrote that it doesn't matter whether the listener's unaware of the musical processes involved in composing, since that's the composer's domain. And I recall Tony Arnell asking me if I'd recognised in his Sixth Symphony the reference he'd made in it to Beethoven's final string quartet; I hadn't, and he was somewhat pleased at this. The composer probably *is* more concerned than the listener with the business of how music is made and put together, but we shouldn't assume that the listener (defined as the amateur, for the purposes of this argument) isn't interested in this at all. The issue is whether knowledge of the music's construction enhances or hinders the aesthetic experience of listening to it.

On the other hand, it may be that the composer himself doesn't always have a full understanding of what he's doing in his work because the subconscious takes over while he's doing it. I recall that Alan Walker makes this point in his book *A Study in Musical Analysis*, and I believe that Copland refers to it in his book *What to Listen for in Music*.[2]

Our response to music is, I believe, essentially subjective. And it has to be, because music is an art form whose basis is emotional response, not scientific proof. (Again, I know that many people would completely disagree with me, and for a variety of reasons.) If this weren't so, it would beg the question 'So is it then *music* – in the widely accepted definition of the word?' Perhaps all I can add is that I echo Malcolm Arnold's sentiment: 'I write the kind of music that I'd want to listen to.'

A number of factors will tend to determine whether a composer has success early in his career. They include time, the availability of resources, opportunities and possibly luck, and they're available to only a small minority. So the notion of early success is, to me, rather contrived. I

---

[2] Alan Walker, *A Study in Musical Analysis* (London, Barrie & Rockliff 1962); Aaron Copland, *What to Listen for in Music* (New York, McGraw-Hill Book Company, 1939; revised 1957).

can see that it might also be a double-edged sword. One of the main advantages of early success is that with youth comes the energy to cope with it and to exploit the results, but it might also put pressure on a young composer to repeat or better that success before he's ready to. The benefit of age, usually, is that it brings experience; but that's perhaps a little undervalued in our culture. A composer friend told me recently that he keeps quiet about his age for fear that it might have a detrimental effect on encouraging performances of his music!

For me, success as a composer isn't measured in fame or fortune. It's about obtaining performances of my music. Sadly, the two things are often inextricably linked, and I think I would have found it helpful to experience a little 'success' earlier in my career. I can't say that many performances of my music have materialised since making all these recordings – especially performances of my orchestral works – but at least the music can now be heard. For me, that's what it's all about, and it encourages me to carry on composing.

Appendix:
Advice for the Young Composer

Joseph Phibbs's remark about being inspired by the discovery of Paul Griffiths's *New Sounds, New Personalities* in his school library encouraged me to hope that the present collection of interviews might have a similar influence on budding British composers of the future. So, for those who will read this as they are either considering whether to enter the profession or are already trying to make their mark in it, I invited the contributors to offer their most important piece of advice.

Julian Anderson: Listen widely, read widely. Whether you prefer to improvise or notate your music, learn Western music notation, because it's a wonderful and flexible tool, especially nowadays. You can always decide not to use it for a time, but there's much more freedom in knowing than in not knowing. Young composers, like anyone else, need skills and tools to express themselves properly.

Don't be restricted by the first music you liked. Even music you initially hate may turn out to be vitally important to you. So when you get to know a new piece of music always try to listen three or four times before forming any judgement. When you have a piece of your own played, listen carefully to the result, as if it was by someone else. If it doesn't excite or attract you, there's something wrong somewhere.

Simon Bainbridge: You have to have absolute faith in what you're writing. At the same time, a composer's life is one of discovery, and you mustn't get so fixed in one area of work that it becomes a comfort zone. You've got to keep moving forward, constantly testing boundaries and finding new directions for your work. And this will become more and more difficult as you get older. Above all, you must think about your audience but *never* write down to them.

Sally Beamish: Keep writing, even if what you write seems like rubbish, because you have to keep flexing the muscle. Students often say things like 'Is this okay?' and 'I don't want to be too obvious', or they may have a really strong idea but sort of fuzz it around the edges because they feel the music has to have something different in every bar. But why not stick with one good idea for a whole piece? Switch off that self-critical voice a bit and just tap into what's inside you. Don't be embarrassed or ashamed; be prepared to make mistakes and to learn.

George Benjamin: Love music. Study new music – *all* music, in fact. Be curious, be determined, be daring, be patient. Trust but nurture your instinct. Find something of your own to do, and follow your own path. Get as much technique as you can. And, unquestionably, train your imagination to *hear* in your mind everything you write.

Michael Berkeley: Have open ears *and* eyes. Don't confine yourself to the language of music, but take in contemporary writing, contemporary theatre and contemporary visual art as well. And, above all, have the courage to be yourself. We live in a world in which the notion of celebrity seems to determine whether or not things are good, and in which people feel they should jump on a particular bandwagon; but you have to resist this if you're going to be original. So do what excites *you* even if it's not fashionable.

More practically, encourage your friends to play your music, write for what's available to you so that you get to hear it, and learn technique so that you can put what you want to say on the page in such a way that it comes *off* the page. The other thing I would say to a young composer is: don't feel frightened if it takes you time to find your own voice. Unless you're prodigiously gifted, you won't find it instantly. You'll have to work at it.

Judith Bingham: It's very hard when you're a young composer. There are so many people willing to give you unhelpful advice. And worrying all the time about not writing the right sort of music, or not being in the right group or being made to feel that you're not very talented like the whizz-kid over there who's the next Mozart can really hold you up. So try not to listen too much to all the chatter that's going on around you. Zone that out a bit and focus on your internal voice – what your own imagination wants to do.

Harrison Birtwistle: Do you want the cynical answer? Don't expect anybody to like what you write!

Howard Blake: Keep writing. And don't give up your day job! If you want to compose, compose; but don't expect miracles. It will be a very hard road, because people won't fall over you and say, 'What a marvellous thing you're doing', and they won't say, 'We'd like you to write a symphony.' You'll do it because you love doing it.

Gavin Bryars: First, listen to as much music as you can, and always with an open mind, not with a predisposition for or against it. However alienating a piece might seem, see if you can find something of use in it. Second, keep yourself mentally agile. Don't get stuck. Always prepare to bounce in a new direction. Third, and above all, consolidate your craft. Make sure that you have enough technique to express what your mind and heart want to say.

Diana Burrell: Young composers are always tempted to think, 'So-and-so's doing incredibly well, writing that sort of music, so *I* should be writing it, too.' But they need to find the courage to do their own thing. There are a million composers in the world and we don't really *need* any more music, so there's no point in writing any unless it includes something of you that's special, something that no-one else has got. Otherwise, composing involves pasting on something that you don't have – and that's not being true to yourself.

Tom Coult: Apart from 'Ask someone older', you mean? Get some good pencils – that's important! I'm not sure that I can offer anything more substantive than that. The thing is, I don't feel I have enough perspective to be anything other than flippant. I'm still waiting for my older self to give my current self the advice! But if I were to give advice to a younger version of me, I'd say, 'Listen to as much music as possible.' I don't think there's any excuse not to do that, really. It's what made me a musician and what makes me a better composer.

Gordon Crosse: Your performing abilities matter. You won't get on very well as a composer if you can't play at least one instrument. I never did, and this hasn't been helpful. In general, what helps is having a partner or spouse whose aim in life is to make life smooth for you; but that, almost by definition, is a difficult thing to achieve in a marriage. And it probably explains the number of divorces that there are!

Jonathan Dove: Write the music that you want to hear. And say yes to any project that seems interesting, regardless of whether it was something you were expecting to do and regardless of how well it's paid. When I was starting out, the most interesting projects were paid nothing, but they taught me everything. Doing interesting work is how you grow.

David Dubery: Composing isn't easy to teach to people who are trying to develop their own musical personalities and styles. What they need is practical knowledge about the techniques that make their music playable. When I study the scores of revered works I'm struck by their clarity – even *The Rite of Spring* isn't as complex to the eye as it sounds to the ear. So give thought to the musicians you're writing for, and don't have expectations that are beyond their capabilities. And be sure to make your intentions as clear as possible in your scores. It's rather like coaching an actor: 'Speak clearly so that we can both hear and understand you.' *That's* communication. Remember that if you don't have your music performed no-one will know it exists, and you may never know whether or not your score works. And if it's poorly performed, its potential may never be recognised. So choose your works and their performers accordingly.

Finally, a word of caution. Learn as much as you can about how the music industry operates and be aware of those who would try to control or manipulate your music in order to raise their own profiles or commercial interests. It's a ruthless industry overbrimming with insatiable egos – in many camps.

Michael Finnissy: Learning is a responsibility. The sacred fire must be kept alight, and one should try to find ways of handing something on. It is, however, impossible to learn 'composition'; you can only learn the handling of it, the tools involved and how to fall down without causing too much damage. So the advice I would offer is: follow your nose. Which means: believe in, and be, yourself.

Cheryl Frances-Hoad: As long as you're okay being by yourself, can learn to fill in lots of application forms, can learn to be a shameless self-publicist and don't mind being incredibly poor at least some of the time, you'll be okay as a composer! So never give up. If you're really passionate about what you do, it will all work out in the end. Just write what you want and (within reason) don't give a toss about what anybody else thinks – but *always* take every piece of advice given to you by really good performers. They're the only people you should always take notice of.

Alexander Goehr: I can offer one piece of advice: when I first joined the staff at Cambridge I suggested putting up a banner over the Music Faculty that read, 'Here we do not "express ourselves"!'

Howard Goodall: Don't be precious. I think it's a myth that great art is achieved by people who stand their ground and do what they want to do, against the whole world. Even if that *was* once the case, it certainly isn't now. In Mozart's time there were so few key people involved in making European culture that most of them actually met each other – it was a small world. Today, that's simply not the case. There are millions of us and we're all doing different things. What's more, we live in a world in which art is collaborative – and that includes the audience. So it's probably good not to think that what you're doing is going to change the world. Just do your bit, and do your best. I wish someone had said this to *me*!

Christopher Gunning: My advice is *almost* 'Don't do it.' Almost, but not quite. It's 'Don't do it unless you're absolutely, 100 per cent committed to it.' And even if you're totally committed, have some other option up your sleeve because, due to the way things work in this country and in Europe generally, it's going to be very, very difficult to make a living from composition. You've got to be practical as well as idealistic.

Morgan Hayes: Write from an inner compulsion, from what drives *you*, rather than from thinking, 'This is the kind of music that will enhance my career because it's what the London Sinfonietta would like.' But don't be afraid to model yourself on other composers, because that's probably the best way of developing any kind of individual voice. It's *not* copying. If you were to ask four composers to write, say, a Bach chorale, each of them would approach the task slightly differently even though they weren't doing so in idiosyncratic ways. And the differences in the music that resulted would be interesting. So, whichever composers you decide to model yourself on, go into their music in a very deep way by exploring a lot of their works.

Robin Holloway: Several people have told me, with amusement, that when they were at Cambridge, aged eighteen or nineteen, the best thing I did for them was to show them that they weren't composers.

There's got to be the deed as well as the will; and if you can't do the deed, the will's neither here nor there. So sometimes the best advice is: 'Don't do it!' And if that advice is wrong, it will probably be a spur – they'll respond, 'Sod him! I *am* a composer, and I'll prove it.' More generally, I can't do better than repeat what Stravinsky said: we have a duty towards music – to compose it. As well as we can; and true to the inner vision, whatever its nature.

Oliver Knussen: Take in as much as you can of what's going on around you, and find yourself a good (and tough!) teacher. And write, write, write while you've got the freedom to make mistakes away from the limelight. By writing as much as you can now, you'll exercise your imagination and acquire the experience and technique to stand you in good stead when life becomes more problematical later on – as it will.

John McCabe: I wouldn't wish to put anybody off being a composer. I've loved every minute of it. But it's very much harder than it was even thirty years ago to get a second performance. A lot of obstacles are put in your way, like soloists and orchestras who won't play a piece that was written for somebody else. There's a lot of that kind of thing, and it doesn't help music at all. So listen to advice, take from it what you find helpful and then write what you absolutely have to write. Never consider the audience, never consider your bank balance. And then, if you're lucky enough to have an idea that's successful, good!

James MacMillan: Always stay close – physically, practically or professionally – to your fellow musicians. Even just being friends with them is important, because they'll be your first interpreters. And maybe the students that you spend a lot of time with will be the first people who commission a piece from you. The other important relationships for a composer are with artists in spheres other than music, because they can be a huge intellectual inspiration.

Colin Matthews: I don't know whether I can go any further than saying: Be absolutely certain that this is what you want to do, and about what it entails, because it's not easy!

David Matthews: I see quite a lot of young students' music, and much of it is post-Birtwistle or post-Adès in style. This suggests that it's very difficult today to write openly romantic music in an unselfconscious way, if that's what you feel you have to do as a composer. Yet it shouldn't be impossible. It's also quite difficult to write pieces that are consciously happy without falling into clichés. For a long time I thought my music was rather unfashionable – it was *very* unfashionable when I started writing – but times have changed, and I feel much more secure now about what I do. So I'm going to say what every other contributor to this book will probably say, which is: try to find your own voice. It's very important, I think, to hold fast to one's inner vision and not get led astray by trying to be fashionable.

Peter Maxwell Davies: I would answer this question with just two words: Alexander Goehr. Getting to know how he thought about music was the most constructive influence on me as a student because it had a rigour that I found nowhere else at college and university – not in other students and not in the staff. He didn't give me advice; he simply set, by example, a standard of thinking about music which, in my experience, was unprecedented. And I don't know how young composers today can find and maintain that kind of rigour. So I would say to them, 'Don't take notice of any advice that I, or anybody else, might give you. Just be yourself. But be it *absolutely*, and with rigour – which will involve a hell of a lot of work.'

Thea Musgrave: Make friends with performers. They're the people who are going to play your music, so get to know them and their instruments, and pick their brains about all the practical aspects of realising your music. There's always a lot to learn about your craft!

Roxanna Panufnik: It's what my father and mother have always said to me: be yourself, because it's the only way you'll stand out from the crowd. It's not difficult for me to say this now that I'm older, because with age comes confidence. When I was younger I was just plain stubborn, and I was helped further by being given plenty of moral support by my nearest and dearest. It's the case that, whatever field you choose to work in, you can do *anything* if you have love, support and optimism.

Anthony Payne: To feel that you're not quite in tune with the times, and not in the same musical world as most of your contemporaries, can be painful. You look around and see that composers of a certain style are getting all the breaks, and you think, 'Why aren't they asking *me*? It's because they think I'm old-fashioned.' But you mustn't worry about things like that. You can only really be yourself, so just write your own music. If you're an original person, it'll turn out to be original. And if you're not, it won't. And if you get to the age of forty and you're *still* not getting performances, carry on anyway. It's rather simple advice, I know, but who's to say that your music won't be performed in, say, forty years' time? Think of how people used to react to Rachmaninov: he was considered a second-rate old Romantic, fifty years out of date. Now we just think of him as an extremely good composer.

Elis Pehkonen: My immediate response is to think of Schoenberg's remark, 'There is still plenty of good music to be written in C major.' Maybe few readers of this book will recall Terry Riley's *In C*, but the point still needs to be made! Otherwise, I've only one observation, really. I know this sounds hackneyed, but you have to be true to yourself. Don't be too swayed by what other people are doing. Follow your instinct.

Joseph Phibbs: I think there are still stylistic pressures on young composers. They feel they have to adopt a certain way of writing in order to fulfil expectations, whether at university level or beyond. There *are* fashions and there *are* fads, and there will always be certain promoters and institutions and performers and so on who are only going to like a certain type of 'new music' – whether it's simple or complex. But worrying about this can be destructive and it can also be very limiting in preventing composers from really blossoming in an authentic way. So, if I were to give any advice, it would probably be to have the courage to do your own thing musically.

Gabriel Prokofiev: There's no such thing as waiting for inspiration. So having a habit and a routine in composing is very important. Try to make sure that you're always composing – just creating material all the time, even if it's not for a specific project. One reason is that the more you do this the more likely you are to come up with interesting material; another reason is that ideas don't always come even when you're facing a deadline, and so it's useful to have a battery of sketches to refer to. I've often done this and it has proved invaluable. Sometimes I'll find old sketches from a year ago and think, 'Did I write this, or did someone else sneak it in here?' That can be very exciting because I can look at the material in a more objective and critical way.

The other thing I'd say is: try to stay in touch with what *you* want to hear. Don't feel that you need to compose in a particular way or in the style of a particular teacher or composer. It's fine to be inspired and influenced by others, but if you start to follow them you're not necessarily being true to yourself. So don't feel that there's a correct way or a true path. There isn't one. When we study musical history we see that there have been these 'schools' and directions in music, but history is written after the event.

John Rutter: I'm sorry, but the most important advice is pure cliché. It's: be true to yourself. Write the music that you really want to write, regardless of what anybody thinks of it and regardless of what the fashion is. Having said that, you should experiment as widely as you can in as many genres as possible. If you know you're a specialist, then okay, specialise; but my belief is that one branch of music informs another. So if you're offered a film score and you don't think of yourself as a film composer, don't turn it down, because you'll learn things from doing it. Next, take every opportunity you possibly can to get your work performed, because that's more instructive than any number of composition seminars.

And the last bit of advice is to get your work out there – but not too soon. I see composers who are gifted but whose work isn't ready for the public: they're getting performances even though they have rather too little knowledge of how to write. And all this does is harm, because people remember something that doesn't work. So first try to be the best composer you can be, and *then* market what you're writing.

Robert Saxton: Frank Bridge advised the young Britten, 'Find yourself, and be true to what you find', and I'm not sure there's a better piece of advice than that. I would add that whatever you've got to say as a composer you must know your craft, because you're communicating your ideas through performers. So work very hard at fulfilling your ideas in as technically professional a way as you can.

John Tavener: You have to believe, almost to bursting point, that you have something that you've absolutely got to write down. I don't think it matters what's going to become of it, and whether or not it's ever recognised; you just have to reach that state where you're bursting to write it down – for some mad reason!

Judith Weir: Young composers often feel that they must constantly be sending their scores here and there – to panels and so on – and therefore they believe that a piece should *look* impressive on paper. And I don't blame them for this. But it's up to those who are reading a score to use their knowledge and judgement in making what will anyway be just a personal opinion. A score is just a blueprint. You can't forget about it when you've spent so many months writing it, but what you should be looking for is that moment when performers first sit down and make some sounds, or maybe even when the music reaches the ears of an audience. The score is just something that gets you to that point.

More generally, you should think of something that you want to do, and do that thing. At least, don't feel that you have to do everything or even several things at once if you don't want to. Listeners and performers may want a particular thing to come out of your piece and – preferably – will be able to explain what they take from it; but they may not take what you thought you'd given them! So the best composition is one in which you do a particular thing in your own way.

Debbie Wiseman: There are a lot more people wanting to enter the profession than there are commissions, and it's incredibly difficult to get a foot in the door now, I think. And being a composer is all-consuming: there's very little social life, certainly when you're building a career, and a lot that you have to give up. So you have to want to do it for the right reasons – not in order to be famous or to have lots of money but simply because you want to write music more than you want to do anything else. Because at the end, that's all there is: it's just you and your music, and that has to be fulfilling in itself. So the most valuable quality that you can have is tenacity. Just keep going, and try to develop your own voice – something that you feel is *you*. There are opportunities to just copy something that's been hugely successful, but that doesn't produce interesting new music.

Christopher Wright: All my life I've been given professional advice, some of it well intentioned. On more occasions than not I've taken that advice, and none of it has been of any worth. So my advice is: don't take any advice, because it will probably reveal more about the giver than be of use to the recipient! And also, of course: be yourself.

Index

Actors Centre, xiv
Adams, John, 151, 287, 318, 441
Adès, Thomas, xvii, 58, 129, 237, 261, 287, 482
   Asyla, 400
Aimard, Pierre-Laurent, 49
Alchemist, The (Ben Jonson), 142
Aldeburgh Festival, ix, xiii, xvii, 25, 138, 238, 300, 301
Alexander Korda Award, xxiii
Almeida Theatre, xiv
American Academy of Arts and Letters, xv
Anderson, Julian, ix, 129, 173, 197, 254, 261
   (Interview 8–16)
   Alhambra Fantasy, 14
   Diptych, ix, 13, 14
   Fantasias, 15, 16
   Khorovod, 13, 14
   Stations of the Sun, 14, 15
   Symphony, 11–12
   The Bearded Lady, 14
   The Discovery of Heaven, 11
   Tiramisù, 14
Aphex Twin, 126
Aprahamian, Felix, 60
Archbishop of Canterbury, xxii, 61
Arditti, David, 162
Arditti Quartet, 86
Arnell, Richard, xxiii, 469, 474
   Symphony No.6, 474
Arnold, Sir Malcolm, 30, 110, 474
   Overture: *Tam o'Shanter*, 30
   Overture: *The Roots of Heaven*, 274
Arts and Humanities Research Council, 187
Arts Council England, 337
Association of Professional Composers, 231

Atkinson, Rowan, 218
Atonement (Dario Marianelli), 462
Austin, Christopher, 241
Austrian Cultural Forum, London, xiii
Avengers, The, 92, 95

Babbitt, Milton, xix, 235, 240, 262, 264, 301
Bach Choir, xxi
Bach, J. S., 49, 50, 95, 105, 122, 126, 128, 163, 174, 178, 198, 210, 218, 219, 226, 230, 240, 249, 386, 387, 388, 396, 399, 410, 425, 426, 481
   Brandenburg Concertos, 179
   Magnificat, 413
   The Art of Fugue, 250, 436
   The Well-Tempered Clavier (48 Preludes and Fugues), 180
Bacon, Francis, 87, 205
BAFTA (British Academy of Film and Television Arts), xvi
Bailey, Derek, xii
Bainbridge, Simon, ix, xvi, 244
   (Interview 20–26)
   Ad Ora Incerta, 25
   Double Concerto, ix
   Fantasia for Double Orchestra, ix, 21
   Horn Concerto 'Landscape and Memory', ix
   Music, Space, Reflection, 21
   Spirogyra, ix, 25
   String Quartet No.2 'Mehretu', 23
   Three Pieces for Orchestra, ix
   Toccata for Orchestra, ix
   Viola Concerto, ix, 20, 21
Balakirev, Mily
   Symphony No.1, 274
Band of the Coldstream Guards, 211

Index

Barbican Centre, 331, 343
Barbirolli, Sir John, 81, 274
Barrett, Richard, 237
Barry, Gerald
   Chevaux de Frise, 236, 239
Barry, John, 462
Bartók, Béla, 57, 98, 161, 174, 199, 227,
   249, 312, 314, 361, 373, 387,
   422, 426, 470
   Mikrokosmos, 204
BASCA (British Academy of Songwriters,
   Composers and Authors), xv,
   xvi, xxiii, 191, 231
Bassey, Dame Shirley, xvi
Bath Spa University, xii
Bavarian Academy of Fine Arts, x
Bax, Sir Arnold, 359
   Symphony No.3, 274
BBC (British Broadcasting
   Corporation), xv, xx, 9, 60,
   107, 110, 121, 205, 231, 260,
   299, 302, 316, 325, 335, 337,
   349, 351, 359, 362, 373, 374,
   383, 397, 409
   BBC Choral Society (BBC Symphony
      Chorus), xi
   BBC Concert Orchestra, xxi
   BBC Music Magazine, 193, 467
   BBC National Orchestra of Wales, xi
   BBC Philharmonic Orchestra, xviii
   BBC Promenade Concerts (Proms),
      x, xvi, xx, xxi, 11, 42, 69, 82,
      87, 107, 116, 119, 122, 144,
      149, 155, 217, 237, 248, 261,
      285, 300, 317, 337, 364, 385,
      426, 440
      'Last Night of the Proms', xi, 87,
      383
   BBC Radio 3 (formerly 'Third
      Programme'), xi, xii, xix, xxi, 8,
      11, 63, 81, 110, 217, 311, 335,
      337, 350, 374, 427
      Essential Classics, 438
      Fifty Years of British Music, 8
      Music Matters, 311
      Private Passions, xi, 55, 63
   BBC Reith Lectures, xv
   BBC Scottish Symphony Orchestra,
      337
   BBC Singers, xi, 335, 336
   BBC Symphony Orchestra, xiii, xvi,
      xvii, 21, 149, 335, 336, 383, 388,
      426

BBC Young Composer Competition,
   xv
Beach Boys, The, 179
Beamish, Sally, x, 139
   (Interview 30–37)
   Cello Concertos, 37
   Commedia, 33
   Knotgrass Elegy, 31
   No, I'm Not Afraid, 33
   Spinal Chords, x, 33, 34
   Suite pour Violoncelle et Orchestre, 36
   Symphony No.1, 32
   Violin Concerto, 31
   Violin Sonata 'Winter Trees', 37
Beatles, The, 127, 442
   The White Album, 396
Becket, Samuel, 106
Beethoven, Ludwig van, xxii, 48, 50, 95,
   161, 163, 174, 178, 273, 274,
   290, 312, 422, 439
   Hammerklavier Sonata, 274
   String Quartet No.16, 474
   Symphony No.5, 96
   Symphony No.9, 328
Bellini, Vincenzo, 366
Benjamin, George, x, xiii, 125, 129, 197,
   261, 287
   (Interview 42–51)
   Into the Little Hill, 46
   Ringed by the Flat Horizon, x, 10, 42
   Three Inventions, 47
   Upon Silence, 47
   Written on Skin, 42, 43, 44, 46, 51
Benjamin, Walter, 176
Bennett, Alan, 254
Bennett, Sir Richard Rodney, xi, xvi, xx,
   57, 60, 61, 137, 140, 161, 163,
   225, 335, 338, 362, 374
   Richard Rodney Bennett Professorship
      of Music, xvii
Berg, Alban, 47, 49, 57, 59, 204, 237,
   252, 262, 314, 315, 361, 424,
   474
   Chamber Concerto, 266
   Lulu, 59, 251, 262
   Wozzeck, 59, 424
Berio, Luciano, xxii, 24, 31
   Sinfonia, 260
Berkeley, Sir Lennox, x, xx, xxii, 31, 55,
   56, 57, 58, 60, 374
Berkeley, Michael, x
   (Interview 56–64)
   Clarinet Concerto, 61, 62

Concerto for Orchestra, 61
Listen, Listen, O My Child, 61
Meditations, 57, 62
Oboe Concerto, 60, 62
Organ Concerto, 61, 62
Berlin Philharmonic Orchestra, x
Berlioz, Hector, 48, 70, 178, 424
   Benvenuto Cellini, 424
Bernstein, Leonard, 161, 163, 212, 411
Bingham, Judith, xi
   (Interview 68–75)
   Chartres, xi
   The Everlasting Crown, 71
Birmingham Festival Choral Society, 375
Birtwistle, Sir Harrison, xi, xv, xxi, 24, 31,
      57, 59, 61, 128, 137, 139–140,
      143, 197, 204, 260, 287, 288,
      361, 362, 378, 410, 421, 440,
      442, 482
   (Interview 80–88)
   Antiphonies, 84
   Carmen Arcadiae [Mechanicae Perpetuum], 87
   Earth Dances, 280
   Gawain's Journey, 280
   Love Cries, 61
   Panic, xi, 87
   Punch and Judy, xi
   Secret Theatre, 87
   The Moth Requiem, 82
   The Second Mrs Kong, 61
   The Triumph of Time, xi, 280
   Verses for Ensembles, xi
   Violin Concerto, 82, 84, 139, 440
Black, Cilla, xvi
Blackheath Concert Halls, 397, 401
Blake, Howard, xii
   (Interview 92–99)
   A Month in the Country, xii
   Benedictus, xii, 96
   Diversions, 95
   Piano Concerto, xii, 96
   The Duellists, xii, 95
   The Riddle of the Sands, 94
   The Rise of the House of Usher, 99
   The Snowman, xii, 91, 96
   Violin Concerto, xii, 98
Blake, William, 68
Bliss Prize, xv
Boosey & Hawkes, 86, 441
Booth, Claire, xiii
Borges International Electroacoustic Competition, 398

Borromini, Francesco, 332
Boston Conservatory of Music, ix
Boston Symphony Orchestra, xix
Boston University, 197
Bostridge, Ian, 307
Boulanger, Nadia, xix, 23, 57, 180, 337, 338
Boulez, Pierre, x, 10, 24, 42, 47, 49,
      57, 127, 130, 175, 197, 243,
      260, 302–303, 315, 360,
      375, 388
   Improvisations sur Mallarmé No.2, 264
   Le marteau sans maître, 261, 386
   Piano Sonata No.3, 362
   Pli selon pli, 10
Bowman, James, 160
Brabbins, Martyn, 326, 335, 336
Bragg, Melvyn, 218
Brahms, Johannes, 126, 199, 274, 388, 429
   Ein Deutsches Requiem, 408
   Saint Anthony Variations (Variations on a Theme by Joseph Haydn), 250
   Viola Sonatas, 20
   Violin Concerto, 98
Brakhage, Stan, 178
Brecht, Bertolt, 175
Brendel, Adrian, 86
Brian, Havergal, 9
   Gothic Symphony, 9
Bridge, Frank, xx, 359, 361, 485
Brighton Festival, 149
Britain's Got Talent, 209
British Composer Awards, xx, xxi
British Council, 106, 372
British Music Information Centre, 9, 237
Britten, Benjamin, x, xviii, xix, xx, xxi,
      xxii, 25, 30, 55, 56, 57, 58, 59,
      60, 61, 74, 138, 139, 140, 141,
      142, 144, 151, 161, 162, 163,
      188, 198, 200, 217, 227, 259,
      261, 262, 264, 265, 268, 281,
      287, 288, 292, 299, 301, 302,
      311, 312, 315, 316, 318, 328,
      350, 361, 367, 372, 373, 374,
      379, 385, 387, 388, 399, 421,
      439, 441, 449, 468, 470, 485
   Abraham and Isaac, 441
   Cello Symphony, 138
   Death in Venice, 59, 144
   Noye's Fludde, 441
   Peter Grimes, 141, 281, 372
   Phaedra, 59

490 Index

Serenade for Tenor, Horn and Strings, 372
Canticle: *Still Falls the Rain*, 317
String Quartet No.3, 59
The Turn of the Screw, 140
The Young Person's Guide to the Orchestra, 8
War Requiem, 217, 281, 400, 441
Young Apollo, xiii
Britten Estate, xviii, xxi, 299, 301
Britten Sinfonia, xiii, xix, 22
Britten-Pears Foundation, xviii, 299
Britten-Pears Young Artists Programme, xvii
Brough, Paul, 336
Brownjohn, Alan, 174
Bryars, Gavin, xii
   (Interview 104–111)
   After the Underworlds, 107
   Cadman Requiem, 108
   Cello Concerto 'Farewell to Philosophy', 103, 105, 106
   Double Bass Concerto 'Farewell to St Petersburg', 106
   Jesus's Blood Never Failed Me Yet, 103, 111
   Piano Concerto 'The Solway Canal', 106
   The Sinking of the Titanic, 103, 111
   The War in Heaven, 110
   To Gain the Affections of Miss Dwyer Even For One Short Minute Would Benefit Me No End, 106
   Violin Concerto 'The Bulls of Bashan', 106
Burrell, Diana, xii
   (Interview 116–122)
   Clarinet Concerto, 121
   Das Meer, das so groß und weit ist, da wimmelt's ohne Zahl, große und kleine Tiere, 118
   Dunkelhvide Månestråler, 121
   Gold, 122
   Landscape, xii
   Missa Sancte Endeliente, xii
   Symphonies of Flocks, Herds and Shoals, 121
   The Hours, 122
Burroughs, William
   Cities of the Red Night, 239
Bush, Alan, xi
Bush, Geoffrey, xx
Busoni, Ferruccio, 107, 180

Byrd, William, 288, 420, 421

Cadman, Bill, 108
Cadogan Hall, 326
Cage, John, xii, 57, 103, 175, 180, 205, 292, 301
   4'33", 292
   Piano Concerto, 57
Cambridge Composers' Competition, xv
Cambridge Singers, xxii
Cardew, Cornelius, xii, 301
Cardiff University, xvii, xxiii
Carewe, John, 70
Carter, Elliott, 260, 362, 385, 387
   ASKO Concerto, 260
   String Quartet No.3, 22
Cartier-Bresson, Henri, 428
Carver, Robert, 288
Casken, John, xviii
Cézanne, Paul
   Mont St Victoire, 424
Channel 4 TV, xiv
   Sinfonietta, 237
Chappell's, 94
Charles, Prince of Wales, 85
Charpentier, Marc-Antoine, 70
Cheltenham International Festival of Music, xi
Cheltenham International Violin Course, xxiv
Chin, Unsuk, x
Chopin, Frédéric, 48, 68, 163, 235, 274, 441
   Mazurkas, 439
   Nocturnes, 434
   Preludes, 439
Cirencester Grammar School, xix, xxi
City of Birmingham Symphony Orchestra, ix, xxiii
City University of New York Queen's College, xix
Classic CD Magazine, 285
Classic FM, xvi, xxiii, 209
Clerks, The, 420
Cleveland Orchestra, ix, xix
Cobbett Medal, xiii
Colchester Institute Music School, xxiii, 468
Cole, Nat King, 161
Collegium Records, xxii
Collins, Cecil, 442
Concertgebouw Orchestra, x
Connolly, Justin, 365

Conseil Musical de la Fondation Prince
    Pierre de Monaco, ix
Conservatoire de Paris, x, 49
Cooke, Deryck, 299, 301, 311
Copland, Aaron, xix, 411
    Rodeo, 274
    What to Listen For in Music, 474
Cornell University, xxi
Coult, Tom, xiii, 185
    (Interview 126–134)
    Codex (Homage to Serafini), xiii
    Four Perpetual Motions, xiii, 133
    Moto Perpetuo, 133
    The Chronophage, 132
Country Life, xx
Craxton, Harold, xii
Crimp, Martin, 46, 48
Cross, Jonathan, 128
Crosse, Gordon, xiii, 316, 446
    (Interview 138–146)
    Ariadne, 138, 143
    Meet My Folks! (Theme and Relations), xiii
    Memories of Morning: Night, 138, 140, 143
    Oboe Quintet, 141, 142
    Sea Psalms, 137
Crowthers, Malcolm, xvi
Croydon Music Festival, xiv, 174
CTS Studios, 457
Cumnock Tryst, The, 287

Da Ponte, Lorenzo, 424
Da Vinci, Leonardo, 179
Dadd, Richard
    The Fairy Feller's Master Stroke, 263
Daily Telegraph, The, xx, 138, 156, 359
Dalby, Martin, 30, 373
Dallapiccola, Luigi, 264
Dante, 435
    Farewell to Beatrice, 435
DARE, xv, 192
Darmstadt, 366
Dartington College of Arts, xii
Dartington International Summer School, xix, xxii, 30, 32, 83, 261, 338, 442
Davis, Carl, xix
De Leeuw, Reinbert, 266
Deal Festival, xix
Debussy, Claude, 31, 36, 48, 161, 218, 305, 312, 363, 470
    Clair de Lune, 181

La Mer, 50
Prélude à l'après-midi d'un Faune, 50
Préludes, 306, 307
Degas, Edgar, 178
Delius, Frederick, 227, 328, 359, 360, 361, 362, 363
Dench, Chris, 237
Dennis, Brian, 373
Deutsche Symphonie Orchester
    (Schoenberg Prize), x
Diana, Princess of Wales, xii, xiv, xxiii, 96, 439
Dillon, James, 188, 237
DJ Yoda (Duncan Beiny), xxi
Donizetti, Gaetano, 366
Dove, Jonathan, xii, xiii, 185, 445
    (Interview 150–156)
    Diana & Actaeon, 150
    Flight, xiv, 149, 153
    Flute Concerto 'The Magic Flute Dances', 154
    Gaia Theory, 149
    Man on the Moon, xiv
    Mansfield Park, 149, 154
    On Spital Fields, xiv
    Seek Him that Maketh the Seven Stars, 378
    The Adventures of Pinocchio, 149, 154
    The Enchanted Pig, 153
    There Was a Child, 149, 150
    Tobias and the Angel, 149
    When She Died, xiv
Drummond, Sir John, 87
Dubery, David, xiv
    (Interview 160–169)
    Cello Sonata, 167
    Cuarteto Iberico, 167
    Love Sonnets/Sonetti d'amore, 160
    Mrs Harris in Paris, 159
Dunstaple, John, 422
Dutilleux, Henri, 49
Dutton Vocalion, 467
Dvořák, Antonin
    Symphony No.9 'From the New World', 37
Dylan, Bob, 127, 133

Edinburgh Festival, 285
Edinger, Christiane, 98
Eggert, Moritz, 241
Eisler, Hanns, 175
Elgar, Sir Edward, 85, 98, 117, 118, 200,

227, 312, 328, 360, 362, 366, 421, 439
  Pomp and Circumstance March No.6, 359
  Symphony No.3, xx, 306, 359
Elgar Estate, 359
Eliot, T. S.
  Four Quartets, 386
Elstree Film Studios, 95
Elysian Quartet, 403
English Chamber Orchestra, xix, 25
English Music Festival, xxiv
English National Ballet, xvi
English National Opera, 104
English Opera Group, 264
Eno, Brian, 33
Ensemble Intercontemporain, Le, x
Ensemble Moderne, x
Ernst von Siemens Music Prize, xi, 85
Evans, Bill, 22
Exon Singers Festival, xxi

Faber Music, xix, 41, 44, 311
Fauré, Gabriel, 23
  Piano Trio, 23
  Requiem, 414
Feldman, Morton, 440
  Coptic Light, 12
Fenby, Eric, xi
Fenice, La, 109
Ferguson, Howard, xii, 94
Ferneyhough, Brian, 188
Field, John, 68
Finale (software), 337, 341, 377
Finnis, Edmund, ix
Finnissy, Michael, xiv, xvi, 9, 32, 235, 237, 239, 241
  (Interview 174–181)
  Après-midi Dada, 174
  Casual Nudity, 174
  Necessary and More Detailed Thinking, 174
  Not Envious of Rabbits, 174
  Piano Concerto No.2, 237
  Red Earth, 236, 237
  Sea and Sky, 10
  That Ain't Shit, 174
Foss, Lukas, 261
Frances-Hoad, Cheryl, xv
  (Interview 186–193)
Francis, Connie, 286
Fricker, Peter Racine, xx, 277
Fuchs, Kenneth, 161

Fulbright Arts Fellowship, xxii

Gál, Hans, xix, 337
Gance, Abel
  Napoléon, 267
Garner, Alan, 142
Gaudeamus International Composers Prize, xxii
Genesis Foundation, 286
Gerhard, Roberto, 274, 360
  Concerto for Orchestra, 276
Gibbons, Orlando, 235, 288, 421
Gilbert, Anthony, x
Gilbert & Sullivan, 299
  Iolanthe, 151
Glasgow Academy, xi
Glass, Philip, 145, 151, 213
  Einstein on the Beach, 401
Glock, William, 9, 302, 338
Gluck, Christoph Willibald, 109
Glyndebourne Festival Opera, xiv, 151, 426, 438
Goehr, Alexander, ix, x, xv, xvii, 3, 10–11, 24, 137, 139, 260, 361, 442, 483
  (Interview 198–206)
  The Deluge, 205
Goehr, Walter, 197, 198
Goldsmith, Jerry, 462
  Papillon, 274
Gomez, Eddie, 22
Goodall, Howard, xv, xxiii, 163
  (Interview 210–219)
  Bend It Like Beckham, 211, 216
  Blackadder, 209, 217
  Eternal Light: A Requiem, 211, 216, 217
  Every Purpose Under the Heaven, 214
  Mr Bean, 209, 211, 217
  Q.I., 209
  Red Dwarf, 209
  The Hired Man, 218
  The Seasons, 213
  The Vicar of Dibley, 209
Górecki, Henryk, 292
  Symphony No.3, 350
Gould, Clio, 463
Gowers, Patrick, 412
Goya, Francisco, 326
  Los Caprichos, 326
Grainger, Percy, 305
  Country Gardens, 111
Gramophone magazine, 383
Gramophone Company, The, 201
Granados, Enrique, 238

Grant, Julian, 153, 343
Green, Gordon, xvii
Grieg, Edvard, 161
Griffiths, Paul, 2, 3, 4, 248, 300
   New Sounds, New Personalities, 2, 3, 7, 80, 125, 248, 299, 383, 419, 477
Grime, Helen, ix
Grisey, Gérard, x, 10, 130
Groag, Lilian, 341
Guardian, The, 210, 259, 336, 445
Gubaidulina, Sofia, 292
Guggenheim Fellowship, xix
Guild of Church Musicians, xxii
Guildhall School of Music and Drama, ix, xii, xvi, xxii, xxiii, 151, 237, 241, 242, 244, 335, 336, 344
   Lutosławski Prize, xvi
Guinness Prize, 57
Gunning, Christopher, xvi, 457
   (Interview 224–232)
   Agatha Christie's Poirot, xvi, 231
   Firelight, xvi
   La Vie en Rose, xvi
   Middlemarch, xvi
   Night Voyage, 228
   Oboe Concerto, 223
   Piano Concerto, 228
   Porterhouse Blue, xvi
   Rebecca, xvi
   Saxophone Concerto, 228, 229
   Symphony No.1, 228, 229
   Symphony No.2, 229
   Symphony No.3, 223, 229
   Symphony No.4, 223
   Symphony No.5, 229
   Symphony No.7, 229
   Under Suspicion, xvi
Gutman, Stephen, 241

Hahn, Reynaldo, 243
Haitink, Bernard, 279
Halbreich, Harry, 9, 178
Hallé Orchestra, xviii, 70, 306
Handel, George Frideric, 210, 288, 374, 424
Harle, John, 87, 228
Harris, Roy, 274, 373
Harvard University, ix
Harvey, Jonathan, 292
Harwich Festival of the Arts, xiii, 115, 116
Hastings Music Festival, xii
Haydn, Joseph, 161, 164, 226, 421

Hayes, Morgan, xvi
   (Interview 236–244)
   Lute Stop, 242
   Opera, 238
   Port Rhombus (Squarepusher), xvi
   Shirley and Jane, xvi-xvii
   Strip, xvi
   Violin Concerto, 238, 240
   Völklinger Hütte, 239
Heights Restaurant, The (London), 7, 185
Hendrix, Jimi, 127
Henze, Hans Werner, 260
Hesse Scholarship, xiv
Het Residentie Orkest, xvii
Hickox, Richard, 121
Highgate School, xxi, xxii, 409
Hilliard Ensemble, 108
Hindemith, Paul, 81, 186, 428, 470
   Mass, 273
Hinkins, Chris, 110
Hockney, David, 177, 178, 325, 424
Hoddinott, Alun, 253
Holloway, Robin, xiii, xvii, xxii, xxiii, 42, 67, 153, 197, 407, 451
   (Interview 248–255)
   Brand, 253
   Debussy and Wagner, xvii
   Fifth Concerto for Orchestra, 248
   First Concerto for Orchestra, 254
   Second Concerto for Orchestra, 10
   Third Concerto for Orchestra, 250, 251, 255
   Trio for Oboe, Violin and Piano, 251
   Violin Concerto, 235
Holst Estate, 301
Holst Foundation, xviii, 300, 301
Holst, Gustav, 312, 327, 328, 360, 470
   Terzetto, 470
   The Evening Watch, 470
   The Planets, 306, 470
   Uranus, 316
Holst, Imogen, xviii, 299
Honegger, Arthur, 276
Hong Kong Philharmonic Orchestra, xx
Horszowski, Mieczysław, 20
Houdini, Harry, 263
Howarth, Elgar, 324
Howells, Herbert, 415
   Missa Sabrinensis, 273, 277
Huddersfield Contemporary Music Festival, 122, 238
Hughes, Ted, xiii
Hume, Cardinal Basil, xii, xx, 351

Humperdinck, Engelbert
   Hansel und Gretel, 151

Ibert, Jacques, 366
Ibsen, Henrik
   Brand, 253
IFMCA Awards, xxiii
Imperial War Museum North, 21
Incorporated Society of Musicians, xviii
   ISM Distinguished Musician Award, xviii, xxiii
Independent, The, xx, 359
International Record Review, 467
International Society for Contemporary Music, xv, 261
International String Orchestra Composition Competition, xv
Ipswich Wolsey Orchestra, xxiv
Ireland, John, 3, 359
Isserlis, Steven, xxiii, 2, 36
Ives, Charles, 174
   Symphony No.4, 260
Ixion, xv, 238

Jackson, Harold, 205, 206
Jacob, Gordon, 94
Janáček, Leoš, 140, 373
   String Quartet No.2 'Intimate Letters', 58
Jane's Minstrels, xx
Jarrett, Keith, 235
Jenkins, Karl, 415
Jerusalem Symphony Orchestra, xx
Jessell, Camilla (Lady Panufnik), 347
Jeyasingh, Shobana, 403
John of the Cross, 435
Josefowicz, Leila, 307
Josquin des Prez, 437, 440, 441
Joyful Company of Singers, xx, xxii
Juilliard School, x, 275
Jungle, 400
Jurowski, Vladimir, xxi

Kagel, Mauricio, 24
Kaipainen, Jouni, 371
Kalinnikov, Vasily
   Symphony No.1, 274
Kancheli, Giya, 292
Katholieke Universiteit Leuven, xv
Keller, Hans, xi, 70, 367
Kim, Earl, xix
King's College London, x, xiii, xv, xxi, 44, 86, 125, 388, 440

King's Lynn Festival, xxi, 374
King's Singers, The, 280
King's Speech, The (Alexandre Desplat), 462
Klemperer, Otto, 243
Knussen, Oliver, x, xvii, xviii, 9, 10, 30, 31, 33, 51, 129, 203, 252, 287, 326
   (Interview 260–269)
   Flourish with Fireworks, 263
   Ophelia's Last Dance, 265
   Requiem – Songs for Sue, 265
   Symphony No.1, 260, 264
   Symphony No.3, 9, 10
   Two Organa, 266, 267
   Violin Concerto, 265
Kodály, Zoltán, 227
Kokkonen, Joonas, 371
Korngold, Erich Wolfgang
   Symphony, 273
Koussevitzky Award, xix
Kreppein, Ulrich, ix
Kubrick, Stanley
   Barry Lyndon, 95
Kurtág, György, 204

Lachenmann, Helmut, 10
Lady Sovereign
   Public Warning, xxi
Lambert, John, ix, xvii, 10, 11, 23, 263
Lambeth Doctorate of Music, xxii
Landon, H. C. Robbins, 211
Lankester, Michael, 362
Lanza, Mario, 161
Lauridsen, Morton, 212
Lee, Laurie, 374
Leeds College of Music, x
Leicester Polytechnic (De Montfort University), xii
Leipzig Gewandhaus Orchestra, xix, 300
Leppard, Raymond, 57
Lesley Boosey Award (RPS/PRS), xviii
Levi, Primo, 25
Libeskind, Daniel, 21
Ligeti, György, x, 16, 24, 47, 49, 126, 204, 260, 360, 366, 434
   Études for Piano, 9
   Trio for Violin, Horn and Piano, 25
Lincoln Center, xxiii
Linstead, George, 105
Liszt, Franz, 163
Lloyd-Webber, Julian, 105
Locatelli, Pietro, 68

Logic (software), 229, 402
London Bach Choir, 375
London Chamber Orchestra, xviii
London College of Music, xi, xviii
London Contemporary Dance Theatre, 179
London Mozart Players, xx
London Philharmonic Orchestra, ix, 15, 24
London School of Contemporary Dance, xiv, 237
London Schools Symphony Orchestra, 151
London Sinfonietta, x, xiii, xvi, xvii, xxii, 31, 107, 260, 261, 306, 426, 481
London Symphony Orchestra, xiii, xviii, 24, 225, 260, 263, 264, 279, 301, 409
Loriod, Yvonne, x, xv, 41
Los Angeles Chamber Orchestra, xx
Lumsden, David, 434
Lutosławski, Witold, 57, 360, 384, 387
Lutyens, Elisabeth, xxii, 3, 144, 204, 315, 421

McCabe, John, xvii, 137
   (Interview 274–281)
   Cloudcatcher Fells, 280
   Edward II, 276–277, 280
   Notturni ed Alba, 279
   Oboe Quartet, 276
   Scenes in America Deserta, 280
   Symphony No.2, 280
   Symphony No.7 'Labyrinth', 280
   Symphony on a Pavane, 280
   Tenebrae, 276
   The Chagall Windows, 278, 279, 280
   Variations on a Theme of Karl Amadeus Hartmann, 276
McCartney, Sir Paul, 106, 127
MacMillan, Sir James, xviii, 111, 253
   (Interview 286–295)
   Cello Concerto, 294
   Oboe Concerto, 289
   Percussion Concerto 'Veni, veni, Emmanuel', 285, 294, 318
   Piano Trio No.2, 289
   St Luke Passion, 293
   The Confession of Isobel Gowdie, 285, 290, 294
   Tryst, xviii
   Violin Concerto, 285
Maddocks, Fiona, 259

Maderna, Bruno, 260
Magnus Liber Organi, 266
Mahler, Gustav, 48, 49, 70, 81, 120, 144, 151, 163, 199, 212, 273, 312, 315, 361, 373, 400, 439
   Symphony No.2, 43
   Symphony No.8, 130
   Symphony No.9, 251
   Symphony No.10, 299, 301, 311
Mahler Chamber Orchestra, x, xiii, 51
Manchester School of Music, xiv
Manning, Jane, xx, 359, 364
Mantovani, 174
Mark, Peter, xix, 335
Martin, Sir George, 127
Martino, Donald, 264
Martinů, Bohuslav, 117
Master of the Queen's Music, xix, xxiii, 3, 219, 324, 445
Matthews, Colin, xvii, xviii, 252, 311, 315
   (Interview 300–307)
   Fourth Sonata, 311
   Grand Barcarolle, 300
   Hidden Variables, 306
   No Man's Land, 300, 305, 307
   Pluto, 306
   Suns Dance, 306
   Violin Concerto, 307
Matthews, David, xviii, 4, 252, 280, 299, 300, 348
   (Interview 312–320)
   A Vision and a Journey, 314
   Concerto in Azzurro, xix, 348
   Landscape into Sound, xix
   Symphony No.1, 316
   Symphony No.2, 316
   Violin Concertos, 319
Matthias, William, 253
Maw, Nicholas, xviii, 137, 275, 301, 315, 362
Maxwell, Melinda, 83, 86
Maxwell Davies, Sir Peter, xv, xix, xxi, xxiii, 24, 30, 137, 139, 140, 144, 197, 204, 219, 260, 261, 286, 288, 361, 362, 378, 420, 421, 442, 445
   (Interview 324–332)
   A Mirror of Whitening Light, 330
   An Orkney Wedding, with Sunrise, 327
   Ave Maris Stella, 330
   Caroline Mathilde, 330

Eight Songs for a Mad King, 140, 325
Farewell to Stromness, 327, 330
Miss Donnithorne's Maggot, 325
Naxos String Quartets, 331
Sonata for Trumpet and Piano, 324
Symphony No.4, 326
Symphony No.6, 323, 324, 326, 330
Symphony No.8 'Antarctic', 306
Symphony No.10, 331, 332
Worldes Blis, 325
Mehretu, Julie, 22
Mendelssohn, Felix, 218
Mendelssohn Scholarship, xv
Messiaen, Olivier, x, xv, 31, 41, 47, 48, 49, 130, 198, 260, 292, 360, 422, 440
MIA (Music Industries Association)/Classic FM Award, xvi
Millennium Dance, 237
Milne, Lisa, 343, 390
Milner, Anthony, xviii, 315
Milstein, Nathan, 98
Milstein, Silvina, 186
Mitchell, Donald, 11
Monteverdi, Claudio, 169, 209, 421
    Vespers, 209
Monty Python's Flying Circus, 231
Moore, Dudley, 225
Morgan, Darragh, 241, 244
Morley College, 204
Morricone, Ennio, 462
Movie Music UK Awards, xxiii
Mozart, Wolfgang Amadeus, 49, 105, 163, 179, 211, 226, 243, 262, 274, 290, 367, 391, 396, 424, 436, 439, 440, 441, 478, 481
    Cosí fan tutte, 151
    Le nozze di Figaro, 438
    Symphony No.41 'Jupiter', 86
Munrow, David, 472
Murail, Tristan, ix, 10, 130
Musgrave, Thea, xix
    (Interview 336–344)
    Green, 343
    Harriet, The Woman Called Moses, 342
    Horn Concerto, 336, 338, 339, 340, 344
    Rorate Coeli, 338
    Simón Bolívar, 341, 342
    Songs for a Winter's Evening, 343
    Space Play, 338
    The Story of Harriet, 343
    Turbulent Landscapes, 339

Music Theatre Ensemble, xv
Music Theatre Wales, xvi
Musical Times, 236, 306
Mussorgsky, Modest
    Pictures at an Exhibition, xvi

Naomi Sargant Memorial Award, xvi
Nash Ensemble, 365
National Anthem, 86
National Film and Television School, 351
National Film Theatre, xii, 94
National Theatre, xiv
National Youth Orchestra of Great Britain, xxi
Netherlands Radio Chamber Philharmonic Orchestra, xviii
Neue Einfachheit ('New Simplicity'), 178, 253
'New Complexity', 107, 178
New England Conservatory, xv, xix
New Music Manchester, xv, 197
New Music 20x12, x
New York Shakespeare Festival, xiv
Newman, Barnett, 106
Nicolson, Alasdair, x
Niculescu, Ştefan, 13
Nielsen, Carl, 117, 122, 281
    Symphony No.5, 281
Nietzsche, Friedrich, 435
Nimbus Records, 42
NMC Recordings, xviii, 235, 242, 300, 301, 306
Nonclassical, xxi, 395, 403
Nono, Luigi, 21, 175
    Prometeo, 21
Northern Ballet School, xiv
Northern School of Music, xiv
Not The Nine o'Clock News, 218
Novello, Ivor, 161
    Ivor Novello Award, xiv, xvi, xxiii
Nyman, Michael, 462
    The Piano, 462

Oare String Orchestra International Composer's Competition, xxiv
Ockeghem, Johannes, 290
Ogdon, John, xv, 324
Ojai Music Festival, xix
Old Dominion University, xix
Open University, 410
Opera Lab, xxii
Opera North, xv, 192
Orff, Carl, 202

Orr, Buxton, xxiii, 460
Owen, Martin, 336, 340, 343
Oxford Playhouse, 142
Oxford University Press, xxii, 318
Oxley, Tony, xii

Padmore, Mark, 87
Palestrina, Giovanni Pierluigi da, 105, 186
Palmer, Christopher, 415
Panufnik, Sir Andrej, xx, 348
Panufnik, Roxanna, xx
    (Interview 348–355)
    Beastly Tales, xx, 352
    Cantator and Amanda, 347, 352
    Dance of Life, 352
    Olivia, 352
    Summer Dance, 351
    The Music Programme, xx
    Westminster Mass, xx, 349, 352
Pappano, Sir Antonio, 332
Paradiso (Amsterdam), xxi
Park City Film Music Festival, xiv
Park Lane Group, xxii
Parrott, Andrew, 68
Parry, Sir Hubert, 85, 359
Pärt, Arvo, 318, 440, 441
Patterson, Jeremy, 375
Patterson, Paul, 70
Payne, Anthony, xx, 137, 275, 306, 440
    (Interview 360–368)
    Spring's Shining Wake, 362
    String Quartet No.2, xx
    The Spirit's Harvest, xx, 363–364
    Time's Arrow, xx, 363
    Wind Quintet, 365
Payne, Cynthia, 253–254
Pears, Sir Peter, 441
Pehkonen, Elis, xx, xxiv, 467, 484
    (Interview 372–379)
    Amor Vincit Omnia, 375
    Buccinate Tuba, 375
    Concerto for Two Pianos and Orchestra, 373
    Everyman, xx, 374
    Missa Pro Defunctis, 374, 378
    Russian Requiem, xxi, 375
    String Quartet No.1, 373
    Three Songs, 374
Penderecki, Krzysztof, 126, 127
Percy Buck's Practical Harmony, 94
Performing Right Society, xii, xviii, 9, 29, 231

Pérotin, 11, 266
Persichetti, Vincent, 275
Petrassi, Goffredo, xix
Phibbs, Joseph, xxi, 4
    (Interview 384–391)
    Clarinet Concerto, 389
    Lumina, xxi, 383, 384, 385
    Rivers to the Sea, xxi
    The Canticle of The Rose, 390
Philadelphia Orchestra, xx
Philharmonia Orchestra, ix, x, xii, xiii, xviii, xix, 15, 96
Philips Records, 30
Picasso, Pablo, 81, 178
Pick of the Week (BBC Radio), 82
Pierrot Players (later The Fires of London), 24
Piston, Walter, 274
Pitfield, Thomas, xvii
Plath, Sylvia
    Winter Trees, 37
Plato, 92
Plymouth University, xii
Polish National Opera, xx
Ponsonby, Robert, 9
Porter, Dame Shirley, xvii
Poulenc, Francis, 57, 243, 366
    Concerto for Two Pianos and Orchestra, 243
Pousseur, Henri, 24
Powell, Jonathan, 235, 241
Presteigne Festival, xxi, xxii
Previn, André, 279
Price, Julie, 347
Primrose, William, 30
Princeton University, xi, xix
Prix de Rome, 209
Prokofiev, Gabriel, xxi
    (Interview 396–404)
    Cello Multitracks, 403
    Concerto for Bass Drum and Orchestra, 402
    Concerto for Turntables and Orchestra, xxi
    Nonet for Cellos, 403
    String Quartet No.1, 403
    String Quartet No.2, 403
    Journeys of a Cattle Herd, 398
    Violas Can't Dance, xxi
Prokofiev, Oleg, 395
Prokofiev, Sergei, 163, 281, 395, 397
    Symphony No.5, 401
    Symphony No.6, 401

Psycho, 59
Puccini, Giacomo, 141, 149, 366
Purcell, Henry, 109, 154, 227, 288, 421
Purcell School, xvi, xxi, xxii, 242
Puttnam, David, 95

Queen Elizabeth Hall, xxii, 24, 231, 260
Queen's Hall, 7
Queen's Medal for Music, xxiii

Rachmaninov, Sergei, 58, 163, 373, 484
Radiohead, 126
Radulescu, Horatiu, 10
Rambert Dance, xv, 211
Rameau, Jean-Philippe, 70, 241
Ratushinskaya, Irina, 37
Rauschenberg, Robert, 178
Ravel, Maurice, 31, 48, 57, 92, 97, 305, 387, 470
Rawsthorne, Alan, 274
    Symphony No.3, 274
Reeves, Camden, 128
Reich, Steve, 145, 151, 373, 375
Ridout, Alan, xx, 374
Rihm, Wolfgang, x
Riley, Terry, 301
    In C, 484
Robert Helps International Composition Prize, xv
Rodgers & Hammerstein, 212
Rolling Stones
    Satisfaction, 111
Rose d'Or Festival, xiv
Rostropovich, Mstislav, 294
Royal Academy of Music, ix, x-xi, xiii, xv, xvii, xx, xxii, 19, 23, 24, 25, 56, 70, 94, 122, 323, 324, 329, 349, 350
Royal Albert Hall, 9, 325
Royal Ballet, xiii, 96
Royal College of Music, ix, xiv, xviii, xx, xxiii, 10, 24, 25, 44, 92, 144, 175, 180, 301, 373, 374, 462
Royal Festival Hall, xiii, xxi, 10, 21, 110, 375
Royal Liverpool Philharmonic Orchestra, 375
Royal Manchester College of Music, xv, xvii, xix, 197
Royal National Theatre, xi
Royal Northern College of Music, x, xi, 197
Royal Ontario Museum, 21

Royal Opera (Covent Garden), 441
Royal Philharmonic Orchestra, xix, 24, 323, 326, 463
Royal Philharmonic Society, ix, xii, xiii, xiv, xv, xvii, 300
Royal Shakespeare Company, xiv, 95
Rubbra, Edmund, xvi
Rumi, 435
Russian National Orchestra, xix
Rutter, John, xxi, 137, 185, 212, 217
    (Interview 408–415)
    'All things bright and beautiful', 415
    'For the beauty of the earth', 415
    Gloria, 411, 414
    Hymn to the Creator of Light, 415
    Magnificat, 413
    Requiem, 408, 413, 415

St Asaph Festival, 58
St Endellion Festival, xii, 121
St John's Presbyterian Church, Kensington, xxii
St Magnus International Festival, Orkney, xviii, 323
    Composers' Course, x
St Mark's Coptic Orthodox Church, xxii
St Paul's Cathedral, xvii
Sallinen, Aulis, 371
Salonen, Esa-Pekka, 287
San Francisco Symphony Orchestra, xix, xx
Sanders, John, xxi
Satie, Erik, 174
    Gymnopédies, 111
Saxton, Robert, xvi, xxii
    (Interview 420–429)
    Five Motets, 420
Scarlatti, Domenico, 238
Schafer, Murray, 1, 2, 3, 371, 446
    British Composers in Interview, 1, 3, 4, 300, 324, 388
Schenker, Heinrich, 388
Schnittke, Alfred, 292
Schoenberg, Arnold, xx, 43, 81, 107, 131, 144, 178, 197, 198, 199, 202, 204, 226, 237, 249, 255, 266, 275, 290, 291, 302, 314, 315, 361, 362, 388, 409, 434, 471
    Jacob's Ladder, 204
Schönberg Ensemble, 266
Schott, 109, 110
Schubert, Franz, 161, 274, 387
Schuller, Gunther, ix, xvii, 260, 264

The Visitation, 109
Schuman, William, 274
Schumann, Robert, x, 48, 249, 250, 366, 439
Score, The, 144
Scott, Cyril
  Piano Concerto, 9
Scott, John, 225
Scott, Sir Ridley, 95
Scottish Chamber Orchestra, x, xi, xviii, xix, 326
Scriabin, Alexander, 50
Sculthorpe, Peter, xviii-xix, 315
Searle, Humphrey, xiv, 175, 315
Second Viennese School, 57, 204, 290
Service, Tom, 197, 205, 335, 336, 343, 445
Sessions, Roger, xix
Seth, Vikram, xx
Shakespeare, William, 352
Shankara, Adi, 435
Sheppard, John, 439
Sherlaw Johnson, Robert, xxii
Shostakovich, Dmitri, xxii, 161, 292, 318, 325
Sibelius (software), 24, 62, 97, 143, 144, 166, 189, 243, 303, 314, 337, 341, 377, 390, 402, 425, 460
Sibelius, Jean, 199, 253, 281, 312
  Symphony No.2, 328
  Symphony No.3, 328
  Symphony No.4, 325
  Symphony No.6, 328
  Symphony No.7, 239, 328
Simpson, Mark, ix
Sing Up, xvi
Sir Charles Groves/Making Music Prize, xvi
Sixteen, The, 286
Skempton, Howard, 145
Small, Jonathan, 375
Smalley, Roger, 373
Smith College, xix
Society for the Promotion of New Music, xviii, 9, 25, 151, 301, 316, 324
Solomon, 441
Solstice Quartet, 145
Sondheim, Stephen, 215, 216
South Bank Centre, xvi, xxii, 134, 176, 186
South Bank Show, The, xxiii
Southwark Cathedral, 433

Spectator, The, xvii
Spektrum, 398
Spitalfields Festival, xii-xiii, xxiii
Squarepusher, xvi, 126
Stanford, Sir Charles Villiers, 201, 275
Stevens, Bernard, xiv, 175, 176
Sting, 213
Stockhausen, Karlheinz, 15, 24, 70, 83, 144, 175, 303, 360, 361, 373, 401, 440, 441
  Gruppen, 15, 261, 386
  Licht, 262
  Stimmung, 401
Strad, The, 467
Strauss, Richard, 64, 107, 163, 293–294, 305, 361, 362
  Der Rosenkavalier, 151
Stravinsky, Igor, 37, 46, 74, 95, 128, 140, 144, 199, 218, 251, 262, 265, 276, 291, 304, 373, 385–386, 388, 437, 440, 441, 470, 482
  Abraham and Isaac, 441
  Ave Maria, 291
  Cantata, 128
  Credo, 291
  Fireworks, 263
  Huxley Variations, 263
  Mass, 128, 291
  Requiem Canticles, 441
  Symphony of Psalms, 128
  The Flood, 441
  The Rite of Spring, 8, 43, 57, 69, 144, 202, 480
Stucky, Steven, xxi
Sumner, Alaric, 180
Sun River Composition Prize, xv
Sunday Times, The, 60
Suoraan, xv
Swedish Chamber Orchestra, x
Sweeney, John, 235, 237
SXSW Festival, xxi
Sydney Festival, xi
Sylvester, Victor, 174
Syntax Error, 397
Szymanowski, Karol, 250
  Violin Concerto No.1, 250

Takahashi, Aki, 326
Takemitsu, Toru, 250, 260
Tallis, Thomas, 421, 439
Tanglewood Music Center and Festival, ix, xv, xvii, xix, 260, 264
Tate Modern, 59

Tavener, Sir John, xxi, xxii, xxiii, 292, 350, 409
  (Interview 434–442)
  Chamber Concerto (Piano Concerto), 434
  Gnossis, 436
  Song for Athene, xxiii, 435, 438, 439
  The Beautiful Names, 435
  The Death of Ivan Ilyich, 437
  The Lamb, 435
  The Protecting Veil, xxiii
  The Veil of the Temple, 435, 436
  The Whale, xxii
  Thérèse, 441
  Three Shakespeare Sonnets, 433
Taverner, John, 439
  Gloria Tibi Trinitas, 420
Taylor, John C., 132
Tchaikovsky, Piotr Ilyich, 58, 98, 176, 199, 255, 305, 415, 429
Temple Festival, xxii
Thatcher, Margaret, 202
The Rest is Noise Festival, 134
Thoreau, Henry David, 179
Three Choirs Festival, xxi, 375
Tilson Thomas, Michael, 255, 263
Times, The, 359
Tippett, Sir Michael, xix, 117, 176, 199, 261, 288, 305, 312, 315, 318, 361, 373, 387, 470
  A Child of Our Time, 281
  The Vision of St Augustine, 422
Tobutt, Jonathan, xiv
Tolstoy, Leo, 437
Toop, Richard, 178, 237
Toovey, Andrew, 236
Tormé, Mel, xvi
Trampler, Walter, ix, 20
Trapani, Chris, ix
Trinity College of Music, xi, xxiii
Tubman, Harriet, 342
Tuckwell, Barry, 340
Turnage, Mark-Anthony, 128, 261
Turner, J. M. W., 48, 339
Turner, John, 138

University of Adelaide, xix
University of Birmingham, xiii, xxi, 397
University of Brighton, 95
University of California, xix
University of Cambridge, x, xii, xiii, xv, xvii, xxiii, 10, 42, 120, 193, 197, 202, 204, 205, 247, 248, 409, 410, 412, 440, 481
  Clare College, xxi
  Corpus Christi College, 132
  King's College, xiii
University of Cincinnati, xviii
University of Durham, xvi, xviii, xx
  St Cuthbert's Society, xx
University of Edinburgh, xviii, xix, 337, 338
University of Essex, xiii
University of Florida, xv
University of Glasgow, xix
University of Leeds, xv, 192, 197
University of London, ix
University of Louisville, xi
University of Manchester, xiii, xvii, xviii, xix, 128
University of Melbourne, xviii
University of Nottingham, xviii, 311
University of Oxford, xiii, xxii, 410, 419, 425
  Christ Church, xv
  New College, xv
  Worcester College, xxii, 419
University of Sheffield, xii
University of Southampton, xv, 197
University of Sussex, xv, xviii
University of York, xxi

Valencia (Architecture Biennale), xii
Van Gogh, Vincent, 304
Vàrese, Edgard, 49, 174, 360, 362
  Amèriques, 260
Vaughan Williams, Ralph, 74, 85, 139, 140, 185, 227, 281, 287, 312, 318, 327, 328, 350, 359, 360, 361, 362, 366, 420, 422, 470
  Four Last Songs, 359
  Symphony No.5, 328
  Symphony No.6, 274, 318, 328
  The Lark Ascending, 74
Vaughn, Henry, 470
Verdi, Giuseppe, 275, 424
  Falstaff, 424
  Rigoletto, 151
Verlaine Duo, xiv
Vir, Param, xxi, 388, 390
Vivaldi, Antonio, 176
Vivier, Claude, 13
Vlad, Roman, xiv
Volkov, Ilan, 236

Von Meck, Nadezhda, 305

Wagner, Richard, x, 43, 49, 74, 85, 107, 249, 251, 274, 366, 373, 428
  Der Ring des Nibelungen, 151
  Tristan und Isolde, 408
Walker, Alan
  A Study in Musical Analysis, 474
Wallfisch, Raphael, xxiv
Walton, Sir William, 30, 140, 161, 281, 312, 373, 388, 413, 470
  Belshazzar's Feast, 277
  Cello Concerto, 281
  Symphony No.1, 281
  Viola Concerto, 30
Warlock, Peter (Philip Heseltine), 439
Watkins, Huw, ix
Watkins, Richard, 20, 25
WDR (Westdeutscher Rundfunk), 178
Weber, Carl Maria von, 161
Webern, Anton, 47, 50, 107, 199, 204, 237, 274, 361, 375, 434, 442
Weill, Kurt, 212
Weir, Dame Gillian, 99
Weir, Judith, xvii, xxiii, 219, 253, 398
  (Interview 446–454)
Welby, Most Revd and Rt Hon Justin, 61
Wellesz, Egon, 144
Westminster Cathedral, x, xii, xx, 58
Westminster Choir College, Princeton, xxii
Westrup, Sir Jack, 410
Whitacre, Eric, 212
White, John, xii
White, Michael, 138
Whitman, Walt, 179
Whittall, Arnold, 236
Wickham, Edward, 420
Wigmore Hall, London, ix
Wihan Quartet, 347
Willcocks, Sir David, xxi, 375, 409
William Alwyn Festival, xxi, xxiv, 312, 376
William Yeats Hurlstone Composition Prize, xiv

Williams, John, 273
  Cello Concerto, 273
Williams, Roderick, 307
Winchester College, xv
Wiseman, Debbie, xxiii, 224
  (Interview 458–464)
  Arsène Lupin, xxiii, 457, 463
  Flood, xxiii
  Jackanory, 457
  Judge John Deed, 457
  The Promise, 457
  Tom & Viv, xxiii, 457
  Wilde, xxiii, 457, 461
Wittgenstein, Ludwig, 426
Wonder, Stevie, 213
Wood, Hugh, 362
Woolrich, John, 30
Wordless Music, xxi
Worshipful Company of Musicians, xiii
Wright, Christopher, xxiii
  (Interview 468–475)
  Munrow's Muse, 472
  Oboe Concerto, 472
  Patterns, xxiv
  Spring Overture, 470
  String Quartet No.1, xxiv
  String Quartets Nos 1–4, 472
  Violin Concerto 'And then there was silence', 467, 472
  Wind Quintet, 472
Wright, Frank Lloyd, 181
Wright, Roger, 9
Wright, Ruth, 467

Xenakis, Iannis, 117, 126, 240, 326

Yale University, x, xv, 197
Yehudi Menuhin School, xv, 186, 192
Yonsei University, Seoul, x
YouTube, 176, 351

Zawose, Hukwe, 398
Zimmer, Hans, 213
Zimmermann, Walter, 178